Intentional Behaviorism
Philosophical Foundations of Economic Psychology

Intentional Behaviorism
Philosophical Foundations of Economic Psychology

Gordon Foxall
Cardiff University, United Kingdom
Reykjavik University, Iceland

Academic Press is an imprint of Elsevier
125 London Wall, London EC2Y 5AS, United Kingdom
525 B Street, Suite 1650, San Diego, CA 92101, United States
50 Hampshire Street, 5th Floor, Cambridge, MA 02139, United States
The Boulevard, Langford Lane, Kidlington, Oxford OX5 1GB, United Kingdom

Copyright © 2020 Elsevier Inc. All rights reserved.

No part of this publication may be reproduced or transmitted in any form or by any means, electronic or mechanical, including photocopying, recording, or any information storage and retrieval system, without permission in writing from the publisher. Details on how to seek permission, further information about the Publisher's permissions policies and our arrangements with organizations such as the Copyright Clearance Center and the Copyright Licensing Agency, can be found at our website: www.elsevier.com/permissions.

This book and the individual contributions contained in it are protected under copyright by the Publisher (other than as may be noted herein).

Notices
Knowledge and best practice in this field are constantly changing. As new research and experience broaden our understanding, changes in research methods, professional practices, or medical treatment may become necessary.

Practitioners and researchers must always rely on their own experience and knowledge in evaluating and using any information, methods, compounds, or experiments described herein. In using such information or methods they should be mindful of their own safety and the safety of others, including parties for whom they have a professional responsibility.

To the fullest extent of the law, neither the Publisher nor the authors, contributors, or editors, assume any liability for any injury and/or damage to persons or property as a matter of products liability, negligence or otherwise, or from any use or operation of any methods, products, instructions, or ideas contained in the material herein.

British Library Cataloguing-in-Publication Data
A catalogue record for this book is available from the British Library

Library of Congress Cataloging-in-Publication Data
A catalog record for this book is available from the Library of Congress

ISBN: 978-0-12-814584-5

For Information on all Academic Press publications
visit our website at https://www.elsevier.com/books-and-journals

Publisher: Nikki Levy
Acquisitions Editor: Joslyn Chaiprasert-Paguio
Editorial Project Manager: Ali Afzal-Khan
Production Project Manager:
    Sujatha Thirugnana Sambandam
Cover Designer: Matthew Limbert

Typeset by MPS Limited, Chennai, India

Dedication

For Helen and Charlotte

Contents

Preface   xi

Part I
Introduction   1

1. Orientation   3
   1.1 Economic behavior   3
   1.2 Levels of exposition   5
   1.3 Outline   7

Part II
Foundations   15

2. A kind of consilience   17
   2.1 Intentional behavior   17
   2.2 Insight into insight   21
   2.3 Radical behaviorism and intentionality   25
   2.4 Beyond the extensional   29
   2.5 Rationale   32
   2.6 Endnote   37

3. The basis of the intentional stance   41
   3.1 Cognitive explanation   41
   3.2 Intentional explanation   43
      3.2.1 Intentional phenomena are real   44
      3.2.2 Irreducibility   47
      3.2.3 Behaviorism has failed   48
      3.2.4 Psychology must be intentionalistic, but . . .   49
   3.3 Realism revisited   50
      3.3.1 Extensional science and intentional ascription   51
      3.3.2 The ascription of content   52
   3.4 Prelude to ascription   55
   3.5 Endnotes   57
      3.5.1 Crossing the divide   57
      3.5.2 "Conscious" and "unconscious" awareness   59

4. **The basis of the contextual stance** — 63

    4.1 The nature of radical behaviorism — 63
    4.2 Four-term contingencies — 69
    4.3 The contextual strategy — 72
    4.4 Stances compared — 75
    4.5 Extensional behavioral science — 77
    4.6 Behavior theory — 82
    4.7 Radical behaviorism's claim to uniqueness — 85
    4.8 Endnote — 89

Part III
Imperatives of Intentionality — 91

5. **Behavioral continuity and discontinuity** — 93

    5.1 Beyond the stimulus field — 93
    5.2 Symbolic behavior — 99
        5.2.1 Stimulus equivalence revisited — 99
        5.2.2 Schedule insensitivity — 102
    5.3 The appeal to physiology — 103
    5.4 The appeal to private events — 106
    5.5 The appeal to rules — 109
    5.6 The appeal to verbal analysis — 109
    5.7 Endnote — 110

6. **The personal level** — 111

    6.1 Acknowledging personhood — 111
    6.2 Skinner's third-person account — 113
    6.3 More on first-person accounts — 114
    6.4 First- and third-personal perspectives — 122
    6.5 Endnote — 126

7. **Delimiting behavioral interpretation** — 127

    7.1 Behavioral interpretation — 127
    7.2 What kind of interpretation? — 130
    7.3 Interpretive stances — 133
    7.4 Vague analogic guesses? — 136
    7.5 Teleological behaviorism — 140
    7.6 The scope of radical behaviorist interpretation — 141
    7.7 Endnote — 145

Part IV
Intentional Behaviorism 149

8. The intentional behaviorist research strategy 151

8.1 Intentional Behaviorism 152
8.2 From theoretical minimalism to psychological explanation 152
    8.2.1 Theoretical minimalism 153
    8.2.2 Psychological explanation 158
8.3 Intentionality, extensionality, intensionality 163
    8.3.1 Intentionality 163
    8.3.2 Intensionality and extensionality 165
    8.3.3 Criteria of extensionality 165
    8.3.4 The nature of intentional objects 166
    8.3.5 Truth value of intentional states and intensional statements 167
    8.3.6 Derived intentionality 167
    8.3.7 Some objections 169
8.4 Being human 170
    8.4.1 The intensional criterion 170
    8.4.2 Cognitive uniqueness 174
8.5 Endnotes 176
    8.5.1 Psychological agency 176
    8.5.2 Economic agency 177

9. Ascribing intentionality 181

9.1 Modeling consumer choice 181
    9.1.1 The extensional model of consumer choice (BPM-E) 181
    9.1.2 The bounds of behaviorism in consumer psychology 185
    9.1.3 The imperatives of intentionality 188
    9.1.4 The intentional model of consumer choice (BPM-I) 189
9.2 Predictability: attitude−intention−behavior 194
    9.2.1 Predictive validity 194
    9.2.2 The attitude revolution 197
9.3 Consumer heterophenomenology 209
    9.3.1 The nature of heterophenomenology 209
    9.3.2 Consumer heterophenomenology 213
    9.3.3 Heterophenomenology in the context of Intentional Behaviorism 215
9.4 Endnote 219

10. Grounding intentionality 221

10.1 Evaluating the intentional interpretation 221
10.2 Janus-variables and valuation 225

10.3	Relating the levels of exposition		229
	10.3.1 Micro-cognitive psychology as a basis for picoeconomic interaction		229
	10.3.2 Picoeconomic analysis: the determination of V_2		236
	10.3.3 Macro-cognitive psychology as a basis for picoeconomic interaction		247

Part V
Conclusion 251

11. The explanatory significance of Janus-variables 253

11.1	Janus-variables and the intentional consumer-situation	253
	11.1.1 Intentional objects populate the intentional consumer-situation	253
	11.1.2 Decision-making	255
	11.1.3 Bundling revisited	257
11.2	The broader explanatory significance of Janus-variables	260
11.3	Endnote	263

Bibliography	265
Index	287

Preface

Explaining economic behavior is a multidisciplinary task. Economic psychology and behavioral economics concentrate on two of the most relevant disciplines but, in addition to economics and psychology, the task requires elements of neuroscience and neuroeconomics, picoeconomics, and marketing science: at the least! The research program with which this book is concerned has embraced all of these and has always recognized that forging a genuinely *inter*-disciplinary study of economic and social choice also requires a philosophical component. An important reason for this is that attempts at interdisciplinary work often pick out current schools of thought in the areas they seek to bring together, without taking into consideration that, in the "parent" disciplines, the chosen schools represent only one of several or many alternative ways of approaching their subject matter. Combining disciplinary perspectives to elucidate the areas of human activity such as the economic is, therefore, dependent on an overarching philosophy that facilitates the fruitful meeting of separate worldviews. Bridging concepts that make possible the required meeting of minds can then be more sensitively developed. Philosophical analysis also contributes to the critical evaluation of such concepts, identifies how explanatory systems might benefit from the extension of their conceptual outlook by the devising of new ideas and variables, and assesses the success of the entire venture. This book is concerned with the philosophical analysis of Intentional Behaviorism that brings together behavioral and intentional schools of psychology, behavioral economics, and marketing science into a unique perspective on human economic and social behavior.

It examines the philosophical foundations of Intentional Behaviorism, which reside in the justification of intentional explanation and the continuing relevance of psychological behaviorism to economic psychology. It discusses the interdependence of these philosophical bases, as well as their limitations and the consequent need for conceptual development. And it shows how Intentional Behaviorism employs them innovatively to fashion novel approaches to the empirical analysis of economic behavior and, in particular, its explanation. Intentional Behaviorism combines both extensional behavioral science and intentional theory in a sequence of theoretical argument that brings all of the disciplines mentioned previously together in the explanation of economic and social choice.

The book is centrally concerned with the intractable difficulty that has become known as the mind–body problem that embodies an apparent conceptual duality: the necessity of finding constructs that bridge the biconditionality represented by subjective perceptual experience, knowledge by acquaintance, and third-personal conceptual understanding, knowledge by description (McGinn, 2004). McGinn's view is that the devising of such biconditionality-spanning constructs is beyond human cognitive imagination; hence, the name his position has acquired, the "new mysterianism." While such skepticism is persuasive, the mysterian conclusion is not intended to impede inquiry: while no single concept may be capable of embracing both subjective experience and objective descriptiveness, there are means of coming to terms, albeit gradually and incrementally, with the impasse. Needless to say, the book does not accomplish the leap in cognitive capacity that McGinn identifies as necessary. But it attempts to lay out how linguistic differences between the extensional and intentional modes of explanation may be reconciled. Even this modest goal has impressive antecedents. The problem of bidirectionality is precisely that which Dennett (1981) seeks to overcome in his use of the notion of *illata*, physical entities that can, he claims, be intentionally characterized. This bold move alone justifies the *abstracta–illata* distinction on which his work rests in spite of the arguments of critics that it ought to be dispensed with. Where Dennett's formulation breaks down is in his, to my mind, too cursory assumption that we can use the intentional stance where the physical or contextual stance ought to suffice or at the subpersonal level of exposition. Rather than assuming that we can simply flip between levels and stances, we need to search out an alternative approach. This quest has stimulated two further innovations presented here for the first time. The first is the concept of *Janus-variables*, in which ordinary language terms such as value, which have multiple meanings, each uniquely compatible with a specific level of exposition, are examined in pursuit of what they imply for the unification of these levels. Second is the *economic justification* for the use of these terms and their interrelationships across levels of exposition. Economic analysis provides a theoretical and empirical basis for the use of Janus-variables.

I have drawn on material previously published in my *Context and Cognition: Interpreting Complex Behavior* (Foxall, 2004) which was intended for the small audience of behavior analysts and contained no reference to economic behavior or the essence of my empirical research program, which has developed considerably in the intervening years. That earlier material, revised and updated, now undergirds the argument that reaches its apogee in Part IV. While the earlier book could argue on philosophical grounds that behaviorism and cognitivism relied upon one another—indeed, that neither made sense in the absence of the other—it is now possible to show in what their interdependence inheres, as they form part of a practicable program of research in economic psychology. I have also made use of parts of my chapter on consumer heterophenomenology in *The Routledge Companion to Consumer Behavior Analysis* (Foxall, 2016c), which has also been updated and largely rewritten for the present work.

I have deliberately, but only occasionally, repeated definitions or explanations of a small number of concepts that may not be familiar to all readers and which, therefore, may need to be described both when they first occur and when they are developed further. This is especially necessary when the various mentions of a topic are separated by several chapters, and I hope it does not prove unduly irritating to polymaths.

I am deeply grateful to my editorial team at Elsevier, who have been exemplary in their encouragement and assistance. My special thanks go to Joslyn Paguio and Dennis McGonagle, in the United States, and Ali Afzal-Khan and Elizabeth Wang, in the United Kingdom.

I want also to express my very special thanks to my wife, Jean, and to our son-in-law, Robin, each of whom has been an indispensable mainstay during this extraordinary year.

Gordon Foxall
Penarth
September 30, 2019

Part I

Introduction

Chapter 1

Orientation

Chapter Outline

1.1 Economic behavior 3
1.2 Levels of exposition 5
1.3 Outline 7

1.1 Economic behavior

Economic behavior is that aspect of behavior which recognizes its instrumentality, its persistence only in the face of reward for which agents exchange work or other valued resources such as money or goods. Economic activity is usually understood to involve the allocation of limited resources among competing ends.[1] In fact, most behavior can be viewed in this way, prompting the idea that there is no behavior that is specifically economic in character as opposed to social, political, romantic, or any other kind of behavior but that the economic perspective can be applied to activity in general in order to understand it and explain it. In the context of consumption, which is our theme, the behavior with which we are concerned is certainly social as well as economic, and this invites the possibility of comparing these perspectives and of exploring their interrelationships. It is inevitable, therefore, that our quest to understand will be interdisciplinary, drawing upon social psychology as well as economics, for instance.

The idea of distributing scarce resources among mutually exclusive objectives is also found in behavioral psychology, especially in the school of behavioral economics to which it has given rise, which I have elsewhere called "operant behavioral economics" (Foxall, 2016d; see also Hursh, 1980, 1984; Hursh & Roma, 2016). Operant psychology is concerned with the allocation of a limited number of responses among competing opportunities for reward; once again, it focuses on a particular aspect of behavior, the amenability of its rate of performance to particular consequences that are known as

---

[1]. See Robbins (1935, p. 16), who defines economics as "the science which studies human behavior as a relationship between ends and scarce means which have alternative uses." Although this is generally accepted among students of economic behavior, it is not without its controversies. For one discussion of these, and the reasons for nevertheless adopting it, see Ross (2005).

reinforcers when the rate increases and punishers when it decreases. Operant behavioral economics connects this school of psychology to microeconomics in order to generate a powerful means of predicting and explaining animal and human behavior in a wide range of circumstances. Behavior corresponds to working or spending, the rewards (and punishers) it produces to the goods (and bads) of economic theory, and the rate at which working or spending earns these outcomes to the wages and prices that influence economic behavior in the workplace and the store. Economic psychology is, therefore, necessarily an interdisciplinary affair: to economics and psychology, we must add philosophy, consumer and marketing research, and neuroscience in order to forge a methodology of economic action.

We are here concerned with a particular aspect of consumer behavior that understands it as *choice*, where choice reflects the allocation of resources among rewards and potential rewards that appear at different times (Foxall, 2017b). In particular, choice is defined in terms of the fact that some rewards, even though they are smaller than others (for which we must wait longer), are so attractive that we select them instead of engaging in the more economically rational behavior marked by patience and, ultimately, higher levels of consumption. Just the imminent appearance of an inferior reward can vastly enhance its desirability, even though we know full well that something better lies in the future. We do not always dismiss the future in this way, of course; sometimes we manage to wait patiently and reap the greater return. It is in the potential conflict that characterizes temporally defined situations of this kind that we understand consumer behavior as consumer *choice* and managerial behavior as managerial *choice* (Foxall, 2016a, Chapter 2). The guiding principle is that the formulation of theory is a matter of how we speak about our subject matter and that the analysis of how the actors whose activity provides our subject matter use language is the key component of our analysis.

Economic activity can be conceived in two ways: as *behavior*, in which case it is explained as the effect of environmental stimuli, especially those that follow it; and as *action*, in which case it is interpreted as consistent with, though not necessarily caused by, desires and beliefs. All three terms in the depiction of activity as action—desires, beliefs, and action—are intentional expressions, whereas behavior and the stimulus field that predict it are extensional constructs. Recognizing this as a guiding principle of one's investigation of economic behavior is to assume a methodological perspective. Methodological explorations are concerned with how we can speak of phenomena as well as what we have to say about them. In investigating the role of intentional explanation in the treatment of economic phenomena, we must confront the mind—body problem, the fact that while we assume a materialist ontology, we can come to terms with it only by employing the language of mentality, desires, beliefs, emotions, and perceptions. This formulation is not antibehaviorist, since it acknowledges that we have only behavior as our subject matter (Dennett, 2005). It simply recognizes that the extensional vocabulary and reasoning of radical behaviorism is insufficient to capture the causation and interpretation of behavior in its entirety. The relationships between the extensional languages of neuroscience and behavioral science and the intentional language of interpretation are the means by which we can attempt to deal with this problem of reconciling personal subjective experience and a world of extrapersonal causes. However, we lack the bridging concepts that belong to both modes of expression and would enable us to conjoin the disparate explanations they provide into a single theoretical framework (McGinn, 2004). Simply switching from one language to another, even if the same words are employed in each case, may amount to no more than intellectual legerdemain. Our task requires a more principled methodology.

This book is concerned with the conceptual development of Intentional Behaviorism as an approach to explanation in economic psychology. As a methodology of social science, Intentional Behaviorism relies on an extensional account of economic behavior to indicate, by its exhaustion as a means of explanation, the point at which an intentional account becomes necessary and the form it should take. It also entails the evaluation of this intentional interpretation by reference to its compatibility with more general psychological theories of cognitive structure and functioning. Since the research process and results have been described in detail elsewhere (Foxall, 2016a, 2016b, 2016c, 2017a, 2017b), I do not rehearse them here, though sufficient description is provided to elucidate the argument. The present purpose is, rather, to examine the viability of this mode of explanation, which brings together behaviorist and cognitive reasoning. The book is concerned with the capacities, first, of radical behaviorism to act as a foundation for the theoretical minimalism that is the initial stage of the research process, and, second, of intentional interpretation to provide an account of economic behavior when the extensional mode of explanation provided by theoretical minimalism has been empirically expended. But there is a deeper ambition.

1.2 Levels of exposition

Given the increasing prevalence of neuroscience and neurophilosophy, behavior is nowadays widely explained at the subpersonal level of exposition that entails neuronal activity, as well as the personal level which is that of individual action and the desires and beliefs that underlie it (Dennett, 1969). We can also identify a superpersonal level of exposition in which behavior is explained according to its sensitivity to its rewarding and punishing consequences (Foxall, 2004, 2016b). Each of these levels has a mode of explanation associated with it: extensional in the case of the sub- and superpersonal levels and intentional in the case of the personal. Hence, the intentional behaviorist paradigm assumes three levels of exposition: the *superpersonal* that comprises the theories and research of behavioral scientists, which shows empirically how patterns of behavior are functionally related to patterns of environmental contingencies; the *subpersonal* that relates neuroscience to patterns of behavior; and the *personal* that deals with behavior or action and the patterns of intentionality associated with their explanation. I have long argued (most recently in Foxall, 2016b, 2017b) that while these levels of exposition and the corresponding modes of explanation are inextricably bound up with one another, the maintenance of their integrity, that is, their conceptual separation is of paramount significance to explaining behavior and action. This remains a cardinal principle, though the questions of how the levels of exposition are related and how they interact in an explanation of action remain. They are of prime concern in the exposition which follows.

A possible model for work of this sort is what Hacker (2007) calls philosophical anthropology, "the investigation of the concepts and the forms of explanation characteristic of the study of man" (p. 4). Hacker describes philosophical anthropology as a *grammatical* inquiry into the "sense- or meaning-determining rules for the use of words," and traces this usage, which is not confined to the syntactical, to Wittgenstein. As such, philosophical anthropology includes but is not limited to the philosophy of mind and the philosophy of psychology. He also makes clear that the job of philosophy is "not to generate novel concepts and conceptual connections for use in the empirical sciences, or for use in everyday discourse" (p. 12). While sympathetic to this orientation, I must point out where I nevertheless depart from Hacker's exemplar: I am specifically concerned with the philosophy of economic psychology and, specifically, with the meanings of concepts as they enter the psychological explanation of economic behavior, and I am primarily concerned with the conceptual basis of Intentional Behaviorism. This requires, of necessity, a willingness to advance novel concepts for the explanation of economic and social behavior.

Hence, an important distinction must be made. The current emphasis is not on the philosophical analysis of mind per se but on the philosophy of a particular approach to explanation in economic psychology. Because I am concerned especially with the conceptual basis of a methodology for economic psychology, the idea of the syntactic structure of the argumentational procedure, the mode of explanation adopted, necessarily looms large. This precludes exclusive concentration on the conceptual implications of specific terms, an undividedly grammatical account. This is in part because, by focusing on a specific theory of human behavior and its empirical confirmation or disconfirmation, one must grapple with concepts that are not simply grammatically feasible from an armchair point of view but have to be implemented in some way in a *process* of behavioral explanation and appraised accordingly. As an exercise in the philosophy of psychology, rather than either of these disciplines alone, this requires the inclusion of novel concepts and methodological recipes for empirical research alongside their critical evaluation. The aim of the investigation of the nature of the explanation proposed is not simply to evaluate it in isolation but to extend and hopefully improve on it. Hence, the work is not simply retrospective in its critical evaluation of work already completed. It seeks the conceptual and explanatory gaps which remain in the intentional behaviorist enterprise and proposes what is necessary to bridge them. What this necessitates is not a conceptual investigation of the whole of economics and psychology; rather, it is confined to the ways in which they combine to explain the economic behaviors that Intentional Behaviorism embraces. Two confessions follow from the last sentence. First, I have alluded to the sphere of economic psychology with which I am primarily concerned: the consumer behavior analysis on which most of the investigation, theoretical and empirical, with which Intentional Behaviorism is concerned. I do not attempt to cover the whole of economic psychology. Second, although the analysis presented here in terms of consumer choice appears equally to fit managerial behavior and the actions of the firm (Foxall, 2014a, 2014b, 2020), I cannot, for reasons of space, treat them in any depth in the present volume. Both are covered in depth elsewhere (Foxall, 2017a, in preparation). Finally, I must note that, as an exercise in the philosophy of psychology, my approach is critical of Hacker's position that "The deepest students of the role of the emotions in human life are the novelists, dramatists, and poets of our culture" (Hacker, 2018, p. xiii). This stance may suffice for the pure pursuit of philosophical anthropology, but to adopt it in the context in which I am working would be to overlook the role of the empirical and theoretical social sciences in favor of romantic speculation.

1.3 Outline

What Intentional Behaviorism seeks is a particular style of rapprochement between antithetical routes to behavioral explanation, namely, radical behaviorism and cognitivism: not a merger, but working together to provide as comprehensive an explanation as is possible, since each is necessary to the accurate articulation of the other's claim to explain. This requires understanding of the antipodal viewpoints these schools of psychology present, the barriers to conciliation, and the advantages of cooperation. These are the themes of Chapter 2, *A kind of consilience*, that offers a general introduction to the argument and interdisciplinary spirit of inquiry. The chapter sets out the conflict between behaviorist and cognitive perspectives on explanation, calling for mutual understanding and rapprochement in order to generate as comprehensive an account of activity (behavior and action) as is feasible. It describes the *contextual stance*, the expectation that behavior is the outcome of environmental stimuli, the reinforcing and punishing consequences of behavior which, along with the behavior itself, constitute the contingencies of learning. It contrasts this with the *intentional stance*, the expectation that behavior is predictable from the desires and beliefs that precede it, that any entity that can be predicted by the ascription to it of the intentionality appropriate to its history and situation is an intentional system, and that all there is to having a mind and its attributes is to be so predictable. Although these perspectives are antithetical in their explanatory capacities, the abovementioned chapter argues that both are necessary to the generation of psychological explanations.

Chapter 3, *The basis of the intentional stance*, and Chapter 4, *The basis of the contextual stance*, examine in greater detail the foundational disciplines, psychological explanation, and radical behaviorism from the philosophical perspectives that underlies them. The rationale for an intentional explanation of economic behavior is taken up in Chapter 3, *The basis of the intentional stance*, that presents a discussion of the early work of Daniel Dennett who has done more than almost any modern philosopher to elucidate the need for an intentional perspective on behavior and the means by which it might be accomplished. Dennett (1987a, 1987b) proposes that there are "three kinds of intentional psychology," what we may regard as a three-stage methodology for refining intentional psychology. It ranges from the level of everyday folk psychology, through *intentional systems theory* (IST) to *subpersonal cognitive psychology* (SPCP), the last providing the kinds of variable that can enter empirical psychology's hypothesis testing phase. IST is the intentional interpretation of behavior based on the intentional stance, the view, as I have said, that all there is to being an intentional system is to be predictable by the attribution of desires and beliefs that are appropriate to the situation. "Having" desires and beliefs reduces, therefore, to being predictable in this manner; it amounts to nothing more. The key concepts that comprise SPCP are *illata* that Dennett designates "intentionally-characterized physical entities," a notion that, if it is acceptable, transcends the integrity (separation) of the personal and subpersonal levels of exposition and overcomes the mind—body problem. The problem with *illata* is that they rest on what Bennett and Hacker (2003) call the "mereological fallacy," the allocation of qualities or entities that properly belong at the level of the whole person to one or other of its parts (say, its neurons). I have written about this move of Dennett's (Foxall, 2007, 2008, 2016b, 2017b) and it is not, therefore, something I shall redescribe at length in this volume. However, it will reemerge as a central element in the argument I shall pursue in Part III which is concerned with the nature of Intentional Behaviorism. Coming back to Chapter 3, *The basis of the intentional stance*: this is not concerned directly with IST or SPCP but provides a crucial prelude to the thinking that underpins them. Although Dennett's intentional stance is easily stated in a short sentence, the reasoning that led to it and the necessity of intentional explanation are often ignored. Chapter 3, *The basis of the intentional stance*, examines Dennett's reasoning in coming to the proposition that the ascription of intentional idioms provides an adequate basis for the explanation of complex behavior. This chapter describes Dennett's justification for adopting the intentional stance. It is not a thoroughgoing critique of Dennett's work but an exposition mainly of his ideas in the first part of *Content and Consciousness* (Dennett, 1969) which concentrates on the justification for the ascription of intentionality to explain behavior.

Chapter 4, *The basis of the contextual stance*, presents an exposition of radical behaviorism and the philosophical stance upon which it rests. Skinner (1974) described behaviorism as a philosophy of psychology and the previously mentioned chapter concerns itself with radical behaviorism as a source of the theoretical minimalism on which Intentional Behaviorism depends. Radical behaviorism is of central concern to the intentional behaviorist research strategy by virtue of its being a rigorous descriptive behaviorism that ascribes the rate at which behavior is repeated to visible contingencies of reinforcement and punishment, that is, environmental stimuli. This chapter shows how the contextual stance was developed as a supplement to the physical, design, and intentional stances proposed by Dennett. It goes on to compare and contrast the intentional and contextual stances and some of the criticisms of radical behaviorism as well as considering its claims to uniqueness as an explanatory medium. Although the contextual stance is an essential component of the intentional behaviorist research process, it is not sufficient to explain all economic behavior.

Chapters 2–4 comprise *Part II: Foundations*.

Part III: Imperatives of intentionality consists of three chapters that examine the limitations of radical behaviorism, identifying thereby the "imperatives of intentionality," which make intentional explanation necessary. Radical behaviorist explanation rests upon a rigorous behavioral syntax as the foundation of its theoretical relevance. It can fulfill its promise as a source of rigorous explanation when the stimulus field on which its explanations repose is available to the researcher. But what is the status of this paradigm when the necessary stimuli are no longer empirically available?

Chapter 5, *Behavioral continuity and discontinuity*, is concerned with the difficulties radical behaviorism encounters when its adherents cannot identify the stimulus field on which it depends for its explanatory success. Behaviorism is preoccupied with the effects of extrapersonal stimuli on the shaping of behavior; as Skinner (1977) famously put it, the variables of which behavior is a function reside in the environment. Nevertheless, radical behaviorism does not deny the existence of what it terms "private events," the thoughts and feelings that accompany and are determined by the same stimuli that occasion public behaviors. Moreover, despite their official repudiation of personal psychological variables, behaviorists frequently make reference to them as causes of behavior but they are far from being either valid or reliable variables in a science of behavior. The contextual stance depends on the investigator's capacity to identify the stimulus field on which radical behaviorist explanation relies both unambiguously and in a manner that allows the behavior in question to be predicted and controlled. This is feasible within the closed setting of the animal laboratory and in some human experimental contexts. But, in relatively open settings, when the stimuli of which behavior is alleged to be a function may be empirically unavailable to the researcher, the logic of radical behaviorist explanation crumbles. This chapter deals with situations in which the stimulus field is not amenable to researchers and radical behaviorists' attempts to overcome this inadequacy by resort to physiology, private events, rules, and verbal analysis.

Attempts by radical behaviorists to explain complex phenomena, usually referred to as cognitive, in terms of the three-term contingency often lead to implausible interpretations. A genuine third-personal account of behavior requires intentional variables that take the intrapersonal causal fabric of behavior into consideration. Chapter 6, *The personal level*, deals with the necessity of adopting a level of exposition which is based on intentionality as embodied in individuals' desires, beliefs, emotions, and perceptions. Radical behaviorism's reliance on interpretation leaves it open to the criticism that its attribution of the rate of behavior to consequences which have not been experimentally shown to control action cannot draw the line between those behavioral outcomes that could legitimately have an influence on behavior and those that may well not.

Chapter 7, *Delimiting behavioral interpretation*, deals with a little-known aspect of this paradigm (at least among many nonbehaviorists), namely, its resort to interpretation when its subject matter is unamenable to a laboratorial or other experimental analysis. This lies at the heart of how we are to understand radical behaviorism and the explanatory role it can contribute as well as its limitations. But when the strict laboratory conditions, and other experimental contexts that are essential to the demonstration of this methodology, are not available, radical behaviorism resorts to behavioral interpretation in which more casual observation gives rise to explanations couched in the theory-language of radical behaviorism but lacking the rigorous demonstration of relationships between stimuli and responses that the experimental analysis of behavior requires. This chapter examines critically the status of explanations based on such behavioral interpretation. The problem it identifies is that consequential stimuli, reinforcers, and punishers, to which resort is made in the process of behavioral interpretation, ramify endlessly in the absence of an understanding of what the actor can reasonably have been aware of at the time of behaving. Only an intentional account can circumscribe the otherwise unwieldy proliferation of the possible outcomes of behavior to which its occurrence and frequency might be fancifully attributed. The chapter therefore, treats the necessity of restricting the identification of behavioral consequences on which behavioral interpretation depends to what could reasonably be assumed to have impacted the interpreted behavior.

Preceding chapters have discussed the foundational philosophies of Intentional Behaviorism and their limitations. The focus of interest turns in *Part IV: Intentional Behaviorism* to economic behavior and to Intentional Behaviorism itself. Chapter 8, *The intentional behaviorist research strategy*, describes the economic-psychological research program that has been employed in its elucidation. The program comprises three stages—theoretical minimalism, intentional interpretation, and cognitive interpretation—which draw on notions of intentionality, intensionality, and extensionality. This chapter describes the three stages of the research strategy and their explanatory functions and raises the question of their interrelatedness. It defines key terms that are central to the book—intentionality, extensionality, and intensionality. Thereafter, it summarizes earlier treatments of Intentional Behaviorism and discusses to which entities intentionality can be ascribed in the course of explanation. The chapter also sets out the basic assumptions on which Intentional Behaviorism is founded. It argues that intentionality can be ascribed only to entities that have first-personal experience of the desires and beliefs that shape its actions, that intentional explanation is applicable only to verbal humans. Underlying these considerations is the question of how subjective experience can assume presence and a role within a universe that is almost universally taken to be wholly materialistic, the so-called mind—body problem, no less. Hence, the argument turns now to the forms of intentional explanation that follows from these limitations of behaviorism.

The ascription of intentionality in the course of explaining action requires all three components of the intentional behaviorist research strategy: an extensional account of behavior, an intentional interpretation, and a cognitive interpretation. Chapter 9, *Ascribing intentionality*, is primarily concerned with the first two and shows how the extensional model of consumer choice has been constructed to allow the explanation of consumer behavior in terms of its antecedent and consequential stimuli, the nature of the bounds of behaviorism that limit the use of a behaviorist account of consumer choice, and the construction of the intentional model of consumer choice to overcome them. Hence, the chapter is concerned with the way in which the intentional interpretation of economic behavior is constructed in accordance with the imperatives of intentionality revealed by the bounds of behaviorism. It examines the concept of contingency-representation, the desires, beliefs, emotions, and perceptions in which the intentional consumer-situation consists. The chapter examines the nature of an extensional model of consumer choice, the specific bounds of behaviorism that impinge on economic behavior, and the subsequent construction of an intentional model of consumer choice. Dennett argues that the validity of the IST can be gauged by its predictive capacity, a position that Intentional Behaviorism has questioned. In view of this the chapter also considers in depth the feasibility of measures of intentionality providing accurate predictions of behavior. It also raises the question of how reliable is the idea that the intentional interpretation can be tested via the accuracy of predictions based on it. The achievement of high correlations between measures of intentionality and measures of behavior depends centrally on the adoption of an extensional model of choice on which to base the behavioral predictions.

The ascription of intentionality has another dimension. Insofar as the formulation of an intentional interpretation relies on extrapolations from an extensional model of economic behavior, it can be tested against consumers' own subjective experience of their private intentionality. But how is this to be accessed? Dennett's (1982, 1991a) proposal of heterophenomenology provides at least a logical guide to how this feat might be performed. It comprises a means of translating knowledge-by-acquaintance to knowledge-by-description through the rigorous verbalization of what the consumer knows of her inner experience. Chapter 9 also describes this method and its application in consumer psychology.

The intentional interpretation must be validated, either through the devising of predictions that can be empirically tested against reality or in terms of its consonance with theories of cognitive structure and functioning. Chapter 10, *Grounding intentionality*, argues that the cognitive theories to which reference has been made in this regard give rise to economic analyses that are relevant to the empirical testing of propositions derived from the intentional interpretation of economic behavior. The chapter introduces the concept of *Janus-variables* as intentional variables that have corresponding measurable variables in the extensional sciences of neuroeconomics and consumer behavioral economics that enable the necessary empirical evaluation of intentional interpretation.[2] Such a variable is the idea of value which, at the intentional level, embodies the economic actor's subjective valuation of economic exchanges and which is related to ideas of value at the subpersonal level (in terms of the comparative rate of neuronal firing) and the superpersonal level (in terms of the manifest exchange values of economic goods for pecuniary consideration.) The chapter also discusses the relationships among the three levels of exposition on which Intentional Behaviorism rests and considers how the intentional interpretation generated by adherence to the intentional model of consumer choice might be tested and evaluated, especially in view of the skepticism that has been expressed over the role of predictive validity in this process. It reviews three sources of cognitive psychology, concerned with intellectual structure and efficacy, within which the intentional interpretation may be evaluated and proposes that economic analyses derived from these cognitive psychologies, namely, neuroeconomics, picoeconomics, and consumer behavioral economics, can supply the empirical means through which the intentional interpretations can be assessed. But the chapter is centrally concerned with the question how the

---

2. Dahler-Larsen (2018) speaks of Janus-variables in a quite different context.

three levels of exposition that are integral to Intentional Behaviorism can be related while maintaining their integrity. Janus-variables, as intentional concepts, are capable of "reaching out" to the levels of exposition represented by the extensional sciences of neuroscience and extensional behavioral science. For example, with regard to the latter, the Janus-variable of value can take objective valuations that are describable in terms of consumer behavioral economics as its intentional objects. In this way the analysis suggests interconnections among levels of exposition.

A key issue that arises from this discussion is the nature and status of Janus-variables, especially vis-à-vis Dennett's *illata*. This is a theme of Chapter 11, *The explanatory significance of Janus-variables*, which comprises *Part V: Conclusion*. First, Janus-variables complement the understanding of the role of the intentional consumer-situation that forms a central theme of my *Context and Cognition in Consumer Psychology* (Foxall, 2016b). Second, Janus-variables, for all their capacity to link the levels of exposition, are themselves wholly intentional conceptions and thus not a species of *illatum*.

Part II

Foundations

Chapter 2

A kind of consilience

Chapter Outline

2.1 Intentional behavior 17
2.2 Insight into insight 21
2.3 Radical behaviorism and intentionality 25
2.4 Beyond the extensional 29
2.5 Rationale 32
2.6 Endnote 37

He who knows only his own side of the case knows little of that.

John Stuart Mill

This chapter establishes the spirit of the investigation that follows. It takes the form of an essay on the need for behaviorists and cognitivists each to appreciate the philosophical standpoint of the other (Section 2.1) and to practice openness in the search for alternative explanations of the phenomena they uncover, transcending the particular framework of conceptualization and analysis to which they normally adhere (Section 2.2). The interdependence of extensional and intentional approaches is the theme of Sections 2.3 and 2.4, and Section 2.5 proposes a rationale of the quest for a kind of consilience. The aim of this quest is not the formation of an overarching behavioral science, which incorporates both philosophical stances, but the formulation of a research strategy, which employs both perspectives in the pursuit of an epistemological foundation of a more comprehensive source of explanation (Section 2.6).

2.1 Intentional behavior

The authority exercised by schools of thought within the social scientific disciplines often seems a counterproductive consequence of the compartmentalization of knowledge, inimical to intellectual vision if only because every way of seeing is a way of not seeing. But there is virtue in strongly held views. For, unlike religious and political ideologies which can be imposed by force upon their chosen adherents, genuinely scientific ideas may naturally evoke their antitheses and do battle with them. Unless an idea is powerfully stated, however, unless the evidence for it is articulated with vigor, it is unlikely to bring forth the combative reaction upon which intellectual progress depends. The view that methodologies come and go over time, replacing one another in a process of paradigmatic conflict and supersession, holds sway over many social scientists. It is a view reflected in the common but superficial understanding that behaviorism has given way to cognitivism in psychology and that there is no going back. However, to the contrary, intellectual progress in social science relies heavily on the clash of extant theories, paradigms, and methodologies as well as on the more linear accumulation of knowledge that takes place within each. The coexistence of competing frameworks of conceptualization and analysis, far from providing evidence that psychology is a preparadigmatic field of inquiry that is yet to attain the status of mature science, is vitally necessary to the growth of knowledge (compare Feyerabend, 1975, with Kuhn, 1970, and Lakatos, 1978). Such growth requires, however, that the adherents of the rival approaches interact, consider their several positions and methods, and are sufficiently open-minded to appreciate the intellectual challenges posed by synthesis and integration as opposed to the cozy acceptance of this or that locally established worldview. Such interaction aids the process in which one paradigm impinges on, but never replaces, another, producing new syntheses, innovative predictions, and more satisfying explanations, none of which would be forthcoming but for the initial clash.

But a clash of ideas is not a war. The intellectual is an arena in which no one need be hurt by friendly fire, and there need be no other kind. An essay is an attempt, neither a treatise nor a manifesto. In so designating what follows, I draw attention to the tentativeness of knowledge and argument. Holding our views tenaciously is essential to the fruitful interaction of our cherished theories with others', but it is not the point of the exercise. A hundred years from now even our most devout disciples, if we had them, would smile at our present schemes: perhaps we have something to learn from them. Hence, the Feyerabendian ideal of critical interaction between paradigms must be tempered by a willingness to see opportunities for rapprochement. In the context of economic psychology, antagonistic interdisciplinary rivalry between extensional and intentional explanations of choice can actually be destructive of our understanding of economic behavior. Intentional Behaviorism strives to overcome this by allocating key roles to each of these approaches that recognize not only their incommensurability but also their mutual indispensability.

While the general wisdom has it that behaviorism is dead, it not only survives but also is intellectually active in areas such as psychological theory, the analysis of language and cognition, and behavioral economics. It is a successful, albeit limited, source of behavioral science. Its chief difficulty arises when its practitioners look out from their laboratory windows and attempt to explain the complexities of human behavior that will never be amenable to direct experimental investigation. Behavior analysis has failed to establish a methodology of interpretation to deal fully with such complexity.

The message of this essay is that it cannot do so without embracing intentional explanation in the form of an interpretive overlay that plugs the gaps in its explanations of life beyond the lab.

The science of which behaviorism is the philosophy has produced not only a unique experimental analysis of behavior but also an array of applications to social and economic practice, and a basis of interpretation from which complex activities such as those involved in human economic behavior can be accurately predicted. It would be a travesty if the general wisdom prevailed to the extent of eclipsing these accomplishments. But the gaps remain: radical behaviorist interpretation is unable to deal with the personal level of explanation (at which an individual knows what pain is without being able to analyze it further, a level on which physiological accounts of pain cannot operate), or with the problem of why behavior persists in the absence of the immediate rewarding consequences that form the central plank in behaviorism's explanatory scheme, or with the need to delimit the range of consequences that can reliably account for complex behavior. The attribution to individuals of desires and beliefs (intentional ascription) can perform these functions in the absence of which behavioral interpretation both founders and flounders. But the resulting methodology, which has the potential to unify aspects of behaviorism and cognitive psychology, is subtle and not without irony.

There seems on the surface little hope of compromise between psychologists who are willing to attribute mental functioning to both humans and nonhumans, and those for whom behavior is always the result of noncognitive learning and environmental history. Nevertheless, despite the tendency of behaviorists and cognitivists to misunderstand and disparage one another when in truth neither of their systems of thought is complete without the other, it is possible to find a new resting place for the debate in which they currently assume opposing positions. The differences between their methodologies, which revolve around the meanings they attribute to the term *intentional behavior*, have also the potential to unite them. The paradox is that the brand of behaviorism, which is an important theme of this book, Skinner's *radical* behaviorism, appears fundamentally antithetical to the approach which can rescue it, Dennett's "intentional stance."

To those behaviorists who define thinking, deciding, believing, and other cognitive activities as behaviors, albeit private, that are ontologically similar and subject to the same causal factors as public behaviors, intentional behavior is no more or less than the behavior that these events constitute. Hence, Skinner (1974) portrays thinking, knowing, believing, and the like simply as "covert behavior." This is of course an a priori assumption necessary to sustain a particular philosophy of psychology as it seeks to broaden its range of application from the experimental laboratory to the interpretation of everyday behavior, and it is not subject to direct empirical evaluation. The other meaning of *intentional behavior* is behavior that can be explained fully only in terms of the ascription of intentional content, particularly desiring and believing. It is not that this behavior is *caused by* cognitive events in some mechanistic fashion: rather that understanding and perhaps predicting the behavior requires the ascription to it of cognitive content or intentionality. In this vein, Dennett (1978, p. 271) defines an intentional system, which might be a person, an animal, or a machine such as a chess-playing computer, as one "whose behavior can be (at least sometimes) explained and predicted by relying on ascriptions to the system of beliefs and desires (and other intentionally characterized features) — what I will call intentions here, meaning to include hopes, fears, intentions, perceptions, expectations, etc."

While this book is generally concerned to clarify the relationship between these understandings of intentional behavior, it is more specifically concerned with the authors mentioned and their explanatory systems: that is, with *radical* behaviorism, a philosophy of psychology that invokes the first definition, in relation to Dennett's intentionally based approach that provides a basis for the currently far more dominant social cognitive psychology. Differentiating the meanings of these portrayals of intentional behavior and appreciating their place in diverse styles of scientific discourse is prerequisite to understanding the symbiotic association between behavior analysis and cognitivism. The methodology of Skinner's paradigm is constructed on what I have called the *contextual* stance (Foxall, 1999), the view that

> *Behavior is predictable and explicable in so far as it is assumed to be environmentally determined; specifically, in so far as it is under the control of a learning history that represents the reinforcing and punishing consequences of similar behavior previously enacted in settings similar to that currently encountered.*

In evaluating the exploitation of this methodological perspective in practice, it is essential to recall that modern behavior analysis, no longer confined to the rat and pigeon psychology that prevailed during the heyday of behaviorism, nowadays treats subject areas that lie at the very heart of cognitive psychology, among them thinking, decision-making and language. Its proponents claim that radical behaviorism is sufficient to deal with these phenomena, indeed with all human and animal behavior, on its own terms. That means without resort to "mentalistic" concepts such as beliefs, attitudes, and intentions which are the very stuff of modern information processing views of behavioral causation. Such views, which predominate in contemporary cognitive psychology, encapsulate an altogether different, indeed incommensurable, stance. The *intentional* stance (Dennett, 1978, 1983, 1987a) claims that

> *The behavior of systems such as people and computers can be predicted from the desires and beliefs, and other intentional, idioms, that can be rationally attributed to them.*

We shall return to both stances. For now, it is enough to draw attention to the quest for consilience that the existence of these opposing *Weltanschauungen* presents us with: for, while a conceptual fusion of these incommensurable approaches to behavioral explanation is not feasible, there is a way in which they can work together in pursuit of a more comprehensive understanding of human choice. As I have argued (e.g., Foxall, 2004), the conceptual independence of neither approach to psychology can be maintained without its practitioners' adopting at some level the countervailing stance in order to predict and explain complex human behavior. This extends the success criterion of behavioral science beyond mere prediction and control/influence into the realm of explanation and understanding. Putting prediction on the pedestal goes too far. As the physicist, David Deutsch (1997, p. 6) puts it, "Prediction is not the purpose of science, it is part of the characteristic method of science." Prediction without understanding the nature of the world is in any case a highly limited goal of science and the elevation of prediction to occupy the sole position of importance in science may be antithetical to progress. As he further says, "Whereas an incorrect prediction automatically renders the underlying explanation unsatisfactory, a correct prediction says nothing at all about the underlying explanation. Shoddy explanations that yield correct predictions are two a penny ..." (p. 65). A catholicity of vision that has not generally characterized behavior theory must become part of the scientific purview of its adherents. Recognition that the psychological theory it provides is unlikely to be of universal and exclusive application, that it has bounds that are defined by its competitors, and that the exploration of those bounds can expedite the growth of knowledge, is essential to intellectual progress.

2.2 Insight into insight

In Wolfgang Köhler's classic experiment, a banana was suspended well above the head of a chimpanzee so that it was inaccessible. After a period of confusion, in which jumping toward the fruit was of no avail, the chimp dragged a box into position, stood on it and reached the banana (Köhler, 1925). For decades, this behavior was widely attributed to the animal's exercise of "insight": the single movement in which Koko, the chimp, manipulated the box and obtained the banana was hailed as problem-solving through "the sudden appearance of novel behavior" (Chance, 1960) that could only be attributed to the ape's mental processes. After all, the sequence of behavior exhibited none of the so-called trial-and-error learning or "behavioral shaping" by which behaviorists liked to explain actions as responses to environmental stimulation. The behaviorists argued that an organism's history of learning could account for its problem-solving behavior, but in the absence of direct experimental evidence, their accounts seemed weak and speculative interpretations rather than genuine explanations (Chance, 1999).

Animals may well learn novel behavior as a result of "insight," but the alternative possibility—that learning history plays the decisive part—received emphatic support only some six decades after Köhler's work had been published. It came in the report of an experiment by Epstein, Kirshnit, Lanza, and Rubin that appeared in *Nature* in 1984. These authors argued that if animals needed to have had specific experiences in order to show novel behavior—the basic behaviorist line—they would have to have acquired two skills: moving objects to specific targets and climbing on those objects to reach other objects. Pigeons usually do neither and thus presented a model opportunity to assess how prior learning might influence problem-solving: in this experiment, pushing and climbing on a box in order to peck a facsimile of a banana. The training histories of the birds were varied in the course of the experiment, the results of which indicated that, if insight were necessary for novel learning, it was highly dependent on experience. Just those birds that had learned both skills succeeded: those which had only learned to climb on to a box and to peck did not solve the problem, but those that had in addition learned to push a box toward a goal, randomly placed in the floor of the experimental chamber in the absence of the banana, did manage to do so. The behavior in question was certainly novel since the pigeons had not encountered the banana until the trial on which they used the box to get at it. But where was "insight"? As Chance (1999, p. 162) points out, "the appearance of a novel solution was shown to be the product of specific learning experiences—to physical, not mental, events."

Between these two pieces of research is suspended an intense debate among cognitive and behaviorist psychologists over the thought processes not of chimpanzees and pigeons but of human beings. It is a debate at the center of the philosophy of psychology between behaviorists and cognitivists who present a bewildering array of perspectives.[1]

Indeed, there are so many behaviorisms, so many cognitivisms, that it is natural to inquire what definitively separates one from the rest. What are their boundaries? Perhaps most important of all, how are they related and what are the implications of one for another? The focus of Intentional Behaviorism is, first, *radical* behaviorism, "the area of philosophy, research and application that encompasses the experimental analysis of behavior, applied behavior analysis, operant psychology, operant conditioning, behaviorism, and Skinnerian psychology" (Vaughan, 1989, p. 97). Its essential methodology is to explicate behavior in terms of its contingent relationships with the consequences it produces, and associated environmental stimuli,

---

1. For a fascinating account of the debate in Pavlov's time, see Todes (2014, especially Chapter 46, Gestalt Pavlov Style.) But, be warned: this 855 page volume, once begun, is unputdownable!

where "A behavioral contingency consists of a stimulus, a response, and the outcome the response produces in the presence of that stimulus" (Malott, 1986, p. 208; for a review, see Staddon & Cerutti, 2003). This is especially relevant to the analysis of economic behavior and neoclassical microeconomics has a natural affinity with operant psychology (Foxall, 2016d).

The reasoning behind this paradigm need not be circular: it states simply that some behavior *operates* on the environment to produce consequences, which govern its future rate of emission, predicting its frequency and providing means for its control. The explanation of this "operant" behavior lies in the contingencies of reinforcement and punishment, that is, the relationships among the behavior, its consequences, and stimuli in the presence of which the behavior is emitted. These *discriminative* stimuli do not elicit the behavior as in classical conditioning but set the occasion for its performance by signaling the consequences it is likely to have. Reinforcing consequences are those which increase the likelihood of the behavior's being emitted again; punishing consequences, those which reduce this probability. A behavioral response, the discriminative stimulus that sets the occasion for it, and its reinforcing and/or punishing outcomes comprise the three-term contingency. But whether this basic device is sufficient to account for all behavior, whether it is possible to make over all of psychology in its likeness, or whether it has boundaries beyond which alternative modes of prediction and explanation must be sought are empirical questions.The bounds of behaviorism are verbal: they can be set only by comparing the locutions employed by radical behaviorists with those utilized by proponents of alternative psychologies. An inevitable consequence of pursuing the bounds of behaviorism is that those of cognitivism will become clearer too since their frontiers are necessarily shared. In order to elaborate my thesis at this stage I must anticipate much of the case with which the remainder of the book is concerned even to the point of employing some terminology which may become clear to some readers only as the argument progresses. But a preliminary statement of what I am asserting and what I am not may nonetheless be useful. In pointing out that the bounds of behaviorism are verbal I wish only to argue that by employing particular locutions we may invite modes of explanation that appear distinct from that with which we started. However, if such a locution and explanatory mode makes no (or minimal) ontological demands and either aids predictive accuracy or fills gaps in our explanations of behavior we might choose to embrace it. At the very least we should be aware of them and the linguistic usages from which they arise. If however we find that we are unable to convey the theories and findings of one explanatory system other than by borrowing the locutions that belong to or imply another, we should give thought to the possibility that our original philosophy of science stands in need of some modification.

Radical behaviorism has sought to differentiate itself from other neobehaviorisms and from cognitive psychology by avoiding locutions that embrace intentionality. This has worked well in its attempts to build an extensional science of behavior based on an experimental analysis. An experimental analysis is almost by definition concerned with behavior occurring in a relatively closed setting. The exclusion of nonoperant explanation of such behavior is favored by the small range of variables that can be shown to control simple responding in such circumstances. The kinds of behavior to which radical behaviorists have sought to apply an interpretation based on the principles gained in the laboratory are again almost by definition subject to a large range of influences from which it is much more difficult to abstract those that are particularly salient in predicting, controlling, and explaining the behavior in question. In moving from the confines of the laboratory to the task of explaining such complexity in operant terms, radical behaviorists have extended the locutions they employ to make possible (not inevitable) an intentional mode of explanation. They have necessarily had to include private events, thoughts and feelings, in their accounts and the forms of language in which these events are described involve *aboutness*, which is a hallmark of the intentional. We do not simply think and feel: we think and feel *about* something. Recognition of this can make available a new dimension to the interpretation of behavior. While this is antithetical to radical behaviorism on one level, it can also complement it in a way that plugs the gaps in its interpretations.

It is, of course, open to radical behaviorists to maintain that thoughts and feelings are simply part of the stimulus setting within which behavior occurs—discriminative stimuli, establishing operations or derived stimuli—that influence interpreted behavior just as these stimuli control responses in the laboratory. I have no argument with this and would not wish to discourage the research programs which stem from these views. But I would point out that an intentional interpretation can be just as feasible and permissible once we admit thinking and feeling to our account of behavior. And it may prove useful in generating some kinds of radical behaviorist interpretation, which at present lack conviction. Such adoption of the intentional is a linguistic phenomenon, one which behaviorist philosophers such as Quine (1960) have simply sought to ignore on the grounds that it cannot be fitted into an extensional understanding of the logic of science. But it is a legitimate one nonetheless for those who can take on board the intensional nature of sentences of a particular form. I wish to show some of the implications of doing this in the context of radical behaviorist interpretation and shall argue that, by embracing the intentional, behavior analysts may secure a more adequate explanation of complex behavior without making ontological concessions to cognitive explanation. Behavior analysis can furnish an extensional science of behavior based on the experimental analysis of behavior in the laboratory. It can also inspire and produce a variety of sources of operant interpretation which retain the extensional stance each with its own sources of substantiation whether based on experimental or nonexperimental method.

But its interpretations, as opposed to its predictions, will not I believe be as comprehensive as they might be without recognition of the implications of an intentional overlay added to the findings and theories of its extensionally based investigations.

The conceptual bounds of behaviorism as opposed to cognitive psychology are demonstrable through comparison of the underlying philosophical and methodological stances on which they respectively rely (Foxall, 1999). The current work again explores the methodological bounds of radical behaviorism in contradistinction to cognitive psychology. It argues further that the eschewal of propositional content is the defining characteristic of radical behaviorism and that this distinction demarcates radical behaviorism from the alternative neo-behaviorisms of Tolman and Hull as well as from cognitivism. This delineation differs from the more usual assertion that it is the avoidance of mediating events and processes that demarcates radical behaviorism. Whereas Foxall (1999) explored the conceptual bounds of radical behaviorism as the means of discriminating this system from cognitive accounts, the present analysis is concerned primarily with the methodological bounds of behaviorism. The earlier account gave rise to the possibility of two psychologies, each providing an inescapable and essential approach to explanation. The present exploration suggests that each of these methodologies is intrinsically contingent on the other, and that a psychology of social complexity requires both.

2.3 Radical behaviorism and intentionality

Despite the seeming plethora of cognitivisms and behaviorisms, and although the stories of all their relationships and connections will prove fascinating when they come to be written, I concentrate here on one example of each: those which need each other the most. Even so, in presenting each as a sine qua non of the other's explanatory completeness, I am critical where necessary of deficiencies that inhere in each. In synopsis the argument proceeds as follows. "Intentional behavior" can mean two things. To Skinnerians, it is the behavior constituted by thinking, feeling, intending, believing, hoping, etc., for radical behaviorism understands these things as behaviors. For Denettians, it is behavior that can be predicted by the use of the intentional stance. Between these alternatives lies a spectrum of varying possibilities for the philosophy and methodology of the behavioral and social sciences. It is the difference between an approach to behavior based on the contextual stance, which in its turn is founded upon an extensional understanding of science and one based on the intentional stance in which a heuristic interpretation is used to overlay extensional findings and theories in order to produce an account of human behavior at the personal level. Radical behaviorism's capacity to generate an extensional experimental science of behavior in is not in doubt: it is when radical behaviorism attempts to provide an account of behavior that is not amenable to an experimental analysis that questions of its explanatory adequacy arise. In particular, the status of private events, the inclusion of which provides the explicit definition of radical as opposed to other behaviorisms, calls for careful examination. The delimitation of scientific schools is a matter of identifying the verbal usages unique to each. Cognitive explanation requires intentional explanation in order to delineate the mental, which is its peculiar preserve, the recognition that mental terms have the characteristic of aboutness. Dennett (1969) proposes that extensional science provides a necessary but insufficient basis for psychology: psychology requires that a personal level of analysis be made available in addition to the subpersonal level provided by physiology. This is done by adding a heuristic level of interpretation to the theories and findings of extensional physiological science. The definitional essence of radical behaviorism, which has not been made explicit by its exponents, is its avoidance of intentional explanation, of intentional idioms as part of its locutions, of propositional attitudes. This demarcates it from cognitivism and also from the neo-behaviorisms of Hull and Tolman. It does not rule out mediating events as part of its interpretations: indeed as the practice of radical behaviorists who have engaged in interpretation indicates such theoretical terms are in fact unavoidable (Foxall, 2009).

Central to my thesis is that these stances cannot operate independently: at some level each makes use of the other. I argue that social cognitive psychology employs the contextual stance as a prelude to its ascription of intentional content. Hence, the user of the intentional stance faces the problem of determining on what the ascription of intentional content should be based. Webb (1994) argues that in humans it must be based at least in part on the verbal behavior of those whose behavior is being predicted. Second, and connectedly, the manner in which attitude theorists and researchers have resolved the problem of a lack of empirically demonstrable attitudinal—behavioral consistency is to solicit verbal responses from those whose behavior they wish to predict, which reflects their learning histories and the stimulus settings they currently face. From these responses they infer their subjects' attitudes and intentions and other cognitive precursors of action. Therefore radical behaviorist interpretation contains explanatory gaps that can be filled only by intentional ascription. Behaviorism's lack of a personal level of analysis leaves gaps in its explanations (though it does not affect its capacity to predict behavior, which is generally on a par with that of intentional psychology). The gaps are (1) an inability to account for the continuity of behavior, (2) the lack of a personal level of explanation itself, which leads to an undue reliance on an empirically unavailable learning history as a basis of interpretation of current behavior, and (3) an inability to delimit the reinforcement context of radical behaviorist interpretations by circumscribing the problem of equifinality. Not to acknowledge the gap, or to blithely assume that it will someday be bridged by the findings of physiological research, seems to evince not a scientific attitude but a dogma. Equally, to jump to the conclusion that a cognitive theory or any particular information processing model fills the gap in some ultimate sense betrays the same assertive stance. The conclusion that has been drawn is, as all knowledge must be, tentative, but it seems the best hypothesis to advance in order first to acknowledge the gap left by behavior analysis, to promote research, which will help fill it with extensional scientific findings, and to promote the cause of radical behaviorist interpretation. All of this can be accomplished without making unwarranted ontological assumptions about the nature of the gap and whatever can conceivably fill it. It is the essence of Intentional Behaviorism.

A rapprochement between the intentional and contextual stances can be accomplished by applying Dennett's logic for arriving at a personal level of analysis but incorporating also the superpersonal level of analysis provided by extensional behavioral science alongside the subpersonal level of physiology. Adding an intentional overlay to the findings and theories of operant psychology leads to a more comprehensive explanation of behavior than either radical behaviorism or Dennett's "physiological psychology" can provide. The incorporation of subpersonal and superpersonal levels into a single scheme of behavioral explanation makes possible a more complete personal level psychology of social behavior. Hence, an extensional radical behaviorist interpretation is perfectly feasible in addition to the social behavioral science proposed here for purposes of prediction, but not as a comprehensive explanation. The resulting social behavioral science is a-ontological: no conclusions are drawn with respect to the veracity of any particular cognitive theory or as Dennett calls them subpersonal cognitive psychologies. By adopting the intentional stance in this way radical behaviorist interpretation does not commit itself to a cognitive ontology: it merely acknowledges that its explanations are incomplete in the absence of the personal level of explanation, which an intentional heuristic overlay makes possible. The result is a new model for radical behaviorist interpretation: *Intentional Behaviorism*, which combines the contextual stance of behavior analysis with the heuristic overlay of the intentional.

Radical behaviorists usually claim, following Skinner (1945), that what distinguishes *radical* behaviorism is its incorporation of private events, thoughts, and feelings. This certainly sets it apart from Watsonian behaviorism and the neo-behaviorisms of Tolman and Hull. However, more important in distinguishing radical behaviorism is its attempt to base psychology on an extensional approach to science, something that sets it apart not only from those neo-behaviorisms but also from any cognitive approach that embraces intentional explanation (Smith, 1994). Two concerns arise. The first is whether the inclusion of private events into the operant account of human behavior sufficiently compensates for its attempted omission of the intentional inner states (whatever the ontological basis on which they rest) that are found in cognitivism and neo-behaviorisms. This is to ask: what is the status of a science of human behavior that treats thoughts and feelings as nonmental private events, collateral responses under the same external contingency control as public behaviors? The second is whether a purely extensional approach, that is, one which excludes from proper scientific discourse terms such as "desiring" and "believing," is sufficient to form the basis of a psychology of human behavior that deals not only with publicly available responses but also responses that are observable only by the person to whom they are occurring—that is, private events again. This is to ask: can intentionality be avoided in a science of psychology that takes private experience as part of its subject matter?

In seeking the bounds of behaviorism and its relationship to intentional psychology, it is impossible to ignore the contribution of Daniel Dennett whose work suggests indirectly a rapprochement between cognitivism and behaviorism, which he fails to take up directly. Dennett (1969) has argued that by attributing propositional content to the findings of an extensional science, namely physiology, it is possible to account more comprehensively for behaviors (such as pain) than is possible within the confines of physiology alone. Yet, despite the fact that such an enterprise is implicit in his criticism of behaviorism to the effect that it is incapable of an adequate explanation of behavior without accepting the intentional idioms into its system, he does not pursue the possibility that behavior analysis can provide an extensional basis for a social cognitive psychology that proceeds by overlaying intentional content on the findings of that science of behavior. Rather, he argues that behaviorism cannot provide a basis for psychology since it has failed as a predictive behavioral science. There is a missed opportunity here. A more critical and systematic approach to the nature and methodology of radical behaviorist interpretation would have revealed to behaviorists and intentionalists alike its shortcomings and its potential as the purported emanation of a fully fledged extensional science. The missed opportunity has not only stymied the development of radical behaviorist interpretation, leaving it open to the ridicule of nonbehaviorists who have drawn attention to its open-ended identification of stimuli and responses as they are required to support the behaviorist account of complexity: it has also had deleterious repercussions for the development of psychology as a whole.

Dennett's *intentional stance* proposes that an organism's behavior is predictable from the beliefs and desires it "ought" to have by virtue of its history and its current position. The use of this stance in, for instance, the realm of cognitive ethology (Dennett, 1983, 1987b, 1988; cf. Allen & Bekoff, 1997; Seyfarth & Cheney, 2002; Shettleworth, 2010) can proceed only by making assumptions—based on observation or deduction—about the organism's learning history and the opportunities presented by its current behavior setting, and this requires the prior exploitation of either the observed temporal and spatial context in which the organism has existed/exists and/or the *contextual stance*, a philosophical position based on the scientific analysis of environmentally determined behavior. Hence, the methodology of the intentional stance requires the prior application of the findings of extensional behavioral science. This is moreover precisely the way in which social cognitive psychology proceeds as witness contemporary attitude theory and research. The increased capacity demonstrated over the last three decades of attitude measures to predict behavior is attributable to their authors' incorporation into their models of variables relating to respondents' learning histories and the social and physical settings in which their behavior takes place (Fishbein & Ajzen, 2010; Foxall, 2005) . This reliance of intentional psychology upon a *contextual stance* suggests a resolution of how the intentional and extensional approaches are related in the context of the psychology of social cognition. The implication for cognitive psychology is that it is logically and methodologically founded upon the ascription of content to the findings of extensional behavioral science. But what are the implications for behaviorism, notably the radical behaviorism that uniquely incorporates private events into its explanatory mode?

Three possibilities arise. First, that radical behaviorism is a necessary but insufficient basis for a psychology of complex behavior; second, that *private events* raise many problems of psychological explanation that they are helpless to solve; and, third, that the social cognitive approach (i.e., the attribution of content to the findings of extensional behavioral science) is essential to the production and evaluation of plausible interpretations based on the findings of behavior analysis. I argue for all three.

2.4 Beyond the extensional

The bounds of behaviorism, as I have mentioned, are drawn in three ways each of which reveals the dependency of radical behaviorist interpretation on the intentional stance. The first is determined by the inability of behavior analysis to account for the continuity of behavior on its own terms. Behavior analysis, an approach to psychology that is staunchly founded upon the contextual stance, cannot in practice do without the intentional stance if its interpretations are to be valid. The second is defined by the level of analysis, which a radical behaviorist interpretation based directly upon the findings and theories of an unreconstructed behavior analysis is capable of generating. A personal level of exposition is inevitable if radical behaviorism is to account for phenomena that its acceptance of private events presupposes. The third is required in order to delimit the context within which the causes of behavior are located in such an interpretation. Taken together, these means of delineating the nature and the scope of radical behaviorist interpretation help define the relationship between behavioral and cognitive psychology and also promote unity among psychologists who for too long have described themselves exclusively as "behaviorists" or "cognitivists" and in doing so have overlooked the interdependencies of these two perspectives.

Those interdependencies arise also from the recent development of social cognitive psychology. The traditional approach has been for social psychologists to seek the explanation of behavior entirely in the mental, in the attitudes and intentions and other cognitive processes that are deemed to prefigure overt action. But, since context is always relevant to explaining behavior, why has it been so often ignored? Is it that psychologists have sought to emulate the "physics that never was" by searching for universal laws which, by definition, are true regardless of context, for example, "when metals are heated, they expand"? There are no such universal or near-universal "laws" in social science simply because context always is important. This, after all, is why the economist is constantly having to speak of "other things being equal." Yet there has been a subtle change in social psychology that has recognized, albeit not always explicitly, the influence of context.

Although there is a traditional tendency for cognitive psychologists to seek a-situational determinants of behavior in intrapersonal mental states and events, social cognitivists who have studied for instance the relationship among attitudes, intentions, and behavior have increasingly adopted the contextual stance, prior to the application of the intentional stance, in order to ensure the accuracy of their behavioral predictions. Just as radical behaviorism is unable to generate interpretations of complex human behavior at the required personal level or to delineate the role of contextual influences on behavior without invoking the intentional stance, so social cognitivism cannot ascertain the appropriate desires and beliefs of the human systems it seeks to predict in the absence of prior knowledge of their learning histories and the stimulus contexts of their current behavior settings.

The relationship between behaviorism and cognitivism is of course many-faceted. Any book-length treatment necessarily delimits its subject matter and I have explicitly confined my terms of reference. While they are inadequate frameworks to discuss and debate cognitive behavior in all its manifestations, they are sufficient to illustrate the implications of an extensional science of behaviorism for cognitive explanation and, more controversially, those of mental ascription for behaviorist explanation. In the process of making explicit the reliance of social cognitivists on the prior exercise of the contextual stance, the analysis draws more clearly the bounds of behaviorism and in the process delineates the cognitive task more sharply.

Malcolm (1977b, p. 85) writes, "... [T]he dispute over the place of behaviorism in psychology is fundamentally a philosophical issue," and although that view is not contested, this book is written from the viewpoint of the psychologist who recognizes the import of philosophy at every turn. Moreover, the location of behaviorism in psychology must, for the sake of the theoretical development of psychology as a science, be treated first and foremost as a psychological issue, one related to the methodological sophistication of psychology. There is virtue in Dennett's approach and belief that it is capable of contributing to a problem in psychology that is particularly important and apparently intractable: how to present an acceptable interpretation of "complex" behavior, that which is not susceptible to an experimental analysis, according to the principles derived by behavior analysts from their laboratory-based studies of simpler behavioral systems.

The approach to the growth of knowledge assumed here is explicitly in consonance with the methodological pluralism advocated by Feyerabend (1975) while stopping short of his "anything goes" dictum. Against the popular view that scientific progress is the straightforward result of the continual accumulation of facts within a given framework of conception and analysis, Kuhn (1970) hypothesizes that "mature" sciences, notably physics, develop by means of dramatic paradigmatic supersession. The revolutionary replacement of a previously productive paradigm has profound implications for the concepts that are deemed relevant, the canons of theoretical judgment, which are applicable and the appropriate practical methods of data collection, techniques of analysis, and procedures of interpretation. The paradigm that provides the current framework for "normal science" tends to become a fiercely protected and restrictive superstructure to which the scientific community compels obedience. By contrast, Feyerabend (1970) argues that competing theories proliferate not intermittently, during the periods of crisis that precede the revolutionary overthrow of one paradigm by another, but all the time as a constant feature of scientific investigation and discovery. Hence, he writes, "Science as we know it is not a temporal succession of normal periods and periods of proliferation; it is their juxtaposition. Science has its normal and proliferative modes, but their relationship is accurately described as one of simultaneity and interaction" (p. 209). The deliberate proliferation of competing theories produces an active interplay of various tenaciously held views, which is necessary to progress, at least in the sense of the growth of knowledge (Feyerabend, 1975). This method has three components (Valentine, 1992, pp. 98–99): *counter-inductivism* (the evidence required to test one theory may be adduced only through the agency of a competing, even incompatible, theory), *the principle of proliferation* (it is important to provide a critical counterpoint from which theories can be evaluated in order that they may be developed and refined), and *a pluralistic methodology* (the growth of knowledge depends on innovativeness in the development of theoretical and technical approaches). Feyerabend (1962) shows that only the advent of the kinetic theory revealed the inadequacies of classical thermodynamics, for instance. Brown (2001, p. 89) points out, "No amount of direct testing [of the kind proposed by Popper] would have sufficed to make its problems manifest." Hence, "*Theory testing is comparative*. We do not take a theory directly to nature to test its correctness. Instead we test a theory comparatively in the sense that we look to both nature and its rivals. A phenomenon becomes evidentially relevant to some theory when a rival theory can account for it." (Brown, 2001; italics in original). While, as Brown notes, the "epistemological anarchy" that Feyerabend came to advocate contains elements of trivialization of what scientists do, his principle of pluralism is valuable, and it is within this approach to the growth of knowledge that the present argument proceeds.

Among the attacks on behaviorism that have proliferated over the last century, there have been a handful of thoughtful rebuttals, among which that of Zuriff (1985) stands out. However, there is little to be gained by rehearsing the standard philosophical arguments for and against intentionalism and behaviorism for their own sake. More important is to concentrate on the practical difficulties of conducting a radical behaviorist interpretation of complex behavior without invoking the intentional stance. In the course of doing this, it will become apparent that intentionalists are forced to use the contextual stance; hence, the symbiosis, which is the inevitable relationship between these philosophies of explanation.

2.5 Rationale

Resolving the contradiction that behaviorist and intentionalist standpoints present might still seem a matter of empirical science alone, especially as both behaviorism as presented by Skinner and intentionalism as presented by Dennett are pragmatic approaches that rest on the accurate prediction of behavior. It might be argued that the theoretical stance that gives rise to the more accurate predictions and the more effective means of controlling behavior ought to be judged the more acceptable approach to explanation. Why, then, if the ultimate criterion is empirical science, should behavior analysts and cognitive psychologists get involved in the philosophical bases of these methodologies? There are five reasons that seem particularly apposite to the present investigation.

The first is that radical behaviorism rests upon a distinctive explanatory basis, and this has implications for theoretical and empirical work in both behavior analysis and cognitive psychology. It is valuable for researchers within both frameworks to appreciate what radical behaviorism uniquely entails (if only to comprehend fully its implications for the interpretation of their findings). This is what is meant by "delineating radical behaviorism." But it cannot be done in a vacuum. Because scientific explanation is verbal behavior, the bounds of behaviorism are necessarily linguistic. But our own verbalizations are insufficient to the task. Because psychological science is competitive, radical behaviorism contends with alternative explanatory systems to provide a plausible and comprehensive account of a subject matter to which many other than ourselves also lay claim. Any analysis of scientists' verbal behavior, which attempts to delimit one of the available approaches, must, therefore, take the form of a comparative examination of the locutions of practitioners from rival schools.

Second, this unique explanatory stance is the source of a profound philosophical disagreement between radical behaviorism and cognitive science.

The intentional stance which underpins cognitivism claims, in essence, that the behavior of intentional systems can be predicted based on the desires and beliefs that can be rationally attributed to them. This is a mentalistic philosophy of science that seeks to understand and predict the behavior of individuals and other systems by attributing to them interpersonal states and events. By contrast, the contextual stance on which radical behaviorism is founded is based on the understanding that behavior is predictable in so far as it is shown to be environmentally determined. Behavior is to be understood and predicted in terms of the stimulus conditions that are consequent upon it and which signal its likelihood. In spite of claims that little if anything nowadays separates radical behaviorist and cognitive psychologies (e.g., Overskeid, 1995), there are fundamental differences in the ways in which these philosophies approach the explanation of behavior, which render them incommensurable (Foxall, 1999). The difference is verbal. Different languages mean divergent modes of explanation. It will be necessary to elaborate the nature of this verbal criterion in Chapter 8, *The intentional behaviorist research strategy*, when discussing intentionality, extensionality, and intensionality more rigorously, but the rudiments are germane to the present discussion and deserve brief mention here: As a working approximation, which will be elaborated further in Section 8.3, intentional explanation deals in sentences that are *about* something else, sentences that say that the subject believes *that* something is the case, or thinks *about* our vacation, and so on. The philosophical meaning of intentionality with which we are concerned here is that it refers to this *aboutness* of our verbal expressions. Hence, sentences based on the intentional idiom typically take the form: "Mary believes *that* the man at the desk is Neil Armstrong."

Such intentional sentences are said to be referentially opaque meaning that a term that is equivalent to "Neil Armstrong" may not be substitutable for this name in the sentence. We cannot say, having heard the sentence about what Mary believes, that "Mary believes *that* the man at the desk is the first man to step on the moon," for Mary may not know that Neil Armstrong was the first man on the moon.

However, sentences within the extensional idiom that marks the contextual stance display referential transparency: "That planet is the fourth from the sun" can be consistently substituted for "That planet is Mars." This linguistic difference has given rise to a dichotomy between the mental and the physical that is often used to differentiate the realm of natural science from that of psychology including the science of behavior.[2]

---

2. Among highly accessible introductions to these ideas are those of Dennett (1969, 1996), Heil (1998), and Symons (2002). For broader discussion, see Rosenberg (2016). For contrary positions to Dennett's, see, again among several (Dretske, 1988; Stich, 1983; Searle, 1999). For contextualization, see Lyons (1995).

Third, it is widely and persuasively argued that an extensional science of behavior is infeasible, that psychology is necessarily intentional. Admittedly, the claim that a science of behavior resting on the philosophical terms proposed by radical behaviorists is logically and methodologically impossible comes predominantly from cognitivists. But, except in behavior analytic circles, the cognitive argument is winning the battle. As Schnaitter (1999) intimates, part of the reason for that is behavior analysts' disdain for philosophical involvement. The issue of intentionality reveals the tendency of behaviorists to show either flight or fight reactions to the philosophical question it raises rather than to assert their unique explanatory position, the *contextual* stance. Faced with making sense of intentional explanation, some behaviorists tend either to dismiss the whole question as beneath their consideration, a meaningless intellectual escapade of cognitivists, or to attempt to meet the intentional position head on by trying to refute it. Sometimes they simply get on with the job of showing by experimental means that a nonintentional approach to behavioral science can work, leaving philosophy to those who have the time.

The challenge to behavior analysts is to demonstrate the capacity of radical behaviorism, as a philosophy of psychology, to show how an empirical behavioral science can predict its subject matter without resort to the propositional attitudes that are the stock in trade of intentionalism. If it can go further, by demonstrating (rather than merely asserting) that the contextual strategy is methodologically prior to the intentional strategy that underlies cognitive psychology, it will have begun to redress the philosophical balance that is undoubtedly tilted at present in favor of intentional explanation. Moreover, the resolution of this issue has implications for the procedure of radical behaviorist interpretation, which behavior analysts cannot ignore if their science is to have significance beyond the walls of the laboratory. The challenge to cognitivists, as contenders for the prevailing paradigm, is to appreciate that they can similarly benefit from understanding the role of the contextual stance in their empirical and theoretical work. Unfortunately, exponents of the normal science component of knowledge are not so pressed as other contenders to underpin their paradigm philosophically. By rubbishing behaviorism rather than appreciating and meeting its arguments and the content of the science it produces, cognitive psychologists are in danger of missing the contextual basis of their endeavors. Most critics of behaviorism from a cognitivist viewpoint base their understanding of behavior analysis on a pre-1960s version of "Skinnerism" that is confined to the analysis of contingency-shaped behavior, including Skinner's (1957) extrapolation from the animal laboratory to the complexities of human verbal behavior. It is rare for critics to have any awareness of Skinner's (1969b) conceptualization of rule-governed behavior, let alone knowledge of recent empirical and theoretical work on verbal behavior as symbolism such as is contained in the stimulus equivalence (Sidman, 1994), relational frame theory (Hayes, 1994), or naming (Horne & Lowe, 1996, 1997) paradigms. The number of scholars who speak of "Watson and Skinner's radical behaviorism" and otherwise show no understanding of the role of private events in the definition of radical behaviorism is dispiriting to say the least.

Fourth, through noninvolvement, behavior analysts are losing by default a debate to which they have much to contribute and from which they may gain substantially; equally, cognitivists are presenting a view of behavior which leaves it unsituated when both their empirical methodology and their required theoretical contribution require that behavior be appropriately contextualized. The level of debate, and hence of understanding, on both sides is often unsophisticated and uninformed. So, Skinner says of Dennett, "The underlying terms in Dennett's statements ... are apparently offered as referring to cognitive and intentional states or acts. They can all be interpreted as referring to consequences." (Skinner, 1963, p. 378). As it stands, this is no more than an assertion that is unsupported by detailed argument, as is what Dennett says of Skinner: "Skinner's experimental design is supposed to eliminate the intentional, but it merely masks it." (Dennett, 1978, p. 15). The difference is that cognitivists can afford not to take behaviorists seriously because cognitivism now provides the normal science component of psychological science. But it is not in the interests of behaviorists to ignore the debate. This requires a more philosophically engaged approach than has usually been the case. As Schnaitter (1999, p. 239) puts it: "At the very least behaviorists should consider the problem of intentionality to be a most interesting case of verbal behavior, not to be dismissed but to be explored and understood. The standard behavioristic line that the mental is the fictional is just not good enough."

Finally, there is the goal of intellectual diversity and the intellectual progress that is the result of the active interplay of competing theories (Feyerabend, 1975). There are times when behavior analysis and intentional psychology reach the same conclusion (e.g., with respect to third-person accounts). It is important to understand how each system reaches this conclusion in its own way if we are to appreciate the differences in logical reasoning and methodology that each employs. It is also important to recognize that mutual agreement with respect to a conclusion does not necessarily mean that the conclusion should not be further examined. Philosophers and psychologists who belong to neither the cognitive nor the behaviorist camps may have a third take on the material that led to that conclusion and may conclude differently. We should know why. If they are wrong, we shall have strengthened our reasons for adopting and maintaining our own perspective; if they are right, we have much to gain by knowing why and, if warranted, by incorporating their reasoning. Moreover, if one system of interpretation produces a particular state of affairs, perhaps a limitation of its capacity to explain some aspect or other of complex behavior, we may simply put that down to the inadequacies of that specific theoretical system. However, if more than one methodology is limited in this way, we have an opportunity to learn more about either methodology in general (and, perhaps, how it can be improved) or about the subject matter of which we are concerned to make sense. Our scientific integrity and our intellectual credentials demand the plurality of methodologies implicated in our quest.

The urgency of our addressing these themes is apparent from even brief consideration of the likely state of affairs should we fail to do so. The problem is not so much that intentionalists and contextualists have ignored one another but that they have avoided intellectual engagement of the kind necessary to resolve issues. The question of the relationships between the intentional and the contextual stances, for example, is important because the principal exponents of each position appear to think that their own approach is so inherently superior as to automatically refute the other without detailed consideration of its basis and ramifications. But where is the interpretation, where the examination of how cognitivists actually use intentional idioms, where the delineation of the crucial underlying differences in the philosophies of psychology offered by each school that recognizes that we come to know our own thesis only by knowing its antithesis? It is assertion of this kind that brings inquiry prematurely to an end. Dennett often offers little more than counterassertion, too; he claims, for instance, without extensive argument, that establishing *what has happened?* or *what is the history of reinforcement?* is impossible "with a 'pure' (utterly non-interpretivist) investigation, without, that is to say, a healthy helping of adaptationist (or intentionalist) assumptions. This is because without answers to 'why' questions, we cannot begin to categorize *what has happened* into the right sort of parts" (Dennett, 1987a, p. 278). This is not an unimportant point, but it is a stance-laden remark unlikely to impress the implacable contextualist who can assert differently from the standpoint of the contextual stance. But elsewhere Dennett's attack rests less upon straight assertion, more on a line of argument that cannot be answered by mere counterassertion.

The intentional and contextual stances carry within themselves ontological and methodological assumptions that determine to a degree what is observed and how it is interpreted. It is not necessary to adopt the entire philosophical paraphernalia that accompanies the idea of the theory-ladenness of observation to appreciate that scientific behavior is somewhat influenced by a priori reasoning. The act of translation inherent in moving between a data language that describes observed phenomena and a theoretical language that renders them intelligible in a broader framework of analysis necessarily relies upon the guiding role of some philosophy of science or other. Only by making explicit the philosophical foundations of our work and by being aware of their alternatives can we rest assured that our interpretations are sensible. As we do so, the interdependencies of the intentional and the contextual are revealed: the way forward is not by battle and conflict alone but by mutual understanding and cooperation.

2.6 Endnote

The possibility that environmental determination and intentional explanation can be reconciled has been raised by several social and behavioral scientists. Among them, Lewin's (1936) well-known formula to the effect that behavior (B) is a function of both the person (P) and the environment (E)—$B = f(P, E)$—deserves elaboration, if only because it reveals the complexities involved in even the apparently simplest resolutions. The practical difficulty with this self-evident proposition lies in deciding on the relationship between P and E. How does each influence behavior, given the active presence of the other? What is their proportionate effect on behavior? Do they influence one another, and if so, how? In general, theories of behavior have simplified by concentrating on just one explanatory variable. Some behavioral scientists have seen behavior as predominantly determined by what goes on within the individual; while they have not neglected entirely the context in which the person behaves, they have sought the mainsprings of human action in their personalities, attitudes, intentions, and perceptions. Other behavioral scientists have concentrated on the environment as the determinant of human behavior; while they have not omitted personal characteristics from consideration, they have emphasized the consequences of behavior, the rewards and punishments produced by the environment, in explaining why people act as they do.

Abandoning the attempt to explain behavior in terms of the unidirectional influence on behavior of either the environment, as would radical behaviorism, or personal factors, as would an extreme personality psychology, Bandura's (1977, 1978, 1986) principle of reciprocal determinism posits that each of these three continually operates on the other two. Environment influences behavior but is influenced by it and by the person since E is not an autonomous factor but one that is itself molded by patterns of behavior instigated by the individual. Behavior is also influenced by personal influences such as goal selection, contemplation of the outcomes of past behaviors, the range of behavioral possibilities currently available and their merits and demerits, and active choice among the alternatives. The person is influenced in turn by the effects of prior behaviors on desires, beliefs, emotions, and perceptions of the situation. The problem that Bandura seeks to overcome by simply assuming that all of the elements of Lewin's formula influence one another, is not that with which we are primarily concerned, however.[3] The present task stands one step behind his practical solution to empirical behavioral science: it is to determine how systems of explanation cohere in rendering economic behavior intelligible. In our context, reciprocal determinism is premature.

The explanation of economic behavior we seek necessitates two psychological approaches, two languages of explanation, which, despite their differences, can each in its own way be labeled behaviorist. The first is typified by *radical behaviorism* (Skinner, 1945) in which behavior is held to be explained by the identification of the antecedent and consequential stimuli that control its rate of emission. This paradigm has the merit that, when experimental analysis permits, it enables the rigorous demonstration that the behavior of a single subject is a function of environmental variables that render it predictable and controllable. Behavior is unambiguously the subject matter of a psychology based on this philosophy, which allows no resort to unobservable explanatory variables that cannot be readily specified and controlled by the experimenter. Where this methodology obtains it must surely be considered the gold standard of experimental psychology.

It is, nevertheless, not universally applicable since there are instances where we cannot identify the stimuli of which behavior is a function. We must in such cases, perhaps *faute de mieux*, resort to the intentional language of beliefs and desires in order to complete out explanation of behavior. This is the point at which the second source of explanation becomes operative. We still have only behavior as our subject matter, we still adopt a materialist framework of conceptualization and analysis, and our interpretations of behavior are still subject to the rigor of the findings of behavior analysis, economics, and neuroscience wherever these can be brought to bear.

---

3. Even as it stands, and assuming that it is intuitively correct, it requires elaboration if it is to be turned into a useful paradigm for empirical behavioral investigation. It is necessary, for instance, to consider each of these components of reciprocal determination as molar variables: it is *sequences* of behavior, *sequences* of reinforcing and punishing consequences, and *sequences* of personal attributes that give rise to individual differences which influence rather than individual instances. It is not my watching a particular TV program right now that influences the station to broadcast it; rather, patterns of molar behavior audience behavior have an effect on patterns of broadcaster decision-making and activities (cf. Bandura, 1983, 1986; Phillips, 1987; Phillips & Orton, 1983). (My use of "molar" implies that the behavior of each party is aggregated in two ways: first, in the sense that a single viewer watches many iterations of this program or similar offerings, and, second, in the these sense that many viewers are involved in influencing media output, which is sensitive to audiences and advertisers. Similarly aggregated behavior sequences of broadcasters and sponsors influence TV station outputs.) The three variables are, therefore, to be considered temporally dynamic, processes rather than molecular elements of a simple formula. The consumer's learning history influences the procedures involved in his/her formulating an overall attitude toward future behavior, which encapsulates beliefs and norms about the likely consequences of that behavior, and of an intention to behave in a particular way should situational cues indicate that those consequences would be forthcoming (Foxall, 1997a, 2005).

We can regard this endeavor, *Intentional Behaviorism*, as behaviorist in terms both of its practitioners' intent and many of the procedures they follow.[4] Intentional Behaviorism's initial stage incorporates radical behaviorism in order to ascertain its unique explanatory contribution to economic psychology and to establish its own limitations, which indicate the necessity of an intentional explanation and the form it must take. Thereafter, it employs intentional interpretation and cognitive psychology as well as economics in order to underpin its idealized portrayal of economic behavior and to provide economic hypotheses for its ultimate empirical evaluation. The explanation of economic behavior requires all of these methodological approaches, which are demarcated by their own peculiar languages of exposition. Appreciating the differences between these modes of explanation is central to this book and it is to them that we now turn.

---

4. I realize that for most radical behaviorists this is a grave heresy and that it smacks of all that they reject as cognitivism and mentalism. But, as I have argued (Foxall, 2009), radical behaviorists themselves readily resort to such an intentional mode of explanation when circumstances demand, notably in their analyses of private events and rule-governed behavior.

Chapter 3

The basis of the intentional stance

Chapter Outline

- 3.1 **Cognitive explanation** 41
- 3.2 **Intentional explanation** 43
  - 3.2.1 Intentional phenomena are real 44
  - 3.2.2 Irreducibility 47
  - 3.2.3 Behaviorism has failed 48
  - 3.2.4 Psychology must be intentionalistic, but . . . 49
- 3.3 **Realism revisited** 50
- 3.3.1 Extensional science and intentional ascription 51
- 3.3.2 The ascription of content 52
- 3.4 **Prelude to ascription** 55
- 3.5 **Endnotes** 57
  - 3.5.1 Crossing the divide 57
  - 3.5.2 "Conscious" and "unconscious" awareness 59

Dennett's intentional philosophy of psychology represents one of the most penetrating and pervasive justifications of intentional explanation (Section 3.1). His conceptions of physical, design, and intentional stances have become fundamental to the discussion of the character of mind and action. Sections 3.2 and 3.3 examine the argument he makes in his first book, *Content and Consciousness*, and lead to the conclusion that many of the later themes he pursues exist in embryonic form in this pioneering volume. Section 3.4 deals with the implications of Dennett's thought for the ascription of intentionality, while Section 3.5 provides evidence of his willingness to transcend the subpersonal and personal levels of exposition in pursuit of behavioral explanation.

3.1 Cognitive explanation

Cognitive explanation begins with the "poverty of the stimulus," the view that only by positing unobservable mental events can psychologists account for the richness of the repertoire of response outputs available to humans given the parsimony of the stimulus inputs that behaviorists insist are sufficient to explain behavior (Fodor, 1983). The argument is familiar to those who know Chomsky's (1959) review of Skinner's (1957) *Verbal Behavior*:

surely, only some kind of inner processing, transformation, and computation can possibly account for this stimulus—response discrepancy (Plotkin, 1997; see also Pinker, 1997; cf. Fodor, 2000). Behavior analysts also have ready a counterargument. They point out the poverty of cognitivists' understanding of modern behaviorism—Plotkin's idea that "behaviorists believed that psychological explanation reduced entirely to a rather fancy theory of reflexes" (1997, pp. 130–131), for instance—and contrast this with the sophisticated treatments of private events, internal states, rule-governance, and stimulus equivalence that now characterize behaviorists' assault on whole areas of behavior that are no longer ceded *faute de mieux* to cognitive psychologists (e.g., Hayes, Barnes-Holmes, & Roche, 2001; Hayes & Ghezzi, 1997; Sidman, 1994; Staddon, 2001a, 2001b).

Stated thus, however, both arguments lack a clear understanding of what demarcates cognitive from behaviorist explanation and how the two approaches are related in practice. Moreover, some of the more elaborate behaviorist explanations of complex behavior appeal to (private) events taking place within the skin, be they behavioral or physiological. However, well behavior analysts may think that they have handled the cognitivist onslaught, nonbehaviorist psychologists can argue eloquently that little if anything nowadays separates radical behaviorist and cognitive psychologies. That the message has not got through is due in part to some behavior analysts' deliberate avoidance of the philosophical basis of the two psychologies (Schnaitter, 1999) and partly to a laxity in the use of words such as "attitudes," "intentions," and "beliefs" by some behavior analysts whose work extends into applied fields. Words such as these as they are used in cognitive psychology as well as everyday discourse carry within themselves a whole universe of explanation that is as essential to cognitive science as it is antithetical to orthodox behavior analysis.

Defining that essence and its antithesis is not a simple task. In contrast to the intentional stance that underpins cognitive psychology, a contextual stance can be identified which is the concomitant foundation of radical behaviorism (Foxall, 1999). To appreciate the role and implications of that contextual stance, we must first delve more deeply into the role and implications of intentionality. As previously noted, the intentional stance maintains that the behavior of systems such as people and computers can be predicted from the desires and beliefs that can be rationally attributed to them (Dennett, 1987a). It is useful to understand how Dennett arrives at this stance. He, in fact, distinguishes three stances by which we may seek to make systems intelligible. The *design* stance is used to "make predictions solely from knowledge or assumptions about the system's functional design, irrespective of the physical constitution or condition of the innards of the particular object" (Dennett, 1978, p. 4). The information provided by this stance leads us to define what an object will do, what its function must minimally be, regardless of its form.

From the *physical* stance, we make predictions on the basis of the physical state or conditions of the system; it depends on knowledge we have in the form of laws of nature. Predicting that when the bough breaks, the baby will fall involves using the physical stance, as does forecasting that the atmospheric conditions that are about to bring rain will also bring on my lumbago. It is through the recognition that the best chess-playing computers now defy prediction by either of these stances that Dennett arrives at the third: the *intentional* stance. In using it, "... [O]ne assumes not only (1) that the machine will function as designed but (2) that the design is optimal as well, that the computer will 'choose' the most rational move" (Dennett, 1978, p. 5). Note that rationality here means optimal design relative to goal, and that prediction is relative to the nature and extent of the information the system has about the field of endeavor. "One predicts behavior ... by ascribing to the system *the possession of certain information* and supposing it to be *directed by certain goals*, and then by working out the most reasonable or appropriate action on the basis of these ascriptions and suppositions. It is a small step to calling the information possessed the computer's *beliefs*, its goals and subgoals its *desires*" (Dennett, 1978, p. 6, emphasis in original). "Lingering doubts about whether the chess-playing computer *really* has beliefs and desires are misplaced; for the definition of intentional systems does not say that intentional systems *really* have beliefs and desires, but that one can explain and predict their behavior by *ascribing* beliefs and desires to them ..." (p. 7, emphasis in original). "The decision to adopt the strategy is pragmatic, and is not intrinsically right or wrong" (Dennett, 1978). This is reminiscent of Skinner's claim that using the radical behaviorist interpretive stance is "neither right nor wrong, merely useful." It shows that in each case, we are using an interpretive stance that is founded on ascriptions and suppositions. The statement of the contextual stance makes these explicit.

Hence, as we have noted, the contextual stance maintains that behavior is predictable in so far as it is assumed to be environmentally determined; specifically, in so far as it is under the control of a learning history that represents the reinforcing and punishing consequences of similar behavior previously enacted in settings similar to that currently encountered (Foxall, 1999). While the intentional stance proceeds by the attribution of propositional attitudes to a system that is assumed to be rational in order to reveal the intensionality of its behavior, the contextual stance is methodologically extensional, seeking to explain behavior exclusively by reference to its environmental determinants.

3.2 Intentional explanation

In elucidating the nature of intentionality, my account is largely limited to Dennett's exposition of content that he covers principally but by no means exclusively in the first part of *Content and Consciousness* (1969) and in *The*

Intentional Stance (1987a).[1] We have already covered the basic idea but it will be useful having briefly restated it to elaborate upon its meaning in preparation for the ensuing argument. The "intentions" that Dennett urges we ascribe to systems in order to predict them are words portraying actions which are *about* something else. A person does not simply hope or fear or decide but hopes *something*, fears *something*, and decides *something*: Mary hopes *that* the bus will come soon, fears *that* the age of miracles is past, decides *that* she will learn to drive, searches *for* a driving school, and so on. Sentences containing these intentional idioms are said to contain propositions or propositional content and the mentalistic terms preceding those propositions such as *hopes* and *fears* and *decides* and *searches* are known as propositional attitudes.

The intentional stance, or something much like it, underlies our everyday experience in which we try to make the behavior of other people (animals, things) intelligible and predictable. Folk psychology of this kind is resilient. The argument can be made, moreover, that the intentional stance is fundamental to cognitive science, including cognitive psychology. As Dennett further points out, (1998, p. 313), "[I]ntentional systems theory is an attempt to provide what Chomsky, no behaviorist, calls a competence model, in contrast to a performance model. Before we ask ourselves how mechanisms are designed, we must get clear about what the mechanisms are supposed to (be able to) do."

3.2.1 Intentional phenomena are real

The import of Dennett's restatement of what he calls "the ontological status of mind" (1969, Ch. 1) is that it transforms Brentano's thesis that the intentional denotes a separate, nonextensional reality or ontology into the view that the correct distinction is *solely* one between sentences. "Intentionality is not a mark that divides phenomena from phenomena, but sentences from sentences" (Dennett, 1969, p. 27; cf. Viger, 2000). And the import of this transformation in the present context stems from the inference Dennett draws to the effect that there can be no extensional science of psychology, a claim that he employs to fashion a powerful critique of the behavioristic enterprise. Dennett's logical progression in reaching this conclusion requires

---

1. See also Dennett (1996). Cf. Stich (1981), Churchland (1981), and the peer commentary on "Intentional systems in cognitive ethology" (Dennett, 1983). More general peer commentary can be found in Dahlbom (1993a, 1993b), Philosophical Topics (1994), Ross, Brook, and Thompson (2000), and Brook and Ross (2002). Reviews of *Content and Consciousness* include Anon (1970), Audi (1972), Blake (1969), Dent (1970), Franklin (1970), Gunderson (1972), Kane (1970), Kelley (1990), McKim (1970), Nagel (1995), Rice (1971), Smart (1970). Alternative accounts are presented by Anscombe (1957), Chisholm (1957), and Searle (1983). A recent set of commentaries on Dennett's *Content and Consciousness* 1969), together with Dennett's responses is to be found in Munñoz-Suárez and De Brigard (2015).

elaboration. He initially admits that the logic of science is generally said to be "blind to intensional distinctions; the intersubstitution of coextensive terms, regardless of their intensions, does not affect the truth value (truth or falsity) of the enclosing sentences" (pp. 29–30; otherwise unidentified page numbers are henceforth to Dennett, 1969). He argues that *intentional phenomena nonetheless exist*. The evidence he adduces for this claim appears unusual to those who have imbibed the traditional canons of (extensional) scientific judgment. "Our evidence that 'there really are' Intentional phenomena", he writes, "coincides with our evidence that in our ordinary language we speak as if there were, and if a science of behavior could be successfully adumbrated without speaking as if there were these 'things', the insistence that there really are Intentional phenomena would take on a hollow ring" (p. 33).[2]

It is difficult at first to get a fix on Dennett's philosophical position because he has at various times accepted and denied labels attributed to him such as instrumentalist and realist (Ross, 2015).[3] At times, he seems to be simultaneously accepting these labels and repudiating them (much as he seems, albeit reluctantly, to invite being described as a "behaviorist" and at the same time abhorring the designation; see, e.g., Dennett, 2005). The claim that he is an *instrumentalist* derives from his maintaining that no system we predict by means of the intentional stance, including ourselves, actually contains intentional content. Nevertheless, he claims to be a *realist* of sorts because he maintains that the patterns of behavior that the intentional stance predicts are real. Moreover, the intentional entities he posits (actually which are posited by folk psychology) are real in the sense that "dints" and "sakes," "miles" and "voices," "centers of gravity," and "electrons" are real. None of these terms refers to objects in the sense that the language of science would identify them, but each is useful, nonetheless, in navigating our way around the world. It is a mistake to ask, for instance, whether "sakes" really exist: they exist in the sense that our ordinary language treats them as though they exist; similarly with "minds" and other mentalistic terms. No one believes that centers of gravity exist physically, and yet their usefulness in predicting the behavior of physical entities lends a reality to them that is generally accepted even by physicists (See, inter alia, Dennett, 1981, 1991a). They do not exist in the way that trains and boats and planes exist but the reality of

---

2. In *Content and Consciousness*, Dennett employs the device of capitalizing the initial letter of intentional when it refers to the philosophical concept, thereby distinguishing it from everyday intentionality. Although he did not retain this usage in later writings, he maintained it in the second edition of *Content and Consciousness* and it is thus retained in the quotations from that source. I have generally avoided, in this book, the term "intentionalistic," except in direct quotations. Instead, for purely stylistic reasons, and for the sake of the euphony achieved by those who will read this book out loud, I have used "intentional."
3. Among views on this difficulty, see Hornsby (2000), Ross (2015), De Brigard (2015), Elton (2000), and Bermúdez (2000).

such physical artifacts is not the only mode of reality. Only by positing the intentional stance can we obtain certain kinds of useful knowledge—knowledge beneficial for the prediction and partial explanation of real behavior, that is—and this makes the ascribed entities real. "Realist," however, is another label that Dennett is reluctant to accept (see, however, Dennett, 1991a). For his ascription of intentionality to systems in order to predict them is not dependent on the intrinsic structure of those systems but on external, environmental matters, the system's context. He is then not so much opposed to the idea that the ascribed intentions are real but to the idea that they are real internal states of the system. Beliefs are objective phenomena but not objective *internal* phenomena. They are ascribed on the basis of the relationship of behavior to its environment (Bechtel, 1988, p. 72). Bechtel finds Dennett's instrumentalism a problem that he attempts to overcome by treating intentional states "realistically," that is, as "states of the system that are adaptable to features of the system's environment" (p. 78).

Also of interest is Dennett's positioning of behaviorism within this configuration. "Behaviorism would attempt to discover the extensional laws governing the occurrence of events (animal − including human − motion) that are *initially* given extensional, non-intentional characterizations. If a truly predictive science of animal and human behavior (specified in pure 'motion' terms and including all human verbal behavior) could be produced, then the existence of Intentional idioms could be safely explained away as a peculiarity of natural languages, perhaps on a par with noun genders and onomatopoeia. Allowing working science to serve as ontological arbiter, one could claim that there really aren't any Intentional phenomena, and hence no science of Intentional phenomena is needed" (p. 33, emphasis in original).

By way of commentary, it is necessary to make four points. First, we must note that in saying that intentional phenomena exist, Dennett is merely making an observation on our linguistic usage. The intentional−extensional distinction is a verbal one; it is about sentences, not things, and we *do* use sentences in a way that can be construed as invoking the intentional idiom; moreover, the delineation of any system is a verbal matter. Second, *contra* Dennett's insistence that behaviorism is about S−R relationships, we must emphasize first that *radical* behaviorism invokes the R−S contingency in which the repetition of *emitted* behavior is determined by its consequences; in addition, its orientation tends toward the molar rather than the molecular (Baum, 1973). Third, it is necessary to emphasize that behaviorism's starting point is the *functional* consequences of words in sentences, terms, predicates: not their intentions or meanings but their effects or functions. This provides the basis of an extensional science of behavior that is not derivative of the intentional, that does not translate, interpret, or paraphrase it but proceeds independently of it. Finally, but most significantly, the assertion that behaviorism has failed in its predictive objective may be true of the Hullian endeavor that was collapsing as Dennett wrote but fails to do justice to the capacity of behavior analysis based on radical behaviorism to predict and control behavior at least in the closed setting of the laboratory and the relatively closed settings of hospital, prison, and therapeutic community. The claim that an extensional explanation of psychological phenomena in the absence of intentional input is necessarily incomplete is as I hope to show more defensible; meantime, Dennett's assertion as it stands is mystifying in light of the experimental successes of operant behaviorism.

3.2.2 Irreducibility

Dennett sharply dichotomizes the intensional and the extensional and argues that statements in the former idiom cannot be reduced to statements of the latter kind. This "irreducibility thesis" goes back at least to Brentano. "Intentional sentences do not follow the rules of extensional, truth-functional logic, and hence they are intensional." Moreover, and this is the central claim of intentionalism, "Intentional phenomena are absolutely irreducible to physical phenomena ... [that is,] Intentional sentences cannot be reduced to or paraphrased into extensional sentences about the physical world." This rules out the possibility of an extensional account of intensional phenomena. "The claim goes beyond the obvious fact that Intentional sentences are intensional, and hence cannot be, as they stand, extensional — to the more remarkable claim that no sentence or sentences can be found which adequately reproduce the information of an Intentional sentence and still conform to the extensional logic" (Dennett, 1969, p. 30). "The Intentionalist claim is that no extensional sentence — or longer paraphrase — could reproduce the sense of an Intentional sentence." (pp. 30–31). Intentional phenomena are absolutely irreducible. "If so overt an activity as saying that something is the case is not subject to behavioral, extensional paraphrase, what hope is there for such hidden, private phenomena as believing and imagining?" (p. 31) Note that this absolute pronouncement derives not from empirical observation but from the underlying stance that Dennett has adopted. As he admits, the irreducibility thesis is impossible to demonstrate since this would require a demonstration that intentional idioms could *always* or never be reduced to extensional idioms and this is impossible; all one can do is contend strongly that this is the case.

Dennett's thesis does not go unopposed in philosophical circles: analytical behaviorists argue that it is feasible to paraphrase intentional language in extensional terms (e.g., Ryle, 1949). Let us, nevertheless, accept the irreducibility thesis for the sake of argument. This is not to argue *contra* Dennett that such translation is possible or legitimate. It is, as I shall contend, that while making strong claims about the predictive use of the intentional stance requiring knowledge of the environment within which behavior occurs, he hints at but fails to develop a vital level of analysis. That level is the extensional analysis of behavior (which supplies a superpersonal level of understanding of behavior) coupled with an intentional interpretive overlay. Thereby, he stymies the development of a comprehensive social psychology of human action. While he sometimes implies that the understanding of environment–behavior relationships is an inevitable part of even an intentional psychology, he fails to elaborate this thesis, partly because he is of the opinion that behaviorism has failed, partly because he seems to misunderstand some vital components of modern behaviorism.

3.2.3 Behaviorism has failed

We have already noted Dennett's insistence that behaviorism has failed. Contrary to the aim of a science of behavior, "so far the attempts to produce such an austere Stimulus—Response science have been notably unsuccessful. While behavioristic research on animals and men over the last several decades has been undeniably fruitful from the point of view of crucial data obtained, these gains have been achieved independently of − and, in many instances, in spite of − the theories the experimenters were intended to confirm or disconfirm. One could even make a case for the claim that the value of experimental results has been in inverse proportion to the extent to which the shibboleths of orthodox behaviorism have been honored" (Dennett, 1969, p. 33). This claim is repeated, without evidence, by Dennett and Haugeland (1987, p. 385): "Dispensing with intentional theories is not an attractive option, ... for the abstemious behaviorisms and physiological theories so far proposed have signally failed to exhibit the predictive and explanatory power needed to account for the intelligent activities of human beings and other animals. A close examination [which is not presented] of the most powerful of these theories reveals intentional idioms inexorably creeping in − for instance in the definition of a stimulus as the 'perceived' stimulus and the response as the 'intended' effect, or in the reliance on the imputation of 'information-bearing' properties to physiological constructs. Moreover, the apparent soundness of information-processing theories, and their utility in practice has strengthened the conviction that somehow we *must* be able to make sense of the ineliminable intentional formulations they contain without compromising thoroughgoing materialism" (emphasis in original). Moreover, while Dennett's argument here may apply to the deductive systems of Tolman and Hull, it misrepresents research in Skinner's radical behaviorist tradition, which has been stolidly inductive, seeking theories only after the accumulation of many results and then only in the form of empirical regularities (Skinner, 1950).

Dennett shifts tack at this point deemphasizing prediction and raising a question of explanation: "The difficulty the behaviorist has encountered is basically this: while it is clear that an experimenter can predict rate of learning, for example, from the initial conditions of his mazes and experience history of his animals, how does he specify just *what* is learned?"

(1969, pp. 33—34, emphasis in original). "What [the animal in the maze] learns, of course, is *where the food is*, but how is this to be characterized non-Intentionally? There is no room for 'know' or 'believe' or 'hunt for' in the officially circumscribed language of behaviorism; so the behaviorist cannot say that the rat knows or believes that his food is at x, or that the rat is hunting for a route to x" (p. 34, emphasis in original). He still fails to appreciate the essential contribution of extensional behavioral science to a comprehensive psychology of complex behavior. Based on its empirical research, behaviorism can tell a story about behavior that is both successful and independent of the physiologists' story about behavior. Both the behavioristic account and the physiological are extensional, they may deal more with what Dennett calls motion than with action, and they may need an intensional overlay in order to encompass some human experiences. But that is not the same as saying that behaviorism has failed, unless behaviorists insist that their approach is sufficient to account convincingly for all human behavior, private as well as public.[4] (I have discussed Dennett's points here at some length in Foxall, 2016b.)

3.2.4 Psychology must be intentionalistic, but ...

Dennett argues that intentional science is the only game in town. Now begins his real assault on behaviorism: his view that psychology *must* be based on the intentional and that an extensional psychology is impossible. He is tentative, but there is no doubt where his argument is leading: "This strongly suggests, but does not prove, of course, that psychological phenomena *must* be characterized Intentionally if they are to be explained and predicted, that no science of behavior can get along without the Intentional idioms" (p. 34, emphasis in original). His rejection of an extensional science of behavior is getting stronger, though he is actually talking about the difficulties of an intentional science. In moving toward a position where an intentional approach must somehow deal with and use the extensional, he evinces the attitude that de facto rejects extensionality when it derives from behavioral science, though not when its origins are in physiology.

However, he notes that a *purely* intentional psychology is also impossible, since it cannot specify its causal variables (beliefs, etc.) in ways that are conceptually independent of the behavior it seeks to explain or predict. "It follows directly from the Intentionalist's irreducibility hypothesis that no independent characterization of an Intentionally characterized antecedent is ever possible" (Dennett, 1969, p. 35). Hume's second approach to causality cannot be fulfilled, therefore. So Dennett rejects the phenomenological approach to explanation as surely as he rejects behaviorism. In sum, unbounded intentionalism cannot provide the basis of a scientific theory of

---

4. Nevertheless, see Ross's (2015) discussion on this point.

behavior because its intentional characterization cannot have an independent referent/specification/characterization; however, this line of reasoning has come about because of the impossibility of the intentional being reducible to the extensional and extensional has been understood as referring to the external. But what if an *internal* basis of extensional characterization were possible that could be shown to have *content* and thus be specifiable in intentional terms? The obvious candidate is physiology and the route to its understanding is brain evolution. Dennett's claim is that it is reasonable to postulate intelligent mental processes as long as an evolutionary explanation can be provided of how and why the mind acquired them (Bechtel, 1988, p. 74).

3.3 Realism revisited

Before turning to how he accomplishes the task of intentional ascription, it may be useful to summarize here the implications to this point of Dennett's thought for radical behaviorist interpretation. Dennett does not ask the traditional ontological questions about mind such as what beliefs are, where they reside, or what they are made of. The formalization of his approach to intentionality in the intentional stance justifies the attribution of intentional idioms such as desires and beliefs to any entity whose behavior can more easily be predicted by virtue of that strategy. Such intentions are said to be real in the sense that they are bound up in the behavior so predicted. This strategy is invaluable to behavior analysts whose interpretations require the assumption of intentionality in order to overcome the problems of purely extensional accounts of complex behavior. There is no need to ask the standard questions of cognitive ethology which are concerned with another, stronger, kind of realism, which by their very form alienate behaviorists, and which may in any case be incapable of answering. Shettleworth (1998, p. 477) summarizes the issues raised by Griffin's path-breaking book *The Question of Animal Awareness* (1976) as follows: "(1) Do animals show behavior that can be taken as evidence of intentions, beliefs, deception, and the like? (2) If they do, do they have subjective states of awareness like those a person would experience while engaging in functionally similar behavior?"

There is no need to become entangled in essentially philosophical problems about the ontology of intentionality if, like Dennett, one simply adopts the strategy of rationally predicting and partially explaining behavior via the ascription of an interpretive layer that not only fulfills these functions but, with particular regard to the present argument, permits the gaps left by other systems of explanation to be filled—not by the kind of premature physiology that is based on blind faith in a particular sphere of scientific endeavor but by current intentionalism.

3.3.1 Extensional science and intentional ascription

Dennett explores physiology as a candidate extensional science to which propositional content might be added. The search for an extensional physiology that can be said to have content and therefore be understood intentionally begins with the claim that "[n]o creature could exhibit Intentional behavior unless it had the capacity to store information" (Dennett, 1969, p. 45). It is the intelligent storage of information that is required of such a system that is the capacity of the entity to *use* information for its own ends. "... the information stored can be *used* by the system that stores it, from which it follows that the system must have some capacity for activity other than the mere regurgitation of what is stored" (Dennett, 1969, p. 45, emphasis in original). Noting that many definitions of information storage fall short of specifying information use, he quotes MacKay (1956): "any modification of state due to information received and capable of influencing later activity, for however short a time." Dennett's definition emphasizes *intelligent* information storage: "We should reserve the term "intelligent storage" for storage of information that is *for* the system itself and not merely *for* the system's users or creators" (Dennett, 1969, p. 46, emphasis in original). Evolution plays a central role in this argument. "The useful brain is the one that produces environmentally appropriate behavior, and if this appropriateness is not utterly fortuitous, the production of the behavior must be based somehow on the brain's ability to discriminate its input according to its environmental *significance*" (Dennett, 1969, p. 47, emphasis in original). This means the brain must respond differentially to stimuli, distinguishing stimuli inputs on the basis of their appropriateness to the environment that they "herald"; else "it will not serve the organism at all." The capacity of the brain to do this does not depend on its size or physical structure. Rather, it is the brain's capacity to make appropriate linkages between its afferent (input) and efferent (output) functions that matter.

But environmental significance is "not an intrinsic physical characteristic." The brain cannot use physical tests to sort its inputs (Dennett, 1969, p. 48). Therefore the only remaining hypothesis is that it does so by chance: "if such fortuitous linkages could in some way be generated, recognized and preserved by the brain, the organism could acquire a capacity for generally appropriate behavior". The sorting of physical structures must be done by an analog of natural selection, though this cannot operate via a principle of physical fitness. What Dennett calls an excursion into elementary hypothetical evolutionary history helps. The upshot of this is that the organism makes blind responses to stimulation but "the response that *happens* to be appropriate is endorsed through the survival of the species that has this response built in" (Dennett, 1969, p. 49, emphasis in original). "As the evolutionary process continues, the organisms that survive will be those that happen to react differently to different stimuli — to discriminate." Although discriminatory behavior is "only blind, dumb-luck behavior; that is, it is the fortuitous and unreasoned result of mutation, the appropriateness of which is revealed by the survival of the strain" (Dennett, 1969, p. 50), it is through this process that "a variety of simple afferent-efferent connections can be genetically established, and once they are firmly 'wired in' the afferent stimuli can be said to acquire *de facto* significance of sorts in virtue of the effects they happen to have, as stimuli-to-withdraw from and stimuli-to-remain-in-contact-with." (Dennett, 1969). This, some would say, is no more than a "just-so" story, though probably typical of adaptationist evolutionary thinking; if so, it ought to be acceptable on that basis to radical behaviorists who often subscribe to such interpretations of natural selection (Skinner, 1981). On the other hand, it ought not to be acceptable as a kind of behavioral science to radical behaviorists, who reject such physiologizing when it is done by Hullians, for example. Dennett traces how this brain processing of stimuli might be carried out via neural firings. The remainder of his chapter is given over to an account of goal-directed behavior.

3.3.2 The ascription of content

It is one thing to propose that a psychological theory requires the assertion of content to a preexisting extensional theory such as that provided by physiology, quite a trickier endeavor to justify the proposed level of analysis in psychologically relevant terms, lay down procedures for the process of ascription, and specify the relationship between the two. So Dennett finally explores the manner in which content might be ascribed to physiological systems. This is the crux of his argument against behaviorism and for a psychology that proceeds by ascribing content to the extensional facts of physiology. The personal level of explanation which is Dennett's focus here and which he contrasts with the subpersonal level at which physiology operates is that of "people and their sensations and activities" rather than that of "brains and events in the nervous system" (Dennett, 1969, p. 93; for discussion, see, inter alia, Bermúdez, 2000, Elton, 2000; Gardner, 2000; Hornsby, 2000; Roth, 2015; Wilkinson, 2015). The subpersonal level provides mechanistic explanations, but these are not appropriate to the explanation of so-called mental entities such as pain. While there is a good understanding of the neurological basis of pain, Dennett raises the question whether the presumed evolutionarily appropriate afferent−efferent networks underlying this understanding are sufficient (they are certainly necessary) to account for the "phenomena of pain." This resolves itself into the question whether pain is an entity that exists in addition to the physical questions that constitute this network (Dennett, 1969, p. 91).

There are no events or processes in the brain that "exhibit the characteristics of the putative 'mental phenomena' of pain" that are apparent when we speak in everyday terms about pain or pains. Such verbalizations are nonmechanical, while brain events and processes are mechanical. It is unclear, for instance, how an individual distinguishes a sensation of pain from a nonpainful sensation. The only distinguishing feature of pain sensations is "painfulness" that is an unanalyzable quality that allows of only circular definition. But people can do this, and the personal level is the level at which pains are discriminated, not the subpersonal. Neurons and brains have no sensation of pains and do not discriminate them. Pains, like other mental phenomena, do not refer to the following: our speaking of them does not pick out *anything*; pain is simply a personal-level phenomenon that has, nevertheless, some corresponding states, events, or processes at the subpersonal, physiological level. This is not an identity theory: Dennett does not identify the experience of pain with some physical happening; he maintains two separate levels of explanation: one in which the experience of pain, while felt, does not refer, and one in which the descriptions of neural occurrences refer to actual neural structures, events, and states in which the extensionally characterized science deals.

The task now becomes that of ascribing content to the internal states and events. The first stage is straightforward: since intentional theory assumes that the structures and events they seek to explain are appropriate to their purpose, an important link in this ascription is provided by hypotheses drawn from the natural selection not only of species but also, as we have seen, of brains and the nervous system. A system which through evolution has the capacity to produce appropriate efferent responses to the afferent stimulation it encounters, clearly has the ability to discriminate among the repertoire of efferent responses it might conceivably make. Its ability so to discriminate and respond to the stimulus characteristics of its complex environment means that it must be "capable of interpreting its peripheral stimulation," to engender inner states or events that cooccur with the phenomena that arise in its perceptual field. In order for us to be justified in calling the process intelligent, something must be added to this afferent analysis: the capacity to associate the outcomes of the afferent analysis with structures on the efferent portion of the brain.

For instance, in order to detect the presence of a substance *as food*, an organism must have the capacity not only to detect the substance but, thereafter, to stop seeking and start eating; without this capacity to associate afferent stimulation and efferent response, the organism could not be said to have detected the presence of the substance *as* that of food. Dennett uses this point to criticize behaviorists for having no answer to the question how the organism selects the appropriate response. There is a need to invest the animal that has discriminated a stimulus with the capacity to "know" what its appropriate response should be. (In fact, behaviorists have ducked this problem by designating it a part of the physiologist's assignment and drawing the conclusion that the behavioral scientists need be concerned with it no longer. The conventional behaviorist wisdom over the kind of cognitive ascription to which Dennett refers is that it amounts to no more than "premature physiology.")

The content of a neural state, event, or structure relies on its stimulation *and* the appropriate efferent effects to which it gives rise, and in order to delineate these it is necessary to transcend the extensional description of stimulus and response. It is necessary to relate the content to the environmental conditions as perceived by the organism's sense organs in order that it can be given reference to the real-world phenomena that produced the stimulation. And it is equally important to specify what the organism "does with" the event or state so produced in order to determine what that event or state "means to" the organism. An aversive stimulus has not only to be identified along with the neural changes it engenders to signify that it means danger to the animal; in addition, the animal has to respond appropriately to the stimulus, for example, by moving away. Failure on its part to do so would mean that we were not justified in ascribing such content to the physiological processes occurring as a result of the stimulation. If we are to designate the animal's activities as "intelligent decision-making" then this behavioral link must be apparent. Only events in the brain that appear appropriately linked in this way can be ascribed content, described in intentional idioms.

How are the intentional ascription and the extensional descriptions related then? This ascribed content is not an additional characteristic of the event, state, or structure to which it is allocated, some intrinsic part of it discovered within it, as its extensionally characterized features are discovered by the physiologist. They are a matter of *additional interpretation*. The features of neural systems, extensionally characterized in terms of physiology or physics, are describable and predictable in those terms without intentional ascription which makes reference to meaning or content. Such a scientific story, consisting in an account of behavior confined to talk of the structure and functions of neural cells and so on, is entirely extensional in character. But such an extensional story could not, according to Dennett, provide us with an understanding of *what the organism is doing*. Only an intentional account can accomplish this, "but it is not a story about features of the world *in addition to* features of the extensional story; it just describes what happens in a different way" (emphasis in original). Such an extensional theory would be confined to the description/explanation of the *motions* of the organism rather than of its *actions*.

Physiologists, in practice, do not seem able to get along in their account of the function of the central nervous system without viewing neural operations as signals, reports, or messages (for modern corroboration, see, for a typical textbook treatment: Gazzaniga, Ivry, & Mangun, 1998; and *inter alia* for direct research evidence: Angulo, Staiger, Rossier, & Audinat, 1999; Kandel, 2001). As Dennett (1969, p. 79) puts it, "Were the physiologist to ban all Intentional coloration from his account of brain functioning, his story *at best* would have the form: functional structure A has the function of stimulating functional structure B whenever it is stimulated by either C or D ... No amount of this sort of story will ever answer questions like why rat A knows which way to go for his food. If one does ascribe content to events, the system of ascription in no way interferes with whatever physical theory of function one has at the extensional level, and in this respect endowing events with content is like giving an interpretation to a formal mathematical calculus or axiom system, a move which does not affect its functions or implications but may improve intuitive understanding of the system" (emphasis in original). The required ascriptions of content would thus not comprise intervening variables within a physiological theory but a "heuristic overlay" on the extensional account. Such a centralist theory would have two components: "the extensional account of the interaction of functional structures, and an Intentional characterization of these structures, the events occurring within them, and states of the structures resulting from these. The implicit link between each bit of Intentional interpretation and its extensional foundation is a hypothesis or series of hypotheses describing the evolutionary source of the fortuitously propitious arrangement in virtue of which the system's operation in this instance makes sense." The ascription of content to afferent and efferent operations is necessarily imprecise, since it depends on the inexact locutions we use in everyday life.

3.4 Prelude to ascription

Dennett's (1983) intentional stance is the attribution of prebehavioral mental events to human and nonhuman animals in order to predict their behavior. Dennett claims that ascribing beliefs, attitudes, and other mentalistic thought processes to individuals is a legitimate scientific endeavor as long as it results in more accurate predictions of overt behavior than would otherwise be possible. The intentionality of which he speaks is that of the philosopher and merely indicates that these processes are "about" something. (We shall gain a more sophisticated understanding of the nature of intentionality in Chapter 8, *The intentional behaviorist research strategy*.) The intentional stance may thus facilitate a richer understanding of behavior since it is possible to speculate what the individual is thinking about and, in the case of more than one person, to conjecture the interpersonal cognitive contingencies made possible by people's thinking about each other (Dennett, 1987a, pp. 239–240).

The distinctiveness of Dennett's theory can be more clearly understood in terms of its contradistinction to physicalist theories of the mind–brain relationship. He contrasts it with *type identity theory* on the one hand and what he calls *Turing machine functionalism* on the other. Identity theory relates (identifies) each mental event to a physical brain event and claims that individuals who share a mental event (say, believing that grass is green) also share a physical brain event. The brain events in question are it is claimed "physically characterizable *types* of brain events" (Dennett, 1978, pp. xiv–xv, emphasis in original). The claim that mental events are identical with brain events retains its credibility, Dennett argues: it amounts only to the nondualistic view that there is no need for a category of nonphysical things to account for mentality. But the notion that there are types of physical brain event that account for the commonality of mental events is no longer tenable: it proposes too strong a view of the mind–brain relationship. What physical things have in common is not commonality of physical components or design (compare the manual, gasoline-driven and electric forms of lawnmower) but their function or purpose.

Turing machine functionalism conserves the idea of mind–brain identity but has a novel take on the question of commonality. In it the physical predicate corresponding to a mental predicate must abstractly specify functions and functional relationships. The language by which computers and programs are described fits this requirement. Software can be functionally described in the abstract, that is, independently of the description of the physical hardware that constitutes the computer. There is no need to argue that two organisms, both of which believe that grass is green, must be physically similar, but they must share a "functional" condition or state (or, more accurately, be specifiable as such in functional language) (Dennett, 1978, p. xvi). This is still too "strong" for Dennett who argues that the notion that it is highly speculative to claim that individuals who share a common mental state could ever be described such that they would be in "the same logical state whenever they shared a mental epithet" (Dennett, 1978, p. xvi; see also Dennett, 1978, Ch. 2).

Dennett's answer is *token functionalism*: two people who share a belief in the color of grass have in common simply that they can be "predictively attributed" this belief, that is, their behavior can be more accurately predicted if this belief is ascribed to them. He avoids the charge of epiphenomenalism by retaining the assumption that every mental event is a physical event. The role of intentional systems is to legitimize (at least in part) mental predicates. Dennett avoids the view that our speaking ordinarily of mental events such as beliefs and desires picks out real corresponding entities. We can speak of *fatigues* for instance without there being any corresponding entities—this is much as he pointed out in the opening chapter of *Content and Consciousness* that "voices" and "sakes" do not refer. "For me, as for many recent authors, intentionality is primarily a feature of linguistic entities – idioms, contexts – and for my purposes here we can be satisfied that an idiom is intentional if substitution of co-designative terms do not preserve truth ..." (Dennett, 1978, p. 4).

More specifically, the attribution of intentionality to organisms assumes that they are rational and that their behavior can be explained on some level in terms of what their mental processing is *about* (Dennett, 1987a, pp. 240–242). Dennett proposes several orders of intentional system, applied in his illustration, to the behavior of vervet monkeys. The assumption having been made that the behavior of the vervet can be better understood/predicted by attributing to it prebehavioral beliefs, desires, and other mentalistic constructs, the question is *which* of these notions should be attributed? Given that the animal is assumed rational, the following hierarchy can be employed. *First-order intention* simply incorporates beliefs, desires, etc.: "*x* believes that *p*." If, however, *p* itself contains an intentional idiom, that is, beliefs about beliefs, the elaboration of the intentional system is increased: "*x wants y* to *believe* that *x* is hungry" is a *second-order* intentional system. And so on: in principle, humans could presumably cope with a level of sophistication approaching infinity, but reaching beyond a handful of levels is probably impracticable (Dennett, 1987a, p. 243).

What is even more interesting is that Dennett contrasts these levels of intentionality with *zero order*, "the killjoy bottom of the barrel: an account that attributes no mentality, no intelligence, no communication, no intentionality at all to the vervet" (Dennett, 1987a, p. 246a). Dennett's strategy is to argue against the antiadaptionism of evolutionary biologists such as Lewontin and Gould, but in the process he ascribes to behaviorism this fundamental position in the classification of explanations. So why proceed beyond the zero-order level? An entirely descriptive psychology would presumably devote itself to providing reports of observed behavior, unelaborated by unobservables invented for the purpose of giving a more anthropomorphic account. Dennett's answer implies that the search for a more elaborate interpretation is motivated by a desire for enhanced predictiveness: "Lloyd Morgan's canon of parsimony enjoins us to settle on the most killjoy, least romantic hypothesis that will account systematically for the observed and observable behavior, and for a long time the behaviorist creed that the curves could be made to fit the data well at the lowest level prevented the exploration of the case that can be made for higher-order, higher-level systematizations of the behavior of such animals. The claim that *in principle* a lowest-order story can always be told of any animal behavior (an entirely physiological story, or even an abstemiously behavioristic story of unimaginable complexity) is no longer interesting. It is like claiming that in principle the concept of food can be ignored by biologists — or the concept of the gene or the cell for that matter — or like claiming that in principle a purely electronic-level story can be told of any computer behavior. Today we are interested in asking what gains in perspicuity, in predictive power, in generalization, might accrue if we adopt a higher-level hypothesis that takes a risky step into intentional characterization." (Dennett, 1987a, pp. 246—247, emphasis in original).

3.5 Endnotes

3.5.1 Crossing the divide

Several commentators on Dennett's early work have assumed that the distinction between the personal and subpersonal levels was maintained with high integrity in *Content and Consciousness* (1969) but abandoned by the time Dennett published *Brainstorms* (1978) and *The Intentional Stance* (1987). However, this is not so. The rationale and process of ascribing intentionality at the subpersonal level, albeit refined in later writings, is thoroughly argued in the first of these books. As a more detailed appreciation of the subtlety of *Content and* Consciousness shows, it was always part of his strategy. His reasoning is as follows: first, Dennett criticizes "S–R theorists" for being unable to show how a novel stimulus can arrive at or select the appropriate response.[5] He continues by pointing out that an animal might detect a stimulus but not "know" what the appropriate response is (the stimulus in question could as well be a discriminative stimulus as an unconditioned one or a classically conditioned one). No afferent can be taken by the brain to have significance A unless it is recognized by the efferent side of the brain has having it, that is, until the brain has produced the appropriate response (Dennett, 1969, p. 74). The content of a neural event or state depends not only upon its "normal state of stimulation" but also whatever additional efferent effects it produces. The determination of these factors necessarily takes us beyond the extensional description of stimuli and responses.

Content can be ascribed to a neural event only when it is a link between an afferent and an efferent—and not just that but a link in an *appropriate chain* between afferent and efferent. The content is not something one discovers within this neural event but an extra interpretation. The ultimate justification for such ascription is provided by evolutionary thinking—the intelligent brain must be able to select the appropriate response to a specific stimulus. Why should this be less the case for the link between extensional operant analysis and the personal level of analysis than for that between physiology and that level? A totally biological theory of behavior would still not be able, Dennett claims, to account for *what the person is doing*. Intentional ascription simply describes what a purely extensional theory would describe, nothing more, but in a different way. This different way may be useful to the physiologist, however. Neuroscience that does not view neural events as signals, reports, or messages can scarcely function at all. No purely biological logic can tell us why the rat knows which way to go for his food and nor, incidentally, can any purely contextualistic logic reveal this in the absence of some sort of "heuristic overlay." In neither case does the proposed intentional ascription detract from the extensional version of events but adds an interpretation that provides greater intuitive understanding of the system.

---

5. Although behavior analysts are immediately likely to interpret reference to "S–R theorists" as not applying to them, the following argument is just as applicable to operant psychology as to S–R psychology and it is clear that Dennett is including operant and respondent behaviorisms in the same category here.

All of this is argued in *Content and Consciousness* (Dennett, 1969). Dennett later elaborated by proposing the intentional stance and arguing that its adoption invokes an intentional strategy by which it may be put into operation (Dennett, 1987a, p. 17): First, treat the object whose behavior is to be predicted as a rational agent; second, figure out what beliefs that agent should have given its place in the world and its purpose; do the same for its desires; third, predict how it will act to further its goals in the light of its beliefs. The use of the intentional strategy is a deductive process: it proceeds from the a priori ascription of rationality to the system whose behavior is to be explained. There is one application of this stance that could revolutionize behavioral science. Dennett proposes a physiological psychology in which content is ascribed to the findings and theories of neuroscience.

According to Dennett, an extensional science of psychology is infeasible. That is, an extensional science could not deal with intensional phenomena—no paraphrase or translation is possible that captures the intentional idiom in extensional language—rather than that an extensional science can have no existence at all. But he obviously sees intensionality as the very heart of psychology. Extensional behavioral science just is not psychology. It is, however, entirely possible to argue that an extensional science is feasible, and that the contextual stance on which it rests is the antithesis of the intentional stance on which intensional behavioral science (cognitive psychology) is based. That this extensional behavioral science cannot provide a universal explanation of behavior is, however, not only a route to an intentional psychology but also a more rounded approach to behavioral explanation.

3.5.2 "Conscious" and "unconscious" awareness

I should like to conclude this chapter with a reminder of Dennett's style of reasoning with respect to what he came to refer to as the intentional stance explanation, since Chapters 8–11 will adopt an alternative line of understanding intentionality and its implications. The following is instructive as to how, even in *Content and Consciousness*, Dennett anticipates his "three kinds of intentional psychology" (Dennett, 1981). Much of his later reasoning is apparent from his examination of the use of "awareness" in ordinary language and distinguishing awareness$_1$ from awareness$_2$. He writes, (Dennett, 1969, pp. 118–119):

1. *"A is aware$_1$ that p at time t if and only if p is the content of the input state of A's speech centre at time t."*
2. *"A is aware$_2$ that p at time t if and only if p is the content of an internal event in A at time t that is effective in directing current behaviour."*

The first of these is awareness in which we can report on what we are experiencing; the second is a source of behavioral control on which we have no means of commenting. I may drive in such a way as to avoid an obstacle and be able to report verbally that I am doing this. This is to be aware$_1$. But I can also avoid obstacles when driving and not be capable of giving such a report even to myself. Yet I am still avoiding the obstacles and must be aware of them in some way. This is to be aware$_2$. In awareness$_1$ the individual is able to articulate what he is doing; in awareness$_2$ he is aware at some level of the driving conditions in which he is operating his car but unable to articulate them. Note that quite complicated behavior patterns can be affected without awareness$_1$: for example, the behavior of a pianist playing a a piece of music who is not aware of notes, pages of music, even the sounds produced. Hence, perception by exception, for example noticing a wrong note, can cause a retreat from "automatic" playing to playing on which the pianist concentrates in striving to improve. It is worth noting in passing that behavior influenced by awareness$_1$ is what radical behaviorists classify as rule-governed behavior, while that influenced by awareness$_2$ is contingency-shaped behavior (Skinner, 1969b). The latter is directly controlled by the contingencies of reinforcement and punishment, while the former is determined by verbal instructions, promises, exhortations, and so on that specify a set of contingencies that must be followed. (The nature of contingency-shaped and rule-governed behaviors will be clarified in Sections 4.1 and 4.4.) At the purely descriptive level of behavior analysis favored by radical behaviorists, this suffices to account for behavior without any recourse whatever to notions of awareness or consciousness.

However, we must not be sidetracked from Dennett's analysis. "The more important concept, awareness$_1$," he writes, "is restricted to creatures that can express, or in other words, speaking creatures ... Of course any machine that, like our perceiving machine, had a speech centre attached would be aware$_1$ of the content of the input to this speech centre ..." Dennett admits this might be intolerable to those who are attached to the "folklore" of the ordinary word "aware." He maintains that there is nothing wrong with the idea that a machine is "aware$_1$ of certain things if *all* this means is that it can express these things correctly" (Dennett, 1969, p. 121, emphasis in original). Since he argues that awareness$_1$ and awareness$_2$ subsume all the meaning of the ordinary use of awareness, he concludes that there is no possibility of a third concept, awareness$_3$, that is relevant only to people and excludes machines.

What Dennett appears to be doing here is, first, ignoring subjective mental awareness which is a component of ordinary awareness and of awareness$_1$; and, second, equating human awareness and inanimate machine awareness simply on the grounds that a suitably programmed machine can emit verbal behavior as can a human. Being verbal may be a *sine qua non* of being aware$_1$ but being aware$_1$ does not consist only in being able to emit verbal behavior, especially when this is not spontaneous but only in accordance with programming by humans. The innovative nature of language which Chomsky (e.g., Chomsky, 2006) describes is not reflected in the limited speech functions of a machine. Searle's (1980) thought experiment of the Chinese Room is also instructive here: a machine's speech center can be syntactically programmed but has no semantic awareness.[6]

Crucially, Dennett (1969) claims that the concepts, awareness$_1$ and awareness$_2$, bridge the gap between the personal and subpersonal levels: they take persons (whole systems) as their subject but employ subpersonal criteria. There may be no need, however, to make this jump. We could maintain the personal level location of awareness by arguing that A is consciously aware when aware$_1$ and subconsciously aware when aware$_2$. This emphasizes that awareness is a phenomenon that exists at the level of the whole person, that is, the intentional level. Such experience is obviously instantiated at the subpersonal level but is not found there; hence, we avoid the mereological fallacy.[7]

Dennett's *perceiving machine* is a device "that would report its 'mental experiences' with the infallibility of human introspectors" (Dennett, 1969, p. 104). However, a machine has no mental experiences. Dennett puts the phrase in scare quotes either because he is eliding the human subjective capacity to appreciate content and the functioning of an inanimate object or he is denying that subjective experience actually exists and that it distinguishes human capacities from those of machines. Dennett posits an *awareness line* between the two functional parts of such a "perceiving machine": the afferent analyzer (which embraces perceptual inputs) and the speech center (which produces and emits language-based outputs). In the case of a physical machine, this can be achieved but it is less obvious in the brain. However, a *theoretical* line can be proposed. A human within whom a signal fails to cross this line cannot express the content of the signal, since she is not aware$_1$ thereof (Dennett, 1969, pp. 122–123). Once again, Dennett seems to conflate having a speech center with having access to content and, more importantly, understanding of content. And once again, the response must be that the kind of machine he describes, including human brains, are syntactic engines, not semantic ones. He argues that such a signal could, nevertheless, contribute through initiating a reflex response to the organism's welfare.

---

6. This is not an argument that impresses Dennett, however. See Dennett (2013 pp. 319–329).
7. For a rebuttal to Dennett's usage of terms such as "consciousness," see Strawson (2019).

Chapter 4

The basis of the contextual stance

Chapter Outline

- 4.1 The nature of radical behaviorism 63
- 4.2 Four-term contingencies 69
- 4.3 The contextual strategy 72
- 4.4 Stances compared 75
- 4.5 Extensional behavioral science 77
- 4.6 Behavior theory 82
- 4.7 Radical behaviorism's claim to uniqueness 85
- 4.8 Endnote 89

The character of radical behaviorism as an extensional philosophy of science governed by the demonstration of contingent relations among behavior, its antecedents and consequences may be said to reflect the contextual stance. Section 4.1 elaborates this observation by arguing that radical behaviorism rests upon the principles of third-personal corroboration of observation and a correspondence theory of truth. The recognition that the contingencies of reinforcement and punishment are more than the commonplace three-term formulation admits leads to the idea of *n*-term contingencies as the explanatory mode of the paradigm (Section 4.2). Section 4.3 discusses the consequent pursuit of the contextual strategy of behavioral explanation, while succeeding sections treat the comparative nature of contextual and intentional stances, the character of behavioral science and behavior theory, and radical behaviorism's claim to uniqueness in its inclusion of private events.

4.1 The nature of radical behaviorism

Radical behaviorism is a philosophy of psychology, which seeks to explain behavior in extensional language that describes the environmental consequences that influence the future rate at which the behavior is emitted (Skinner, 1974).[1] Although this is sufficient to predict and control much behavior, especially that occurring in the operant laboratory and similarly

---

1. In the case of operant conditioning, a response is *emitted* by an organism; the rate of its repetition depends on its consequences. In respondent (or classical or Pavlovian) conditioning, a response is *elicited* by a prior stimulus.

relatively closed settings, some aspects of behavior are not amenable to an operant account. These include characteristics of the continuity/discontinuity of behavior, the personal level of exposition that involves private events, and the scope of radical behaviorist interpretation. When this is the case it is necessary, for reasons of clarity and intellectual honesty, to employ the intentional language of desiring, believing, perceiving, and feeling. But the ascription of intentionality must be circumscribed to conform to the principle of "selection by consequences," including evolution by natural selection and the ontogenetic selection of behavior by the environment. This means that the aspects of behavior that are interpreted intentionally must be consistent with neurophysiological−behavioral patterns and molar environmental−behavioral sequences. Like radical behaviorist explanation, the interpretation of behavior in intentional language so-circumscribed is governed by pragmatism and constitutes a linguistic rather than an ontological procedure.

We have noted that the three-term contingency of radical behaviorism comprises a behaviorally antecedent setting stimulus in the presence of which the organism discriminates its behavior by performing only responses that have been previously rewarded (or, more precisely, reinforced) in the presence of this discriminative stimulus. Hence, the three-term contingency can be described as $S^D: R \rightarrow S^r$, where a discriminative stimulus, S^D, sets the occasion for reinforcement via a reinforcing stimulus, S^r, consequent on the performance of a specific response, R. The colon denotes that the discriminative stimulus increases the probability of the response, while the arrow indicates that the response inevitably leads to the reinforcer and that the probability of R's repetition is increased. In the case of an aversive consequence of behavior, S^p, the three-term contingency would be written $S^D: R \rightarrow S^p$, indicating that the behavioral consequence has the effect of reducing the probability of R being repeated in similar circumstances, that is, a similar array of discriminative stimuli and motivating operations (MOs). This setting is also known as the stimulus field. This formulation defines the contingencies of reinforcement and provides the basic explanatory device of radical behaviorism. Sometimes reference is made to a "four-term contingency," which describes the situation when an additional environmental stimulus, an MO, precedes or accompanies the S^D and this has the effect of enhancing the relationship between the response and the reinforcer (see Skinner, 1938, 1945, 1969a, 1969b, for expositions of radical behaviorism; Michael, 1982, for the conceptualization of MOs; Fagerstrøm, Foxall, & Arntzen, 2010; Fagerstrøm & Ghinea, 2011; Fagerstrøm, Stratton, & Foxall, 2015, for the relevance of MOs to consumer choice; Foxall, 2016a, 2016b, for the relevance of radical behaviorism to consumer research). In the theoretical minimalist stage of the Intentional Behaviorism research program, we are really asking how far behaviorism explains behavior, in order to establish the bounds of behaviorism, and inquiring of the necessity and, if required, the shape of an intentional explanation. The research paradigm selected for this purpose is radical behaviorism.

Operant conditioning provides a means of predicting and controlling the behavior of organisms in relatively closed settings such as the operant chamber (the so-called Skinner box), and in other experimental and quasi-experimental situations where environmental control can be unambiguously observed (Skinner, 1938).[2] The principles of behavior established in these "favorable" contexts may also be employed to "plausibly" interpret patterns of behavior that cannot be studied in this way because they are simply not amenable to an experimental analysis (Skinner, 1957, p. 13, 1969a, p. 100, 1984, p. 207). The experimental and interpretational analyses of these phenomena comprise one aspect of the school of psychology known as behavior analysis. The philosophical dimension of behavior analysis is radical behaviorism (Skinner, 1974). The essence of radical behaviorist explanation is that behavior is followed by consequences, some of which are in turn followed by an increase in the rate at which the organism emits this and similar behaviors, while others consequences are followed by a reduction in the rate at which behaviors of the type that precede them are emitted. The first class of consequences is known as "reinforcers" since, metaphorically, they strengthen the behavior and the second, as "punishers." The relationship between behavioral responses and the reinforcing and aversive consequences that are said to predict and control them is correlational (Skinner, 1931). Stimuli in the presence of which these behavior−consequence correlations are established may also come to exert control over responding; such "discriminative stimuli" do not elicit behavior in the way in which an unconditioned stimulus generates an unconditioned response in Pavlovian or respondent conditioning. Rather, in the case of operant conditioning (so-called because it concerns behavior that "operates on the environment to produce consequences" (Skinner, 1971, 18), the organism emits responses, originally in a somewhat random fashion, some of which through reinforcement come to be included in its behavioral repertoire. When the stimulus conditions that predict and control behavior have been identified and can be experimentally manipulated to modify the behavior in predictable ways, the behavior has been explained.

Skinner's system of explanation has been distinguished from other behaviorist schools and from cognitivism by its repudiation of the explanatory fictions that masquerade as theoretical terms (Skinner, 1950, 1963) and by its

---

2. Skinner rather disarmingly points out that he "does not write as *the* behaviorist" (Skinner, 1974, p. 3), nor, presumably, even as *the* radical behaviorist, but I have taken what I understand his view of radical behaviorism to be as my starting point because it is one of the most extensively articulated accounts, developed over decades, and is familiar to specialist scholars and others as forming a definite school of psychological theory. Not all who describe themselves as radical behaviorists would wish to be uncritically associated with Skinner's views.

acknowledgement of thinking and feeling, that is "private events," as part of its subject matter (Skinner, 1974). But the dimension that actually demarcates radical behaviorism from these other approaches to behavioral explanation is more subtle. Radical behaviorism does not actually avoid theoretical terms (Zuriff, 1979); nor is its treatment of private events, viewed originally by Skinner as responses but subsequently and necessarily construed by other radical behaviorists as (causal) consequences, robust. Rather, its distinctiveness inheres in its attempt to base a methodology of behavioral explanation on a particular linguistic usage, namely the exclusive employment of extensional language to describe responses, the stimulus elements held to be responsible for their rate of emission, and their relationships. The truth criterion of this explanatory device (the three-term contingency consisting of a discriminative stimulus, a response, and a reinforcing stimulus) is a pattern of intersubjectively observed relationships among events in the laboratory or other closed setting.[3] Skinner strove to maintain this linguistic usage throughout his career. His request that his doctoral dissertation consist of a series of linguistic clarifications based on operational definitions of psychological terms was denied (Skinner, 1979) but his early papers attest to his meticulousness in the use of language to define stimulus—response relationships and ultimately a novel psychology (Skinner, 1931, 1935). Some of his last work was still concerned with delineating radical behaviorism from cognitive psychology on the basis of the meanings of words (Skinner, 1989). An example of the care he took in defining expressions so that they excluded intentional explanations of behavior is found in his depiction of the meaning of "in order to" as when we speak of a fisherman spreading his nets in order to catch fish. For Skinner, the order is to be understood purely in terms of the temporal sequencing of spreading and catching, not in any mentally held purpose or plan to snare fish (Skinner, 1971).

Radical behaviorism is, then, an extensional language psychology. There are in nature no such things as stimuli and responses: there are only environmental and behavioral events to which psychologists and others attach the terms "stimulus" and "response," usually on the basis of interobserver agreement about the causal nature of their relationship. In radical behaviorism, as in other forms of strict behaviorism, when one event is intersubjectively observed to be a function of another (a response is recorded as a function of a stimulus or stimuli), then the response has been explained. The three-term contingency marks radical behaviorism as an extensional language psychology.

---

3. Intersubjective agreement was not held by Skinner to be an essential of scientific methodology: an individual who observes his or her own private events is acting in the same manner as an observer whose observations can be verified by others. However, in practice, scientific research undertaken and reported within the purview of radical behaviorism adheres to the third-personal reproducibility of its results.

Further investigation requires that we characterize radical behaviorism more specifically. Radical behaviorism purports, for instance, to be a pragmatic theory of truth. Following James (1907/1975), Skinner apparently thinks that "A statement is true if it 'works'." Hence, "a proposition is true to the extent that with its help the listener responds effectively to the situation it describes" (1974, p. 235). A truer proposition leads to "more effective behavior" (Skinner, 1953, p. 139) and enables the scientist to "operate successfully on his material" (Skinner, 1945, p. 293).

So what is effectiveness and how do we measure it? One avenue is to investigate values. For Skinner what is good/valuable is what is reinforced. As Zuriff (1980, p. 348) characterizes it,

> *Verbal behavior R1 is true if it has the feature T (effectiveness). Methods generated by the science specify that the behavior R2 is necessary for determining if R1 has T. If the truth of R2 also had to be determined in the same fashion, then [an] infinite regress would be generated. However, the truth of R2 does not have to be determined in that fashion, for the truth criteria are accompanied by a set of methods that specify how R2 is to be carried out (e.g., what observations are to behavior made, what measurements are to be taken, what apparatus is to be used, and under what conditions all of these occur. If R2 is carried out properly, then its results are accepted, and the determination ends. This does not mean that R2 is infallible but that science itself justifies much of its own methodology, or as Quine (1969, chap. 3) puts it, epistemology is naturalized.*

But this begs more questions. It seems to rely on both a correspondence theory of truth and truth by agreement. And "science" surely is shorthand for "the scientific community." Crucially, *whose* verbal behavior are we speaking of here and who decides what constitutes the verbal behavior arising from conducting an experiment that will be indicative of the experiment's outcome? Surely the "methods generated by the science" are those established by scientists' intersubjective agreement and the specification that the behavior R2 is required in order to determine if R1 has T similarly relies on third-personal consonance. Reference to truth criteria, methods, and observations must specify whose determinations are germane to this methodology: the response must surely be that they are those of the scientific community, and that this implies truth by agreement. The requirement that R2 be "properly" conducted points to scientists' acting in concert according to common agreement.

So the very means by which Zuriff attempts to extricate radical behaviorism actually enmeshes it further in a need for both a correspondence theory of truth and intersubjective agreement on the significance of the outcomes of scientific research. The repudiation of truth by agreement may be accepted as an abstract principle when one is trying to emphasize the continuity of private and public observation, but it hardly forms the basis of scientific progress through researchers' successive investigations. Zuriff argues that "methods generated by the science" decide that behavior R2 is able to determine whether R1 has T. Moreover, he claims, an infinite regress is avoided because the truth of R2 does not have to be decided in the same way (i.e., by R3 and that of R3 by R4). A series of techniques is specified that states how R2 will be conducted: that is, the observations to be made, the measurements taken, the apparatus employed, and the circumstances under which the research will be conducted. Then, if R2 is properly undertaken, its outcomes are accepted as the results of the research, and the process comes to an end. Hence, "science itself justifies much of its own methodology" (Zuriff, 1980, p. 348).

However, this scarcely puts the matter beyond considerations of truth by correspondence and the intersubjective agreement of scientists: for how are the methods of science generated other than through the agreement of scientists? Whose truth criteria are accepted as sufficient and on the basis of whose observations are they deemed to have been fulfilled? Similarly with respect to apparatus, measurements, and conditions: who sets the criteria and decides they have been fulfilled? "Science" does not justify anything; scientists do, acting in concert, in harmony, by agreement. Underlying this procedure are both the idea of truth by correspondence (that is what the setting and monitoring of the methodological criteria is all about) and truth by agreement (since the scientific enterprise is impossible without third-personal acquiescence that the proper canons of scientific enquiry have been adhered to and that the reported research is replicable by other scientists). Has any empirical paper on operant psychology been accepted by a journal on criteria other than these? The Skinner–Zuriff approach would result in the infinite individualization of science, each scientist acting as their own methodologist, judge and critic: who but the individual investigator is empowered to set the criteria for "effectiveness" and to determine whether they have been met? Moreover, the criterion of effectiveness can be used "only because humans have evolved to the point at which they already accept certain things as true without that explicit criterion. Thus effectiveness works as a criterion only for organisms that already accept things as true but not on the basis of considerations of effectiveness" (Zuriff, 1980, p. 349). It is difficult to see how any such program could be carried out in the absence of a correspondence theory of truth and truth by agreement.

It seems reasonable, therefore, to characterize the radical behaviorism program in practice as reflecting that the events depicted as stimuli and responses are those environmental and behavioral events, which are so designated through interobserver agreement about how they are related. When one is observed to be a function of another (a response of a stimulus), then the response has been explained through agreement that the criteria have been met. Moreover, radical behaviorism is surely *in practice* a correspondence theory of truth. A central tenet of logical positivism is the establishment of truth through intersubjective agreement (Smith, 1986). However, radical behaviorism does not recognize truth by agreement as a necessary component of scientific procedure, differing in this respect from the other behaviorisms we have mentioned (those of Spence, Hull, and Guthrie, and presumably that of Tolman). What cognitive scientists take as their central focus is, according to radical behaviorism simply behavior; hence, "[t]o know, is to behave in a particular way" (Zuriff,1980, p. 342), as is to believe, to trust, to think, and so on. Zuriff proposes that there are two kinds of behaving would be consistent with this, only one of which is consistent with Skinner's radical behaviorism.

4.2 Four-term contingencies

There have been exciting developments in behavior analysis over the last several decades of which many of its critics remain unaware. Radical behaviorism *promises*, via its inclusion of private events and rule-governed behavior, to embrace a hierarchy of behavioral complexity, including the explanation of language, within its explanatory purview. There is no need to exclude thoughts and feelings, language and calculation, or the generation of novel behavior from its range of interpretation, nor to confine its accounts to simple responses in uncomplicated environments. The contextual stance is capable of accounting for the interpretation of human behavior in ways that make its prediction and/or its at-least-plausible interpretation on an operant basis, as long as the intersection of the individual's learning history and the stimuli composing the current behavior setting remain the building blocks of its explication.

The operant interpretation looks to increasingly complex contingencies to explain increasingly complex behavior. Nor is such science confined to three-term contingencies. Sidman (1994) proposes that n-term contingences can be invoked to explain increasingly complex behavior. In the three-term contingency, R the basic $R \rightarrow S^r$ relationship ("performing a response, R, produces consequence S^R" which makes future enactment of R more likely) comes under the control of a discriminative stimulus, S^D such that S^r follows R only when S^D is present. If the presentation of an S^D sets the scene for reinforcement contingent upon the performance of R, then S^r will be produced only when S^D is present and R is enacted. The enactment of a response other than R (i.e., not-R) will not produce S^r even when S^D is present. When the prebehavioral stimulus is other than S^D (i.e., not-S^D), neither R nor not-R will produce S^r. The four-term contingency places this whole relationship under the control of a further stimulus. The discriminative stimulus, S^D, now controls the relationship between the response, R, and the reinforcing consequence, S^r, only when a further antecedent stimulus, A, is present. The presence of any other antecedent stimulus (not-A) means that neither R nor not-R will produce S^r. In the presence of A, R will produce S^r only when S^D is also present.

All of this may possibly strike Dennettians as at least a little higher than the bargain basement level but when it is applied to verbal behavior its capacity to illumine a considerable range of human behavior that behaviorists have long ceded to cognitive psychologists becomes apparent. The *n*-term contingency does not have to be discussed within the confines of verbal behavior but some of its most significant implications for human behavior arise in this context. The fourth term, A or antecedent stimulus, in the four-term contingency may be considered what Michael (1982, 1993) calls an *establishing operation* (EO). An EO is a "function-altering stimulus," one, that is, which causes another stimulus to take on reinforcing functions. An advertisement for an antiperspirant might make claims that using this product will reduce or eliminate sweating; in other words, it presents a rule for action based on the three-term contingency: the product becomes the discriminative stimulus, the proposed response repertoire involves buying and using it, and the promised consequences are a lower rate of perspiration and less social embarrassment. If the product is an entirely new brand, of which consumers will not have heard, they cannot by definition have established responding appropriately to these contingencies. Given the competitive nature of the antiperspirant market, there is no reason for thinking that this product will work any better than those currently in use and thus no special reason why the rule presented in the ad should be motivating. If, however, the message is presented by a famous sports personality, his or her presence may become an EO, changing the words into a motivating message by turning the rule into an augmental. The presence of this antecedent stimulus means that the rule has a greater likelihood of being acted upon.

Some behaviorists have turned, relatively recently, to the analysis of *stimulus equivalence* (Sidman, 1994), a phenomenon that has far-reaching implications for behavior theory as well as the experimental analysis of behavior. Nonhumans have proved capable of learning complex relationships if they are appropriately reinforced but generally do not innovate by initiating relationships they have not been explicitly taught (Sidman, 1994; for a selection of recent research, see, inter alia, Arntzen, 2012; Arntzen & Liland, 2019; Arntzen & Nartey, 2018; Hansen & Arntzen, 2018). By contrast, even young humans display the emergent behavior of relating A to C having been trained that A is related to B and that A is related to C (i.e., their selection of the appropriate response has been reinforced). This capacity for transitivity is one of three criteria used to establish *stimulus equivalence*, a phenomenon which appears peculiar to human animals. The other criteria are symmetry (matching A to A), and reflexivity (matching B to A having learned that A relates to B). The implication is that these stimuli (A, B and C) belong to the same *stimulus class*, since they evoke the identical response: for instance, a picture of a car (A), the written word "car" (B), and the written word "auto"

(C) are all likely to evoke the oral response "car." The role of stimulus equivalence in radical behaviorist interpretation is particularly interesting as it participates in relational frame theory. According to Sidman (1994) stimulus equivalence is a basic or primitive (i.e., unanalyzable) occurrence, the result of the contingencies of survival encountered in the course of phylogenic evolution rather than something acquired by learning. In this it resembles the phenomena of reinforcement and discrimination: we are just "built that way" (Sidman, 1994, p. 389).

However, relational frame theory (Hayes, Barnes-Holmes, & Roche, 2001; Hayes & Hayes, 1989) seeks to extend the analysis inherent in the study of stimulus equivalence. It emphasizes that the functions of a stimulus can be transferred to other stimuli, indeed that such a function can be understood only in terms of its relationships with other stimuli. A stimulus may come to reinforce behavior depending on whether it is greater than, less than, or equal to another stimulus that has already received the capacity to reinforce via a training procedure. Language can be understood in this way as a symbolic process in which the functions of one stimulus are transferred to another, which comes to stand for it. Because of the ubiquity of such transfers, the problem of the "poverty of the stimulus" is overcome: depending on the context, a pairing of stimuli can acquire numerous meanings and functions. An immensely wide range of linguistic abilities can thus be acquired. Relational responding of this kind is portrayed in relational frame theory as operant behavior, an overarching response class. Relational frames such as "equal to" or "fatter than" are defined in terms of three properties, which partially overlap with those Sidman employed to define stimulus equivalence. The three properties that are peculiar to relational frames are (1) mutual entailment, (2) combinatorial entailment, and (3) the transformation of functions (for an accessible introduction to relational frame theory, see Hayes, Strosahl, & Wilson, 1999).

Mutual entailment is the symmetry of stimulus equivalence: the derived bidirectionality of stimulus relations. The relationship A→B entails the relationship B→A. *Combinatorial entailment* is the transitivity and the equivalence of stimulus equivalence: when in a particular context A→B and B→C, and also a relation is entailed between A and C and another between C and A. For example, if A is harder than B and B is harder than C, then a harder than relation is entailed between A and C and a softer than relation between C and A. *A transformation of stimulus functions* occurs when the function of one stimulus is transferred to another stimulus, which is a comember of a relational network. If we have enjoyed a play by a particular author and are told that she has written a sequel, we are more likely to show marked approach behavior toward the new play: reading reviews, checking out where it is on stage, going to see it, and so on. If one hears that a scholar who has produced interesting research on the behavior analysis of environmental spoliation and conservation is now doing work on verbal behavior one is more likely to show similar attention to the later work. As these examples show, the transfer of function is highly situation- or context-specific, depending on how concepts such as "play," and "sequel," "environmental conservation," and "verbal behavior" participate in various relational frames that have become part of one's operant repertoire. In everyday discourse, we would say that the likelihood that one would exhibit the approach behaviors in question depends on one's interests and aspirations.

4.3 The contextual strategy

The contextual strategy that follows from the contextual stance is inductive: it makes no a priori assumption about the rationality of the system that is to be predicted but assumes that its behavior is environmentally determined. The environment is the agent. The procedure in which this strategy consists is as follows: first, treat the behavior to be predicted as environmentally determined; second, figure out the past contingencies that have shaped that behavior; third, predict how present and future contingencies will influence the continuity of that behavior. Steps two and three require figuring out the system's learning history, including the capacity of its behavior to be contingency-shaped and rule-governed. Step three predicts the susceptibility of future enactments of the behavior to rules and contingencies and thereby requires an assessment of the motivating or inhibiting nature of the behavior setting.

This strategy results in levels of explication which can range well beyond the purely descriptive. The zero-order level of analysis would be well illustrated by basic empirical regularities. In this case, the analysis *is* purely descriptive and makes no demands on higher level constructs to explain it. Even from a radical behavioristic viewpoint however it is incomplete: it fails either to explain observed behavior by relating it to the environmental conditions that shape and maintain it, or even to interpret it in these terms. Even a radical behaviorist analysis requires a first-order level of explanation which achieves this. An operant psychology would need to relate observed individual behaviors systematically to the patterns of reinforcement and punishment by which they can be explained and to the discriminative stimuli under whose control they might come. *But our analysis can go further still.* Radical behaviorism has long proceeded beyond the analysis of contingency-shaped behavior (its first-order level) by considering the (causal) role of private stimuli and the rule-governance of most if not all human behavior. Although in both cases the contingencies themselves have been held to provide ultimate control of human behavior, the interpretation of complex human behavior has in fact increasingly relied upon theoretical entities located within the individual. In contrast to the primitive radical behaviorism cited by Dennett (cf. Dennett, 1995), recent formulations deny that any but the simplest human behaviors can be considered entirely contingency-shaped—tapping one's fingers absentmindedly, for instance. The unlikelihood of operant conditioning occurring in humans without conscious awareness has long been noted (Brewer, 1974), casting doubt on whether the word "conditioning" is justified or useful. Most if not all human behavior is influenced by rules that specify setting−response−outcome contingencies which, at the most basic level, arise from the verbal behavior of others.

When the individual lacks a relevant learning history and therefore rules for performing a given behavior, decision-making is required. In the dual-process cognitive depictions of this, behavior is said to be preceded by "deliberative processing" or "systematic processing" or the "central route to persuasion" (Petty & Cacioppo, 1986). In a radical behaviorist interpretation, such behavior is governed by "other-rules" embodying social pressures. Lacking a learning history, the individual uses other rules as a surrogate. As he or she develops experience, a history of reinforcement and punishment prompts the generation of self-rules that take the place of others' formulations of the situation. Finally, this person's behavior is characterized by apparent spontaneity as the discriminative stimuli that compose the behavior setting evoke self-rule-governed responses. The higher levels of operant analysis which the contextual strategy makes possible apparently undermine Dennett's insistence that behaviorism cannot handle postdescriptive accounts of human choice.

An individual faced with a situation that is new to her has no specific learning history with respect to the behavior that is socially appropriate to such circumstances. However, in proportion to her having a learning history for rule-following, she is likely to seek out and act on "other-rules," those made available by members of her verbal community. As a result of her consequent actions, she acquires a learning history. Thereafter, reasoning with respect to her newly acquired behavioral experience will lead to the formation of "self-rules," those she formulates by reasoning about the situation and her performance within it and these rules will henceforth guide action without constant deliberation. The initial lack of a relevant learning history prompted a search for other-rules; the acquisition of such a history means that self-rules can be extracted from experience. This account is entirely consistent with radical behaviorism. However, once we acknowledge the individual's capacity to make self-rules, her behavior cannot be predicted (let alone controlled) by someone whose knowledge of her is confined to the contingencies of reinforcement in operation. Her capacity to think beyond the contingencies, to create her own history of reinforcement, even her own fantasies that bear no relation to her actual learning history, renders the behaviorist program of predicting and controlling behavior unfeasible (Garrett, 1996).

More generally, people have the capacity to create learning histories for themselves, to misrecall the past, and to act as though the resulting imaginings were true. People can reinterpret their past (and present) and act upon their deliberations even though (1) this is against their learning history and what it would lead one to predict they would do or (2) it is not the only course of conduct open to them. People join religious sects for instance having convinced themselves that their entire lives were leading up to this moment of conversion (rather than to running the gangland empire they seemed to have been moving toward since age 14, or becoming the professor of art history their postdoctoral studies had seemed to be preparing them for). This does not mean cognitive processes are autonomous since, except in cases of psychosis, the imagined history or potential course of behavior must come from somewhere, must have been described by others, for instance. However, such "mental simulation" or "personal rule formation and following" means that behavior is not necessarily the result of learning history. If we recognize that behavior can result from rules or descriptions of contingencies never encountered then we are justified, in the absence of a known learning history, in ascribing intentionality in order to try to predict behavior more accurately. The standard radical behaviorist response to this is twofold.

First, these imaginings, if real, are caused—and caused by external contingencies. But can this be empirically demonstrated? It would be necessary to demonstrate a one-to-one correspondence in order to do this. In fact, we have no access to an adult's learning history, which would be necessary to make such a demonstration, nor to her imaginings since they are, by definition, covert events. Second, the real contingencies will take over control of behavior once the individual is exposed to them. Again, can this be demonstrated empirically rather than asserted as an act of faith? What are the "real" contingencies? In the animal laboratory, they are obvious enough. In the world of naturalistic settings, the complexity of different environmental impingements on an individual, the fact that her behavior is "multiply determined" even in the behaviorists' terms, that several schedules of reinforcement may have brought her here, and so on, makes it impossible to know what the actual contingencies are with any greater accuracy than we can determine what the imagined contingencies are. Chomsky's review put paid to the idea that the precision available in the laboratory is equally available to the interpretive operant psychologist.

A system like radical behaviorism which posits prediction and control as the criteria for scientific success falls short as a comprehensive explanatory system if it can be shown that its subject matter cannot be predicted. The above argument implies not simply that, given the present state of knowledge and investigative technique, particular behaviors cannot be predicted, but that a certain class of behavior is inherently unpredictable. Rule-governed behavior often cannot be predicted: this is so whenever the individual acts upon covert rules that are not based on simple cost−benefit analysis and are not therefore directly amenable to others who are faced solely with the cost−benefit facts (Garrett, 1996; Prelec & Herrnstein, 1991).

4.4 Stances compared

While the intentional strategy provides a logical basis for understanding the philosophical underpinnings of cognitive psychology, radical behaviorism is a natural starting point for delineating the contextual strategy (Foxall, 1999). The equation of the contextual idiom that underlies radical behaviorism with its portrayal of psychology as nonintentional is not always precisely what is meant by "contextualism," though Pepper's (1942) account of contextualism provides a philosophical treatment that is clearly contiguous with the present exposition of the contextual stance. Pepper (1942, pp. 232–233) points out, for instance, that the contextualist is not interested in past events per se but in "the event live in its present. What we ordinarily mean by history, he says, is an attempt to *re-present* events, to make them in some way alive again ... It is not an act conceived as alone or cut off that we mean; it is an act in and with its setting, an act in its context." The act in context is the *root metaphor*, as Pepper puts it, of contextualism; we should, today, more likely call it a *global paradigm* (for detailed discussion of contextualism, see Hayes, Hayes, Reese, & Sarbin, 1993). There is no conflict here, but presenting contextualism as a philosophical *stance* (in parallel with the intentional *stance*) makes possible some emphases that are not explicit in Pepper's account. It also facilitates direct comparison with the intentional stance. However, there are certain advantages in presenting the argument from contextuality in terms of a *stance*, especially since the present aim is to compare this position with that which arises from the argument from intentionality.

Like the intentional stance, the contextual stance is a preempirical philosophy of science, a means of conceptualizing how the world may work prior to directly investigating it. It states, as we have noted, that *behavior is predictable in so far as it is assumed to be environmentally determined; specifically, in so far as it is under the control of a learning history that represents the reinforcing and punishing consequences of similar behavior previously enacted in settings similar to that currently encountered.* It is the prediction and explanation of behavior in terms of the interaction of the current behavior setting and the individual's learning history that is at the heart of the contextual stance. Behavior setting and learning history intersect to define the *situation*, which is the immediate determinant of the probability of responding. By prefiguring the likely positive and aversive consequences of behavior, the situation promotes or facilitates the kinds of response that the individual has previously enacted in similar settings.

Dennett's *intentional stance*, as we have noted, predicts behavior by attributing suitable desires (goals) and beliefs (information) to "intentional systems," those entities, including humans and nonhumans, and computers, that are amenable to second-guessing of this kind. The contextual stance, by contrast, predicts and explains behavior by attributing it to its environmental effects, the rewards and sanctions it tends to produce. The intentional strategy, by identifying the propositional attitudes necessary for the organism's adaptation to its environment, provides social cognitivism, the dominant paradigm, with a rationale for its research program. The contextual stance, by contrast, proposes that the behavior of a system can be predicted from knowledge of its current *behavior setting*—that is the opportunities open to it to behave and the consequences of so behaving, and its *learning history* that gives salience to some elements of the behavior setting by permitting the individual to value/evaluate those consequences (i.e., by comparing the *costs* of performing the behavior with its *rewards*). Hence, it is closely associated with radical behaviorism and provides a vehicle through which the nature of radical behaviorist interpretation can be explored.

Recall that the intentional strategy predicts the behavior of a *rational* system (Dennett, 1987a, p. 17) by, *first*, treating the object whose behavior is to be predicted as a rational agent; *second*, figuring out what beliefs that agent should have, given its place in the world and its purpose; do the same for its desires; and *third*, predicting how it will act to further its goals in the light of its beliefs. The contextual strategy makes no a priori ascription of rationality to the system but predicts its environmentally determined behavior. The test of this strategy rests on its capacity to elucidate learning history and hence reveal the vulnerability of the individual's behavior to the setting variables to which it is exposed. Both strategies entail objective, third-person stances. Dennett (1978, pp. 3—4) states "… a particular thing is an intentional system only in relation to the strategies of someone who is trying to explain and predict its behavior." There is no assumption in the intentional stance that the system *really* has beliefs and desires—only that its behavior is better predicted if these are ascribed to it. Hence, "The decision to adopt the strategy is pragmatic, and is not intrinsically right or wrong" (Dennett, 1987a, p. 7), words that echo Skinner's claim, already quoted, that the truth criterion of radical behaviorist interpretation inheres in its usefulness (1988e, p. 364). The contextual stance, by contrast, works not by ascribing internal mental operations to a system but by observing external environment—environment regularities. The sources of information on these regularities are threefold: first, by observation and inference of contingency-shaping; second, by observation/inference of rules expressed by other persons to the system in question, or articulated by the system in question; and, third, by inference from the regularities of context in context observed of the system.

These inferences and observations are never of "what is going on in the system's mind"; nor are they intentional ascriptions. They are observations or inferences of n-term contingencies (Sidman, 1994), of which the "three-term contingency" is the most familiar explanatory device within this paradigm. The difference between teleology and contingency is further clarified by consideration of the former's assumption of rationality on the part of the agent whose behavior is to be predicted or explained. Dennett (1978, pp. 6—7) states that an intentional system is rational in that it *optimally* achieves its designated/ascribed goals. Hence, "one predicts behavior ... by ascribing to the system *the possession of certain information* and supposing it to be *directed by certain goals*, and then working out the most reasonable or appropriate action on the basis of these ascriptions and suppositions" (p. 6). "It is a small step to calling the information possessed the computer's *beliefs*, its goals and subgoals its *desires*" (Dennett, 1978). The behavior of a contextual system is contingent upon the prior environmental consequences produced by its behavior; it is contingent, not necessarily rational in the sense of optimizing, though it may be rationalized in the sensed of reasoned out where "reasoning out" is understood to be a behavior (Skinner, 1974).

The intentional system is not autonomous—otherwise it would not be predictable. Indeed, Dennett (1987a, p. 49) claims that "A system's beliefs are those it *ought to have* given its perceptual capacities, its epistemic needs and its biography." "A system's desires are those it *ought to have*, given its biological needs and the most practicable means of satisfying them. Thus intentional systems desire survival and procreation, and hence desire food, security, health, sex, wealth, power, influence...." "A system's behavior will consist of those acts that it *would be rational* for an agent with those beliefs and desires to perform." The use of the intentional stance, therefore, depends on teleological reasoning by one intentional system about the needs, beliefs, desires, epistemology, biology and circumstances of what it takes to be another such system. This depends on common ground between the systems: the predicting system may generalize from its own needs, beliefs, and desires to those of the target system. It may also rely on observation and reasoning. But the key component is the assumption that the target system is rational in the pursuit of its desires. Not that Dennett (1988) claims that intentional systems are fully rational at all times; but they are "marvelously rational" (p. 52), rational enough that is for this to be a reasonable assumption for this stance. The contextual stance does not rule out rationality but understands it as a special case of contingent behavior. The focus in the contextual stance is on the actual control of behavior by its environmental consequences. There is no a priori reason to expect that this will accord with optimization; however, the empirical behavior analysis involving the matching law indicates that it usually will in practice (Herrnstein, 1997). It is now possible to consider at greater length the special nature of radical behaviorism.

4.5 Extensional behavioral science

It is usual to portray the defining characteristic of radical behaviorism as its avoidance of mediational terms, be they intervening variables or hypothetical constructs (cf. Amsel, 1989; Moore, 1998). This is not an isolated opinion: Staddon (2001b, p. 148) states unequivocally that "for radical behaviorism as well as for the earlier Watsonian variety, 'internal states' are a no-no." The argument is that since the explanatory ideal of radical behaviorism is to account for behavior exclusively by reference to its contingent environmental consequences and their associated observable stimuli, the contingencies at its heart neither require nor permit mediation by cognitive, neural, or hypothetical states, events, or constructs (Skinner, 1963). Radical behaviorism is said moreover to be unique in its avoidance of terms that mediate stimuli and response: on this basis radical behaviorism can be delineated not only from contemporary cognitivism but equally from the neo-behaviorist approaches of Tolman and Hull. Skinner's oft-quoted statement in favor of the kind of theory that consists in empirical generalizations and avoids "theoretical terms" sums up the position. His objection to *theory* is an objection to "any explanation of an observed fact which appeals to events taking place somewhere else, at some other level of observation, described in different terms, and measured, if at all, in different dimensions." (Skinner, 1950, pp. 193–194). For Skinner, the practice of science consists in "a search for order, for uniformities, for lawful relations among the events in nature. It begins ... by observing single episodes, but it quickly passes on to the general rule, to scientific law" (Skinner, 1953, p. 13). Such a descriptive science is not antitheoretical, though its theoretical concentration is on the establishment of empirical regularities rather than on explanations that employ unobservables (such as attitudes, intentions and traits of personality) which are alleged to exist at some other level than the observed data (Skinner, 1950).

The suggestion has been made that radical behaviorism does not in practice avoid mediational terms and that its "private events" are simply theoretically underdeveloped mediational constructs (Staats, 1996). If this were accepted, it would be difficult to avoid the conclusion that radical, Tolmanian and Hullian systems differ only in degree rather than kind and that they have similar implications for the relationship between behaviorism and cognitivism and, indeed, for the origins of cognitive psychology. This issue is important at least in its implications for the relationship between behaviorism and cognitivism. For the argument has been made that cognitivism has its origins in the mediationism of both Tolman and Hull (e.g., Leahey, 1987, p. 390; Schnaitter, 1999, p. 217): while cognitivism is cast as a natural successor to the mediational systems of both of these men, Skinner's radical behaviorism is portrayed as the natural offspring of the behaviorist ideal (e.g., Lee, 1988).

My argument that the avoidance of intentional explanation rather than the avoidance of mediational processes is the hallmark of radical behaviorism has two components. First, radical behaviorism does indeed employ mediating events and that they are moreover essential to its conception of private events. Second, it is in this respect distinct from the neo-behaviorisms of Tolman and Hull, which do employ propositional content. Definitively support for either of these arguments would require an exhaustive analysis of the entire output of Skinner: if such an analysis revealed a single instance in which he employed propositional attitudes, the thesis would fail.

The argument, therefore, takes the following form. First comes the proposition that radical behaviorism has demonstrated that it can explain behavior without recourse to propositional content, thereby demonstrating the logical independence of the contextual stance as it manifests in radical behaviorism. Second, it is argued that radical behaviorism, nevertheless, employs mediating variables in order to achieve its explanations. Third, the neo-behaviorisms of Tolman and Hull are shown to employ not only mediating events but also mediating events that are propositional in nature.

The first proposition concerns the logical independence of the contextual stance. Skinner's assertion that there can be an independent science of behavior rests upon the capacity of behaviorism to demonstrate that it can deal nonintentionally with the phenomena usually attributed to "mind." The claim of the contextual stance, as a philosophical basis of behavioral science, is that radical behaviorism can indeed cope with all the phenomena that fall within its purview without recourse to intentional idioms. That is, it can describe them extensionally, without resorting to propositional attitudes or opacity of reference. This is true of contingency-shaped behavior, the verbal behavior of the speaker, and that of the listener. As the following analysis shows, the language describing each of these is referentially transparent.

Behavior analysis is an extensional science that does not rely on the attribution of propositional content to any of the elements of the three-term contingency. It describes both contingency-shaped and rule-governed behaviors in terms of "a system of functional relationships between the organism and the environment" (Smith, 1994, pp. 127−128). Hence, an *operant response* "is not simply a response that the organism thinks will have a certain effect, it does have that effect." Further, a *reinforcer* "is not simply a stimulus that the organism desires to occur. It is a stimulus that will alter the rate of behavior upon which its occurrence is contingent." And a *discriminative stimulus* "is not simply a stimulus that has been correlated with a certain contingency in the organism's experience. It is one that successfully alters the organism's operant behavior with respect to that contingency." Descriptions of contingent behavior do not take propositions as their object; rather their object is relationships between an organism's behavior, its environmental consequences, and the elements that set the occasion for those contingent consequences. So behavior analysis does not attribute propositional content to any of the elements of the three-term contingency. "Instead of accepting a proposition as its object, the concept of reinforcement accepts an event or a state of affairs - such as access to pellets - as its object" (Smith, 1994, p. 128). Mentalistic description takes the form, "The animal desires that a pellet should become available." The behavior analytic description is not "The animal's lever presses are reinforced that a pellet becomes available." It is "The animal's lever presses are reinforced by access to pellets." A discriminative stimulus would not be described as a signal *that* something will happen but simply that a contingency exists. "It attributes an effect to the stimulus, but not a content." Whereas the substitutability of identicals fails in mentalistic statements (such statements are said to be logically opaque), behavioral categories are logically transparent, suggesting that "behavioral categories are not a subspecies of mentalistic categories" (Smith, 1994, p. 129).

Neither is the proposition that "reinforcer" merely denotes "desire" feasible: desires are not equivalent to reinforcers, nor reinforcers to desires. Commonsense notions imply that if a stimulus is (positively) reinforcing it is desired, and if it is desired it is because it is a (positive) reinforcer but in fact neither holds. Objects of desire may not be attainable (the fountain of youth, perpetual motion) and so cannot be (linked to) reinforcers. Nor are reinforcers necessarily desired: on FI schedules, electric shock maintains responding for monkeys, pigeons, and rats. The shocks are easily avoidable, but are not avoided. They cannot be "desired," yet they reinforce behavior. Nor yet do functional units of the speaker's verbal behavior such as mands and tacts (Skinner, 1957) have propositional content. They are simply statements of contingencies that account for an individual's behavior in the absence of his or her direct exposure to those contingencies. A mand is "a verbal response that specifies its reinforcer" (Catania, 1992, p. 382): for example, "Give me a drink" plus the unspoken, "You owe me a favor," or "Else I shall ignore your requests in future." Even if this is expressed as "I desire that you give me a drink...," it is actually no more than a description of contingencies. A tact is "a verbal discriminative response... in the presence of or shortly after a stimulus" (Catania, 1992, p. 399): "Here is the bank." Even if this were expressed as, "I want you to see the bank," its function would be confined to establishing the stimulus control of the word "bank," as when the listener replies, "Oh, yes, the bank." More technically, the *mand* denotes the consequences contingent upon following the instructions of the speaker or of imitating his or her example. Much advertising consists of mands—"Buy three and get one free!" "Don't forget the fruit gums, mum"—which indicate contingencies that are under the control of the speaker. *Tacts* present a con*tact* with part of the environment and, depending on learning history, a potential for behavior on the part of the recipient. A trade mark or logo may be followed by making a purchase or entering a store. The definitive source is Skinner's (1957) *Verbal Behavior*.

The functional units of the listener's verbal behavior, as proposed by Zettle and Hayes (1982), similarly describe contingencies rather than express propositional content. Pliance, for instance, is the behavior of the listener who complies with a verbal request or instruction; hence, "Pliance is rule-governed behavior under the control of apparent socially mediated consequences for a correspondence between the rule and relevant behavior" (Hayes, Zettle, & Rosenfarb, 1989, p. 201). Pliance is thus simply the behavior involved in responding positively to a mand. Tracking is "rule-governed behavior under the control of the apparent correspondence between the rule and the way the world is arranged" (Hayes et al., 1989, p. 206). It involves tracking the physical environment as when following instructions how to get to the supermarket. Once again, its form—for example, "Turn left at the traffic light" plus the unspoken "And you'll get to Sainsbury's"—is a basic description of contingencies rather than an expression of propositional attitudes. Precisely as Smith has concluded with respect to contingency-shaped behavior, we may conclude with respect to rule-governance: "Beliefs and desires have propositional content. ... Designations of discriminative stimuli and reinforcing stimuli, by contrast, do not accept *that*-clauses." (Smith, 1994, p. 128). A third functional unit of listener behavior has no corresponding unit for the speaker: the *augmental* (Zettle & Hayes, 1982) is a highly motivating rule that states emphatically how a particular behavior will be reinforced or avoid punishment. "Just one more packet top and I can claim my free cell phone!"

Nor does radical behaviorism attribute propositional content to the "inner world we subjectively observe" (Smith, 1994, p. 138). This is interpreted as a "world of events." "Beliefs, desires, intentions, etc., have propositional content but are not the objects of subjective awareness, whereas inner speech, feelings, images, etc., are objects of inner awareness but do not have propositional content." While we undoubtedly have the thoughts and feelings we report, there is no reason why these inner events must give rise to inferences of beliefs, desires, and other propositional content. Indeed, as long as we are willing to assume analytically that there is no ontological discontinuity between the within-the-skin world, to use Skinner's terminology, and the outer, then we are entitled to treat the inner simply as a series of stimuli and responses, albeit private rather than public. In other words, they can be represented in an extensional way if they are simply understood as constituted by discriminative or other stimuli for particular behavior. We do not, therefore, have to speak of thinking and feeling in intentional terms and can thus pursue an extensional approach, at least toward the prediction and control of behavior.

We have reached the crux of the argument. On one hand it has emerged that it is legitimate to treat private events as stimuli and responses, that is, extensionally (though this entails the analytic assumption of ontological continuity between these private thoughts and feelings and publicly available elements of the three-term contingency). What I hope is equally clear is that this formulation is a function of the way in which we use language. Since there is more than one way to use language, it is equally legitimate to someone who accepts the logical distinction between extensional and intentional sentences to argue that the thinking and feeling which Skinner characterizes as private events can be alternatively viewed as intentional because they are necessarily about something: we feel *something*, we think *of* or *that*, and so on. They can be represented as mental, therefore, in the sense that a different kind of linguistic form is needed in speaking of them. As long as we can avoid that linguistic form, we may succeed in formulating an extensional behavioral science; when we employ intentional idioms, we are necessarily invoking intentional explanations. I shall argue that from a pragmatic point of view, each approach leads to similar (if not identical) levels of prediction and influence, if only because the intentional stance relies fundamentally on the contextual in order to achieve these functions. And I also shall argue that at the level of providing as comprehensive and logically consistent an explanation of behavior they also converge, this time because the contextual stance is fundamentally dependent on the intentional in order to accomplish this. Before this, however, it is important to distinguish radical behaviorism's avoidance of intentional terms (and consequently its prerogative as the basis of an extensional science) from the more familiar justification of its uniqueness, its avoidance of mediational or theoretical terms per se. Here, I think, radical behaviorism has been less clear-cut in maintaining its distinctiveness.

4.6 Behavior theory

For, whatever its exponents claim, theory is inevitable in radical behaviorism, at least at the interpretational end of its explanatory spectrum. The view that radical behaviorism does not in practice rely on mediational terms has been countered on several grounds. First, inferred events are actually employed in radical behaviorist explanations. In a review of Donahoe and Palmer's (1994) *Learning and Complex Behavior*, Shull (1995) argues that the inclusion of inferred events may make it possible

> to conceptualize some behavior as occurring due to the presentation of a discriminative stimulus or a conditioned aversive stimulus, even though no such stimulus can be found in the environment. Internal events may be inferred to play those roles. Without inferred events, the occurrence of the behavior may be traced to observable antecedents, but the demonstrated molar relationships can often have an ad hoc character instead of being expressions of familiar behavioral processes. For someone who highly values conceptual integration as a scientific goal, then, accounts that rely on inferred events may hold some attractions.

Shull goes on to argue that

> Skinner, of course, made extensive use of these sorts of inferred events in his interpretations of complex phenomena such as "self-awareness", "self-control," "problem-solving," and verbal behavior (for example, Skinner, 1953, 1957, 1969a, 1969b). Autoclitic verbal behavior and editing, for example, were conceptualized as being evoked by stimulation (sometimes conditioned aversive stimulation) arising from the incipient stages of other verbal behavior. Other examples of behavior-analytic accounts based on inferred response and stimulus events include Schoenfield and Cumming's (1963) analysis of perceptual

phenomena, Hefferline's (1962) and Sidman's (1989) analysis of "defense mechanisms" such as repression, Sidman's (1989) interpretation of "conscience," Keller's (1958) analysis of skill learning, and Dinsmoor's (1985) interpretation of attentional phenomena.

In this, Skinner appears to differ not as sharply as radical behaviorist philosophers of psychology have suggested from neo-behaviorists such as Hull, Guthrie, and Miller. All of these

made skillful use of inferred internal responses and stimuli to construct parsimonious accounts of complex behavior in terms of acquired S—R relationships. Interestingly, Skinner's approach has sometimes been distinguished from those of the S—R theorists on the grounds that Skinner was unwilling to infer internal stimulus and response events to mediate temporal gaps between environmental cause and behavioral effect. It is indeed true that Skinner was often critical of such practices, especially when he was in his "prediction and control" mood. But he sometimes displayed a "conceptual integration" mood as well, and his interpretations, at least in their general style and purpose, would be hard to distinguish form those of Hull, Guthrie, Miller and kindred behavior theorists (see the exchange between Zuriff and Skinner in Catania & Harnad, 1988, pp. 216—217).

Zuriff (1979) notes Skinner's insistence that "postulated inner processes do not provide adequate explanations of behavior. At best they are merely collateral by-products of the environmental variables controlling behavior." (Zuriff, 1979, p. 1). Nevertheless, he notes Skinner's ingenious interpretations of complex human behaviors in terms of covert stimuli and responses. Zuriff's argument is that "insofar as these covert behavioral events exert control over observable behavior, they qualify as inner causes." He provides 10 examples from Skinner's work of internal stimuli and responses acting as inner controlling variables; often these are intermediate links in a causal chain that has external variables as its ultimate causes. "Nevertheless, in each example, an inner event is hypothesized to play a causal role, acting as a link in a causal chain, albeit an intermediate one." (p. 2).

Behavior analysts' interpretations are even more prone to the assumption of inferred entities. The analysis of verbal behavior, for instance, incorporates as causes unuttered verbal stimuli. The analysis of the *autoclitic* is a case in point. In Skinner's analysis of the autoclitic, the speaker is said to tact his or her own behavior before it is uttered, thereby transforming it into a discriminative stimulus. The discriminative stimulus in question is, however, nothing less than an inferred unobservable. Smith (1994) concludes that Skinner's theory of verbal behavior falls between a behaviorist and a cognitive account. Other examples can be found, among which the "automatic reinforcement" of playing the piano to oneself stands out so strongly that it is acknowledged as a theoretical term by some radical behaviorists

(Parrott, 1986; Reese, 1986) as well as mentalistic critics (Chomsky, 1959). Nor are such inferences confined to the operant interpretation of verbal behavior. The private events of others, a concept central to the demarcation of radical from methodological behaviorism, cannot but be inferred.[4] They attract all the philosophical problems long associated with the inference of "other minds." Yet Skinner consciously infers the private verbal and emotional responses of others and acknowledges that they may serve as proximal (noninitiating) causes of behavior (see Skinner's, 1988a, 1988b, 1988c, responses to Mackenzie, 1988; Schnaitter, 1988; Stalker & Ziff, 1988). Even if the inferred events are cast by nonbehaviorists as cognitive, their lack of propositional content implies that they are not equivalent to the mental entities posited by the intentional stance. Moreover, to the extent that they point to the kind of equivalence proposed by Overskeid (1995), the argument that they are necessarily cognitive is unproven. Smith's assertion that verbal behavior involves cognitive events seems at this stage an a priori assumption that is backed up by nothing more than assertion of the conventional folk wisdom of cognitivism in the face of a lack of a more convincing alternative.

The private events of others have in common with intentional attributions that they are inferred entities. In parallel with the operation of the intentional stance, they are ascribed by adherents of the contextual stance on the basis that they are the private events (the thoughts and feelings) that an organism *ought* to have, given its position and behavior, that is, given its behavior setting and learning history. They may be self-reported but then so can be propositional attitudes. This raises enormous difficulties for radical behaviorist interpretation. First, we have to recognize that, in providing an account of the behavior of others, *any* appeal to private events is a matter of constructing theoretical variables to account for observed behavior. Second, the status of an individual's privately experienced covert events *as scientific data* must be acknowledged. Kitchener (1996, pp. 116–120) dissects Skinner's categorization of theoretical terms as referring to events (1) taking place somewhere else, (2) occurring at some other level of observation, (3) described in different terms, and (4) measured if at all in different dimensions. Even one's own private events are, *contra* Skinner, (1) taking place *somewhere else*—that is, somewhere beyond the observation of the scientific community and, therefore, even if accepted within that community as relevant to scientific inquiry, of a different epistemological status from other scientific facts; (2) *at some other level of observation*—the evidence for the nature and function of these events is of a different order from that of other scientific facts

---

4. If it is feasible in radical behaviorism to infer the private events of other people in order to render their behavior more intelligible, then of course one could of course ask why the strategy cannot be extended to the private events of nonhumans or machines. However, "sufficient unto the day..."

(those amenable to public scrutiny); they are not open to experimental analysis, for instance; and are (3) *described* and (4) *measured in different terms*—clearly the terminology is identical to that used for publicly available stimuli and responses, but the measurement can only be different. In the case of both my own and others' private events, I must make a leap of faith in assuming ontological continuity between the kind of stimuli and responses that can be manipulated in the experimental setting and those that are private. The lack of experimental analysis of private events renders their measurement qualitatively different.

Third, we have to resolve the difference between the private events of radical behaviorist interpretation and the propositional attitudes of intentional explanation. They are epistemologically distinct: private events, because they are *treated as* (i.e., spoken of and used as) physical stimuli and responses, belong to an extensional approach to explanation, while propositional attitudes are part of an intensional psychology. These are incommensurable approaches to explanation and there is no question of combining them in some way or of one providing an explanation of events that can simply be substituted for the other. Let us not imagine that behaviorism and cognitivism are converging. However, the general criticisms that behaviorists make of mentalistic explanation—the three main ones are the surplus meaning of the construct, the short-circuiting of explanation, and the tendency toward vacuous explanation—can be applied to attempts at interpreting behavior in terms of private events.

4.7 Radical behaviorism's claim to uniqueness

It is the avoidance of propositional content, not that of mediational events, which serves to distinguish radical behaviorism from other neo-behaviorisms. The foregoing analysis does not put radical behaviorism on a par with other neo-behaviorisms such as those of Tolman and Hull, differing from them by degree but presenting the same kind of mediational explanation. Its import is that we must look beyond mediation per se for the essential difference between radical behaviorism and other neo-behaviorisms. The essential distinction is not between systems that employ mediation and those that do not but between those that employ explanatory terms that have propositional content and those that are nonintentional. In view of this claim, it is hardly surprising that those other neo-behaviorisms are the ones that gave rise to cognitivism. The following examination suggests that radical behaviorism is the only neo-behaviorist psychology to provide a basis for an extensional science of behavior.

Tolman's concepts generally appear to have propositional content. Despite his early efforts to operationalize *purpose* in terms that were anchored to observable reality, his later cognitive turn seems to have put him beyond the scope of descriptive behaviorism. Purposes are inferred entities.

If a stimulus is present but the organism does not respond, behaviorists such as Guthrie or Skinner would say that no learning had taken place. But Tolman posits cognition as an intervening variable: "The stimulus is perceived but the response does not occur because it is not in accord with the organism's purpose" (Bry, 1975, p. 56). *Latent* learning may nevertheless take place, which may serve the organism's purpose as well as stimulus-induced learning. Reinforcement is not necessary to learning, though it may lead to the *expectations* that guide further behavior. Tolman's distinction between learning and performance meant that he needed to make no direct link between stimulus and response. This positing of intervening variables is sometimes said to be more parsimonious than an account that looks for one-to-one connections between stimulus and response.

MacCorquodale and Meehl (1954) find evidence of intentionality in Tolman's conceptualization. They distinguish a data language to which Tolman's dependent and independent variables conform and belong, and a quasidata language to which some of his intervening variables, those which take the form of hypothetical constructs (i.e., have surplus meaning) belong. Tolman (1932) stated that he wished to avoid hypothetical constructs, "in which a construct acquires attributes which exceed the original defining operations," and stressed that his use of intervening variables such as "cognition" and "expectancy" were to be understood in terms of the "EOs," in which an intervening variable is functionally related to both an empirically specified dependent variable and an empirically specified independent variable. Intervening variables are, therefore, ideally, theoretically neutralized. MacCorquodale and Meehl (1954, p. 183) find, however, that the empirical support Tolman adduces for his intervening variables relies for its power on "the common-sense kind of surplus meaning [that is] informally attached to these theoretically 'neutralized' terms." In order to account for the observed behavior of rats in mazes, Tolman (1932, p. 175) attributes to them the capacity to recognize one part of the maze as the other end of another part. MacCorquodale and Meehl (1954, p. 184) comment: that

> *recognize is not defined here, nor does it appear in the glossary or index; and surely it is not a word in the data language. The other end of A is a phrase ordinarily in the data language, but used thus only when it describes facts about the maze. In this sentence, however, it occurs in a clause following the word as, where the whole sentence of which it is a part says something, not about the maze, but about the rat's state (or recognition).*

We have already noted that Skinner's covert events do not contain propositional content. As Kitchener points out (Kitchener, 1977; cf. Kitchener, 1979, 1996; Ringen, 1976), however, Hull's do. Not only does Hull have to treat an r_g as an ordinary response, subject to reinforcement, extinction, etc., he is also forced to treat it as "expectation ordinarily understood," so that it cannot be an ordinary response at all. As Deutsch (1960) argues, a fractional goal response must be reinforced by the goal response of which it is a part. Thus an r_g is not an ordinary response but an expectancy. "If this is correct, then the Hullian r_g–s_g mechanism for explaining purposive behavior must be judged to be inadequate since it presupposes teleological and cognitive concepts from the start and therefore cannot derive them as 'secondary principles' from neutral a-teleological concepts" (Kitchener, 1977, p. 54).[5]

The intentional nature of anticipatory goal response seems also to be apparent from Zuriff's (1985, pp. 126–127) account in which he uses this concept as a means by which behaviorists deal with the apparent foreknowledge that organisms have of future events. Zuriff, however, seems unaware of the implications of the philosophically intentional nature of r_g when he states "... behavior under the antecedent control of anticipatory goal reactions not only shows the marks of purposiveness but also can manifest the foreknowledge, expectations, and intentions of human action." (p. 127).

Yet there is good reason for both the dichotomous approach that Shull attributes to Skinner and the unequivocal attitude of other behavior analysts toward the inclusion of mediating events in a science of behavior and in radical behaviorist interpretation. The explicit admission of mediation often leads quickly to the inclusion of intentional idioms, as mediating events cease to be mere building blocks within a theory and take on explanatory functions that necessitate their being about other events or entities. So it is quite easy for an account of behavior in terms of classical conditioning to lead to the understanding that the conditioned stimulus (CS) is a *signal for* the unconditioned stimulus, that what a stimulus (S) gives rise to is not a response but to

---

5. Kitchener's (1977, p. 54) full comment here is instructive: "The most damaging criticism of the r_g–s_g mechanism for purposive behavior is an objection raised by J. A. Deutsch (1960). Deutsch argues (convincingly in my opinion) that Hull is forced to treat r_g as an ordinary response, subject to the well-established experimental laws of conditioning, extinction, etc. At the same time, however, Deutsch claims, Hull is also forced to treat an r_g as an expectation ordinarily understood and, consequently such a response cannot be an ordinary response at all. [Comment by Foxall: Compare Hull's remarks: "When $r_g \rightarrow s_g$ leads to $S_g \rightarrow R_g$, i.e., when the anticipation of food leads to the actual eating of food, we have what we shall call the *realization of an anticipation*" (1952, p. 133). See also Amsel and Rashotte (1984) and Rossiter and Foxall (2008).] For example, Hull believed an r_g (e.g., salivation) was an "anticipatory response" to the goal stimulus (food). However, Deutsch suggests, responses can be reinforced in various ways and one way of reinforcing the r_g in question would be by means of the goal stimulus water. Water should therefore reinforce an r_g (even though this r_g is a fractional part of the original goal response of eating). But such an account is inadequate to explain certain kinds of maze behavior. The results can only be explained, according to Deutsch, if it is assumed that a fractional goal response must be reinforced by the goal response it is part of (and not by different goal responses). But to assume this is to assume an r_g is not like an ordinary response at all but rather is equivalent to the ordinary notion of expectancy (along with the associated notions of the confirmation or frustration of such an expectancy). If this is correct, then the Hullian r_g–s_g mechanism for explaining purposive behavior must be judged to be inadequate since it presupposes teleological and cognitive concepts from the start and therefore cannot derive them as 'secondary principles' from neutral a-teleological concepts."

an *expectation of* reinforcement (Bolles, 1972),[6] that mediating stimuli and responses can account for cognitive (i.e., representational) phenomena (Staats, 1996),[7] and so on. The safest means by which such semantic drift

---

6. Berridge (2000) makes the progression from mediationism to intentionalism clear in his description of the history of behavioral psychology. Bolles's (1972) account of behavior in terms of the expectation of hedonic consequences of Bolles follows the S—S theory of Tolman rather than the S—R theory of Hull but suggests that what is learned are S—S associations of a particular kind and function: an association is learned between a CS and a subsequent hedonic stimulus (S*) that elicits pleasure. The first S does not elicit a response but an expectation of the second S (S*). This explains why animals sometimes act as though they have received a reward when they have not: for example, the raccoon that washes a coin as though it were food, presumably displays "misbehavior," or autoshaping, or schedule-induced polydipsia. Berridge (2000) argues that useful as this is it fails to explain why the animal still approaches the reinforcer (say food) rather than waiting for it to appear and enjoying the S* in the interim. He discusses the approach of Bindra (1978) who proposes the hedonic transfer of incentive properties to the CS. Bindra accepts the S—S* theory but argues that the S does not simply cause the animal to expect the S*: it also elicits a central motivational state that causes the animal to perceive the S as an S*. The S assumes the motivational properties that normally belong to the S*. These motivational properties are incentive properties, which attract the animal and elicit goal-directed behavior and possibly consumption. Through association with the S*, the S acquires the same functions as the S*. An animal approaches the CS for a reward and finds the signal (S) attractive; if the CS is food, the animal wants to eat it. If it is an S for a tasty food S*, the animal may take pleasure in its attempt to eat the CS (Berridge, 2000, p. 236; see also Bouton & Franselow, 1997). But if CSs were incentives one would always respond to them whether or not one were hungry. The question is to explain how CSs interact with drive states. Toates (1986), therefore, builds on the Bolles—Bindra theory by positing that both cognitive expectancy and more basic reward processes might occur simultaneously in the individual. All of these theories are necessarily intentional since they deal in expectancies.

7. Staats (1996) goes beyond the Skinnerian and Hullian systems to propose an approach to human environment that incorporates both classical and operant conditioning. The contribution of Staats's behaviorism is that it combines the roles of classical and operant conditioning into a single system in which a stimulus performs three functions. The first function of a stimulus is to elicit an emotional response (S→r). In classical conditioning the emotion-eliciting function of an unconditioned stimulus is transferred to a neutral (subsequently conditioned) stimulus and, in higher conditioning, this function may be further passed to any number of originally neutral stimuli that become in turn conditioned elicitors. Emotion-eliciting stimuli are those that reinforce motor responses enacted prior to their presentation (R→S). This is the second function of the stimulus; it is thus the capacity of a stimulus to elicit an emotional response that determines what can be a reinforcer. These two functions of a stimulus show how classical and operant conditioning are related in the environmental production of emotional and motor responses. The third function of a stimulus inheres in its ability to elicit approach-avoidance. Associated with each emotional response is an emotional stimulus or stimulus function, which elicits the motor response (S→r→s→R). Approaching an object that elicits a positive emotional response is often reinforced. As a result, any positive emotion-eliciting stimulus will come to elicit approach. This mechanism, once learned, generalizes to any stimulus that elicits a positive emotional response. While a stimulus that elicits positive emotion elicits approach, avoidance is elicited by a stimulus that elicits negative emotion. In this incentive or directive function, the stimulus brings on approach-avoidance, which thus follows it; contrast this with reinforcement in which the stimulus follows the environment it strengthens. Although he goes further than most behaviorists who embrace cognitive phenomena in anchoring cognition in behavior, Staats nonetheless proposes a theory in which representative images (which are *of* or *about*) other phenomena cause behavior.

can be avoided is to deny the relevance of mediating events altogether, even though on other occasions, notably those of interpreting complex behavior with the tools made available by a relatively simple experimental analysis, their usefulness can be acknowledged. Sometimes the drift is made light of, as in Bolles's (1979, pp. 85–87) account of Tolman's going beyond the definition of learning as the strengthening of S–R connections, involving a single syntactical unit that is both simple and of universal applicability, to posit an organism's map-reading capacity, something that requires description in a syntactically looser form that necessitates the use of terms relating to perception and the formation of expectancies. While admitting the "frankly mentalistic" import of Tolman's words, Bolles seeks to deflect the criticism they attracted to their author by arguing that since he defined terms such as "expectancy" and "demand" behaviorally, that as intervening variables they constituted an explanatory device that was peculiarly psychological in nature and which referred to neither physiological or mental events. Be this as it may, it misses the point that it is the use of intentional language that is at issue here and which marks the deviation from a purely extensional approach to explanation. After all, behaviorism's bounds are not ultimately ontological or methodological.

4.8 Endnote

Three aspects of radical behaviorist interpretation expose shortcomings of the genre when it is judged not in terms of its predictive capacity but rather of its explanatory completeness. Explanatory completeness is central to the plausibility of an interpretation. Any purely extensional operant interpretation of behavior raises three difficulties for a comprehensive psychology of complex human behavior: providing an account of the factors responsible for *behavioral continuity*, the accommodation of what Dennett designates the *personal level of analysis*, and dealing with the problem of *equifinality* and the need to delimit operant accounts of complex human behaviors. In the case of behavioral continuity, the problem is that radical behaviorism lacks a mechanism to account for the continuity of behavior between situations and over time. Continuity is sought in the discriminative and other setting stimuli that are constant from setting to setting. The problem that arises in connection with the personal level of analysis is that neither physiological theories (which operate at a subpersonal level) nor environment-behavior theories (which operate at a superpersonal level) capture what the person as a whole knows (what pain is, for instance). Finally, the problem stemming from considerations of equifinality and delimitation is that of ambiguity surrounding the behavioral response enacted, the precise discriminative stimuli that should be held responsible for it, and the particular consequences that should be implicated in its shaping and maintenance. Any radical behaviorist interpretation must address not one of these problems but all three. They are taken up in Chapters 5–7.

Part III

Imperatives of Intentionality

Chapter 5

Behavioral continuity and discontinuity

Chapter Outline

5.1 Beyond the stimulus field 93
5.2 Symbolic behavior 99
   5.2.1 Stimulus equivalence revisited 99
   5.2.2 Schedule insensitivity 102
5.3 The appeal to physiology 103
5.4 The appeal to private events 106
5.5 The appeal to rules 109
5.6 The appeal to verbal analysis 109
5.7 Endnote 110

A fully extensional behavioral science must be capable of demonstrating the lawlike interactions of behavior and the variables of which it is assumed to be a function (Section 5.1). When the stimulus field that comprises those variables is not empirically available, then behavioral science has reached the conclusion of its explicatory journey. Circumstances in which this occurs are discussed in Section 5.2 which makes reference to the phenomena of stimulus equivalence and schedule-insensitive behavior, both of which are important components of radical behaviorist analysis. Radical behaviorism has appealed to a variety of proxy variables which might account for lapses in the explanation of behavioral continuity and discontinuity, including physiology (Section 5.3), private events (Section 5.4), rules (Section 5.5), and verbal analysis (Section 5.6). In the absence of convincing empirical evidence, however, these appear to be explanatory fictions, unless behaviorism reconfigures its explanatory stance.

5.1 Beyond the stimulus field

The scientific stance of radical behaviorism rests on a rigorous application of a syntax of explanation. We have discussed this in terms of the n-term contingency, but a more formal treatment is useful before discussing radical behaviorist interpretation in detail. The syntax of an extensional explanation comprises two terms, E1, a prior event, and E2, a subsequent event (see Foxall, 2016b). If E1 is a behavior or response, its performance only when it has been previously followed by E2, a rewarding occurrence, allows us to say that E1 is a function of E2. We might also say that E2 is the cause of E1 if we can establish that E1 is repeated if and only if it has been followed in the past by E2. It is also possible that another class of events, setting stimuli that coincide with the performance of E1 or the presentation of E2, can evoke E1 even when E2 is not consequent on its performance, at least for periods of time. This third kind of event, E0, can thus control E1, even though it is not its cause—since unless E2 is occasionally presented contingent upon the performance of E1, E0 will lose its power to control behavior. This is the logic of explanation contained within the three-term contingency. There is no attempt in this kind of explanation to argue that the organism that performs E1 *wants* the reward, E2, or *believes* that it will follow the performance of E1, or *remembers* that E1 has occasioned E2 in the past. The language employed is entirely extensional (see Dickinson, 1980, for the basic reasoning employed here; Smith, 1994, for an exposition of the use of extensional language in radical behaviorism; Foxall, 2016b, for an application of the logic of extensional explanation to consumer choice). E0 is simply a stimulus that sets the scene for the rewarding of a particular response, E1 is a bit of behavior, E2 is an event that follows E1 and is itself followed by a repetition of E1. Similar syntax of explanation is apparent in the case of events whose following a response eventuates in E1 being performed less often. We may say that the behaviorally consequent event, call it E2′, *punishes* the behavior by making it less probable. We are not alluding to the organism's being punished, only to its rate of behaving being reduced. If E2 ceases to follow the performance of E1, E1 will eventually cease or, in the jargon of behaviorism, extinguish. Radical behaviorists are free, of course, to vary or relax their adherence to their logic of explanation, as we are to question how far the resulting accounts of behavior have departed from scientific canons of judgment.

The plausibility of an extensional radical behaviorist interpretation depends vitally upon its capacity to account for the continuity of behavior by reference to the learning that an organism has undergone in terms of its history of exposure to antecedent and consequent stimuli which have accompanied its behavior pattern. Radical behaviorist interpretation raises interesting questions. Why should behavior that has been followed by a particular (reinforcing) stimulus in the presence of a setting stimulus be reenacted when a similar setting is encountered? Why should a rule that describes certain physical or social contingencies be followed at some future date when those contingencies are encountered? Why can I tell you now what I ate for lunch yesterday? The whole explanatory significance of learning history is concerned with the continuity of behavior between settings, and this implies some change in the organism, some means of recording the experience of previous behavior in such a way that it will be available next time similar settings are encountered. There is no other way in which the individual can recognize the potential offered by the current behavior setting in terms of the reinforcement and punishment signaled by the discriminative stimuli that compose it. Broadbent's *Behaviour* (1961/78) remains a most readable and authoritative account of what amount to problems of behavioral continuity and the theoretical and empirical ingenuities to which they led in the history of behaviorism. It is the fascinating story of behaviorists' attempts to explain the emission of behavior in the rat that has not been previously reinforced, but which is nevertheless consistent with an intentional account. Similar difficulties arise in the purely operant explanation of human choice, all of which raise the specter of accounting for behavioral continuity.

Although he does not use the term "behavioral continuity," Bandura (1986) provides a clear description of the problem. The arguments against radical behaviorism he puts forth center on the impossibility of providing an account of behavioral continuity that does not refer to cognitive processing. So long as people are assumed to act automatically in response to the environmental consequences of their past behavior or their thoughts are conceptualized as no more than intervening events themselves under environmental control, so long will any "internal link in the causal chain" be eschewed and agency assumed to reside in the environment (p. 12). Yet there are instances in which environmental causation is assumed to act without any mechanism by which it produces behavior over time being shown to operate.

First, consider his treatment of the fundamental behaviorist principle that behavior is controlled by its immediate consequences. Bandura points to Baum's (1973) demonstration that the rate of emission of behavior is related to the aggregate of its consequences. Such "molar" behavior is actually a feature of Skinner's own approach since it is learning history rather than present stimuli alone that determine behavior. In fact, it was Herrnstein (1997) who most obviously defined and built upon this phenomenon. Defining choice not as an internal deliberative process but as a *rate* of intersubjectively observable events that are temporally distributed, Herrnstein's dependent variable was not the single response that needed contextual explication in terms of a single contingent reinforcer: it was the relative frequency of responding that he explained by reference to the relative rate of reinforcement obtained from the behavior. Animals presented with two opportunities to respond (pecking key A or key B), each of which delivers reinforcers (food pellets) on its own variable interval (VI) schedule, allocate their responses on A and B in proportion to the rates of reward they obtain from A and B. This phenomenon, known as "matching," has been replicated in numerous species, including humans, and has found applications in behavior modification and organizational behavior management, to name but two relevant fields. In particular, it provides a framework for the behavioral analysis of consumption (Rachlin, 1989, 2000). However, Baum's (1973) molar approach to which Bandura makes reference is sufficient to suggest that organisms use data on how often a response is reinforced over a long period of time and that their behavior is then regulated according to the aggregate level of reinforcement. Such integration, Bandura asserts, requires cognitive skills. It actually suggests the need for a subsumptive level of analysis, cognitive, environmental, physiological, behavioral or otherwise such as that for which Smith (1994) called. The absence of any convincing evidence for these (when cognitive is given a specific ontological status) leaves the ascription of intentional content as the only safe possibility given the current state of knowledge.

A second consideration to which Bandura draws attention is that when behavior is learned on intermittent schedules, only a small proportion of responses receive reinforcement and reinforcements are occasional: perhaps only every 50th or 500th response is reinforced. Yet the behavior strengthens for very long periods and eventually diminishes or is entirely extinguished. The question is whether such integration or behavioral continuity can be explained without positing some nonenvironmental determinant, presumably cognitive. Something other than external causation is necessary to account for what happens in between. Bandura invokes the distinction between the acquisition of a skill and its performance which in turn evokes the question of what is learned. Cognitive processes are again implicated. Despite the fact that reinforced performance is uncommon on such schedules, skill is acquired which nevertheless permits the behavior in question to continue.

Bandura points out too that most complex behavior is learned by modeling rather than by experienced reinforcement (Bandura, 1986, pp. 74–80). He is highly critical of operant attempts at interpreting observational learning within the framework of the three-term contingency, which portray the process as the one in which the modeled stimulus (S^D) is followed by an overt matching response (R) which produces a reinforcing stimulus (S^r). The elements of the three-term contingency are often missing from actual instances of observational learning. When the observer performs the matching response in a setting other than that in which it has been modeled, when neither the model's behavior nor that of the observer is reinforced, and when the modeled behavior is performed by the observer after the passage of time (which may be several months), the operant paradigm is unable to explain the behavior. As Bandura (1986, p. 74) points out, "Under this set of conditions, which represents the pervasive form of observational learning, two of the factors ($R \rightarrow S^r$) in the three-element paradigm are absent during acquisition, and the third factor (S^D, the modeling cue) is absent from the situation in which the observationally-learned behavior was first performed." Observational learning of this kind also requires some mechanism to aid integration of vast amounts of information. Acquisition of novel behavior particularly requires such integration of modeled information. Bandura maintains that learning through modeling requires four processes: attentional, retentional, reproductive, and motivational. Certainly, observational learning is a process that must be comprehended at the personal level of analysis. Neither the subpersonal nor the superpersonal level of exposition can cope with it.

The social learning approach which Bandura (1986) promotes assumes that the exposure to modeled behavior engenders symbolic processes that account for learning in the absence of reinforcement. If reinforcement plays a part in this process, it is *expectation of reward* that influences what is observed (as opposed to the many modeled stimuli that go unnoticed because they lack salience for the individual). Hence, while behavior is often enacted in the absence of immediate reinforcement in the external environment, some is controlled by anticipated outcomes. Much, however, is under the control of what Bandura refers to as "self-reward control" (pp. 341−349). This means that people set criteria for their own behavior, which they monitor so that they can bestow reward or punishment on themselves. This is what controls their behavior. "The criteria that together constitute a self-rewarding event include self-bestowal of freely available rewards contingent on performances that meet adopted standards." (1986, p. 366).[1] Self-regulated reinforcement exerts regulation of behavior principally via its motivational function. Self-reward is thus contingent on the attainment of a certain level of performance. Past achievement builds self-appraisal via its influence over the setting of standards for personal performance.[2]

Learning that involves rule acquisition and following must also require these four procedures in some way or other. The individual acquiring rules from others must pay attention to the behavior of others, verbal or nonverbal. Somehow this has to be retained, compared for instance with earlier gained knowledge and experience. Then it must somehow be translated into overt behavior when the situational immediacy that makes the behavior in question possible or even likely becomes apparent. For Bandura, all of this argues for cognitive representation and processing, and it becomes all the more urgent to develop this line of reasoning if understanding rather than prediction and

---

1. In an earlier statement, Bandura (1977, p. 130) refers to "self-reinforcement" rather than "self-reward" and states that it "refers to a process in which individuals enhance and maintain their own behavior by rewarding themselves with rewards that they control whenever they attain self-prescribed standards."

2. In an attempt to rescue observational learning from cognitive psychology and to counter-propose an operant view, Fryling, Johnston, and Hayes (2011) point out that the association of stimuli and responses occurs in the environment rather than in the cognitive processes of the behavior. However, this cannot be the case for verbal behavior. In the case of verbal behavior, the elements of the tricomponential model of radical behaviorist explanation are not associated in the environment but in the utterances of the instructor. The stimuli and responses to which these words refer may never have existed in an environment encountered by the listener, for example, when she is instructed to perform a novel response in order to obtain a reinforce she has not previously received. As a result of hearing these words, the instructed individual encapsulates the rule in her thought and since thought is intentional we can describe the rule in intentional language. In doing so, we leave behind the dimensional system of radical behaviorism, not because we are arbitrarily abandoning it in order to proffer unscientific explanations but because we are following the logic enjoined upon us by radical behaviorists who explain behavior as rule-governed.

control is the primary goal of scientific endeavor, though it is an empirical question whether the inclusion of cognitive processing will increase the predictability of behavior. In fact, we must keep an open mind on whether they add to predictive accuracy. Their primary aim is to aid understanding, to allow a complete account of human behavior acquisition and maintenance. The environmental variables alone *might* contribute more to simple prediction and control. However, the evidence is that, alone, cognitive factors add little to prediction (Foxall, 1997a).

Can the required account of behavioral continuity be achieved by introducing the moderating effect of thought into the explanatory scheme? Bandura argues that a fundamental principle of radical behaviorism is that thought cannot affect action. He argues that, contrary to this, most external influences on behavior act via cognitive processing. People develop beliefs about what is happening to them (i.e., the likely consequences of their behavior), and the beliefs come to influence their behavior. Moreover, "One can dispense with the so-called internal link in causal chains only if thought cannot affect action" (Bandura, 1986, p. 13). It is a moot point, however, whether thought's influencing behavior is or is not part of radical behaviorist explanation. Strictly, thought is a collateral response, the effect of the same environmental events that determine the overt responses with which the thoughts are associated. However, even Skinner came to recognize thoughts and other private events as "noninitiating" causes in the sense that they might act as discriminative stimuli for covert and overt behaviors but remained ultimately dependent on external environmental stimuli for their power as did the events of which they were local or proximal causes. Other radical behaviorists, as we have seen, have held that a private event can function as any of the elements in the three-term contingency—hence, a thought can reinforce other covert or overt behaviors—though this remains a subject of deep controversy. More particularly, however, the role of thought in rule-governed behavior is of interest here. Rules may inhere in thought and thought, like other verbal behavior that embodies or expresses rules, may thus control responses. This is an interesting departure from the behaviorist view that behavior can predict other behavior but not be the cause of it.

As it stands, Bandura's claim that cognitions determine behavior is not substantiable since, especially if the last-mentioned causal statement of radical behaviorism is allowed, the overt behaviors to which he refers might be caused by covert behaviors rather than mental events. However, given that the ontological status of thought and its empirical availability are not obvious, the situation is open to rational cognitive ascription since there may be no other means to establish behavioral continuity and predict future actions. It seems of little importance to the argument whether we simply ascribe intentionality as does Dennett on the basis of rational behavior or make the ontological claims for it that Bandura does on the basis of empirical psychological research: the imperative of behavioral continuity that is raised here requires one or other of these solutions. In the absence of ontological certainty, the first seems preferable, but either way the argument is one that radical behaviorists must face up to.

In his final criticism of radical behaviorism, Bandura draws attention to the principle that behavior is influenced by its enactive consequences. He argues that, on the contrary, the *anticipated* consequences are more effective in predicting and controlling behavior. Hence, "When belief differs from actuality, which is not uncommon, behavior is weakly influenced by its actual consequences, until more realistic expectations are developed through repeated experiences" (Bandura, 1986, p. 13). There is ample corroborative evidence for this from studies of rule-governed behavior in behavior analysis as well as from more cognitively based investigations. The question is how the findings will be interpreted.

5.2 Symbolic behavior

5.2.1 Stimulus equivalence revisited

On one interpretation, stimulus equivalence presents a stark example of the inability of radical behaviorist extensional logic to provide an explanation, other than a redescription, of observed phenomena (Sidman, 1994). Recall that experimental analyses have established that training is not necessary to select particular stimuli. If an individual is trained to select stimulus B on the presentation of the stimulus A, and then to select stimulus C on the presentation of B, it becomes apparent that the untrained relationship involving the selection of C on the presentation of A is demonstrated. On the basis of its necessary syntax, radical behaviorism cannot provide an explanation of a response (selecting C) when there has been no presentation of a stimulus which has previously set the occasion for reinforcement consequent on the individual's having responded by selecting C in the past. Operant psychologists' answer to this conundrum is to argue that the sole interest of behaviorism is in behavior and that they take the phenomenon as they find it without further speculation as to why it occurs. It is, they argue, a "fundamental" behavioral finding (Sidman, 1994) or a framework that comprises a single operant (Hayes et al., 2001).

Relational Frame Theory (Hayes et al., 2001), which builds on the findings of stimulus equivalence research, attempts to overcome the difficulty by proposing that when A, B, and C are verbal stimuli, they "participate" in a single operant unit, a relational frame, that is a fundamental operant and, therefore, not to be analyzed further. Behaviorists who simply want to describe behavior without explaining it may well be satisfied with this, but most behavioral scientists will concur with the present writer that the A—C relationship requires explanation through the ascription of intentionality to the experimental participant. There is no alternative but to explain stimulus equivalence in terms of the beliefs of the individual, including her perception of A and C as associated by dint of her mental operations over the events involved in her previous training of A to B and B to C. This is a clear example of the inability of radical behaviorism, in the absence of an appropriate stimulus field, to provide an explanation of the continuity/discontinuity of behavior. The whole area cries out for a cognitive interpretation.

The salient import of the phenomenon of stimulus equivalence is that the emergent relations have not been reinforced in the course of subjects' training. Sidman's attribution of equivalence to the basic process of reinforcement begs the question posed by Rumbaugh (1995, p. 369): "reinforcement of what?" As Rumbaugh further points out, "There is no 'equivalence' response in the traditional sense to be reinforced during training. Although equivalence relations do emerge, they are neither obviously nor directly reinforced as such during training, during which time other very specific responses are, indeed, selectively reinforced" (Rumbaugh, 1995). His solution is to propose a third type of behavioral response: in addition to respondents and operants, there are *emergents* (Rumbaugh, 1997). Sidman's understanding of equivalence as the result of evolutionary contingencies implies that the brain is responsible for the production of emergent behavior. Rumbaugh (1995, p. 372) finds that his cognitive view closely resembles Sidman at this level: "Frankly, I believe that my view that the brains of many animals, and primates in particular, have been selected via evolutionary pressures to organize (e.g., relate) sensory and perceptual input and to coordinate those, in turn, with response systems for successful adaptation appears to be far more compatible with Sidman's view than I had earlier thought." Both seem close, at this fairly general level, to Dennett's view of the brain producing evolutionarily appropriate efferent responses to afferent stimuli by the exercise of intelligence.

Dennett's reasoning with respect to the personal and subpersonal levels of analysis is also pertinent. The discrimination of emergent relationships is a phenomenon that can occur only at the personal level: it is something that the personal as a whole does. It is, moreover, unanalyzable. There is no way in which the subject to the training summarized above can tell why C is the "correct" answer when the stimulus is A. The similarity to the experience of pain as a personal-level phenomenon is strong: *knowing* that A must be matched with C, C with A, is something that the person just does. There is no way to explain it, whatever neuroscience comes to reveal, that can deal with this personal level except the appropriate mental language.

Now the present analysis is not intended to offer a critique of relational frame theory or competing explanations of symbolic behavior such as the naming account of Horne and Lowe (1996) per se: as extensional science and interpretation, they will stand or fall in terms of their capacity to predict and control/influence behavior. These are appropriate goals for an extensional account and where these accounts are in conflict with one another a choice can be made between them based on their comparative predictive validities. The point is that when we are called upon to make an interpretation of complex behavior that is more than merely plausible, it is necessary to attend to the problem of how continuity between learned relational frames and current situations comes about. There will naturally be correlates of these temporal and spatial relationships that can be expressed in terms of physiology, rule-governance, verbal behavior, and so on, but since each of these is itself a component of the extensional enterprise, none can fill the gap. That gap requires an additional level of interpretation which must necessarily be intentional. The difficulty faced by a purely extensional account is conveyed by Biglan's (1995, p. 67) summary of the positive functions performed by the phenomenon of functional transformation:

> *Much of the power of the concept of relational framing is in the concept of the transfer of function. The concept specifies how language comes to establish the functions of stimuli that have never directly been experienced. A person's sensitivity to the world increases enormously as framing introduces a huge number of connections that were never directly trained. Events become reinforcing through relational framing even though the person has had no direct experience with them. An event becomes aversive after the listener is told it is like another event that already has that effect. An event becomes a discriminative stimulus simply because of its verbally mediated relationship to another event.*

Descriptively this works; pragmatically it fulfills the goal of extensional science that phenomena be predictable and subject to influence or control. There is no argument with that. But it is essential that the behavior analyst acknowledge here that it brings us back to the problem of explaining how behavior is acquired in the absence of reinforcement, back to the realm of Skinner's "automatic reinforcement," "seeing in the absence of the thing seen," and whatever else cannot be accounted for within the strict confines of laboratory science. Filling in the gaps requires that we resort to intentional idioms that propose what the individual whose target behavior is to be explained rather than just predicted and influenced believes and desires.

Nor does the claim that relational framing itself accounts for the temporal and other gaps that must be filled if behavioral continuity is to be explained (Biglan, 1995; Hayes, 1992) identified carry weight. For, of itself, it invokes intentional interpretation:

> *Hayes (1992) suggests that relational framing may account for human abilities to bridge such temporal gaps. When an organism does something to achieve a long-delayed consequence, the organism must somehow be able to discern that the delayed event was relevant to a given behavior. He points out that all instances where nonhuman species are able to make this connection involve processes that narrow the possible relations between the consequent event and*

behavior. For example, nonhuman organisms have been shown to avoid foods that make them ill hours later. Presumably, organisms responsive to such contingencies could be selected because such responsiveness did not interfere with responding to other features of the environment. In other words, ingestive behavior could be sensitive to long-delayed responses of the alimentary canal because such sensitivity contributed to the avoidance of poisoning and did not prevent responses to other contingencies (Biglan, 1995, p. 69; emphasis added).

It is entirely consistent with the behaviorist thesis that knowing can be understood as behavior. But, even if "knowing that" is redescribed in terms of relational framing which identifies it with different sources of environmental control from those that govern "knowing how" (Hayes, 1992; see also Hayes, 1997), there remains room for an understanding of knowing which alludes to the personal level of experience on which the individual can describe his or her knowing that but cannot further analyze it. This accounts for the individual being able to make the relational connections between verbal expressions in ways that lead to their being treated as equivalent (or whatever) in which they have similar behavioral consequences, and which delimit the range of applicability (content) of the relational frame. This is the function of the heuristic overlay to which Dennett refers.

It might be objected to this analysis that even if intentional idioms are required pro tem as we await the ability of physiology or more elaborate principles of verbal behavior to provide more complete explanations, they need not become a permanent feature of behavioral analysis. This would be to misunderstand the role of the intentional overlay which is to provide access to a level of explanation beyond that of extensional science. Whatever advances physiology and the analysis of verbal behavior make to extensional behavioral science, they will not address this level which refers primarily to explanation, plausible interpretation, and the inevitability of gaps that can be filled only by an a-ontological ascription of intentionality. Let us examine these elements of extensional science in greater detail.

5.2.2 Schedule insensitivity

Another example of the inability of radical behaviorism to account for the continuity/discontinuity of behavior is provided by the insensitivity of human participants' behavior to changing schedules of reinforcement in the course of matching experiments. Matching experiments involve variable interval schedules of reinforcement that provide reinforcement contingent on at least one response being performed in a programmed time period; the temporal intervals vary between the presentations of the reinforcer. Matching is a phenomenon in which an animal responding on two manipulanda each governed by its own interval schedule of reinforcement distributes its responses on manipulandum X compared with those on manipulandum Y in the same ratio as the reinforcements actually obtained (not programmed) by the experimental procedure on each of the manipulanda (Herrnstein, 1997; see also Foxall, 2016a for an extended account in the context of Intentional Behaviorism).

Of course, the really interesting outcome of matching, one to which radical behaviorists give not a scintilla of thought, is how the animal *knows* or *computes* that it is time to switch responding from one key or disk to the other in order to temporarily maximize its returns. How does it come to allocate its responding between the keys or discs on the basis of computations of when the sooner reinforcement can be expected? In the absence of a stimulus field that actually governs switching rather than simply scheduled performance on each manipulandum, we have to accord the switching phenomena to the animal's beliefs, including perceptions, about the contingencies governing the performance of the behavior.

But, while behaviorists do not concern themselves with this kind of revealed preference of rats and pigeons, they have been more exercised by the finding that humans who, as well as animals, display the equivalence behavior known as matching, show insensitivity to changes in the schedule parameters while rats, pigeons, and other animals do not. Animals quickly adjust to the new contingencies, but humans tend to continue responding as though the original schedules were still in force. Neither learning history, which has just altered radically, nor schedule of reinforcement can provide an explanation and some radical behaviorists have turned to the possibility that private events in the form of strategizing and planning about how the contingencies are operating must be the causal mechanism. An individual human participant in a matching experiment comes to work out a cognitive representation of the contingencies and how her behavior should be allocated in order to achieve the maximum reward on offer. When the scheduled contingencies change, she continues to act on the basis of this strategy, ignoring the actual contingencies until a new plan is formulated that accommodates the novel situation. The possibility that language is behind this otherwise anomalous behavior (as we would understand it, private verbal behavior about the contingencies that invites intentional explanation) has been raised by some behaviorists, though not followed up (Lowe, 1983; for a detailed analysis, see Foxall & Oliveira-Castro, 2009).

5.3 The appeal to physiology

The radical behaviorist does not deny that change occurs within the organism as a result of behavior but maintains that it is physiological change. The nature of Skinner's reasoning on this point is interesting and germane to the argument pursued here. He notes that Pavlov was "interested in how the stimulus was converted into neural processes and in how other processes carried the effect through to the muscles and glands... The 'physiological activity' was inferential. We may suppose, however, that comparable processes will eventually be described in terms appropriate to neural events. Such a description will fill in the temporal and spatial gaps between an earlier history of conditioning and its current result." (Skinner, 1953, p. 54). This hope that physiology will fill in the gaps "eventually" was expressed some 50 years ago. Has it done so? Can it perform this role?

Still, in 1974, Skinner was prophesying that "some day the physiologist will give us all the details" (Skinner, 1974, p. 249). Midgley and Morris (1998) argue that Skinner can deal with the problem of behavioral continuity by reference to "a changed organism," "temporal gaps," and "causal chains." They trace his explanation to phylogenic and ontogenic contingencies of selection of which innate and acquired behavior are functions. Organisms were biologically changed by their exposure to such contingencies: phylogenic contingencies promote genetic differences among organisms, while ontogenic contingencies promote neurological changes that ensure organisms are "different from their earlier selves" (Midgley & Morris, 1998, p. 121). "In both cases, biologically changed organisms (and replicated genes, with phylogenic contingencies) fill the temporal gap in the causal chain between past contingencies and current or future behavior" (Midgley & Morris, 1998). They quote Skinner: "The physiologist of the future will tell us all that can be known about what is happening inside the behaving organism. His account will be an important advance over a behavioral analysis, because the latter is necessarily 'historical' — that is to say, it is confined to functional relations showing temporal gaps. Something is done today which affects the behavior of an organism tomorrow. No matter how clearly that fact can be established, a step is missing, and we must wait for the physiologist to supply it. He will be able to show how an organism is changed when exposed to contingencies of reinforcement and why the changed organism then behaves in a different way, possibly at a much later date. What he discovers cannot invalidate the laws of a science of behavior, but it will make the picture of human action much more nearly complete" (Skinner, 1974, pp. 236–237).

The same reasoning is derived from Skinner by Lee (1988) who speaks in terms of "action at a distance" to describe the problem of accounting for behavioral continuity: "Skinner insisted that the temporal gap between past contingencies and current performance at the psychological level is mediated by the physiology of the organism. Presumably, past contingencies change the organism so that it behaves differently now. Describing this physiological mediation of the effects of past contingencies is properly the task of the physiologist" (Lee, 1988, p. 162).

Burgos and Donahoe (2000) make the same point backed by the same quotation. But their attempt to delineate the behavior analytic from physiology and cognitivism is more elaborate, and their use of experimental physiology more sophisticated. Setting themselves the task of explaining why retention occurs as part of selection by consequences, they argue that three possibilities arise for explicating complex behavior: first, principles of behavioral variation and selection may themselves be sufficient to offer a complete explanation in which case there is no problem of explaining retention; second, inferences about what is happening within the organism may be drawn in the absence of an experimental analysis; and third, retention principles can be drawn from an experimental analysis of the internal processes. The first they characterize as just saying nothing, which appears to be the familiar Skinnerian strategy of just leaving things to the physiologists and trusting that the answers will one day appear in the neuroscience laboratory. The second they designate bizarrely as "cognitivism" which "violates the thesis according to which retention principles must be derived through a direct experimental analysis" (Burgos & Donahoe, 2000, pp. 40−41). The third, their chosen strategy, seeks the required retention principles in the experimental analysis of neuroscientific phenomena. But before examining this what are we to make of their understanding of cognitivism expressed in the second option? Of all the branches of psychology to make advances in the last half century, the study of neurocognition stands out precisely because of its exponents' willingness to embrace experimental method in the attempt to understand the internal physiological processes that account for overt behavior. While it is difficult to see how cognitive neuroscience could conceivably be characterized in this way, more important is the third strategy these authors identify, one which has formed the basis of a broad approach to interpretation in the behavior analytic tradition (Donahoe & Palmer, 1994).

The difficulties with this are twofold: first, although a materialist philosophy of science must put its faith in a physiological basis of continuity, even though it is not presently demonstrable, that physiology will produce the kind of linkages Skinner seeks from it can right now be no more than faith; the device seems like one designed to bring inquiry to an end while stipulating what cannot be admissible as a gap-filling element. It would be more in keeping with what we know of the tentative nature of science to acknowledge this than to argue and act de facto as though the necessary scientific findings were a current fact. Second, while it may be reasonable to believe in general terms that neuroscience will identify the physiological correlates of behavior at the level of extensional science, there is no reason to believe that such science can produce the kind of interpretive device required to produce explanations of behavior at the personal level. In fact, Dennett has argued persuasively that it cannot, and his arguments have not been convincingly met by behaviorists. It may be useful here to remind ourselves of Dennett's reasons for making the distinction between the subpersonal level revealed by physiology and the personal level which is the realm of psychology. Action at a distance is repudiated as a genuinely scientific explanation by other behavior analysts. Malott and Malott (1992, p. 244) are of the opinion that "the notion of distant, physically-separated causes just does not seem plausible, though one can argue in support of their possibility, just as one could argue in support of the possibility of ghosts." Of course, there may well be physiological change when behavior occurs that his implications for the way in which the organism will behave when it next encounters similar stimulus conditions. The question is whether knowledge of this is sufficient to explain the behavior on subsequent occasions including its prediction and control. We have already noted Dennett's objection to the use of physiology as an exclusive basis of psychology, that the heuristic overlay of intentional concepts adds an interpretive level that makes what is going on more intelligible. I do not wish to advocate that at this stage save to point out that it seems self-evident: it adds an interpretive overlay that not only makes the activities of the nervous system more intelligible in terms of ordinary language but may well make them and the behavior of the organism at the personal level more predictable. This remains an empirical matter for now, but it is one to which we shall return.

The most intriguing fact about Skinner's embracing physiological mediating events is that he uses this as a device to bring inquiry to a premature end by denying the need of an intentional analysis, thereby precluding the search for explanations of behavior as opposed to descriptions. Physiology is the concern of the physiologist, not that of the psychologist or behavior analyst. The behavior analyst's job is done when the physiologist has been presented with an "assignment" that reflects the environmental determination of behavior. Thus Skinner avoids speculation about the kind of theoretical structures, events, or states that he abhors, be they mental, neural, or hypothetical. But if physiology is an uncertain means of establishing a basis for behavioral continuity, what other constructs might fill the gap? The leading remaining contenders are private events and rules.

5.4 The appeal to private events

Can radical behaviorism rely on private events to provide or support an extensional interpretation of complex behavior by accounting for the continuity of behavior? Malott and Malott (1992) pose the question whether private events should be included in the causal chain. They note that some behaviorists such as Hayes and Brownstein (1986) and Rachlin (1974) hold the view that private events cannot be considered the causes of public events. Hayes and Brownstein argue, for instance, that only those events that can enter into the prediction and control of behavior can be considered the causes of behavior and, as we have seen, this exempts private events from this category. Others, however, have argued the reverse. Malott and Malott (1992, p. 250) conclude for instance that private events can sometimes function as causes, for example, in mental arithmetic where each response serves as a covert cue (discriminative stimulus) for the next. Malott's view is that Hayes and Brownstein are right to insist that the analysis of covert events make contact between the private elements in the chain of causation and the environmental events that control/cause both the private event and the overt/public responses associated with it. This is fine, but Malcolm (1977a) makes the good point that, although there must usually be some public events associated with (what he calls) psychological sentences, other, intentional usages are automatic, not associated with anything internal or external that can be observed, monitored, or have conclusions drawn from it. Nevertheless, if there is to be a radical behaviorist interpretation of complex behavior that is itself extensional in nature and scope then private events must carry much of the burden of the behavioral construal of events that are not amenable to an experimental analysis. If *radical* behaviorism is to give an interpretive account of complex behavior, it must resort to inferred entities. There are two options: either extensionally defined but nevertheless inferred and hence explicitly theoretical *private events*, or intentional idioms, which are also theoretical, but which make no extensional claims.

We have already seen that private events are theoretical terms of the kind Skinner repudiated. Since the defining essence of radical behaviorism lies in its eschewal of propositional content rather than of theoretical entities as Skinner defined them, this is not problematic for the present analysis. Their nonintentional nature rests entirely on the kinds of sentence in which we incorporate them, the kinds of explanatory work we make them do. If it is possible to construct interpretations in purely extensional terms, which are more than merely plausible, but in some way testable in terms of the accuracy of the predictions or postdictions to which they lead, then so be it. Are private events up to this task, especially in view of the lack of a substantiable learning history for most of the persons for whom such an interpretation would be sought? Even though Skinner claims that radical behaviorist interpretation is different in several essential respects from the experimental analysis of behavior—he implies, for instance, that interpretation will not be subject to the same canons of scientific rigor as apply to experimental analyses—radical behaviorist interpretation belongs in a radical behaviorist framework only if it adheres to the basic explanatory mode of radical behaviorism, if it shares with the experimental analysis of behavior this philosophy of psychology. Radical behaviorist interpretation cannot do without, at present, some allusion to private events. But, notwithstanding Smith's (1994) inclusion of private events within the extensional framework of radical behaviorism, they remain problematical in this regard. There are several reasons for believing that they do not belong within the framework of extensional behavioral science to which the experimental analysis of behavior aspires and within which it can largely be fitted.

First, private events are cast as responses in behavior analysis, collateral responses to those visible to all that are produced by publicly available stimuli, differing from them only in being private or covert (e.g., Skinner, 1974).

Thoughts and feelings come into this category. But to claim that these are behaviors is to make an ontological assumption that can be neither substantiated nor falsified by scientific analysis (see also Harzem, 2000). Second, private events are not subject to an experimental analysis. Their being apparent to only the person to whom they are occurring has not been seen by radical behaviorists as a barrier to their entering into a scientific analysis since radical behaviorism rejects the requirement of logical positivism that scientific observation be amenable to public scrutiny. This is a fine point because having differentiated his *radical* behaviorism from *methodological* behaviorism on this point (Skinner, 1945), Skinner makes little further use of the private events he has uniquely conceptualized. They rarely enter into behavior analysis because they cannot be experimentally manipulated. In the interpretation of complex (especially verbal) behavior they sometimes perform the role of saving the theory by allowing an extensional account to be given of, for instance, the ways an individual might formulate for him/herself rules of conduct not provided by others. This may be permissible, but it is important that if it is sanctioned by the scientific community, the ontological and methodological status of such events be made explicit. While my own private events may be sufficiently in evidence to me to enable me to incorporate them into some sort of limited analysis of my own behavior, those of other people are at best inferences (Skinner, 1988d). Like the perennial philosophical problem of other minds, which can be resolved only by the most severe application of Occam's razor, the problem of other people's private events can be swept away only if the very notion of private events is abandoned.

Third, private events, therefore, resemble the "explanatory fictions" identified by Skinner as the very conceptual mechanisms that bring inquiry to a premature end. They resemble both the mediating events that are invented to provide explanations for observed stimuli and response patterns, and those which we have seen enter readily into radical behaviorist interpretations of private behavior, verbal behavior, decision making, and so forth. Since they are usually characterized extensionally in the accounts behavior analysts give, they are clearly within the scientific purview of radical behaviorism's distinct approach to the science of behavior. The question for a pragmatic science is, how useful are they in this role? Do they permit prediction? control? plausible interpretation? Fourth, there is no legitimate logic or means by which private events can be ascribed to other people—even if we are capable of accurately discriminating them within ourselves. At best, they can only be inferred from other people's behavior (including verbal) which Skinner among others has resolutely set his face against as an explanatory device. They have no ontological status in this interpersonal context (perhaps none at all if they are not intersubjectively available) that would allow us to justify their attribution as part of an extensionally based behavioral science. Private events simply have no place in extensional science. Fifth, private events are in any case incapable of providing an extensional account: they are by their very nature *about* something else: thinking and feeling are always intentional in this sense. We cannot maintain their integrity as constructs, concepts or variables within a science of behavior.

It appears that, at best, private events are an attempt to come to terms with the need for a personal level of analysis. They cannot succeed because the personal level cannot be accessed through extensional science.

5.5 The appeal to rules

Perhaps the burden ascribed to private events can be assumed by rules. Malott (1989) argues that rules are capable of providing the continuity easily ascribed otherwise to "action at a distance." Since the rules that guide individual action can for the most part in contexts requiring interpretation only be arrived at by speculation, we are hardly on scientific ground when we infer them, often from the very behavior we are attempting to explain by them. The radical behaviorist account of the origin of rule-governed behavior is also dubious since it assumes that rules are simply learned in the course of acquiring a learning history. A history of being reinforced by following the rules laid down by others makes one more likely to follow the rules provided by similar people in similar situations. As Zuriff (1985, p. 129) expresses it, "Both the construction and the following of rules are behavior, and presumably they arise because they proved reinforcing in the history of the community and the individual." This is a plausible surmise but its use in the reconstruction of the environmental factors responsible for any particular sequence of complex behavior is likely to be unamenable to canons of judgment that call for the judicious use of evidence. The belief that rules provide for the continuity of behavior is not usually subject to scientific test and therefore cannot be the basis of a scientific account. Seeking to avoid the rigor that would normally be expected of a scientific statement by calling it interpretation rather than science, to be adjudged according to its sounding plausible rather than there being evidence for it will not do. It is a contravention of the very principle by which Skinner has sought to condemn cognitive and other structuralist accounts of behavior.

5.6 The appeal to verbal analysis

A preliminary case for the necessity of considering radical behaviorist interpretation to be deficient in these respects is made by an examination of behaviorists' treatment of the kinds of sentence by which responses to the questions asked in the course of attitude research were exemplified above. How would radical behaviorists explain this verbal behavior? Can they present, in the language of extensional science, an account of this aspect of human behavior which makes no causal reference to intentionality?

The elements of the three-term contingency are specifiable extensionally and are capable of producing a science of behavior that is logically independent. The question raised here is whether this approach can deal adequately with human behavior that seems to express intentionality and especially with the language of intentional sentences that are rife in the folk psychology that all agree we use daily to make sense of our social interactions or at least to steer us through them. Can it deal also with the kinds of analysis proposed by cognitive scientists whose formulations consist in the verbal ascription of intentionality?

The claim has certainly been made by Schnaitter (1999) that radical behaviorism can deal in an extensional manner with verbal behavior which cognitivists interpret in terms of the intentional idiom. But further analysis must be deferred to Chapter 9, *Ascribing intentionality*.

5.7 Endnote

Even if we had all the facts about an individual's past behavior and the reinforcing/punishing consequences it had produced, it would not be possible to explain fully why a particular individual now has a known probability of again behaving in a given way. Simply to say, as Skinner would, that it does not matter, that it is not a question for the behavioral scientist but can be left to the physiologist has limited merit: whatever the physiologist turns out to be able to contribute here, it will always fall short of accounting for the personal level of analysis. Unless we can ascribe rationality to him, we do not even know which direction he will move in—toward which reinforcer. Since behavior is always simultaneously reinforced and punished (Alhadeff, 1982), the individual always has the options of behaving or not behaving. We cannot possibly predict or explain which one will win out unless we know his goal (desire) and the information he has (beliefs) about the consequences of behaving in a particular way in the current behavior setting. There are three sources of the required intentional ascription: observe past behavior and extrapolate (i.e., project the person's behavioral history), ask him, or attribute intentions on the basis of some logical scheme that relates the behavior of the individual to his position (learning history and behavior setting). We need the contextual stance to describe these positional factors and the intentional stance to ascribe appropriate content.

Chapter 6

The personal level

Chapter Outline

6.1 Acknowledging personhood 111
6.2 Skinner's third-person account 113
6.3 More on first-person accounts 114
6.4 First- and third-personal perspectives 122
6.5 Endnote 126

Accounting for certain facets of behavioral continuity and discontinuity requires, as the preceding chapter concluded, the judicious employment of intrapersonal cognitive variables. This requires a theoretical understanding of the personal level of exposition (Section 6.1). Radical behaviorism has acknowledged this by its forays into third-personal accounts of behavior such as Skinner's interpretation of what is happening when one seeks something that has become lost (Section 6.2), a move that is roundly criticized by Malcolm, among others (Section 6.3). The perspectival interpretations of behavior in terms of first- and third-personal accounts is discussed in Section 6.4, and the chapter concludes that behavioral interpretation poses an intractable problem for radical behaviorism.

6.1 Acknowledging personhood

Radical behaviorist interpretation fails to consider the personal level of analysis as surely as it does the subpersonal analysis provided by physiology. It is simply not a part of the function of either physiology or extensional behavioral science to address this level. Nor is it feasible at the superpersonal level that a purely extensional operant interpretation admits. It should be possible nevertheless to include a personal level of analysis in a framework of interpretation that not only embraces the findings of behavioral science but also admits a further heuristic overlay of intentional interpretation. If neuroscience provides the subpersonal level of analysis on to which ascriptive content can be overlain to arrive at the personal level of analysis required by Dennett's "physiological psychology," then a similar procedure can be followed to arrive at the personal level by ascribing content to the findings of extensional behavioral science. Moreover, a comprehensive social psychology requires it. In this way, we can talk more completely about cognition and affect, thinking, and feeling. The personal level we posit here in contradistinction to the superpersonal level of environment—behavior relations is that which Dennett defines in contrast to the subpersonal level of brains and neurons.

We should understand it, as he does, as "the level of people and their sensations and activities" rather than that of "brains and events in the nervous system" (Dennett, 1969, p. 93), and, we might add, rather than the environment and its reinforcing and punishing events which influence the rate of repetition of responses. The experience of emotion is to be understood at this level rather than that of the stimulus—response or the response—stimulus configuration that has been the focus of its study in operant psychology. Just as there are no neural events or processes that capture the experience of pain as we speak of it in everyday discourse, so there are no environmental events or processes that capture emotionality. Even to speak of mediating stimuli and responses in order to capture this personal level is arbitrary and fails to do justice to the nonmechanical, personal level at which emotion is known. There will of course be environmental correlates of emotionality but their study, as part of an extensional science of behavior, does not embrace the unanalyzable sensation to which emotional language refers. The ascription of emotion requires that extensional level of scientific analysis—indeed it cannot do without it—but it is an overlay necessary to its full psychological understanding. There is an equivalent to knowing what pain is (that is not caught in physiological terms) in the environment-behavior sphere: knowing what reinforcement is in the context of what the behavior setting stimuli signal. This knowing comes from or at least is associated with the person's history of reinforcement and punishment. As the person who has felt pain knows what pain is, so the person whose behavior has been reinforced and punished knows what these effects are. But this knowing is unanalyzable: it is a feature of the personal level rather than either the physiological or environmental level. This personal level is not captured by any extensional analysis, be it biological or behavioral. But that is not the verdict of radical behaviorists, who seem to have complicated the point out of all recognition.

We have distinguished three sources of knowledge into which the results of operant research may enter. The first is that of *behavioral science*, aka behavior analysis, the experimental analysis of behavior. It is extensional and superpersonal in its scope, methodology, and domain. The second is that of *radical behaviorist interpretation* as it has been practiced among others by Skinner, Hayes, and Rachlin. It attempts to provide an extensional account of complex behavior based on the extrapolation of principles of behavior gained in the laboratory to naturalistic settings without incorporating intentional idioms. This strategy fulfills well the predictive purposes of those who embrace it but it fails on three counts to provide an adequate explanation of complex behavior. Third is *Intentional Behaviorism*, an interpretive mode based on the findings and theories of behavioral science plus the heuristic overlay provided by intentionalism. This strategy is not intended to predict behavior but to fill in the gaps left by radical behaviorist interpretation through the addition of an additional layer of intentional interpretation.

This chapter and those following are concerned primarily with radical behaviorist interpretation and why it needs this "heuristic overlay." We begin with Skinner's attempt to make sense of first-person accounts of behavior in terms of operant conditioning.

6.2 Skinner's third-person account

Skinner's approach to interpretation is to seek the explanation of an individual's current behavior in his or her history of reinforcement and punishment, that is, *learning history*. Despite the way in which the three-term contingency is usually symbolized as showing the factors that cause a response as the consequences that necessarily follow it, Skinner does not try to explain behavior by reference to future events. He avoids teleology by explaining current behavior in terms of the consequences that have followed similar responding *in the past*. Hence,

> When we see a man moving about in a room opening drawers, looking under magazines, and so on, we may describe his behavior in fully objective terms: 'Now he is in a certain part of the room; he has grasped a book between the thumb and forefinger of his right hand; he is lifting the book and bending his head so that any object under the book can be seen.' We may 'interpret' his behavior or 'read a meaning into it' by saying that 'he is looking for something' or, more specifically, that 'he is looking for his glasses.' What we have added is not a further description of his behavior but an inference about some of the variables responsible for it. There is no current goal, incentive, purpose or meaning to be taken into account. This is so even if we ask him what he is doing and he says, 'I am looking for my glasses.' This is not a further description of his behavior but of the variables of which his behavior is a function; it is equivalent to 'I have lost my glasses,' 'I shall stop what I am doing when I find my glasses,' or 'When I have done this in the past, I have found my glasses.' These translations may seem unnecessarily roundabout, but only because expressions involving goals and purposes are abbreviations. (Skinner, 1953, pp. 89—90).

It is first necessary to contrast this with Skinner's view of cognitive explanation. Such explanation of behavior by reference to some conception of the inner world of the individual, his or her private experience, becomes under the influence of the behaviorist philosophy of psychology one that refers by contrast to his or her contact with prior contingencies. The strategy of cognitive psychology, according to Skinner (1977), is to move the contingencies of reinforcement inside the person, inside the head. The behavior analyst seeks always, by contrast, to locate the causes of behavior in the environment. So the individual who is "looking for his glasses" is engaging not in an internal problem-solving activity but in behavior that in the past has led to the location of the spectacles (Skinner, 1953, pp. 89−90). The person who thinks such and such or feels this or that is simply in touch with discriminative stimuli that happen to be "within the skin" rather than in the external environment (Skinner, 1974). These stimuli are not autonomous: they have been learned through the operation of the external environment and are therefore no more than "collateral" responses that have been produced by the same external contingencies that are responsible for the overt behaviors that correlate with them. A sportsman's feelings of confidence when he plays tennis well are not the causes of his continued good performance but inner responses that result from the same external events that determine his achievements on court. Although he may find it tempting to report his performance as resulting from his changed beliefs, goals, or emotions, or from his "inner game of tennis," his words would be easily translated by the radical behaviorist interpreter into an account based on his supposed learning history.

But Skinner's insistence on an objective, third-person account in a science of behavior that readily accepts private events raises a more fundamental difficulty.

6.3 More on first-person accounts

The behaviorist strategy of "discovering" a learning history in order to interpret complex behavior evidently accords with the philosophy of behaviorist explanation. Although it eschews the mentalistic fictions Skinner so strongly repudiated, it nevertheless extends the analysis of human behavior beyond the confines of a scientific enquiry. "Looking for" one's glasses thus becomes a reenactment of behavior that preceded their being located in the past. Malcolm (1977a) argues that mental terms do not refer to something that can be observed, whether within or outside the individual: terms such as "intend" are not referential in the sense that they point to something to be observed. Although he does not say so in as many words, his view is consonant with Dennett's position that intentions must be ascriptional, though this tells us nothing about their ontology. It is also reminiscent of the irreducibility thesis (Dennett, 1969, p. 30): no sentence fashioned according to extensional logic can capture the meaning of an intentional sentence. He makes some important deviations from Skinner's—and indeed Dennett's—insistence that science requires that an objective third-person account be given of behavior. By following Malcolm's reasoning here, it is possible to critique both of the central philosophies with which we are concerned, to see their conceptual similarities and contrasts, and to advance toward an *Intentional Behaviorism* that is capable of combining their merits.

Clearly, Dennett and Malcolm come from somewhat different philosophical positions. It is in fact Dennett's third-personal view that is here closer to Skinner's: the view that what we know about ourselves is based on essentially the same information as is what others know of us, something that he develops considerably in his treatment of heterophenomenology and consciousness (Dennett, 1991b; see also Dennett, 2003. An exposition of heterophenomenology is provided in Section 9.3). But that need not detain us here, for here they are arguing something very similar in relation to behaviorism. If Malcolm were taking an unequivocally subjectivist stance with respect to intentionality, I would not pursue the similarities in what they are saying. But although he uses the term "first-person account" which Dennett avoids, there is something in Malcolm's insistence that mental terms must have external referents in the contingencies of reinforcement that ensures his inclusion in this part of my critique of behaviorism's being unable to supply the personal level of analysis. Dennett escapes the problem of how to deal with a personal level of explanation while assuming the third-personal stance of science by being willing to ascribe intentionality to the system whose behavior is to be predicted and explained. But there is no such let out for the radical behaviorist. Malcolm, despite speaking in terms of the first-personal perspective, essentially deals with the way in which that intentionality must be assumed and ascribed.

Malcolm's reasoning in coming to his conclusions is both sympathetic with Skinner's (in particular the insistence that so-called mentalistic terms can and must be traced to their environmental contingencies) and critical of Skinner's argument that the individual's description of his thoughts and feelings and that provided by another person are identical third-person accounts. Hence, he points out first that Skinner does not necessarily deny that people have purposes, intentions, and so on (to which mentalistic terminology refers) but that the terms are to be understood in a particular way. Skinner portrays mentalistic terms as explanatory fictions. It is not that he wants to claim that people are never thirsty or discouraged but that such words usually conceal an appeal to the independent variables that actually determine and explain behavior (see Skinner, 1953, p. 36). This means that statements that appear to explain behavior in mentalistic terms, for example, that it is the result of incentive or purpose are reducible to statements that embody the functional relationships that are fundamental to operant conditioning and thus to radical behaviorist explanation (Skinner, 1953, p. 87).

Malcolm also points out that Skinner is against explanations of (operant) behavior that proceed in physical or physiological terms. Rather than appeal to internal physiology in order to test its propositions about behavior, it should seek confirmation in the external physical consequences and outward behavior. Looking within diverts attention from the actual causes of behavior. "The practice of looking inside the organism for an explanation of behavior has tended to obscure the variables which are immediately available for a scientific analysis. These variables lie outside the organism, in its immediate environment and in its environmental history" (Skinner, 1953, p. 35). Skinner's attempts to reformulate psychology by explaining what mentalistic terms actually *mean* in the sense of the environmental causation to which they refer, is a philosophical contribution that identifies the misleading expressions found in ordinary language. "These expressions have a disguised meaning. They are 'abbreviations'. Skinner's task is to unpack these abbreviations by making explicit the behavioristic variables to which they refer in a 'concealed' way and which give them whatever intelligibility and usefulness they have." (Malcolm, 1977b, p. 94).

Skinner is, of course, entirely right to point this out: as we have seen, even the operation of the intentional stance inescapably requires *some* prior contextual analysis. When he writes that feelings of confidence, or believing, or perceiving, for instance, can be related to the environmental contingencies that are related to behavior (see Skinner, 1974), he is making the valid point usually not considered by cognitive psychologists that a contextual analysis of these events is often possible. Dennett's empirical excursion into cognitive ethology (Dennett, 1988) bears this out as does the work of the social cognitivists of attitude−behavior relations. Indeed, these latter examples suggest that the prior contextual analysis is essential to the use of the intentional stance. However, this does not make the intentional stance invalid: the contextual stance cannot handle all so-called psychological terms simply by means of translating them into the language of behavior analysis. The intensional cannot be so treated.

Skinner is arguing here against introspectionism, "the basic assumption of which is that each of us learns from his own case what pain, anger, fear, purpose, and so on *are*." After Wittgenstein, Malcolm argues that there is no possibility of our understanding each other's psychological language and thus such introspectionism leads to a kind of solipsism: worse, "it leads to the result that one's identification of one's own inner experience might be wrong without one's ever being the wiser" (Malcolm, 1977b, p. 95). The behaviorist refutation of introspectionism shows that "our concepts of mental states and events cannot be divorced from human behavior." Skinner himself admits that we must take on the responsibility to showing how a private event is connected to the person's description of it. "The intelligibility of psychological words must be based on something other than the occurrence of those words" (p. 96).

However, he argues, the fallacy of behaviorism, which is common also to physicalism, is the view that when a person uses a psychological sentence such as "I am excited," he is basing this at least partially on personal observations of states or events in his own body. Malcolm (1977b, pp. 96−97) comments, "The truth is that it would be a rare case in which a person said that he was excited on the basis of noticing that his hands were trembling or his voice quavering. I do not say that it is impossible for such a case to occur.... In the normal case, however, a man does not *conclude* that he is excited. He says that he is, and he is; but his utterance is not the result of self-observation." He also employs the following argument (which is germane also to Rachlin's teleological behaviorism which will be discussed in Chapter 7: *Delimiting behavioral interpretation*): "The point comes out very strikingly when we consider first-person reports of bodily sensations, for example, 'I have a headache.' It would be completely mad if I were to say this on the basis of noticing that my face was flushed, my eyes dull, that I was holding my head, and had just taken some aspirin. If someone were to say, *on that basis*, that he has a headache, either he would be joking or else he would not understand how the words are used. The same is true of a first-person perception sentence, such as 'I see a black dog.'"

He argues further that behaviorists have erred by assuming that a psychological sentence expressed in first-personal terms is identical in content and method of verification to the corresponding third-personal sentence. We verify that another person is angry by the way the veins stand out on his neck, by the redness of his face, and by his shouting. But we do not verify our own anger in this way. We do not as a rule attempt to verify it at all. Despite the ontological differences between Malcolm and Dennett, this echoes to some extent what Dennett is saying about one's knowing what pain is, being able to discriminate pain, but not to be able to give reasons for it or define what is meant by being in pain. Malcolm contends that verification is simply not a concept or operation that applies to many first-person psychological reports, those which are not founded on observation. While introspectionism supposes that they depend on observations of internal mental events, behaviorism supposes them to be founded on observations of either external events or of physical events taking place within the speaker's skin. In this respect, both methodologies are in error as a result of imagining that a first-person psychological statement reports on something the speaker has observed or thinks he has observed (Malcolm, 1977b, pp. 97–98).

An individual's statement of purpose or intention belongs in a different class from one made by someone else on the basis of observing that individual. If we see someone turning out his pockets and recall that on previous occasions he has done this before producing his car keys from one of them, we can reasonably conclude that he is looking for this car keys this time too. But it would be odd indeed if he himself were to work out what he was doing by observing that he was emptying his pockets as he had done in the past when looking for his car keys. If he announced that he must be looking for his car keys at present because he was doing what he had done in the past when finding them had eventuated, we should think him most odd, crazy, to be treated in future with circumspection.

Scruton (2012) makes a similar point in his discussion of I–you relations that arise, for instance, in a dispute between two humans which progresses from an accusation that one has acted deceitfully to a request for the reason for this statement, its denial and refutation by the other, the evaporation of unfriendliness, and a promise to work constructively together in future. Such an interaction, he says,

> *presupposes at every point that you and I both understand and make use of concepts like belief and desire. And it assumes that we each have* first person knowledge *of our beliefs and desires – that we don't have to find out what they are but can summon them immediately and without evidence in response to the questions 'why?' and 'what?'. Use of the first person pronoun confers the ability to describe immediately, on no basis, and with a far-reaching immunity to certain kinds of error, the content of one's present mental state, and also to put oneself forward as accountable for one's deeds (Scruton, 2012, p. 44).*

I imagine that some *might* be tempted to reconstruct such an exchange in terms of a learning history of rule-governed behavior, which is unlikely to be empirically available, and prevailing antecedent stimuli, responses, and consequential stimuli, similarly conjectural. This is unlikely, however, to eventuate in a testable scientific account of behavior or even one the "plausibility" of which convinces someone other than a dyed-in-the-wool behaviorist. An act for a reason is far-removed from the concept of causally conditioned behavior.

Malcolm (1977b, p. 99) also draws attention to speech acts such as "I was about to go home" which for Skinner presents the problem that it "describes a state of affairs which appear to be accessible only to the speaker. How can the verbal community establish responses of this sort?" (Skinner, 1953, p. 262). Skinner's explanation is that as the speaker has previously behaved publicly, private stimuli have become associated with the public manifestations. "Later when these private stimuli occur alone the individual may respond to them. 'I was on the point of going home' may be regarded as the equivalent of 'I observed events in myself which characteristically precede or accompany my going home.' What these events are such explanation does not say." (Skinner, 1953, p. 262). Malcolm comments, "For Skinner 'private stimuli' would mean of course physical events within the individual's skin. The fact that Skinner regards this hypothesis as a possible explanation of the utterances, even though he does not know what the private stimuli would be, shows how unquestioningly he assumes that such a remark as 'I am on the point of going home' must be based on the observation of something." (Malcolm, 1977b, p. 99). But the statement "I am on the point of going home" is not a prediction based on the observation of anything. "The announcement 'I am about to go home' is normally an announcement of intention. Announcements of intention are not based on the observation of either internal or external variables..." (Malcolm, 1977b, p. 99).

Statements of intention are undoubtedly related to external events and someone who said that he was about to go home would normally have a reason for doing so, for example, that it was time for dinner. But this does not mean that going home or making the utterance is under the "control" (in Skinner's sense) of dinner time. In Skinner's technical sense of control, y is under the control of x "if and only if x and y are connected by some *functional relationship*," and if control is given this sense then neither intentions nor statements of intention is "controlled" by anything (Malcolm, 1977b, p. 100). On the one hand, behaviorists' resolution in proposing that psychological language (that which deals with so-called mental phenomena such as believing, intending, and wanting) has to be conceptually linked with public phenomena is entirely correct. (This is what was argued previously, on the basis of psychological practice rather than philosophical argument, in terms of the demonstration that social cognitivists have to use the contextual stance as a starting point.) Otherwise, to put the matter in the terminology of behavior analysis, the verbal community could not teach children to use such terms appropriately. The psychological terms must have some external referent in preverbal behavior. But, on the other hand, "the employment of psychological terms outstrips their foundation in preverbal behavior. Someone who has satisfied us that he understands certain psychological terms begins to use them in first-person statements *in the absence* of the primitive, preverbal behavior that had previously served as the basis for judging that he understood those terms. He tells us that he feels ill, or angry at someone, or worried about something when we should not have supposed so merely from his demeanor. The interesting point is that in a great many cases we will *accept* his testimony. We conclude that he is angry when, if we had been judging solely on the basis of nonverbal behavior and visible circumstances, we should not have thought it. We begin to use his testimony as a new criterion of what he is feeling and thinking, over and above and even in conflict with the earlier nonverbal criteria" (Malcolm, 1977b, p. 101).

There would of course be a radical behaviorist riposte to the effect that through contact with the person who "has satisfied us that he understands certain psychological terms," we had developed a learning history with respect to his verbal behavior that we had tried and tested according to the contingencies. Having done so, we would again accept his verbal testimony, since we had a learning history of doing so. However, the point is that this is an explanatory fiction, an untestable extrapolation of learning principles to a sphere where by its very nature we can have no empirical evidence for or against our assertions. This is not science. In fact, we abandon the contextual stance at this point and rely on the intentional stance. We are using it whenever we "trust" someone or interpret behavior in terms of trust when we have no access to a learning history. We cannot do without the intentional stance any more than social cognitivists can do without the contextual stance. They employ this stance by virtue of their observations of the contingencies to which they add propositional content; behavior analysts employ it (at least in their interpretation of complex behavior) in the absence of observations of the contingencies because the contingencies simply are not empirically available. Hence, "The first-person psychological sentences must be correlated with behavior up to a point. But they quickly go beyond that point. People tell us things about themselves that take us by surprise, things which we should not have guessed from our knowledge of their circumstance and behavior. A behaviorist philosopher will say that if we had known more about their history, environment, and behavior, we should have been able to infer this same information. I do not believe that there are any grounds for thinking so. The testimony that people give us about their intentions, plans, hopes, worries, thoughts, and feelings is by far the most important source of information we have about them. To a great extent we cannot check it against anything else and yet to a great extent we credit it. I think we have no reason to think that it is even a theoretical possibility that this self-testimony could be adequately supplanted by inferences from external and/internal physical variables." (Malcolm, 1977b, 101−102).

"Within the whole body of language the category of first-person psychological sentences has peculiar importance, the puzzling status of human beings as subjects and persons is bound up with these first-person utterances, which possess the two striking characteristics I have pointed out: first, they are not, for the most part, made on the basis of any observation; second, in many cases they cannot be 'tested' by checking them against physical events and circumstances *other than* the subject's own testimony. If we want to know what a man wants, or what he is thinking about, whether he is annoyed or pleased, or what he has decided, the man himself is our best source of information. We ask *him*, and *he* tells us. His own testimony has a privileged status in respect of this sort of information about himself, and *not* 'because he has had an extended contact with his own behavior for many years'" (Malcolm, 1977b, p. 102). "I have argued that behaviorism fails to perceive self-testimony in a true light. It mistakenly assumes that when a man tells you what he wants, intends or hopes, what he says is based on observation and therefore he is speaking about himself as if he were an *object of his own observation*.... In short, behaviorism fails to perceive that self-testimony is not replaceable, even in principle, by observations of functional relations between physical variables" (Malcolm, 1977b, pp. 102−103).

Hayes, Wilson, and Gifford (1999) attempt to show that the concept of private events can address an individual's own account, but they do not answer the specific problems raised in this chapter. The truth is that psychological first-person reports or utterances lie beyond the bounds of behaviorism. They cannot be subjected to a behavioral analysis. We can indeed parse such sentences in functional terms as Schnaitter (1999) has suggested but how does this aid in explaining them or how they are related to the private events that give rise to them? The examples based on the kinds of locutions employed in applications of the theories of reasoned action and planned behavior which were discussed earlier indicate that it is entirely feasible to make the necessary translation of terms. But what can we do with these behavioral translations by way of interpretation without adding inferences that cannot be verified, for example, about the origin of the mands and tacts they include? While the technique makes it possible to specify the rules that people reveal in their responses to standard methods of attitude measurement in extensional language, the question arises: how are we to use this behavioristically consistent locution in interpretation? It may appear to have some advantage in that it may be said to reveal the otherwise-elusive learning histories of those whose behavior we seek to delineate in terms of its environmental correlates. But the burden we place on the extensionalized statements of intentions to reveal a history of reinforcement and punishment is quite unrealistic, leading as it does to untestable propositions about the past.

We could always ask, "Why not confine our interpretations of people's psychological statements" to a functional analysis of their verbal behavior involved in uttering such sentences? This would presumably be on the model of what Schnaitter (1999) suggests, so that a statement like "I believe eating green vegetables is healthy" could be functionally parsed into its autoclitic and tactful components. (Schnaitter's proposal is further examined in Chapter 9: *Ascribing intentionality*.) But these functional categories, though interesting for armchair analysis, have no empirical foundation other than the observational (anecdotal) examples attached to them in *Verbal Behavior*. In other words, they function exactly as do explanatory fictions from other sources, they allay enquiry, and so on. Analyzing a statement as a tact or mand, for instance, is to invent a learning history and behavior setting for the person who uttered it by proposing the contingences that led to the utterance and that will guide behavior based on it. This is sufficient for speculative analysis, but it is not science. Our aim must be to bring science and interpretation closer to one another. Merely translating from one system to another does not bring this goal nearer. Radical behaviorists need to be aware of the two approaches to the use of psychological terms and to determine which they will take. The choice is between believing that I know I have a headache because I look in the mirror and note the way I am screwing up my face or that I base this knowledge on some means that does not involve observing either internal or external phenomena; that I conclude I must be looking for a book because I have observed myself systematically eyeing my bookshelves in the past, or that I simply know that I am searching for the dictionary.

Each of these intentional activities must of course be linked in some way to external events and another person to whom I cannot communicate verbally will judge from my behavior that I am in pain or looking for a book. But this is not the information I use to come to such conclusions. Behavior analysts, in other words, either incorporate the personal level of analysis in their interpretations of complex behavior or confine their analyses to what is externally observable. There is no objection then to radical behaviorists' pursuing the extensional route to interpretation, but none either to the incorporation of an intentional overlay of interpretation being used to supplement this. The entirely extensional approach is surely absurd in this context. The addition of an intentional overlay makes for a more convincing interpretation, a fuller and richer account of what is going on. In a pragmatic spirit, we may pursue both. But let us be aware of the consequences. If we adopt the intentional overlay, we are employing two approaches that in themselves are incommensurable, but we have found a necessary way to incorporate the essential level of analysis for psychology: the personal level. We must not, as Wundt was reputed to do, seek a science more than we seek a psychology.

6.4 First- and third-personal perspectives

The foregoing argument stands, however, in need of some refinement before it can be accepted. First, note that the accounts of Dennett and Skinner are largely identical in that they presume a third-person perspective. Second, Malcolm's account differs from both in proposing a first-personal perspective. The Skinnerian view that first- and third-person viewpoints coincide, that private events are observable in just the same way as are public events, albeit by only one person, suggests a reconciliation that suffices for present purposes between Dennett's views and those of Malcolm. I want to retain elements of the arguments of all three authors, but I emphasize here that Malcolm's view of what he calls a first-personal viewpoint is inescapable insofar as it points to sources of knowledge available to the individual that are beyond those gained by a deliberative examination of the contingencies.

Both Skinner and Dennett argue that we can only know our pains and other private events directly and yet still objectively, that is, as a third person would, even though we are the only one present. I should argue, however, that this applies equally to knowing the kinds of intention that Malcolm posits, even though they are of a different source. There is good reason for retaining and using this third-personal view, but as Malcolm is at pains to point out, this kind of third-personal knowing does not exhaust our knowing of our private events. There are sources of information available to the individual that go beyond those gained by an examination of past behavior and its consequences, and of the current contingencies. Naturally, the radical behaviorist riposte to this is that this source is still the individuals's learning history, an unconscious accumulation based on previous behavior and its consequences, which by appearing to have a spontaneous and immediate effect on behavior gives rise to the notion of an extraenvironmental source of motivation. But the point is not to defend such a mystical source, rather it is to agree with Malcolm that the individual does not contact his or her motivation solely or even usually by a process of third-personal examination of previous behavior and the current contingencies.

Hence, the contradiction that is apparent on one level between the first-person perspective of Malcolm and the third-person perspective of Dennett need not, I think, prove problematical for the present argument. First, note that the argument is aimed at behavior analysts for whom the first-person/third-person distinction is redundant: both are objective, the first based on the availability of data to a single individual rather than a group. Since it is only logical positivism that insists on truth-by-agreement, and behavior analysis does not fall into this camp, the two sources of knowledge coincide methodologically. Both have certain similarities with the radical behaviorist approach they critique. Hence, Dennett argues that the information available to the individual to determine his own beliefs and desires is the same evidence available to others to ascertain them. We can ascertain them through the technique of heterophenomenology that is a process of analyzing the behavior of the target person, including his verbal behavior, what others say of him and how they act toward him. Heterophenomenology is the ultimate strategy that derives from the intentional stance. We have seen that this is the way in which users of the intentional stance use the contextual stance. Malcolm accepts that mental events such as beliefs and intentions must have some external referents which—in our terms—would enter into the learning history and behavior setting. Nevertheless, he denies that the individual examines his own situation in order to conclude what his intentions are: he just knows that it is time to go home; he does not need to work this out from external information: I have always gone home when the light has got dim in my office, etc.

I want to retain elements of all three arguments, but I emphasize here that Malcolm's view of a (possibly first personal) viewpoint is inescapable because there sources of knowledge available to the individual that are beyond those gained by an examination of the contingencies. Radical behaviorists could always argue that this is our learning history, an unconscious accumulation based on our previous behavior and its consequences, which by appearing to have a spontaneous and immediate effect on our behavior gives rise to the notion of an extraenvironmental source of motivation. But I am not arguing that there is such a source of motivation. This is to argue along with Malcolm that the individual does not contact that motivation by a process of third-personal examination of his previous behavior and the current contingencies.

Several implications derive from this:

First, note that the argument pursued here ties in well with the attitude theory and research to be considered in Chapter 9, *Ascribing intentionality* (see also Foxall, 1997a, 1997b, 2005), in which the individual develops spontaneous attitudes through experience with the attitude object (culminating in self-rules acquired in the course of a learning history). Malcolm's intentions are the result of a process akin to what Fazio (1990) calls the spontaneous development of attitudes; the self-examination that Skinner attributes to the man looking for his glasses has much in common with the deliberative approach to attitude and intention formation to which Fishbein and Ajzen have drawn attention. We can combine these into an account of learning that begins with other-rule following and consequent deliberation on events as a surrogate for a learning history for the acquisition of which there has as yet been no opportunity, and which culminates in the development of self-rules that give the impression of spontaneity (Foxall, 1997a, 1997b). At this broad and somewhat abstract level in which we are not directly concerned with an actual person whose behavior we are attempting to explain or predict, such an interpretation is consistent with both extensional behavior analysis (in which deliberation for instance is cast as a behavior) and with an extensional cognitive approach (in which it refers to the intrapersonal processing of information with intentional overtones).

Second, if we are to pursue a radical behaviorist interpretation of a particular individual's behavior, however, it becomes incumbent upon us at some stage to assign particular self-rules to him or her in order to render intelligible his or her past actions and possibly to predict future conduct. Such assigned motivations, even if they reflect the interpreted person's own verbalizations of the rules he or she has constructed and followed, can have no meaning except to the interpreter: he/she has no objective evidence on the basis of which to assign them other than a theory of how the person's assumed experience will have led him/her to accumulate such self-rules. This is no different in essence from the intentionalist's ascription of intentionality. Pragmatically, we are doing the same thing. There are, of course, empirical techniques that may appear to overcome this problem by purporting to provide a purely extensional behavior analytic access to the self-rules that the individual has constructed. One of these is the "Silent Dog technique" (Hayes, 1986) that involves the elicitation of verbal protocols during the performance of a task. Another is through the application of relational frame theory in which we ascertain the emergent relations between words and from which we may claim to reconstruct the self-rules in question. While relational frame theory can claim that it has access to learning history by virtue of the emergent relations, it uncovers that this is an act of faith: the only sure route to knowledge of a learning history is observation/experimentation: all other routes are somewhat conjectural, to be derived from a sure scientific footing by all means, using as far as we can rigorous canons of scientific judgment, but ultimately unconnected to the facts other than by means of a theoretical language (Zuriff, 1985) that has elements of arbitrariness rather than scientific certainty. The same is true of the method of the silent dog. We do not know that we are tapping verbal behavior indicative of the person's learning history: any presumption that we are is based on the prior assumption of a particular explanatory viewpoint. In this case, we have two valid viewpoints and methodologies to which to turn: the contextual stance and the intentional stance.

In both cases, we are making a leap from the words given to us by the individual in a laboratory setting and construing them as indicative of something else. This is precisely the technique of the social cognitivist who attributes attitudes, intentions, and other cognitions to an individual on the basis of his or her verbal responses. In both cases, we ascribe/assign on the basis of what the subject does, says, what is said of him/her, our idea of the behavior (and thus the dispositions or intentions) that would be consistent with his/her having had a particular learning history. We are ascribing to the person whose behavior we wish to pre or postdict verbalizations such as "I think that or I believe that catching an earlier bus to the office in the morning will enable me to complete my assignments before lunch." Yet, doing this is inconsistent with the behavior analytical scientific approach of avoiding explanatory fictions. It is in fact adopting the intentional stance. For self-rules are the domains of intentionality *par excellence.*

In the case of other-rules, the tracks, plys, and augmentals we encounter daily in the social and physical environment can be localized to that external environment: a spouse's admonition to "Take care out there" as one sets out for the academy is a preparation for the slings and arrows of intellectual civilization that can be said to exist in those environments; the road sign that prohibits a particular driving behavior itself contains the rule "No right turn." However, self-rules are not like this. Where are they? In the process of radical behaviorist interpretation which we are discussing they exist in the verbalizations of the investigator albeit generated from the verbal behavior of the interpreted person and other clues. The formulation of these clues into a rule that is attributed to the individual as a motivator of his behavior is either the ascription of intentionality itself or something so close that its recognition should give behavior analysts serious pause for thought. Naturally, it is also the case that there is no way of getting to the intentions that ought to be ascribed to a system without going through exactly the same procedure: that is, constructing a learning history for the person and predicting its reactions to the current behavior setting. As we have seen this is what social cognitive psychology does. However, it is not always possible to construct such a history for the adult human on the basis of either observation or personal verbal report. The use of the intentional stance is inevitable in these circumstances. There are two spheres of inquiry in which this inevitability is especially pertinent for radical behaviorist interpretation: the problem of behavioral continuity, and the problem of equifinality and delimitation which are the subjects of a later chapter.

It is possible from this consideration of the epistemological similarities and dissimilarities of these stances to propose some general conclusions about the interpretation of complexity. Both the contextual stance and the intentional stance make preempirical assumptions about the relationship of private events to overt behavior. The contextual stance assumes that private events are always independent variables, while behavior is always a dependent variable: private events can never therefore be said to cause behavior.

Now, a scientist setting out to discover pragmatically how aspects of the world can be advantageously predicted and influenced could not make such an assumption: his pragmatic approach to the world will turn out to be what it will be, regardless of any a priori assumptions about causality that might be enjoined upon him by this or that preempirical philosophical position. The intentional stance assumes, for purposes of prediction and explanation, a causal relationship between (ascribed) personal events and behavior. Each runs into difficulties. Users of the contextual stance are sometimes forced to adopt private events as causes of behavior, for example, when private discriminative stimuli and private reinforcers are assumed to control private or public behavior, or when the verbal behavior that inheres in rules, especially self-rules, is assumed to act as a discriminative stimulus or establishing operation that enters into the control of other verbal or nonverbal behavior. And adherents of the intentional stance must admit that subpersonal cognitive psychology has proved to be less than reliable as a predictor of behavior. Each comes in practice to resemble the other a little. Perhaps, more than a little.

6.5 Endnote

Dennett's characterization of the intentional has two dimensions. The first is linguistic, based on the nature of intentional sentences (we have seen that he amalgamates the perspectives of Brentano, Chisholm, and Russell into a single account based on the properties of language). Second, he isolates the personal level of analysis that is open only to the individual who, in describing mental events, knows what pain, for instance, is without being able to define or analyze it further. It is, of course, open to behavior analysts to reject both of these on the basis of their philosophy of science. The first can be disposed of as Quine disposes of it by rejecting intentional language because it does not by definition match up to the requirements of science, which is by its very nature extensional. The second can be "retained" by behavior analysts as some kind of private event, acceptance of which is used to differentiate radical from methodological behaviorism, but which is de facto considered no further because behavioral science lacks the technical means to incorporate it into an experimental analysis. Neither of these is satisfactory even at this methodological level. The intentional use of language exists as part of the *parole* that behavior analysts ought by the very dictates of their science to be interested in elucidating; it also produces explanations that cut across those of behavior analysis and which should therefore be of primary interest to the conscious explication of behavior from a radical behaviorist point of view. They have at the very least to show that they can produce satisfactory explanations of both public and private behavior without resorting to the use of intentional idioms. However, the implications of the argument of this chapter are that intentionality poses a problem—and an opportunity—for operant interpretation that is far closer to home.

Chapter 7

Delimiting behavioral interpretation

Chapter Outline

7.1	Behavioral interpretation	127	7.5 Teleological behaviorism	140
7.2	What kind of interpretation?	130	7.6 The scope of radical behaviorist	
7.3	Interpretive stances	133	interpretation	141
7.4	Vague analogic guesses?	136	7.7 Endnote	145

Radical behaviorist interpretation is open to the criticism that it allows the researcher to propose that events that follow a behavior are reinforcing or punishing consequences of which the repetition of the behavior is a function (Section 7.1). The putative relationship between E1 and E2 in the extensional syntax described in Section 5.1 is something that, according to the rigor supposedly imposed on psychology by the behaviorisms of Watson and Skinner, ought to be empirically demonstrable rather than intuited. This chapter discusses the nature of radical behaviorist interpretation and its implications for a scientific account of behavior. Skinner's attempts at third-personal interpretation are critically examined (Section 7.2) and the nature of interpretive stances themselves is the subject of Section 7.3. Chomsky's judgment that Skinner's account of verbal behavior consisted largely in wild extrapolations from the animal laboratory is discussed (Section 7.4) and the methodology of Rachlin's teleological behaviorism is traced in Sections 7.5 and 7.6. The scope and deficiencies of radical behaviorist interpretation are the subjects of Section 7.7.

7.1 Behavioral interpretation

Even among Skinner's earliest formulations of radical behaviorism[1] and its distinctive scheme of explanation, an attempt to fix the essential conceptual

---

1. In examining the nature of radical behaviorism interpretation, I shall often rely on the foundational statements of B. F. Skinner since it is necessary to have a basis for the philosophy of psychology which he, after all, pioneered and sustained for many decades. Some contemporary behavior analysts argue that Skinner does not speak for all radical behaviorists, the implication being that it is wrong to cite him as the authority for the nature of radical behaviorism as a science and an interpretation of behavior. I find this disingenuous. Skinner originated radical behaviorism, not as a psychology but as a *philosophy* of psychology, but no-one has given more consideration to how radical behaviorism provides accounts of those complex modes of behavior that lie beyond the laboratory.

differences between his system and those presented by other behaviorists and cognitivists can be found. The explicit distinguishing feature of radical behaviorism is its admission of thoughts and feelings (private events) into its explanatory system, albeit as responses attracting an operant explanation rather than as causes of behavior (Skinner, 1945). Whereas the *methodological* behaviorism of Watson (1913) placed such phenomena beyond the scope of scientific investigation, Skinner's system refuses to admit that private events differ ontologically or methodologically from those overt stimuli and responses that are open to communal corroboration (Smith, 1986). Private events have nevertheless been of little relevance to the experimental analysis of behavior. Behavior analysts, who have traditionally been involved in laboratory experiments with rats, pigeons, and other nonhuman animals, have had little need of the concept, which has received minimal elaboration in behavioral science even when the explanation of human behavior in nonlaboratory situations has been the objective. The success of radical behaviorism depends, nonetheless, on its ability to make the transition from laboratory to life, and Skinner's answer is neither extrapolation nor theory but "interpretation."

Skinner (1969a) argues that areas of human behavior that lie beyond the rigor of experimental procedure are amenable to an account based on the extension thereto of scientific laws derived from the analysis of simpler behavior patterns observed in the laboratory (see Skinner, 1969a, p. 100). In the study of complex actions, such as everyday verbal behavior, it is usually impossible to ascertain the contingencies that control response rate with the accuracy and precision available to the scientist who can assiduously control and monitor both dependent and independent variables. But it is possible to present a "plausible account" of such complex actions (Skinner, 1957, p. 11) which is essentially "an interpretation, not an explanation... merely useful, neither true nor false" (Skinner, 1988e, p. 364). The behavior analytic interpretation, like those that deal with the evolution of life or the geophysics of the earth's core, is unprovable but preferable, nonetheless, to those which cannot be supported by knowledge of simpler systems gained from carefully executed experiments (Skinner, 1969a, p. 100; 1974, pp. 226–227; 1988c, p. 208). "When phenomena are out of reach in time or space, or too large or small to be directly manipulated, we must talk about them with less than a complete account of relevant conditions. What has been learned under more favorable conditions is then invaluable" (Skinner, 1973, p. 261). Would that it were so straightforward. In terms of methodology, "plausible" is an amazingly weak word to employ here. There is never any problem in rationalizing a plausible interpretation, especially if its main function is to satisfy those who already accept the principles of behavior to which it makes reference, as opposed to an account that is warranted or defensible given the evidence. Skinner seems to have no inkling that what Dewey refers to as a "warrant of assertibility" is required if radical behaviorist interpretation is to have any epistemological merit. The modus operandi of this extrapolation of radical behaviorist explanation beyond the laboratory into the everyday world requires close delineation, since it opens up new vistas of theoretical and methodological concern. Moreover, formulating an appropriate strategy of interpretation brings radical behaviorism inescapably into contact with its borders, notably the interpretive stance inherent in social cognitive psychology. (The problem of interpreting behavior in natural environments in terms of principles gained through experimentation is familiar to ethologists; see, for instance, Kacelnik, 1993; Shettleworth, 2010.) The difficulty is that while sentiments such as Skinner's have promoted the proliferation of somewhat ad hoc and extrapolative interpretations of complex human activity (e.g., Skinner, 1953, 1957, 1971, 1974), radical behaviorists have done little to formulate a *methodology* of interpretation. Although the essential feature of such interpretations is clear—the identification of discriminative antecedents to responses and their relationship of both to the reinforcing and punishing consequences of behaving—no systematic procedure has been evolved that leads plausibly to the unambiguous discernment of these elements of the "three-term contingency." Issues of validity and reliability scarcely arise in so deterministic a system. This neglect gives rise to the criticism that radical behaviorist interpretation consists largely in the "vague analogical guesses" attributed by Chomsky (1959) to Skinner's operant account of verbal behavior (Skinner, 1957). Interpretation cannot be based on an arbitrary procedure but must be capable of judgment based on the criteria to which any scientific hypotheses would be subjected.

The absence of criteria by which to pursue and evaluate "plausible" interpretations leads to dogmatic assertion that environmental element x is or is not an operant response, a discriminative stimulus, or a reinforcer/punisher. This is apparent even to some radical behaviorists, those who refuse to entertain the view that the private events that are not amenable to an experimental analysis are deserving of their scientific acknowledgment. Further, the radical behaviorist principle that discriminative stimulus, operant response, and reinforcer are separate events comes under criticism from those who see a single event as capable of constituting all the three elements of the three-term contingency (Bandura, 1986). The use of these necessarily theoretical terms requires not ontological dogma but a methodology of interpretation and the setting of limits within which the results of applying that methodology can be safely entertained. A more formal construal of radical behaviorism is essential to the appreciation of where experimental science and interpretive system diverge.

Radical behaviorism is an amalgam of positivism, descriptivism, operationism, and pragmatism directed toward the prediction and control of behavior (Delprato & Midgley, 1992; Foxall, 1996/2015; Moore, 1999; Ringen, 1999; Smith, 1986; Smith & Woodward, 1996; Thyer, 1999; Zuriff, 1985). It seeks to explain its subject matter, observed behavior, by relating operant responses to the environmental conditions that have selected and preserved them. Internal events, states, and processes, whether mental, neural, or hypothetical, even if real, are not usually admitted as causes of behavior, though later Skinnerian thought considered them proximal or "noninitiating" causes thereof (cf. Foxall, 1990/2004; Skinner, 1988c). The ultimate causes of behavior, nevertheless, reside always in the environment (Skinner, 1977).

7.2 What kind of interpretation?

Despite Skinner's (1974) view that part of the environment is enclosed within the skin and that the skin is but an arbitrary barrier, here he appears to be thinking of an extrapersonal environment. An alternative view of private events is that the relevant environment is that of the behavior rather than the organism. Similarly, radical behaviorists differ in how far they adopt private events in the interpretation of observed behavior, how far they confine their accounts of complex behavior within the scope of experimental science, or are willing to speculate about the influence of covert actions. Radical behaviorism does not deny the existence of "private events" such as thoughts and feelings—indeed, we have noted that its essential distinction from methodological behaviorism inheres in its acceptance of such events as part of its subject matter—but any proximal control exercised by these covert entities over overt behavior will endure only in so far as it is consistent with the environmental consequences of the overt responding. This is consistent with empirical findings on instructed behavior (Catania, Matthews, & Shimoff, 1982; Hayes, Brownstein, Haas, & Greenway, 1986; Horne & Lowe, 1993). Public or private, events are ontologically identical. Nevertheless, the inclusion of private events in *interpretations* of complex behavior complicates this simple account considerably. In the paper that marks his first use of the term *radical* behaviorism, Skinner (1945, pp. 272–273) writes as follows:

> The response "My tooth aches" is partly under the control of a state of affairs to which the speaker alone is able to react, since no one else can establish the required connection with the tooth in question. There is nothing mysterious or metaphysical about this; the simple fact is that each speaker possesses a small but important private world of stimuli. So far as we know, responses to that world are like responses to external events. Nevertheless, the privacy gives rise to two problems. The first difficulty is that we cannot, as in the case of public stimuli, account for the verbal response by pointing to a controlling stimulus. Our practice is to infer the private event, but this is opposed to the direction of inquiry in a science of behavior in which we are to predict a response through, among other things, an independent knowledge of the stimulus. It is often supposed that a solution is to be found in improved physiological techniques.

Whenever it becomes possible to say what conditions within the organism control the response 'I am depressed,' for example, and to produce these conditions at will, a degree of control and prediction characteristic of responses to external stimuli will be made possible. Meanwhile, we must be content with reasonable evidence for the belief that responses to public and private stimuli are equally lawful and alike in kind.

But are we justified in being so content? Since Skinner's preference was always for radical over methodological behaviorism, his system has since its inception required a dual approach to accounting for human behavior. This duality has become sharper with the passage of time and the extrapolation of radical behaviorist explication from simple animal behavior in the operant chamber to the complexities of human social, economic, political, verbal, and cultural practices. The *experimental analysis of behavior* entails relating simple responses in closely regulated laboratory settings to the environmental events (discriminative, reinforcing, and punishing stimuli) that control them. The success criterion of this inductive behavior science is pragmatic rather than realist (Mackenzie, 1977). This stance derives essentially from the brand of positivism on which it is based—not the logical positivism of the Vienna Circle but Machian positivism founded upon biological expediency (Smith, 1986).

In this philosophy of science to describe is to explain in detail. Science is thus part of the human species' effort to adapt to its environment through predicting and controlling nature. Whatever works in this sense is true; in Skinner's terms, whatever reinforces behavior that ensures the survival of effective cultural norms is "right." Science is not, therefore, neutral: the operant chamber leads inexorably to *Walden Two* (Skinner, 1948) and the design of cultures (Skinner, 1971). The dimensions of science, the operational rigor of its conceptual definitions, and the pragmatic outcomes of its program to predict and control are more than Enlightenment ideals; they are the means to the good life (Flanagan). Though the link may be inexorable, it is not direct. Beyond the confines of the operant laboratory, radical behaviorism's accounts of complexity, notably human behavior, consist in *interpretation*, "an orderly arrangement of behavior derived from an experimental analysis of a more rigorous sort" (Skinner, 1957, p. 11). Principles of behavior gained from the observation of responses in laboratory contexts can be applied to complex behaviors that are not amenable to an experimental analysis in the same way that astrophysicists interpret inaccessible solar events by reference to physical knowledge derived from a more feasible analysis. The success criterion of such behavioral interpretations is as we have seen not their pragmatic contribution to the prediction and control of behavior but their "plausibility" (Skinner, 1969a, 1969b, 1974, 1988a).

The many experimentalists who became behavior analysts in order to investigate the behavior of organisms in the tightly controlled circumstances of the laboratory have made an immense contribution to the derivation of behavior principles by means of which not only the conduct of their experimental subjects may be explained but by which also the behavior of both human and nonhuman animals might be investigated and explained beyond the confines of the laboratory. Many experimenters are content with that and do not seek to extend their scientific analysis outside the experimental space. For them the experimental analysis of behavior has become an end in itself, a means of exploring and explaining animal behavior in closely regulated situations. Others, however, have been drawn to behavior analysis because they sought explanations in terms of behavior—environmental interactions for patterns of nonlaboratory behavior with which they were familiar by virtue of analysis within other disciplines—economics, sociology, consumer science, or whatever. Some of our interest has expressed itself in experimental or quasiexperimental work but by the very nature of its grounding in human behavior beyond the laboratory such interest has also found expression in what Skinner called "interpretation," the application of behavior principles gained in the analysis of simpler systems to environments not amenable to an experimental examination. Looking through the laboratory window at the world of affairs, it is easy to see notional "three-term contingencies" at every turn. Moving from the laboratory to life requires that we modify our conceptual and methodological framework in order to show within what bounds our imported explanations carry conviction. Psychologists of other theoretical persuasions have long sought *rules of correspondence* by which to relate their unobservable explanatory terms to the data language in which they describe their observations. Such rules are not what we seek here but, analogously at least, we require rules of interpretation, means of transcending the expanse between accounts of experimental findings in terms of behavioral—environmental contingencies and operant explications of complex behaviors that are more than merely plausible.

While there had once been a hope—even expectation—that the analysis of the actions of rats, pigeons, and other nonhumans would permit the uncomplicated interspecies generalization of results, the analysis of verbal behavior eventually indicated that extrapolation would be an insufficient means of accounting for the complex interactions of human beings. Between the extrapolative attempts of Skinner's (1957) *Verbal Behavior* and his conceptually innovative account of the rule-governance of much human behavior (Skinner, 1969b) lies at least an implicit recognition of this. We have seen that *Verbal Behavior* attracted the criticism from Chomsky that it made "vague analogic guesses" in its attempt to find equivalences in the complex world of the discriminative stimuli, responses and reinforcers and punishers so readily identified in the laboratory (Chomsky, 1959; see also Broadbent, 1961/1978; Schwartz & Lacey, 1982). The vast interspecies differences between the animals that had typically been studied in the laboratory and those capable of verbal behavior were finally taken into consideration in Skinner's second major contribution to this study, the paper (Skinner, 1969b) in which he dealt with decision-making.

By this time, when the "cognitive revolution" was well under way, it was clear that human behavior could not be comprehensively accounted for in terms of the contingency-shaping that provided a plausible explanation of the behavior of infrahumans at least in the laboratory. Some human behavior undoubtedly is explicable in such terms but the vast majority of its instances are rendered intelligible in operant terms only if they are portrayed as rule-governed, that is subject to the verbal stimuli provided by the actor and, especially, by others in the form of rules, advice, instructions, admonitions, and so on. The complexities of human behavior occurring outside the closed setting of the laboratory experiment, especially when conducted with nonhuman subjects, could not be accommodated within the framework of conceptualization and analysis that had served so well for the explication of simpler patterns of conduct. New explanatory devices were required that were not predictable from the analysis of nonhuman or perhaps even human behavior in the experimental setting. Hence, the origin of rule-governance, a mode of explanation that has resulted in a great deal of empirical and theoretical research that continues to this day and which has taken the analysis of verbal behavior far beyond the (often invaluable, but limited) insights of *Verbal Behavior*.

While verbal behavior is frequently amenable to an experimental analysis, however, this is not always the case. Human interaction in naturalistic settings is often incapable of a reduction to laboratory analogs and experimental analysis: it is at best open only to an interpretation in operant terms. We can seek simple plausibility in such interpretations, in which case we shall undoubtedly succeed. But this is a strategy that from the beginning sees interpretation as a secondary activity compared with experimentation. Alternatively, we can look beyond such simplicity toward the establishment of a system of operant analysis of complexity that rests on a reasoned epistemological foundation.

7.3 Interpretive stances

Interpretation consists in the adoption and application of an analogic stance by which complex behavior, the causes of which are inaccessible to experimental science, is described in terms provided by a causal system that has achieved plausibility when rigorously applied to a simpler behavior system. A stance is, first, an *assertion*. The contextual stance *asserts* that the variables of which behavior is a function can be extensionally characterized (i.e., without recourse to propositional attitudes or other intentional idioms). Second, a stance is a *preempirical* position. This does not imply that it is prescientific, of course: the adoption of a stance is part of the scientific process. Rather, it permits a basis for behavioral prediction to be advanced without prior ontological assumption. Note, however, that as an ideological position that engenders research, a stance is neither true nor false: it gives direction to research by indicating where answers may be found, but it does not guarantee the veracity, usefulness, or superiority of the results to which it leads. However, formulating our strategy by reference to its underlying stance forces us to make explicit the ascriptions and suppositions on which we are basing it. Third, a stance is a *philosophical position*. Dennett continually criticizes behaviorism as a psychology. His remarks about radical behaviorism's *masking* the intentional stance are couched solely in terms of what behaviorism is as a psychological method. It does not recognize that behaviorism is founded on a philosophical stance as surely as cognitivism is. This stance is a means of prediction (and partial explanation). It can be compared with the intentional stance only if it is itself construed as having stance-like qualities. Finally, a stance is *universal of application*. One way of dividing the intellectual landscape would be to claim that the intentional stance applies to open settings (those in which the individual has several to many choices open to him or her so that his or her behavior is difficult to predict), the contextual stance to closed settings (those in which all but one or two behaviors are proscribed by the kinds of consequences they will attract). But our *assertion* is that the contextual stance applies as surely to behavior in open settings as to that in closed.

The rationale for the adoption of such a stance and for its continued application to the complexity in question must be externally derived. In the case of radical behaviorist interpretation, our success criterion must be initially that of prediction and control imposed by the experimental science on which it is based. "Understanding," "explanation," and the provision of a "plausible operant account" are far too vague for a rigorous test. In order to clarify the nature and scope of radical behaviorist interpretation, it is first necessary to delineate radical behaviorism itself as a philosophy of psychology, to understand what sets it apart. Once this has been done, it is possible to explore the relationship between the explanatory basis of radical behaviorism and that which underlies cognitive psychology, the strongest alternative contender as explicator of complex human behavior. Dennett's approach to intentionality (e.g., Dennett, 1969, 1987a, 1987b, 1996) provides a reference point since it is not only generally available, current, and persuasive but engages with behaviorism at a number of points. In this way, it is possible both to facilitate a comparative analysis of Dennett's *intentional strategy* and the *contextual strategy* that is the foundation of the behaviorist enterprise, and to explore the manner by which an operant interpretation of complex human behavior, that is, behavior not amenable to laboratory experimentation, can be accomplished.

The selection of these exemplars of cognitive and behaviorist philosophies of science is not arbitrary. Most cognitive theories, especially those that render prebehavioral events in terms of information processing, rest on the intentional idiom, while the extensional approach that underlies the contextual stance is a necessary component of a genuine behavioristic approach. The endeavor to delineate the bounds of radical behaviorism, in the light of the competing explanations of behavior offered by cognitive psychology, makes necessary the critical comparison of these stances.

The intentionalism encapsulated in Dennett's *intentional stance* is basic to psychological explanations predicated upon information processing. Commenting on the relationship between cognitive accounts, such as Dennett's, that employ propositional attitudes, and those such as the social cognition models, Bechtel (1988, p. 75) challenges "those working on processing accounts to attend to the intentional perspective, in which the behavior of a cognitive system is characterized in terms of its beliefs and desires about the environment. It is this intentional perspective that identifies what aspects of the behavior of a system need to be explained by the processing account." The argument, central to Dennett's (1983) entire enterprise, that the intentional stance elucidates cognitive ethology rests, after all, on the claim that it identifies the mental qualities and capacities of organisms and species. The intentional strategy, by identifying the propositional attitudes necessary for the organism's adaptation to its environment, provides social cognitivism, the dominant paradigm within cognitive psychology (Ostrom, 1994), with a rationale for its research program.

The relevance of the comparison to radical behaviorism is equally compelling. For *contra* Skinner the central fact in the delineation of radical behaviorism is its conceptual avoidance of propositional content. This eschewal of the *intentional stance* sets it apart not only from cognitivism but also from neo-behaviorisms such as those of Tolman and Hull. Indeed, the defining characteristic of radical behaviorism is not that it avoids mediating processes per se but that it accounts for behavior without recourse to propositional attitudes. Based on the *contextual stance*, it provides accounts of contingency-shaped, rule-governed, verbal, and private behaviors that are entirely nonintentional. Its capacity to do so is independent of any prior assumption of intentionality: it is therefore methodologically autonomous. Cognitive explanation by contrast requires the prior application of the contextual stance before its propositions can be translated into an intentional explanation. These ideas are explored on the basis of an examination of recent advances in attitude theory and research, as an exemplar, but there are grounds for believing it to be a universal characteristic of the social-cognitive school of psychology. The import of this is that a social-cognitive psychology can be constructed by ascribing intentional content to the findings and theories of extensional behavioral science. Although this does not affect the pursuit of extensional behavior analysis as a largely experimental enterprise, it has profound implications for the nature of radical behaviorist interpretation. Consideration is given to whether operant accounts of complex human behavior (that which is not amenable to an experimental analysis) can proceed most effectively through such a combination of the intentional and contextual stances or through a reconstruction of intentional idioms in extensional language.

7.4 Vague analogic guesses?

The need for interpretation arises in situations where no stimulus field is available to the researcher to provide the terms of an operant analysis. The standard radical behaviorist response is to construct a behavioral interpretation on the basis of a reconstruction of the learning history and consumer-situations that may have been responsible for the observed behavior. This is neither science nor adherence to the extensional syntax on which radical behaviorism basis its claim to explain behavior in terms of the environmental stimuli of which it is demonstrably a function. The intentional behaviorist response to this is to insist that the interpretation be conducted in intentional terms: first, because this removes the suggestion that the behavior in question has been traced to variables of which it is a function; second, because it draws attention to the appropriation of reinforcing and punishing stimuli that could not possibly have had an effect on the behavior in question; and, third, in order to substitute intentions that refer to what the individual could possibly have known, desired, and believed at the time. Using remote consequences to explain behavior is not only out of kilter with operant analysis (which relies on immediate outcomes) but also spurious in that it is an invitation to invention of uncheckable causes of behavior. If a proposed cause of behavior is not, even in principle, amenable to empirical test is it not meaningless? No need to be a logical positivist to see that this is unscientific. Identifying the nuclear weapons industry as a cause of the splitting of the atom is to confuse remote consequences with environmental variables of which the pioneering scientific behavior in question could possibly have been a function. This is not functional analysis: it is fantasy.

As mentioned, an important plank in Chomsky's (1959) platform of criticism of radical behaviorism was that stimuli and responses that were closely specifiable in the laboratory were translated into "vague analogic guesses" when applied to the interpretation of broad swathes of behavior that was not amenable to experimental analysis. Hamlyn (1970a,b,1990) points out that operant psychologists have stretched the notions of input and output. The idea of a stimulus has been stretched from (1) the application of energy to a nerve ending, through (2) anything that produces some response *by* the organism, to (3) a function of the environment in the presence of which the organism discriminates its behavior. Note that Hamlyn speaks of perception rather than discrimination. However, whether we talk about the organism discriminating its behavior or perceiving, we need a definite mechanism for the translation of a known learning history into a tendency to behave predictably in similar circumstances. Although behaviorists see discrimination in this sense as merely a description of behavior rather than a mental operation, they still need to give an account of why it happens if their interpretations of behavior are to be credible. Similarly, for responses there has been over time a progression from (1) a reaction caused by an (internal or external) environmental element, through (2) a response that may be activated by something in the environment but not caused by it, to (3) an act or action made in relation to something in the environment but not activated by it. The problem with this is that it distends the specific and strict until it fits the amorphous and unwieldy while retaining the terminology of the former. The behavioral interpreter is making pronouncements about causality with the authority of a rigorous experimentalist. The third point appears, essentially, to be action, activity initiated by the organism, perhaps based on a belief about the environment but not a direct function of the environment. If so, a necessary precaution that should accompany the issuance of behavioral interpretations is that of the intentional behaviorist concern with the behaver making her own behavior (action) rather than behavior being simply the result of environmental stimulation (see Hamlyn, 1970, pp. 13–15; cf. Watson, 1970.).

An experimental analysis of behavior, necessarily occurring in a relatively closed behavior setting, makes possible the close delineation of the variables in terms which it proceeds. "Stimulus," and "response," "learning history," and "rate," must be specified sufficiently closely that they can be unambiguously, consistently, and intersubjectively applied to this or that part of the events occurring within the experimental space. Strictly speaking, the results and conclusions of such experimentation apply with total precision and assurance only to that space, and predictions of the generalizability of behavior observed within the experiment will be most accurate when they take the form of projections of acts taking place within similar environments. Interpretation is required when such projection becomes discontinuous, when the terms used with precision in one sphere must be applied elsewhere with less than full assurance that they can be entirely disambiguated, consistently employed, or capable of evoking the high degree of mutual agreement which the operant chamber presents. And, on occasion, terms may be required in the process of interpretation that fails to evoke analogs which can be experimentally tested. The problem of interpretation arises because it is a process that cannot yield the precision of delineation normally available to the experimenter. However, although it is inevitable that interpretation will entail concepts, methods, and criteria that go beyond those appropriate to the experimental analysis of behavior, it is incumbent on the interpreter of complex behavior to delimit the scope of his or her account of complexity, to show how the difficulties inherent in behavior whose various consequences exhibit equifinality have been overcome. If there are no safeguards of this kind, if we cannot circumscribe the range of outcomes of a particular act to which its enactment can be attributed without straining credulity, then we remain unsure what constitutes a cause of the complex behavior we observe outside the laboratory and what does not. And this problem remains, whether our aim is to take our interpretations back to the laboratory or to test them by means of nonexperimental methodologies.

The ease with which we are able to construct interpretations of the everyday actions we behold in the terminology of the three-term contingency compounds the difficulty of reliable delineation. Hence, the behavior of the professor we see entering the faculty club is readily explicable by reference to an easily constructed learning history. Since we have lunch with him there twice a week, the notice "Faculty Club" and the time shown by the clock on the building's façade can safely be said to be discriminative stimuli for his current behavior, elements of the environment that set the occasion for his entering, ordering, and eating a meal leading to an increase in the likelihood that he will enact similar behaviors on other occasions. So far, so good: based on our expert knowledge of these contingencies of reinforcement, we shall make accurate predictions of this professor's behavior in these and similar circumstances. And, although we cannot subject his activities to an experimental analysis, we can interpret what we see of them in terms we have validated in our work. However, he may well be entering the faculty club in order to pursue his extramarital *amour passionel* with the catering manager, something he has done without our knowledge on the remaining days of the working week for the last 7 years. In this case, our prediction will fail and our interpretation of his behavior, though entirely *plausible,* may cause us embarrassment when the catering manager exposes the professor's indiscretion in the tabloids. Our difficulty lies in not having been able to subject the professor to the same rigorous observation in the course of his acquisition of a history of reinforcement and punishment which is available to the animal experimenter.

In experimental studies of the behavior of organisms whose whole world of learning is coterminous with the operant chamber, learning history is often unproblematical. First, it is known: the rats and pigeons typically used in such experiments can be trained from a very early age; all that needs to be known about their history of reinforcement is accessible by the experimenter in whose charge they find themselves. Second, it is simple: the effects of differing schedules of reinforcement and punishment are easily described and taken into consideration in further research. Third, it can often be ignored: the current contingencies represented by the behavior setting are sufficient to determine behavior or at least to render it predictable and controllable by the experimenter. There remains the problem of incorporating the animal's learning history into this account, of course; since learning history is so central an explanatory factor in radical behaviorism, it cannot be right to ignore it altogether. But this does not seem to exercise experimentalists whose scientific goals (prediction and control) are sufficiently fulfilled without recourse to the abstract. But these difficulties cannot go so easily unnoticed by the interpreter of human behavior in radical behaviorist terms, who is left to enquire: how can learning history be taken into consideration in the case of human beings whose previous responding is simply not accessible, and how can we better understand the interaction of that learning history and the stimulus elements of the current behavior setting to produce the situation, the intersection of time and space that explains the response made?

There is simply no means by which the learning history of an adult human can be established even approximately unless he has lived all his life in the most closed of settings. Hence, there is no unequivocal means of deciding what pattern of reinforcement is responsible for the maintenance of an observed pattern of behavior that is amenable only to an interpretive account, that is, the complex behavior that cannot be reduced to a laboratorial analog. The import of this problem of equifinality (Lee, 1988) is that if radical behaviorist interpretation is to mean anything other than vaguely guided speculation, on a par with any other amateur psychology, its practitioners must find a means of bringing to it some greater measure of the scientific rigor characteristic of the experimental analysis of behavior. But if the ascription of terms of contingency to the contextually enrapt behaviors we observe seems easy, it must also be admitted that some behaviors may be neither predictable nor amenable to plausible construal within the bounds of this philosophy of psychology or, for that matter, any other single framework of conceptualization and analysis. If learning histories for the purpose of accurate—as opposed to merely plausible—operant interpretations of complex behavior are not empirically available, we ought surely to be circumspect when proffering constructions of observed activity in terminology we know only from another sphere of inquiry.

An operant class, meaning that group of operant responses that are controlled by the same pattern of reinforcement, is by definition an equifinal class: it may include responses that are topographically quite different but belong together because they are functionally equivalent, that is, produce identical consequences (Lee, 1988, pp. 135–137). Obtaining a product by mail order has a form that is entirely distinct from asking for the same product in a store, but both responses belong to the same equifinal class because they have the same outcome. A response that closely or exactly resembles another belongs to a different equifinal class if it produces functionally different results. Two consumers may enter the same store at the same time in exactly similar manners, but their responses belong to different operant classes if the first is reinforced by the purchase of a product, while the second is reinforced by information about the availability and price of that product. Lee (1988, p. 136) gives the example of seeing a person walking down the stairs at a particular time of the morning. He or she might be going to the library, to morning coffee, or any of a dozen other places of reinforcement. But such equifinality is a problem for the would-be interpreter for it makes ascription of the behavior to a particular operant class difficult if not impossible. Innumerable interpretations might be made: we do not have to go as far as the example of the professor entering the faculty club to recognize that even simple everyday construals of observed behavior in operant terms elude us because we have no access to the person's learning history or even the full complement of stimuli comprising the setting in which the observed individual's behavior is taking place. It is difficult to see how such interpretations as we might venture in these circumstances could carry much by way of plausibility let alone validity and reliability. As I argue in this chapter, in regard to the kind of interpretation proposed by teleological behaviorism, it is impossible to define the bounds of behaviorism other than by the incorporation of intentional idioms.

7.5 Teleological behaviorism

Rachlin's (1994) extensional interpretation of observed behavior, *teleological behaviorism*, follows Aristotle in distinguishing efficient from final causes. Efficient causes precede their effects and consist in the set of internal nervous discharges giving rise to particular movements; they would include internal physiological and cognitive precedents of activity. The analysis of efficient causes yields a mechanism that answers the question "*How* does this or that movement occur?" (Rachlin, 1994, p. 22). Final causes are consequences of behavior and may inclusively fit into one another as the causal web extends outward from the individual who behaves: "eating an appetizer fits into eating a meal, which fits into a good diet, which fits into a healthy life, which in turn fits into a generally good life. The wider the category, the more embracing, the 'more final' the cause" (Rachlin, 1994, p. 21). The analysis of final causes is an attempt to answer the question "*Why* does this or that movement occur — for what reason?" (p. 22). The process of finding the causes of behavior is one of fitting the behavior into an ever-increasing molar pattern of response and consequences. The dependent variable in Rachlin's scheme is not a single response, however, but a temporally extended pattern of behavior. Similarly, the causes of behavior are extended, a series of consequences nested within one another from the closest to the most remote. We have seen that, from these extended patterns of behavior and consequence, can be discerned emotional and "cognitive" behaviors: indeed, the emotion or thinking or believing or knowing *is* the pattern of extended behavior. Rachlin's work in behavioral economics is highly relevant here because an important cause of behavior is the utility function that describes the entire sequence of extended behavior of the individual (Rachlin, Battalio, Kagel, & Green, 1981).

In some respects, this is pure radical behaviorism and for the purposes of this investigation it states very clearly the essential position of radical behaviorism as a philosophy of psychology. It has, therefore, some similarities to the interpretive stance adopted by Skinner, though it also differs from his thought, principally in its treatment of private events. Rachlin is a radical behaviorist to the extent that he avoids dualism and his truth criterion is pragmatic (Baum, 1994, p. 39). Unlike conventional radical behaviorism, however, Rachlin's system has no time for private events or intrapersonal phenomena; yet, unlike both radical and methodological behaviorism, it freely employs mentalistic terminology. The reason is, as we have just noted, that in Rachlin's theory, behavior is always external to the individual even when it is thinking and feeling; its ultimate cause is represented by the individual's utility function, an entirely observable measure of the ultimate range of external consequences it generates (Rachlin, 1989). Rachlin asserts that mind is behavior, sequences, or patterns of behavior rather than single acts. This molar view (common in behavioral economics: see, inter alia, Baum, 1973; Herrnstein, 1997) means that mental phenomena such as attitudes, intentions, and even pain are all defined by extended patterns of behavior. We know that our friend is in pain because of the behaviors he emits: grimacing, groaning, holding his arm, and so on. According to Rachlin, this is exactly the information our friend also has to go on in order to know that he is in pain. Bem (1972) speaks of attitudes in similar vein: I must like brown bread because I see myself eating a lot of it—this is exactly the same information on which my wife bases her view that I like (have a positive attitude toward) brown bread. It is a third-person account that is unconcerned with the first-person access I have to my pain or to my experience of liking brown bread.

Rachlin is not saying that this is the sole permissible ontology: he is simply concentrating on what is of interest to him to the general exclusion of the notion of intrapersonal causation (see also Baum, 2000). That is, he is concentrating on the Aristotelian idea of final (external, succeeding the behavior for which it is responsible) causation as opposed to the more familiar efficient (inner, preceding) causation that underlies cognitivism (Stout, 1996). But he neither rules out the latter nor suggests that it is inadmissible. Teleological behaviorism thus eschews the problems of private events, mediating variables, and propositional attitudes at a single stroke. In insisting on public corroboration of the facts of science, however, it adopts a tenet of logical positivism that is absent from radical behaviorism. Skinner's notion of private events, said by him to be admissible to science because they are observable, albeit by one person, is a very different proposition, though as we have seen it leaves the private events it posits in order to differentiate itself from other (predominantly methodological) behaviorisms almost entirely unanalyzed.

7.6 The scope of radical behaviorist interpretation

There are two reasons why Rachlin's teleological behaviorism cannot provide a comprehensive approach to the explanation of behavior, one that can incorporate both an experimental analysis and a plausible interpretive system. (I am not here offering a comprehensive critique of Rachlin's teleological behaviorism: I merely suggest that interpretations based on his system are unbounded and require an intentional overlay of interpretation in order to be useful. As far as I know, there is little by way of critical comment on Rachlin's system from behaviorists or others, which is a commentary on the level of philosophical debate among behaviorists or about behaviorism. For informed philosophical criticism of Rachlin's book, *Behavior and Mind*, however, see Lacey (1995/1996).) The first is that the search for final causes introduces a degree of imprecision and arbitrariness (since the final causes we advance may frequently be unamenable to empirical examination) that is unacceptable. This is the problem of context, specifically that of finding the appropriate context by which to judge the consequences of the behavior under interpretation. The second is the inability of teleological behaviorism to provide a personal-level analysis of behaviors such as pain. This is the problem of the privacy of personal experience, specifically that of incorporating first-person accounts in a science of behavior.

We have noted that teleological behaviorism is a system of explanation in terms of final causes, the external consequences that determine the rate of behavior and to which the terminology of mental events may be attached. A whole series of final causes may each be nested within one another, diffused over time, the whole sequence being necessary to a full explanation of the behavior that produced them. But, since the events that explain a behavior are temporally extended, the compilation of its explanation may require the elapse of a significant period before the full complexity of the behavior's consequences can be noted and understood (Rachlin, 1994, pp. 31–32). The search for final causes as ultimate explanations may, nevertheless, be convoluted and unscientific in the sense that the propositions employed in explication of a behavior may never be brought into contact with the empirical events that could substantiate them or lead to their refutation. Take, for example, the commonplace idea that Nylon was so-called because of the locations of the laboratories that developed it in *N*ew *Y*ork and *Lon*don. If, as seems likely, this tale is an urban myth, it still provides a final cause for the naming of the material. However, again assuming the story is no more than mythical, there is an important sense in which it is untrue: no one actually had this reason for naming Nylon in mind (or in their verbal behavior) at the time it was named. Its intension must be sought elsewhere. In other words, the extension we might in ignorance attribute to "Nylon" supports the myth (the final cause argument), while the intension of the term does not. The idea that the material was named for the cities of New York and London provides a plausible extension, but one that is untestable. The kinds of final cause that Rachlin enjoins upon us may be like this.

Similarly, pursuing teleological explanation, Stout (1996) quotes Aristotle to the effect that causation lies in identifying what a thing or action is "for the sake of." He comments: "If walking is good for health, and my walking can be explained by that reason, walking about is done for the sake of health. If a flower is for the sake of attracting insects and that is why a plant has one, then the presence of the flower is teleologically explained. If my going to the bank is for the sake of getting out some money, and that explains why I go to the bank, then the action is telelogically explained" (p. 81). So, of course, is the bank. Yet a teleological explanation for the bank in terms of its *being for the sake* of the individual who wishes to get money out of his account is partial to say the least. The intensional meaning of building a bank, and of building it at that particular place, is also required for a full explanation. The frequently misquoted observation that the final cause of the human nose is snuff makes the argument well. (What Coleridge actually wrote was "You abuse snuff! Perhaps it is the final cause of the human nose" *Table Talk*, January 4, 1823.)

Rachlin's search for plausible extensions fails because, first, the extension identified is untestable (at least during the period of the interpretation) and, second, it leaves out of the picture the personal level of analysis that seeks to identify the intensional basis for the interpretation. To say that a or the (final) cause of the physics research undertaken by Rutherford et al. that included the splitting of the atom was the death of millions of Japanese civilians is a travesty. The two events are undoubtedly linked but the invocation of a causal relationship between them is hardly adequate to account for either. More complete explanations must be sought at the intensional level. Of course, this may lead equally to speculative interpretations that are untestable. But, it deduces them (its interpreted "causal" mental mechanisms) from a logical framework of goal-directed activity based on evolutionary reasoning, and it does not ignore the personal level of analysis.

Rachlin gives the example of our seeing a snippet of film showing a man swinging a hammer in order to explain Aristotle's conception of final causation (Rachlin, 2000, pp. 58–59; see also Rachlin, 1994, pp. 82–83, which is the subject of the review by Lacey quoted later). What, he asks, is the man actually doing? He might be swinging a hammer, hammering a nail, joining pieces of wood, laying a floor, building a house, providing shelter, supporting his family, being a good husband or father, or being a good person. All of these may be descriptions of his behavior, all may be true. But in order to arrive at the final judgment of what the man is doing, we must look through the movie of the man's entire life. "The validity of any of the above descriptions may be settled by moving the camera back or showing more film — earlier and later" (p. 59). The whole point of my criticism, the whole problem of the behavioral interpreter, is that there is no such thing as this comprehensive movie, no means of obtaining the complete behavioral history of this individual. We only get snippets of film and we need to find a means of interpreting it that is readier-to-hand than the supposed universal observation. Lacey (1995/1996, p. 69) hints at the kind of extra interpretation that is required: "Insofar as building a house is constituted by an extended behavioral pattern, a particular act is part of the pattern only if it is performed because the builder believes that it will contribute towards her goal of a house being built through her own agency. In this analysis, which is Aristotelian, intentional categories are essential for defining the behavior pattern. The applicability of intentional categories to states of an organism cannot be grounded in the operant processes of discrimination alone."

The mode of expression that Lacey adopts here can possibly be clarified as follows. The behavior of the builder is predictable only insofar as we ascribe to her the desire to build a house and the belief that placing this brick will lead to building a wall; that building the wall will contribute to the fabrication of a room and so on. We need some mechanism for attributing these desires and beliefs: we do so partly on the basis of an idea of rational behavior in the circumstances and partly by inference from the builder's behavior pattern, including her verbal behavior. This displays an initial analysis based on the contextual stance (the operant behavior she displays is likely to result in this consequence which will increase the probability of her doing such and such next...), which is overlain by an intentional heuristic based on optimality, the assumption of desires and beliefs appropriate to the situation, and the ruling out of consequences that are improbable or nonmaximizing, in other words, are impossible ends to attach to her behavior. We can immediately rule out the possibility that she is building a staircase to heaven, therefore, or a marble palace, or a headquarters building for the Society for the Protection of Small Disingenuous Wooden Italians with Extensible Noses. But can teleological behaviorism? It may be significant that the predictive capacity of this approach is greatest in the context of the narrowly defined and measurable utility functions of everyday economic life rather than in broader circumstances.

Perhaps it is a little unfair to criticize the quest for final causes as explanations of behavior: it is the very complexity of the interpretive task that renders precision and warranted assertibility not simply arduous but impossible. It is the apparent unwillingness of the system's exponents to acknowledge this that is the cause for concern. Rachlin (1994, p. 32) observes that "If a behavioral analysis ultimately fails, the failure will be due to the complexity of the task. It will be like the failure to predict and control the weather precisely rather than any intrinsic inaccessibility or opacity of its subject." But it is not the complexity of the task that daunts it; it is the inability of any system on its own to reconstruct all of the relevant elements by which a behavioral interpretation must proceed. In the case of an ultimately intentional approach, the reconstruction of a learning history and the construal of the behavior setting is a vital prerequisite. In the case of an extensional approach such as Rachlin attempts, the bounds of "plausible" causation can be set only by a construal of the intentional meaning of the acts in question. In order to identify the consequences that are relevant to a specific behavior, it is necessary to specify the *context* of the act under interpretation. (One does not have to be a card-carrying contextualist to find the idea of the "act in context" a useful summary of the paradigm.) Radical behaviorism has no mechanism by which to identify the context of any relevant behavior that takes place beyond the closed setting of the laboratory. It has no concept of the open setting and how its influences on behavior can be expected to differ from those obtaining in closed settings. If behavior analysis and the extensional science of behavior which is its basis cannot supply some means of delineating the contextual boundaries of the behavior it seeks to explain, where is such demarcation to come from? At least an approximation to it can be obtained by considering the intensional meaning of the behavior.

The objection is not to the pursuit of final causes as an end in itself—especially one that promises much insofar as it proposes to reduce causality to the economist's device of the individual's utility function—but that it leaves out a level of analysis that is essential to a complete interpretation of human experience. Rachlin (2000, p. 19) is clear on this point: "If other people with all their senses functioning were present, if the lights were on, and if they still could not see or hear you do something, then (according to teleological behaviorism) you have not done it." This is allowing what we claim to be able to see or hear to be determined by a priori assumption and argument rather than by the empirical means available to us. It is reminiscent of scholastic philosophy rather than modern science. Yet what Rachlin is arguing is that our experience is limited by a certain view of what constitutes scientific observation.

7.7 Endnote

Scientific explanation is verbal activity and the boundaries of a particular school of thought are set by the locutions of its practitioners (Skinner, 1945, 1956, 1957). When rival scientific communities lay claim to a common subject matter, as is the case for psychology, delineating any one approach begs consideration of the verbal behaviors of its competitors. Specifically, therefore, this essay compares the linguistic bounds set, respectively, by Dennett (e.g., 1983) and Skinner (e.g., 1945) for the *intentional stance* that claims that mentalistic sentences are distinguished by the referential opacity of their terms, and the *contextual stance* that claims to underpin an extensional science of behavior by virtue of the referential transparency of its statements (Foxall, 1999). Skinner's radical behaviorism uniquely represents the nonintentional approach to psychology and provides the foundation for such a science. Indeed, I have argued that the defining characteristic of radical behaviorism is the avoidance of propositional attitudes—ascribed intrapersonal events and states that are regarded as causes or predictors of behavior by virtue of their intentionality, their being intrinsically *about* other entities. As a consequence, radical behaviorism avoids a distinction between the mental and the physical that is usually traced to Brentano (1874/1995). That approach reaches an apogee in Chisholm's (1957, 1960) sophisticated treatment that distinguishes not mental from physical substances but mentalistic from physicalistic sentences. The distinction between verbal expressions that are referentially opaque and those that are referentially transparent is a distinction between two apparently incommensurable philosophical approaches to behavioral science (Dennett, 1969).

For those who are principally interested in the experimental analysis of behavior, this may have limited relevance. Private events are not amenable to experimental analysis, nor are they essential to a scientific system that is confined to the animal laboratory; they may enter into the interpretation of results obtained in the human operant laboratory, but their role can be only peripheral. Even the phenomena of rule-governance are usually fairly simply dealt with in these circumstances. Those whose principal interest in behavior analysis is the interpretation of complex human behavior, defined as that which is not amenable to a direct experimental analysis, are heavily dependent on private events and on the attribution of rules if they wish to keep their interpretations within the bounds of an extensional behavioral science. The difficulty of the interpretive task is made clearer by considering not only that complex behavior is not subject to a direct experimental analysis, but also that the contingencies of reinforcement that are assumed to operate on the behavior are not specifiable in advance of observation, nor can they be manipulated to isolate their influence. Even the behavior itself may be determined only after observation. Moreover, a comprehensive learning history is not available for the target individual and her target behavior (Lee, 1988).

There is within behavior analysis a natural understanding that knowledge must at some time be derived from or tested by experiment. Even though agreeing with the idea that complex behavior such as verbal behavior cannot itself be subjected to an experimental analysis, Burgos and Donahoe (2000) argue that scientific interpretation can take place only on the basis of principles gained from experimentation. Their citing verbal behavior is interesting because even the theoretical analysis of rule-governance that Skinner (1969a, 1969b) offered was as we have seen the result of a conceptual advance that went beyond the mere extrapolation of learning principles derived from the experimental study of animal behavior. More recent empirical work on verbal behavior (e.g., Hayes, 1989) has also required an a priori conceptual development of the verbal behavior of the listener for instance that is not the result of experimentation but of preexperimental observation and analysis. Undoubtedly, as they point out that experimental analysis has the great advantage of revealing how few variables of the many that might influence a response are actually implicated in its performance: I should be the last to argue against the method per se. But there are no grounds for going as far as claiming that our interpretations of complex phenomena can be considered scientific only if they are directly based on principles derived from an experimental analysis of simpler phenomena. While such principles are a *sine qua non* of the interpretation of complexity, no theoretical enterprise can be confined to terms derived in this way. Moreover, much of the behavior that requires an interpretive analysis leads to explanations that cannot be subjected ex post to an experimental analysis, but which require alternative means of substantiation (Foxall, 1998). Even when this has been done, there will be theoretical terms that simply cannot be so subjected to empirical verification, but which are essential nonetheless in order to fill the conceptual gaps that will be inescapably left by any body of empirical data.

Recognition that such interpretation is an essential component of behavior analysis has not led to the formulation of any systematic approach to understanding complex behavior in operant terms. Whatever the status of our observations of behavior under experimental analysis, as soon as we leave the laboratory to observe and interpret the behavior of our fellow humans engaged in the everyday business of life, we are plunged into the epistemological problems of establishing the validity and reliability of our interpretations (subsumed by Skinner under the label of "plausibility"). The establishment of the grounds of genuine plausibility depends on our knowing what radical behaviorist explanation is and how it is delineated from alternative approaches. That is, it entails an exploration of the bounds of behaviorism. And the irony of that is that it requires first an appreciation of the nature and implications of intentionalist psychology, the very underpinning of cognitive psychology.

# Part IV

Intentional Behaviorism

Chapter 8

The intentional behaviorist research strategy

Chapter Outline

8.1 Intentional Behaviorism 152
8.2 From theoretical minimalism to psychological explanation 152
   8.2.1 Theoretical minimalism 153
   8.2.2 Psychological explanation 158
8.3 Intentionality, extensionality, intensionality 163
   8.3.1 Intentionality 163
   8.3.2 Intensionality and extensionality 165
   8.3.3 Criteria of extensionality 165
   8.3.4 The nature of intentional objects 166
   8.3.5 Truth value of intentional states and intensional statements 167
   8.3.6 Derived intentionality 167
   8.3.7 Some objections 169
8.4 Being human 170
   8.4.1 The intensional criterion 170
   8.4.2 Cognitive uniqueness 174
8.5 Endnotes 176
   8.5.1 Psychological agency 176
   8.5.2 Economic agency 177

The three-part intentional behaviorist research strategy rests on a progression from theoretical minimalism, based on radical behaviorism, to psychological explanation, which entails the construction of an intentional interpretation and its evaluation by virtue of its compatibility with cognitive interpretations (Section 8.1). Section 8.2 traces this progression in terms of the indispensability of an extensional portrayal of economic behavior to the development of an intentional interpretation thereof. In Section 8.3 the concepts of intentionality, extensionality, and intensionality, which were briefly described in Chapter 2, *A kind of consilience*, are elaborated in preparation for the discussions of intentional explanation and cognitive interpretation which are the subjects of Chapters 9–11. The ontological and epistemological bases of Intentional Behaviorism are discussed in Section 8.4 that introduces the intensional criterion as a reaction to Dennett's intentional stance, which is of general application to animate and nonanimate entities. The intensional criterion carries the implication that intentional explanation is appropriate only for verbal humans. This proposition is supported through consideration of the nature of human linguistic capabilities and human agency.

8.1 Intentional Behaviorism

Chapter 1, *Orientation*, pointed out that Intentional Behaviorism proposes a three-stage research strategy in which the necessity of an intentional explanation of economic behavior emerges from the exhaustion of a purely extensional account thereof. The resulting intentional interpretation is suggested by the theoretically minimalist extensional model of economic behavior, but justification is sought for it in the psychologies that indicate the feasibility of a consonant pattern of cognitive structure and functioning. The three stages are, therefore, theoretical minimalism, intentional interpretation, and cognitive interpretation. The research program has been described in detail elsewhere (see Foxall, 2016a, 2016b, 2017a, 2017b, 2017c). Moreover, the use of intentional interpretation within the framework of the model of consumer choice on which these investigations rest has recently begun to receive empirical research attention (e.g., Anninou & Foxall, 2019; Anninou, Foxall, & Pallister, 2016; Laparojkit & Foxall, 2016). This book both critiques and builds upon this foundational work, which is inescapably multidisciplinary. The present treatment is predominantly philosophical, however, critically examining the conceptual basis of Intentional Behaviorism, while seeking to extend and clarify, as necessary, its nature and scope. This chapter draws on the bases of the intentional and contextual stances discussed in earlier chapters to establish the theoretical basis of Intentional Behaviorism. It sets forth the philosophical position occupied by Intentional Behaviorism in light of the critique of the Dennettian conception of intentionality made both in this volume and Foxall (2016a, 2016b), as well as briefly distinguishing it from the positions taken by Searle and Quine.

8.2 From theoretical minimalism to psychological explanation

The intentional behaviorist research strategy embraces both extensional and intentional approaches to the explanation of the human economic activity, paradigms that are usually viewed as antithetical. The extensional theory adopted in Intentional Behaviorism is radical behaviorism that attributes behavior to the environmental stimuli[1] that are associated with its rate of performance. The intentional perspective, cognitive psychology, attributes action to the intrapersonal desires and beliefs that are assumed to be its causes or at least to explain it. Many psychologists and philosophers speak of their recent histories in terms of a paradigm shift in which cognitive science has superseded behaviorism. Behaviorism, at least radical behaviorism, which enjoyed an almost exclusive prominence in the early 20th century, is assumed to have passed away in the wake of the cognitive revolution of the

---

1. It also acknowledges physiological influences which, as we shall see, it then largely ignores.

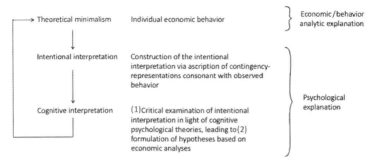

FIGURE 8.1 The intentional behaviorist research process. The psychological explanation aims to formulate an intentional understanding of behavior for which no stimulus field is apparent and to derive from these hypotheses that can be tested by the extensional sciences of neurophysiology and consumer behavior analysis. The first stage proposes an intentional interpretation of the behavior in question basing its suggestion of contingency-representations on the general findings of the examination of the behavior through the theoretically minimalist lens of an operant analysis of consumer behavior in general. The intentional interpretation is tested by reference to its capacity to predict and its consistency with cognitive psychology. The relevant economic analysis is then employed to derive testable hypotheses for empirical research.

1950s and 1960s. Its obituary is premature, however, and some of its most notable contributions such as the analysis of verbal behavior, particularly that of the listener (Hayes, 1989), and operant behavioral economics have become apparent since the mid-20th century (Foxall, 2016d). The use of behaviorism and cognitivism in a single research strategy remains nonetheless controversial and requires justification. That is why we are here.

Before it is possible to examine critically whether the incorporation of both paradigms into a single methodology of explanation is a true marriage, albeit a somewhat distant one, or a spurious attempt to avoid the rigors of philosophical analysis, it is necessary to summarize the intentional behaviorist research strategy that has been described at greater length elsewhere (Foxall, 2017a, in preparation). Subsequent chapters can then inquire of the nature of their relationship in the course of explaining economic behavior.

The intentional behaviorist research process comprises three stages (Fig. 8.1): theoretical minimalism, intentional interpretation, and cognitive interpretation leading to economic analysis based on which hypotheses are generated and tested. This returns us to the first stage that is extensional in nature involving variables that are amenable to empirical testing in experimental and correlational research; the ensuing stages are intentional in nature involving constructs that are not directly amenable to empirical implementation (i.e., they involve entities that are not empirically available).

8.2.1 Theoretical minimalism

The point of the first stage is to employ a theoretically minimal model of economic behavior and to test it empirically to destruction, that is, to the point where it can no longer account for observed behavior. This procedure (1) establishes the extent of extensional explanation (given the current state of our theories, methodologies, and research tools), revealing what we can know of economic behavior in this way, and (2) indicates the need for an intentional explanation and the form it should take.[2] The chosen vehicle for

---

2. Rosenberg (2016, p. 31ff) argues that most social scientists who take an empiricist approach believe that naturalism and interpretivism can be reconciled: they adopt the methodology of the natural sciences and yet strive to accommodate the meaningfulness and significance of human action. Others, however, who espouse antinaturalism or interpretive social science, argue that only interpretivism can achieve the latter. Interpretivism accounts for human action in terms of desires and beliefs: hence (Rosenberg, 2016, p. 39),

[L] *If a person,* x, *wants outcome,* d, *and believes that a particular action,* a, *will lead to* d*'s attainment, then* x *will do* a.

Desires and beliefs are reasons for action, means of rendering it intelligible, reasonable. However, before using [L] to account for action we must face the fact that desire, beliefs, and action rely on one another for their several definitions. Rosenberg (2016, Chapter 3) argues, therefore, that we need an independently specified statement of desires and beliefs before we can use [L] to predict and explain an individual's actions. Theoretical minimalism, especially by its capacity to establish what it is that consumers purchase (namely, bundles of utilitarian and informational reinforcement) seems able to supply the answer. The extensional model identifies the consumer's revealed preferences and from these, we can independently deduce her intentionality.

Rosenberg's argument is one that he has also pursued specifically in the context of economic methodology. Rosenberg (1992) argues that rational choice theory (RCT) in economics depends on the intentional specification of the starting point of predictive analysis and that it is impossible to improve on this beyond the folk psychology that humans have used for millennia. Specifically, Rosenberg claims that the desires (preferences) and beliefs (expectations) that are derived from the observation of revealed preference need to be ascertained independently of this methodology. Although he is right to argue that this cannot be done simply by asking people what they desire and believe (except where there is the closest correspondence between the behavior settings in which opinions are sampled and that in which behavior is ascertained; see Foxall, 2005, and Chapter 9: *Ascribing intentionality*), nor through neurophysiology, which is too coarse-grained for the kinds of decision involved, he does not consider using the agent's history of reinforcement and punishment for this purpose. After all, we cannot sample desires and beliefs, which are theoretical constructs that are unobservable by direct means: we can only sample verbal behavior which we believe to capture them. We ought to consider this. In principle, a history of reinforcement would provide a basis from which to infer preexisting desires and beliefs, viewed as the revealed preferences evinced in behavior. I do not underestimate the difficulty of ascertaining such a history in the case of human consumers. Nevertheless, there is logically a means of overcoming the problem Rosenberg raises by including both extensional and intentional methodologies in a single quest. Furthermore, Rosenberg's question highlights another problem with intentional analysis that only a preceding behavioral analysis can overcome.

For the problem that Rosenberg identifies for RCT is also apparent in Intentional Behaviorism: namely, how is the intentionality on which the intentional interpretation is based to be ascertained other than via inference from observed behavior? The answer has two components. First, the intentional interpretation applies to an idealized system whose behavior in general is apparent from consumer behavior analysis; second, it is based on the intentionality the system ought to have given its circumstances and history. The problem this raises is how to

theoretical minimalism is radical behaviorism, since its instrumental orientation, its fundamental demonstration that behavior is a function of its consequences fits it well for the analysis of economic behavior, and it thus provides the micro-foundation of the psychological explanation that follows. An initial central concern of the present work is to establish whether radical behaviorism in fact provides an adequate model for theoretical minimalism and, if so, how. This requires a thorough investigation of the nature of radical behaviorism, its characteristic mode of explanation and its limitations. Although we are concerned very largely with intentional explanation here, the capacity of radical behaviorism to serve as a foundation for the construction of the intentional interpretation accords it a

ascertain the content of this intentional account. Like the rational choice theorist, the practitioner of Intentional Behaviorism cannot directly sample intentions. The two systems have different ways of approaching the need for incorporating intentionality. Whereas, in RCT, it is the need to obtain a starting-point idea of intentionality, in Intentional Behaviorism, it is the inability to ground an extensional account in the necessary stimulus field for a wholly extensional analysis. Intentional Behaviorism raises an additional question, therefore: given that the stimulus field to establish the prior behavior as operant is not empirically available, how can it be used to provide an account of activity that can be interpreted intentionally? Whilst the interpretive approach is often seen as distinct from and possibly superseding the extensional (Rosenberg, 2016), Intentional Behaviorism demonstrates a means of making definite use of the extensional stage of theoretical minimalism in order to ground an intentional perspective. The solution relies on our perceiving extensional and intentional accounts as complementary, rather than seeing their incompatibility as precluding their joint contribution to the explanation of economic activity.

Intentional interpretation rests on the findings of extensional behavioral science which provide a *generic* account of the factors that shape and maintain consumer choice and which above all render it predictable. We can establish from it that consumers seek to maximize a combination of utilitarian and informational reinforcement, that both of these enter into their preference functions, that their expectations (beliefs about probabilities of outcomes) will be consistent therewith. That is, they will *desire* that combination of products and services that optimizes the bundle of utilitarian and informational reinforcement that is their ultimate aim. They will *believe* that the way of achieving this in the current set of circumstances (contingencies of reinforcement and punishment) in which they are able to purchase and consume is to perform a specific set of actions and to avoid others. And so on. Their desires and beliefs will be a function of their past behaviors (learning history) and the offerings enabled by the consumer behavior setting in which they are operating, namely motivating operations and discriminative stimuli that *promise* a set of outcomes that they judge to be consistent with utilitarian and informational reinforcement maximization. Their actions are not slavishly determined by their learning histories and the setting scope with which they have been presented in the past and which they now similarly encounter—as a radical behaviorist approach must assume to be the case in order to predict and control their current and immediate future behaviors. They can interpret for themselves how the purchase and consumption of a *bundle* of products and services will eventuate in utilitarian outcomes and, more subtly, what social consequences will ensue from these actions. If we combine this generic knowledge with whatever extensional knowledge we have of the prior behavior of the particular system we wish to interpret, we can work out how an interpretational account of this behavior would proceed. We can include samplings of verbal behavior with respect to desires and beliefs in order to supplement this. We can then use this intentionality to predict the behavior/action of the system. Neuroeconomics and extensional behavioral science may enable us to embellish and progress the interpretation further.

continuing role in the shaping and appraisal of both the intentional and cognitive interpretations.

The first concern of Intentional Behaviorism is, therefore, foundational, taking the form of an investigation into whether radical behaviorism (as we have considered it, warts and all) acts convincingly as the basis of a behavioral—scientific methodology by which a fully extensional model of economic behavior can be established, and second, whether the breakdown of this extensional behavioral science, should it occur, can suggest not only the points at which a psychological explanation is required but also the questions it must answer and the form it should take. Enough has been said about the nature and explanatory significance of radical behaviorism to conclude that while it may provide an extensional account of some behavior especially in relatively closed settings such as those represented by the operant chamber, it proves on occasion to be incapable of explaining more complex behaviors. What distinguishes these situations is the presence or absence of a stimulus field that provides the explanatory syntax on which radical behaviorism relies. A theoretically minimal basis for the strategy of identifying the place and nature of intentional explanation by exhausting the explanatory power of a purely extensional approach must predict aspects of economic behavior, allowing the identification of, for instance, what consumers maximize and the environmental stimuli that enable them to do this and/or render their behavior more predictable. The extensional concepts it employs must, moreover, be operationally specifiable, independently of one another. There is abundant empirical evidence on consumer matching, demand analysis, and utility functions that indicate the capacity of radical behaviorism to provide satisfy these criteria (Foxall, 2017a).

In order that it qualifies as an account that is testable via scientific canons of judgment, the truth value of an extensional account based on radical behaviorism must rest on intersubjective agreement, and its empirical contributions to knowledge must rest on truth by correspondence. Chapter 4, *The basis of the contextual stance*, argued that these criteria are also met. In addition, while it makes a contribution to the understanding of behavior in its own right, such an account must not be so vague and general as to appear to explain all behavior. This means that we reserve the right to question its scientific credentials if we are unable to identify its boundaries. Making clear the bounds of behaviorism so that imperatives of intentionality which follow can themselves be adumbrated is a goal in itself. It must then make possible the derivation of an alternative, intentional interpretation to give rise to an intentional account of the behavior. Sufficient has been said also to establish that radical behaviorism, while it is useful insofar as it makes a contribution to understanding economic behavior that is not available elsewhere, is not comprehensive: the bounds of behaviorism lay down limits to its range of applicability.

Previous chapters, and earlier works, have critically examined a central component of the intentional behaviorist methodology, radical behaviorism, drawing attention to its contribution to the advancement of knowledge, which makes it an essential component, and justifying why it is necessary to move beyond it in order to provide a comprehensive explanation. The role of radical behaviorism in the explanation of economic behavior is both subtle and inescapable: subtle because radical behaviorism is generally considered a psychological paradigm that has been eclipsed, even eliminated, by the cognitive revolution; but inescapable because the reality is that the affinity between operant behavior and economic choice has woven these apparently diverse disciplines into a methodology that uniquely makes sense of human economic and social action. Intentional Behaviorism employs this psychological paradigm in two ways: first, to identify the aspects of economic behavior that are amenable only to the investigative strengths of operant behavioral economics and, second, to discover the places at which a cognitive explanation becomes necessary and the form it should take.

The analysis of operant behavior provides a gold standard for determining the relationship between activity and its environmental context, one that is available for rigorous-scientific scrutiny through application of the experimental method. The variables of which behavior is held in this paradigm to be a function, namely, prebehavioral and consequential stimuli, can be isolated and their influence on the shaping and maintenance of behavior demonstrated. The variables posited by cognitivism are by contrast available for scrutiny only after they have been translated into publicly available entities such as behavior and neurophysiological activity. Operant psychology provides a reliable means of understanding environment−behavior linkages because of the direct accessibility it provides to the elements of the three-term contingency that forms on the basis of its explanatory claims.[3]

Radical behaviorism and operant psychology are not of course the final resting place of a science of human action, but they provide a necessary starting point. They can accomplish this, however, only if they are shown to be based on the correspondence theory of truth and intersubjective agreement, neither of which is uncontroversial, even among radical behaviorists. In short, the argument is as follows. The view that radical behaviorism has been methodologically superseded by cognitivism ignores the contribution to science that this approach presents. Operant behavioral economics, for example, attests to the unique insights made available by this paradigm, which consists in employing a syntax of extensional explanation that identifies and relates stimuli and responses. However, radical behaviorism's capacity to explain human behavior is limited by the inability of researchers to identify

---

3. I use the expression three-term contingency to capture operant learning; it is understood that motivating operations may also be at work but in order to the avoid the inelegance of constantly speaking of "three- or four-term contingencies," I opt for the former.

the stimuli and/or responses that comprise its explanatory syntax (Fodor & Piattelli-Palmarini, 2011). These limitations arise in its account of the continuity/discontinuity of behavior and the personal level of exposition that inclusion of private events invites; without recourse to intentional idioms, radical behaviorism is, moreover, unable to delimit its interpretations of complex behavior (i.e., behavior that is not amenable to an experimental analysis). These requirements make intentional interpretation imperative. The use of intentional language (and therefore intentional explanation) is preferable to speculation about the nature of private events that introduces explanatory fictions into radical behaviorism. I argue that in practice, radical behaviorism involves an approach to scientific practice that is based upon the principles of truth by correspondence and truth by agreement. In these respects, it provides an even better basis for Intentional Behaviorism than either its originators or apologists can have imagined.

8.2.2 Psychological explanation

The bounds of behaviorism, as we have seen, are apparent when it becomes necessary to account for the continuity or discontinuity of behavior, to take the personal level into consideration, and to curtail behavioral interpretations that have overstretched the demands of scientific explanation. The bounds of behaviorism that these factors indicate are also the imperatives of intentionality in that they indicate when an intentional interpretation is required and the form it should take. The intentional interpretation treats the individual whose behavior is to be interpreted as an idealized intentional system, one that maximizes the returns to its behavior. It employs what has been learned of this system in the course of applying an extensional framework of conceptualization and analysis during the theoretical minimalism stage of investigation. The intentional interpretation is framed in terms of the desires, beliefs, emotions, and perceptions the system can be reasonably adjudged to act in accordance with given its learning history and current behavior setting.

Hence, the second central concern of Intentional Behaviorism is to examine how the extensional and intentional levels of exposition, on which Intentional Behaviorism draws, and which it strives to keep separate, are related to one another. Why is this of concern? The key enigma that motivates the philosophy of mind is that of accounting for the subjective feel of the world that we appear to have as an inner experience in scientific terms that reflect the assumption of materialism, that we inhabit a physical universe that admits of no substance other than matter. This is sometimes referred to as the mind—body problem. The difficulty that arises in the form of the so-called mind—body problem is that although we often make recourse to concepts that properly belong at the intentional level of exposition that involves personal constructs that refer to action and mental activity, our ontology is confined to the material realm, to the physical. How do we account for the apparent mental sphere in which we perceive, desire, believe, and act when all we have to deal with according to the natural sciences is physicality? What of situations in which we cannot identify the physical causes of behavior and have no resort other than to mental or intentional phenomena? Crossing over from one level of exposition to another seems the only way to accomplish a comprehensive understanding of human behavior; yet this move seems to confound what we know of these levels and the kinds of explanations they can offer.

The attempt at an answer refers to three philosophies of mind that are not usually linked. First is McGinn's exposition of the fundamental conceptual impasse with which we are concerned. McGinn (2004) draws on Russell's (1912) distinction between knowledge by acquaintance and knowledge by description to ground this dilemma, although we can as individuals have direct perceptual experience of the world that can be communicated to others (or to ourselves for that matter) only via the medium of description.[4] While knowledge by acquaintance inheres in direct first personal contact with stimuli, knowledge by description consists in the third personal portrayal of a constructed account. The solution of the mind—body problem would require the devising of concepts capable of bridging both spheres, but according to the new mysterianism adopted by McGinn, such conceptions lie beyond the cognitive wit of humankind. While we may wish to be skeptical of this final conclusion of McGinn—it is surely always too early to rule out future intellectual breakthroughs—it remains evident that we have not to date overcome the conceptual impasse to which he draws our attention.

However, the existence of these two kinds of knowledge is sufficient to show that a mind—body problem is a reality since it entails that there is a personal level of experience that is not directly available to others, for third personal scientific scrutiny, for example. Actually, the problem goes deeper than this because even when we describe to ourselves what we have seen or heard we are using knowledge-by-description rather than the firsthand knowledge-by-acquaintance we received as a result of the seeing and hearing. Qualia present a wholly distinct means of knowing from that available through narrative. If we wish to resolve this problem, we must find concepts that belong to both categories, which capture both the essence of experience that comes through acquaintance and the capacity to represent to others that inheres in description.

Second, Searle (2000) understands that consciousness (knowledge-by-acquaintance) is mental, but it is a particular kind of biological state. Conscious states (1) *have a first personal ontology and are real*. They do not reduce to neurobiology which, by virtue of its being a third personal account,

---

4. Russell (1912) drew a distinction between knowledge we can have by direct acquaintance with the world—perceiving a sunset, for instance—and knowledge we gain through another person's description of the world—telling us about the sunset they witnessed. Knowledge-by-acquaintance is personal, subjective, and above all private, while knowledge-by-description is shared information that is publicly available.

would leave out the first personal nature of consciousness. These (2) *are caused wholly by lower level neuronal processes*. They do not separate entities; nor do they comprise something over and above the neuronal processes. These (3) *are realized in the brain* as features of it at a higher level than synapses and neurons. These (4) *have a causal influence* in the world by virtue of their being real. In a nutshell, "Consciousness is a system-level biological feature in much the same way that digestion, or growth, or the secretion of bile are system-level biological features" (Searle, 2004, p. 80). Desires and beliefs are not only real but causative.

Third is Dennett's (1981) distinction, noted earlier, among "three kinds of intentional psychology."[5] He proposes that after *folk psychology* (that refers to our everyday prediction of and response to our own and others' behavior by positing that it is the result of desires and beliefs), it is necessary to distinguish *intentional systems theory* (IST) and *subpersonal cognitive psychology* (SPCP). IST is an idealized account of behavior in terms of the intentionality an individual "ought" to have given her history and current circumstances. The concepts in terms of which this is achieved are *abstracta* such as desires and beliefs that provide means by which behavior can be predicted and to some degree explained. *Abstracta* are real in the sense in which other theoretical entities that aid prediction and explanation are real, even though we cannot point to them in three-dimensional space: centers of gravity and parallelograms of forces, for instance. The idealized picture so gained is cashed out in SPCP by the positing of another kind of concept, *illata*, which are physical entities that are intentionally characterizable. Neurons, for instance, can be treated in biophysics as material items but can also be accorded desires and beliefs if this renders them more predictable. *Illata* are thus amenable to description by two of three stances that Dennett posits: the physical stance that portrays items in material terms, precisely as does physics, and the intentional stance that proposes that such prediction is facilitated by the ascription to an entity of the desires and beliefs it ought to have as an intentional system. Indeed, all there is to being such as system, to having a mind, is for Dennett to be so predictable.[6]

---

5. I interpret Dennett's distinction between *abstracta* and *illata* and the use he makes of them as a bold attempt to overcome the problem of lack of biconditional concepts. (Dennett's approach predates McGinn's, and does not of course constitute a conscious response thereto.) *Illata*, as physical entities that are intentionally characterizable, are clearly an attempt to provide such concepts. Not literally, of course, since Dennett wrote several decades before McGinn and does not refer to biconditionals per se. However, Dennett's work can be seen as an attempt to overcome the mind–body problem.

6. An interesting corollary is Dennett's insistence that intentional terms are "nonreferring" (see Dennett, 1969, pp. 13–14). As Gunderson summarizes, "... [T]he terms in our mentalistic vocabulary are nonreferring. Rather like 'sakes' or 'miles', [or centers of gravity] mentalistic terms in appropriate contexts tell us something, but succeed in doing so without thereby referring to any entities any more than the words 'sakes' or 'miles' refer to sakes or miles" (Gunderson, 1972, p. 593).

The term *illata* refers to physical entities (such as neurons) but allows them to be additionally characterized by intentionality; this is an ingenious proposal. It rests on Dennett's view that we can apply the intentional stance to these elements of the physical world so long as it increases their predictability. By flipping between the physical stance that treats such elements in the extensional language of the physical sciences and the intentional language that makes them more readily amenable to prediction, Dennett's suggestion comes as close as we currently can to bridging the extensional−intentional chasm. There is nevertheless an important objection to it. The flipping that is central to this methodology maybe just too slippery, especially if one takes seriously the distinction between intentional language's exclusive applicability at the personal level of exposition which precludes its use at the subpersonal level of brains and neurons. Nevertheless, we have here a clue to the only way in which we can explore the personal level of subjective experience while retaining the materialist perspective of science. The ingenuity of the concept of *illata* is that these variables constitute a means of overcoming the mind−body problem by existing at two levels, one extensional and the other intentional. The intentional stance can be applied at either the personal level of intentional phenomena or the subpersonal level of neurons, brains, and electrons. While they are not biconditionals, therefore, they suggest one way of fulfilling the need for such constructs.

For all its merits, Dennett's philosophical basis for psychology is not a perfect model for Intentional Behaviorism. First, Dennett's scheme, based on "three kinds of intentional psychology," has no place for a formal extensional model as a prelude to IST. In Intentional Behaviorism, this is provided by the theoretical minimalism of the extensional model of consumer choice that provides an empirical understanding of the environmental factors of which economic behavior is a function and thereby indicates when an intentional interpretation becomes necessary and what it has to explain. Second, Dennett's proposal commits the mereological fallacy in the third stage of his research strategy (SPCP) in which *illata* clearly belong to the physical stance yet are given an intentional characterization (Bennett & Hacker, 2003; see also Bennett, 2007; Bennett & Hacker, 2007). The mereological fallacy is the application to the parts of a system of attributes that properly belong only to the system as a whole.[7] Desires and beliefs are constructs that belong to properly only at the personal level of exposition, which is the level of intensional explanation, and their ascription to other levels is improper. The means overcoming this problem is to consider the sphere of applicability of intentional explanation and to confine the applicability of intentional reasoning accordingly. This invokes the criterion of intensionality.

---

7. I have dealt with the mereological fallacy in this connection at length in *Perspectives on Consumer choice: From Behavior to Action, From Action to Agency* (Foxall, 2016b).

Intentional Behaviorism avoids this by rigorously maintaining the separation of levels of exposition. Third, Dennett suggests rather vaguely that *illata* will form the variables of actual psychological theories and lead to empirical work. I want to emphasize that the extensional sciences of neuroscience and behaviorology (especially as they eventuate in neuroeconomics and operant behavioral economics) are the vehicles for empirical research and to show how this is possible. However, Dennett is correct in suggesting that there has to be an empirical outcome of the intended research strategy.

The third central concern of Intentional Behaviorism is, therefore, to characterize more precisely the way in which the intentional interpretation can be appraised through the generation of testable hypotheses. The validity of the intentional interpretation is presently sought in its consistency with the theories and findings of cognitive psychologies that relate the structure and functioning of the mind and brain to revealed behaviors. The cognitive psychologies in question refer to the relationships between (1) neurophysiology and action, notably the influence of an impulsive system based in the limbic and paralimbic areas which is responsible for immediate reactions to environmental opportunities and threats and an executive system based in prefrontal cortex which is responsible for action that takes longer term consequences into consideration (this I have called "micro-cognitive psychology"); (2) the operant consequences of behavior in terms of the influence of the contingencies of reinforcement and punishment on the rate at which behavior is performed (macro-cognitive psychology); and (3) the interactions of intrapersonal short- and long-range interests as they strategically seek to dominate overt behavior (meso-cognitive psychology).

The rationale of the intentional interpretation is found, to a limited extent, in its capacity to predict behavior in ways not immediately apparent from the model of economic behavior established within the purview of theoretical minimalism. But it is, at present, generally justified in terms of its ability to be accommodated within psychological accounts of the structure and functioning of cognitive systems. The three cognitive psychologies that are relevant to this task have been identified and described in detail.[8] Micro-cognitive psychology, typified by the neurobehavioral decision systems theory of Bickel (Bickel, Jarmolowicz, Mueller, & Gatchalian, 2011), the tricomponential theory of Stanovich (2011), and dual process theories of mind (Evans, 2010) trace conflictual behavior and specifically the rate at which individuals discount the future to the interactions of an impulsive system, based largely in the limbic and paralimbic systems, of response to environmental stimuli and an executive system based on prefrontal cortex. Macro-cognitive psychology, which relies on theories of collective intentionality

---

8. A comprehensive account is available in *Perspectives on Consumer choice: From Behavior to Action, From Action to Agency* (Foxall, 2016b). See also "Metacognitive control of categorial neuro-behavioral decision systems" (Foxall, 2016d).

that trace the establishment by humans of the social contingencies of reinforcement and punishment that will govern their behavior and the system of societal rules and enforcement processes that will enforce them, is closely related to the establishment of norms of informational reinforcement and their effect on economic behavior (see Foxall, 2016b; Searle, 1995, 2010; Tomasello, 2014). Both of these psychologies give rise to extensional modes of evaluation; the third, however, meso-cognitive psychology, is intentional in character. This is typified by the picoeconomic theory of Ainslie (1992, 2001) that portrays the complexities of impulsive−executive interactions in terms of the strategic conflict between intrapersonal short- and long-range interests. Each of these cognitive psychologies has a theoretical and empirical life of its own and therefore a body of work that seeks to substantiate and amend it.[9] We can be confident in linking our intentional interpretations with these psychological explanations, therefore, given that they are not speculative but rely on rigorous-scientific canons of judgment. However, the relationship between the cognitive psychologies and the explanation of action requires a firmer basis that gives rise to hypotheses that are directly derived and empirically testable. Chapter 10, *Grounding intentionality*, proposes that the necessary links are to be found in economic analyses derived from the micro- and macro-cognitive psychologies (neuroeconomics and operant behavioral economics, respectively) and a basis for intrapersonal interpretation in the case of meso-cognitive psychology.

Before embarking on these deeper concerns, however, it is necessary to provide a firmer conceptual basis for our understanding of intentionality, extensionality, and intensionality, as well as a clearer view of the range of applicability of intentional−behavioral explanation. These are the remaining themes of this chapter.

8.3 Intentionality, extensionality, intensionality

8.3.1 Intentionality

Intentionality is often invoked in psychological discourse, ranging from the everyday folk psychology with which we seek to make sense of and predict our own and others' behavior to formal scientific psychology. Although it was briefly introduced earlier, it is necessary now to refine our understanding of intentionality and to distinguish it from extensionality and intensionality. Central as intentionality is to so much psychological explication; however, we are here primarily concerned with intentionality as it is philosophically understood, a sense that carries a special connotation. It refers not to behavior but to sentences or statements *about* behavior. Moreover, the distinction

---

9. Even though it is largely intentionally constituted, picoeconomics has inaugurated empirical experimental research (Hofmeyr, Ainslie, Charlton, & Ross, 2010).

between physical sentences and mental or intentional sentences has implications for strategies of scientific research and explanation. Some sentences refer simply to physical matters—for example, "That planet is Mars"—while others appear to refer to a mental reality—"John believes that the woman at the podium is the Queen of England." The two kinds of sentence have quite different properties.

Brentano (1874/1995) distinguished the intentional by pointing to the *inexistence* of the object to which mental states referred: the objects to which they refer may not exist, as in "I believe that the golden mountain is in Spain." The crux of Brentano's argument is that mental statements' uniquely exhibiting intentional inexistence points to the means of demarcating physical and mental phenomena. The problem of speaking of inexistent objects raises ontological difficulties, however. Later philosophers like Chisholm (1957) made the distinction on the basis not of objects but the linguistic difference between transparent and opaque statements. Chisholm's view was that in speaking of the physical, there is no need to use intentional language: we can say all we need to say about it without resorting to intentional language. But in order to speak of the mental/psychological (including thinking), we need to use intentional language (cf. Bechtel, 1988, p. 46; Chisholm, 1957, pp. 111–112). The advance here is that Chisholm does not speak of the ontological status of the objects of thoughts, etc. but makes the distinction entirely in terms of language. Like Dennett after him, he argues that the two kinds of sentence differ fundamentally: physical sentences are *referentially transparent* in the sense that, in the sentence we have already considered, a term equivalent to "Mars" can be substituted for it without altering the truth of the statement. We can as easily say "That planet is the fourth from the sun" as "The planet is Mars." "Mars" and "the fourth planet from the sun" are said to have the same *extension* since they name the same red planet, hence the substitutability of the terms. But, as we briefly noted earlier, so-called mental sentences are *referentially opaque* insofar as equivalent terms may not be substitutable. John may well believe that a particular woman is the Queen of England, for instance, but not that she is Elizabeth II: he may simply not know that Elizabeth II is the Queen of England. Hence, while we would be justified in saying, "John believes that that woman is the Queen of England," we could not assert that he knew that she was Elizabeth II. The linguistic approach to defining intentionality, such as Chisholm introduced, may throw up an anomaly of language rather than tell us anything about the nature of intentionality itself, as Searle (1981) points out. But the alternative may be to go back to Brentano's problematic position. Russell (1940) used the term "propositional attitudes" to refer to sentences such as *John wants to use his new washing machine this afternoon* in which the verb is followed by "that" and a proposition. Bechtel points out that an advantage of this approach is that it allows us two degrees of freedom in characterizing mental states, based first on the verb or attitude and second on the proposition. We can believe that John will get to use his washing machine this afternoon but desire that he does not. This suggests a course of action: doing something to prevent his use of the washing machine.

8.3.2 Intensionality and extensionality

To say that Intentional Behaviorism relies on two modes of explanation in order to make economic behavior intelligible is equivalent to saying that it depends on the distinction between the extensional and intensional ways of speaking. The intensional mode assumes the intentionality of the mental realm. These terms require explication before we can proceed. Intentionality is, as a first approximation, the referring capacity or "aboutness" of mental phenomena, experienced qualitatively and subjectively. As Searle (2004, p. 119) puts it, intentionality refers to "that capacity of the mind by which mental states refer to, or are about, or are of objects and states of affairs in the world other than themselves." Intentionality is, therefore, a capability *of the mind*. It does not distinguish the mental from the physical (Brentano, 1874/1995)[10] because some mental events (pain, depression, and anxiety) are not about anything (e.g., Crane, 1998, 2016). But it is nevertheless a *mental* (first personal, subjective, experiential) phenomenon and is not outside the mind (or, if mind is so understood, the brain). Searle (2004, p. 122) continues, "Intentionality-with-a-t is ... that property of the mind by which it is directed at or about or of objects and states of affairs in the world independent of itself." Intensionality is a property of the verbal expression of intentionality as sentences (propositional attitudes) that contain intentional idioms (attitudes), such as *desires* or *believes*, and propositions that refer to an intentional object. Searle (2004, p. 122) says, "Intensionality-with-an-s is opposed to *extensionality*. It is a property of certain sentences, statements, and other linguistic entities by which they fail to meet certain tests of extensionality."[11]

8.3.3 Criteria of extensionality

Searle delineates the meaning of extensionality by describing two criteria. The first we may call the *substitution criterion*. The truth value of a statement is unaffected by the substitution of one term for another providing the two terms refer to the same entity (or, as it is sometimes put, have the same extension). For example, in the sentence "That is the Morning Star," we can

---

10. For Brentano the mental consists in its being "metaphorically speaking, 'directed towards' something, which may or may not exist or may or not be the case" (Hacker, 2013, pp. 60–61).
11. In heterophenomenological terms, we can say that intentionality refers to the subjectively experienced state of desiring or believing while intensionality refers to the third personal verbal expression thereof.

substitute "Evening Star" for "Morning Star" because both these terms refer to the same heavenly body (actually, the planet Venus, which is the extension of all three names for it). Hence, the substitution does not alter the truth value of the statement. "The Morning Star" is said to be extensional with respect to substitution. The sentence exhibits *extensionality*. But, given the sentence, "Janis believes that that is the Morning Star," we cannot say without further information "Janis believes that that is the Evening Star" and maintain the truth value of the sentence because Janis may not know that these two terms corefer (or, as it sometimes stated, are codesignatives). This sentence, which includes a verb relating to a mental state, is said to be *intensional* with respect to "The Morning Star" and fails the test of substitutability (Searle, 2004, p. 123).

Second is the criterion of *existential inference*. The objects referred to in an extensional sentence must exist in the external world for the truth of the sentence to be ascertained. When we say "Janis is meeting her mother at Christmas," the inference is that there exists a person, Janis's mother, whom she will meet toward the end of December. Such a sentence is extensional because its extension, Janis's mother, presents the opportunity to ascertain its truth value: its conditions of satisfaction can be met by determining whether there is an entity existing in the world that is Janis's mother. However, a sentence such as "Janis believes she is meeting Santa Claus at Christmas" does not entail the inference that there must be a person, Santa Claus, who will appear in Janis's life during the holiday season. Janis can believe this whether or not it is the case. Moreover, the conditions of satisfaction of this kind of sentence are not a matter of who or what exists in the real world: they are simply a matter of whether Janis believes something. This sentence fails the test of existential inference and is said to be intensional.

8.3.4 The nature of intentional objects

There is considerable debate about the nature of intentional objects—cf., for instance, Searle (1983) and Crane (2001)—but I would like to propose what seems a straightforward use of the terms *extensional object* and *intentional object*, which I believe is consistent with the understanding of extensionality and intentionality developed here. An extensional object is an existing element of the objective world such as the planet Venus. In linguistic terms, this planet, Venus, is the extension of the term "Venus." It is also the extension of the terms "The Morning Star" or "Phosphorous" or "the Evening Star" or "Hesperus." In sentences such as "Jacob believes that that is the Morning Star," however, "The Morning Star" is an intension (or specific meaning), an element in a sentence embodying a propositional attitude. I propose to refer to this element as an *intentional object*. An intentional object is, therefore, the content of an attitude such as *believes* or *desires* or *loves*. Its existence is within that propositional attitude; hence, it may not have an extension at all. I can believe that Santa Claus is on his way without there being any such being. Dennett (1969, p. 21) notes that, with respect to the term *intentional inexistence*, "... it is not altogether clear whether Brentano meant by his prefix 'in-' that these objects enjoy a form of *non-being*, or existence *in* the mind, or both." For my purposes, an intentional object surely enjoys intentional inexistence in the second of these senses and may also exhibit it in the second.

8.3.5 Truth value of intentional states and intensional statements

Searle (2004, p. 122) points out that there is a connection between intentionality and intensionality because many sentences that are about intentional states tend to be intensional. While the states themselves are intentional (and are therefore representations of their conditions of satisfaction), the statements about these states are not simply representations of these conditions of satisfaction: they are representations of their representations. The truth value of the original intentional states relies on correspondence with some aspect of the world. But the truth value of the sentences lies in what is in the mind of the person to whom they refer. "Hence the truth or falsity of such sentences does not depend on how things are in the real world as represented by the original intentional states, but how things are in the world of representations as it exists in the minds of the agents whose intentional states are being represented [in the sentences]" (Searle, 2004, p. 124).

When one says, "That is the Morning Star," one is talking about Venus and the truth value of what one says relies on there being or not being a heavenly body that fulfills this. But when one writes, "Janis believes that that is the Morning Star," one is alluding not to the Morning Star but to Janis and what she knows. This precludes making the substitution "Evening Star" unless one can be sure that Janis has the required knowledge. This is the import of the substitutability criterion: the truth value of the sentence is a fact about Janis, and it inheres in the contents of her mind. Moreover, when one says, "Janis is meeting her mother," this is an extensional statement about Janis and her mother: its truth value is to be found in facts existing in the real world. But when one says, "Janis believes she is meeting Santa Claus," since there is no such person as Santa Claus, the sentence is intensional. This is the import of existential inference: the truth value of the sentence is not dependent on the existence or nonexistence of Santa but on what Janis is thinking.

8.3.6 Derived intentionality

Now what is clear from this is that intentionality is a property of minds, while intensionality is a property of sentences. Intentionality is the aboutness of mental states. Intensionality is the nature of sentences that do not qualify as extensional. The notion of derived intentionality is that we can wish on to nonmental items an aboutness that is not intrinsic to them. Whatever the initial putative benefits of this strategy, however, it has serious deficiencies.

Clearly, items taken by Searle to possess secondary or derived intentionality, for example, maps, are not *about* anything in the sense in which intentionality was defined previously. They are simply collections of discriminative or conditioned stimuli, formed by association with our verbal expressions of intentionality (in the form of intensional sentences), that now evoke the propositional attitudes in terms of which those expressions are formed. There is nothing in a map that is about anything else because a map does not have desires and beliefs. A map is therefore not intentional. It is a record of our discriminative or conditioned stimuli. Nor is a map intensional. It might be translated into extensional sentences (Birmingham is south of Manchester) but hardly into intensional. Now Searle is not, of course, saying either of these things (that a map is intentional or intensional); only that we can impose intentionality on to it by designating it as about something other than itself. But if we agree that our talking as if a thing has intentionality because we think it is about something else, the concept of intentionality loses its precision and much of its usefulness. If anything can be about anything else with which it is juxtaposed or with which it works in concert, then explaining the world in terms of intentionality becomes so commonplace as to lose its force. Take the example Searle gives of the derived intentionality of bookcases based on the view that a bookcase is about books because we put books on to it. A bookcase is not "about books," however, any more than about anything else in the world that could be put on it. In contrast to mental states such as depression that are about nothing, bookcases are suddenly about everything.[12] I shall for these reasons treat primary, original, or intrinsic intentionality *as intentionality* and avoid the idea of secondary or derived intentionality. This position is close to Strawson's view that while intentionality entails aboutness, it is not the case that aboutness entails intentionality. Moving on from our first approximation of the meaning of intentionality, we can now say that aboutness is necessary but insufficient for intentionality that relies also on conscious experience. As Strawson puts it, "No states of nonexperiential entities are ever really about anything at all" (2010, p. 330,). This means that bees' "flower dances" are not intentional even though they may be about locations or flowers or nectar (unless we

---

12. See Strawson (2010, pp. 231–239). I do not mean to gloss over the difficulties inherent in intentionality, which are sufficiently extensive to take up many volumes of this length. I am making a straightforward distinction between intentionality and extensionality, as well as emphasizing the nature of intentionality as a facet of subjective experience and intensionality as a property of sentences. Searle seems the clearest author in this regard; hence, my exposition follows his. But this is not a matter of paraphrasing without critical involvement. Where I disagree with him, as is the case with respect to derived intentionality, I make this clear.

choose to assume that explorer bees have mental representations in the form of desires and beliefs about the geography of food sources). There is, in my view, no dispute between Searle and Strawson in their initial understanding of intentionality—both take it to be the faculty of the mind whereby it is about other things. But Searle goes on to designate this as *underived* intentionality and to posit *derived* intentionality as that which we ascribe to nonmental entities. Strawson argues that this is untenable in view of the understanding that intentionality is a property of mental states that are clearly absent from instances of so-called derived intentionality. Intentionality is not an automatic result of aboutness: it requires, in addition, conscious experience. As Strawson puts it, "...the paradigm cases of underived intentionality are conscious or experiential states while the paradigm cases of derived intentionality are nonexperiential things like inscriptions, books, road signs, and computers, programmed robots, and so on" (Strawson, 2010, p. 328).

8.3.7 Some objections

A strong argument against the intentional approach is made by Quine (1960, 1969) who assumes the opposite view of intentionality from Brentano. While Brentano argues that the intentional has special significance on account of its different status from the physical—the implication is the "indispensability of intentional idioms and the importance of an independent science of intentionality"—Quine contends that it merely shows the "baselessness of intentional idioms and the emptiness of a science of intention" (1960, p. 221). The result is a behavioristic approach to behavior that has purged the intentional idioms from its language of explanation. Quine's logic has not carried the day where many philosophers, of widely differing orientations, are concerned, however. Bechtel (1978) and Chomsky (1969), for instance, are of the opinion that despite difficulties with intentional explanation, its merit consists in its ability to facilitate explanation of behavior: if it does so, then it belongs to a scientific purview. We have some distance to travel yet before we can endorse this pragmatic solution.

Nevertheless, these fundamental considerations allow us to restate and refine several terms that will be central to the argument. The *extension* of a term or predicate of a sentence is the thing or set of things to which the term refers, whereas the *intension* of that term or language is the particular way in which this thing or set of things is picked out or determined. "Queen of England" and "Elizabeth II" name the same person, the current British monarch, and so have the same extension. But they delineate this entity in different ways and thereby have different intensions or meanings. Referential transparency means freedom to substitute terms that have the same extension. Referential opacity arises out of the different intensions of terms; it occurs in sentences that take propositions as their predicates. Hence terms and predicates that are identical in an extensional sense may not be substitutable because of their differing intensions.[13] These distinctions are not, whatever they seem, a matter of splitting hairs for its own benefit, but vital components of any attempt to separate explanations from one another and, especially, to make clear how apparently incommensurable paradigms may be incorporated into a single approach to explication.

8.4 Being human

8.4.1 The intensional criterion

Much has been written in preceding chapters about the "bounds of behaviorism," the limitations on its sphere of explanatory applicability. It is important to make clear, however, that the intentional behaviorist research strategy may be constrained in terms of the extent of the applicability of intentional explanation. The conclusions summarized in this section derive from and extend previous accounts of Intentional Behaviorism as a methodological basis for economic psychology. They are especially necessary in order to demarcate the sphere to which the following argument properly applies.

In view of Dennett's definition of *illata* as intentionally characterized physical entities, I have argued that his system breaches the mereological principle that intentional language ought to apply solely to the personal level of exposition rather than the subpersonal. Adopting the argument of Bennett and Hacker (2003) to the effect that intentional language applies only at the personal level of exposition, it is impossible to depict electrons and neurons as intentional systems. Dennett's portrayal of nonhuman animals and computer programs as intentional systems also raises questions in view of the definitions of intentionality and intensionality which have been adopted in this chapter. Hence, we require a clearer means of demarcating the entities to which intentionality may be ascribed. The following conservative suggestion proposes for discussion what I term the *intensional criterion*. A brief recap of the earlier definitions may be in order prior to introducing this concept.

Several problems have become apparent with regard to the range of applicability of the intentional stance. Dennett would treat as intentional systems any entities that can be predicted via the attribution to them of intentional states such as desiring and believing. This renders animals, computer programs, and neurons as well as human beings amenable to an intentional explanation. This application of the intentional stance to entities other than human beings is problematical for its committing the mereological fallacy (Bennett & Hacker, 2003), that is, of attributing to parts of a system states that belong properly only to the system as a whole. There are, however,

---

13. See Dennett, 1969, p. 29; 1994; 1996, pp. 38–39; Dennett & Haugeland, 1987; cf. Bratman, 1994; Guttenplan, 1994; Harman, 1998; Perry, 1994; Searle, 1994.

given the nature of intentionality as we have understood it, reasons to doubt the wisdom of employing the intentional stance as Dennett advocates. Searle (2004, p. 119), we noted, argues that intentionality refers to a mental capacity in which desires and beliefs refer to "objects and states of affairs in the world other than themselves." Intentionality is, therefore, a capability of the mind, a personally experienced, subjective occurrence. We have seen that Strawson (2010) points out that aboutness does not necessarily entail intentionality and that while nonexperiential entities have states, these are not about anything else. This rules out Searle's idea of derived intentionality (which, according to Dennett, is the only variety of intentionality there is). Searle points out that many sentences about intentional states are intensional. The states to which reference is made are intentional (and inherent within them are the representations of their conditions of satisfaction); however, the statements themselves are not representations of these conditions of satisfaction but are representations of their representations. While the truth value of the intentional states depends on correspondence with some facet of the world, that of the sentences is to be found in the contents of the mind of the person to whom they refer. We can add to these observations that the sole objective evidence of an entity's having intentional states as Searle understands them is its demonstrated ability to manipulate intensional sentences according to the criteria set out by Searle. This reasoning, which precludes intentional explanation of a number of the so-called intentional systems embraced by Dennett, requires the formulation of an alternative justification for intentional explanation.

What we might refer to as *the intensional criterion* restricts intentional explanation to entities that fulfill three criteria.

1. The first is that intentional explanation must be limited to entities that *lack a stimulus field for the explanation of their behavior*. Theoretical minimalism must have been exhausted in the attempt to explain and predict these systems. Only when the explanation of the entity's activities in terms of the contingencies of reinforcement and punishment has been exhausted, leaving still a deficit in the activity to be explicated, can resort be made to alternative modes of explanation. The possibility of explaining the behavior in extensional terms that make possible an experimental analysis or a correlational examination must be eliminated before resort is made to intentional explanation.
2. The second is that entities must be *intensionally fluent*. There are two aspects to this. The entity must both demonstrate that it can (a) recognize the nature and import of different propositional attitudes in the course of metacognition and (b) recognize the "imperatives of intensionality," namely, the implications of intensional language: understanding the implications of intentional inexistence, of the nonsubstitutability of codesignatives without altering truth value, and the possible nonexistence of

an intentional object other than in the mind of the individual. Part (a) lies at the heart of psychological rationality. It involves recognizing that the intensionality of language is also a metacognitive event.

On what basis do we conclude that the intensional stance can be applied only to entities capable of demonstrating that they can make these distinctions? This question may be rephrased as, What differences do intensional systems—those that can so demonstrate—uniquely exhibit? The answer is that such entities can *show* that their behavior is sensitive to these imperatives. This insistence avoids the temptation to apply intentional explanation at a level of exposition at which it is not appropriate. Clearly, neurons cannot demonstrate intensional fluency any more than can the contingencies of reinforcement. The result is that intentionality is ascribed only to entities that can be said in any sense to have beliefs and desires. This strategy overcomes the instrumentalist or antirealist approach inherent in claiming that being predictable on the basis of ascribed intentionality is all there is to having desires and beliefs, minds, mentality. It is a clear indication for the realist assumption that desires and beliefs exist. And it avoids the mereological fallacy.

3. The third is that entities must *not be amenable to explanation via the physical stance or the contextual stance*. We must consider what other stance we could adopt in explaining the behavior of the system—that is, (a) the physical stance, (b) the contextual stance, and (c) the intentional stance. Parts (a) and (b) are appropriate for physical systems even if they are more complex and verbally cumbersome than the use of the intentional stance in this context; ultimately if the physical stance can be used to predict well, the system is appropriate only to explanation in these terms. Part (c) is no more than folk psychology or at best IST employing *abstracta*—therefore not a scientific approach/or limited because the IST cannot be cashed out. It might be used for animals or things but only on the level of an everyday *façon de parler*. In terms of Dennett's three kinds of intentional psychology, such usage approximates that of folk psychology or, at best, ad hoc IST.

In conclusion, it appears that taking this intensional stance is the only mode of explanation relevant to the scientific analysis of cognitive humans. It allows the explanation of an individual's behavior in intentional terms as long as these are ascribed only at the personal level. A system that can demonstrate that it is capable of behaving in response to the imperatives of intensionality is an *intensional system*. Intensional systems can, moreover, *mis*apprehend the import of the imperatives of intensionality and act accordingly, that is, irrationally or arationally (see, inter alia, Bermúdez, 2003; Brakel, 2009; and for discussion in the context of Intentional Behaviorism, Foxall, 2017b). Inherent in this capacity for misapprehension is a clear understanding of the ontology, nature, and causal efficacy of intentionality.[14] As Tomasello and Rakoczy (2003, p. 123) put it, "Beliefs are fully mental because they are independent of reality in the sense that there can be false beliefs, so that, for example, the truth value of the proposition 'I believe that it is raining' is independent of the embedded proposition 'It is raining'." This suggests they are not simply conditioned entities, the behavior of which is environmentally determined. Belief is cognitively real. In addition, an intensional systems theory avoids the mereological fallacy since it avoids the intentional stance's more comprehensive range of applicability, that is, it rigorously implements the differences between the levels of exposition. In summary, intensional systems can *demonstrate* intensional actions abstractly (verbally) while also having the ability to act counterintensionally (arationally or irrationally). Such misapprehension is not just the absence of correct reasoning: it is another form of reasoning, albeit fallacious. The fact that an individual can formulate an incorrect rule (i.e., one out of accord with the contingencies of reinforcement and punishment) and then act on it is evidence that his behavior is cognitively influenced/necessitates of cognitive explanation.

The import of this reasoning is that it first establishes the basis of psychological rationality in the capacity to make the discriminations required by the rules of intensionality and to distinguish the philosophical attitudes, for example, belief-proper and supposition. Second, it avoids the mereological fallacy. Third, it preserves the integrity of the levels of exposition. Fourth, it properly demarcates the explanatory stance that is most appropriate. And, fifth, it shows that rules are intentional. There are several grounds on which the reasoning behind this criterion might be based: the capacity of humans to

---

14. I make this assertion, especially in regard to intentional causality, not without some hesitation. As Rosenberg points out, "If intentional states of the brain have causal consequences for behavior, there must be a mechanism whereby they bring about these effects. To assert baldly that they do and leave the matter at that is simply the repudiation of science, especially in view of the prima facie difficulty described above" (Rosenberg, 1992, p. 143). Part of the answer is that it is the person not the brain that has intentional states. But saying this does not overcome the problem to which Rosenberg adverts. I believe that a rational person can be expected to act in accordance with her desires and beliefs and that reconstructing these intentional states is a means of explaining the action. It does not follow that there is a direct causal relationship between the intentionality and the action that we can map out in a scientific manner. We can take soundings of the intentionality, not by indexing it directly but by investigations of the verbal and neural behaviors that we understand/assume to be its results; we can subsequently determine how far these are consistent with the over actions of the individual. But this is a long throw from the idea that there is a scientific causation process between intentionality and action. We know that there is a high likelihood of the individual's overt action correlating highly with her verbally stated intention to act (1) when there is a high level of correspondence between the definition and measurement of the preceding intentionality and the action (2) when intentionality is measured at the moment closest to the opportunity to act in accordance with it and (3) when there is little or no situational intervention between the statement of intentionality and the opportunity to act (Foxall, 2005 and Chapter 9: *Ascribing intentionality*).

act in their own right as psychological agents rather than being merely economic agents, and the unique linguistic and cognitive abilities that are peculiar to humans among the primates.

8.4.2 Cognitive uniqueness

Tomasello and Rakoczy (2003) propose that in addition to the belief−desire psychology that humans acquire at around the age of 4, what is often terms "theory of mind," there is an earlier acquisition of "skills of cultural learning and shared intentionality" that occurs at approximately 9 months to 1 year of age. Through this, the child becomes capable of engaging in cultural activities by means of "shared, perspectival symbols with a conventional/normative/reflective dimension − for example, linguistic communication and pretend play − thus inaugurating children's understanding of things mental" (p. 121). On the basis of this empirical finding, these authors make three claims. First, humans are biologically adapted for a kind of social cognition that is unique to mankind as a species. Second, the ability to understand and coordinate their behaviors with intentional agents that humans acquire at about the age of 1 year is a "truly momentous leap in human social cognition" that distinguishes them from other primates. Third, children's ability to understand others as agents who have thoughts and beliefs that may turn out to be erroneous is acquired through several years' linguistic practice (Tomasello & Rakoczy, 2003, pp. 122−123; see also Tomasello, 2019, especially pp. 71−73, and, for an alternative view, see Heyes, 2018). From an evolutionary standpoint, we might say that humans, and only humans, have come by the capacity to understand and reason about the psychological states of persons, even relatively simple ones such as attention. The peculiarity of human cognitive capacity inheres in the ability to understand others as intentional agents and ultimately to engage in collective intentionality. As a result, humans are uniquely able to experience "sharedness," an equivalence of the self with others, and perspectival understanding, the aptitude to construe the same thing under alternative descriptions.

In similar vein, Chomsky observes that in its normal use, language is *innovative, not under stimulus control, and* yet *appropriate to the circumstances* (see Chomsky, 2006, p. 10ff). The behaviorist notions of stimulus and response generalization are simply descriptions of behavioral phenomena. This may be sufficient for behaviorists, whose interests extend no further than the descriptive treatment of observed behavior, but it ignores other intellectual interests. Such behavioristic notions do nothing to explain many aspects of verbal behavior. The fecundity and flexibility of language use, in which, as Chomsky points out, people make "infinite use of finite means"[15]

---

15. Chomsky is here referencing Wilhelm von Humboldt, who used this terminology in the 1830s.

requires for its explanation a view of humans as cognitive animals. Similarly, and as I shall have reason to advert to again, areas of verbal behavior which behaviorists have extensively probed, such as stimulus equivalence, relational framing, and naming, are not given the explanatory depth they require. As Chomsky puts it, "... the method of science ... is typically concerned with data not for itself but as evidence for deeper, hidden organizing principles, principles that cannot be detected 'in the phenomena' not derived from them by taxonomic data-processing operations, any more than the principles of celestial mechanics could have been developed in conformity with such strictures" (Chomsky, 2006, p. 14).[16]

Stimulus freedom and appropriateness are apparent, for instance, in the phenomenon of *misrepresentation* (Bermúdez, 2003), which is the fundamental observation underlying the inability of radical behaviorism to cope with behavioral continuity/discontinuity.[17] The verbal behavior in question is, nevertheless, coherent and meaningful even though it is not related to stimuli. This means not just unrelated to antecedent stimuli but also to consequential stimuli. So Skinner's (1957) notion of meaning as what the verbal behavior accomplishes (e.g., "Give me a drink, please," results in my receiving a glass of water) is sometimes plausibly correct but often difficult to identify. My saying, for instance, "It's a lovely day," does not necessarily evoke any (overt) behavior on the part of the listener, any consequences that establish the meaning of what I have said. It does not even need a listener to be effective. But it is still meaningful, coherent, and appropriate. This requires cognition. Herein perhaps is a clue to the delimitation of behavioral interpretation: in order that behavioral interpretation does not get out of hand, we have to determine the appropriateness of the behavior to the

---

16. Moro (2015, p. 29) points out further in this regard, "The search for simplicity is an important engine for scientific research. Often, this search starts from the astonishment caused in the observation of apparently irreconcilable facts; the search is almost always discretional in the sense that it usually issues from an individual's intuition. The simplicity of a theory is measured according to its capacity to discover new data with the same set of principles of operations. In investigating the facts of the mind, more specifically, the search for simplicity stands out as more than a mere methodological or logical requirement: it becomes psychological. The psychological plausibility of a simple generative—that is, combinatorial (and explicit)—model versus the archive model is intuitively evident".

17. "The essence of a psychological explanation is that it explains behavior in terms of how the creature in question *represents* its environment, rather than simply in terms of the stimuli that it detects" (Bermúdez, 2003, p. 8), and this kind of explanation becomes necessary only when the input—output links on which a conditioning explanation rests cannot be identified (Bermúdez, 2003). *Mis*representation is apparent when a response occurs but the appropriate stimulus is not present or the stimulus is indeed present and registered by the organism but the appropriate response does not occur. Misrepresentation makes psychological explanation necessary, but it has additional theoretical implications. It implies that the intentionality on which psychological explanations depend are both real and causal, since there is no other way to explain why a response occurred. I have discussed Bermúdez's work and the question of misrepresentation in Foxall (2016a).

situation and we do this in cognitive terms, cognitive terms that are, moreover, peculiarly applicable to *human* action.

Even primate "language" is practically entirely devoid of the syntactic complexity of human language. Terrace, Petitto, Sanders, and Bever (1979), for instance, sought chimpanzees' ability to learn the syntax exhibited by human language. But, as Moro (2015, p. 44) sums it up, "Terrace and colleagues showed beyond doubt that the syntax of chimpanzees does not reach the complexity of the syntax of a child that hasn't yet attained linguistic maturity, not to mention the complexity of the syntax of human adults." Adger (2019) uses a principle of Chomsky's called "merge," the mental capacity to join two ideas that can be grammatically processed as a single unit. This is apparently a uniquely human function (Berwick & Chomsky, 2016). Hence, the request, "Pass me the salt and pepper," meets, in the case of a 2-year old human, with both of these items being delivered to the petitioner. In the case of the bonobo, Kanzi, who has demonstrated some verbal behavior through extensive training, it produces random results (Adger, 2019). The capacity to merge is essential to the child's behavior that displays the syntactic prowess required to joining the idea of salt and pepper into a single unit and then applies the verb *pass* to the combination.

Since nonhumans cannot cope display syntax, assess propositional content, or unequivocally display stimulus equivalence, the conclusion must be that individual explanation is not applicable in their case. The reason for our taking the intensional stance is to ensure that the subject accurately distinguishes the kind of propositional attitude (e.g., differentiates a belief-proper from a supposition) that influences/justifies her action. Given the definitions of intentionality and intensionality we have adopted, how can we explain the behavior of an entity that cannot master such differences in intentional terms?

8.5 Endnotes

8.5.1 Psychological agency

An agent is usually thought of as a locus of causation or at least of the factors of which action or behavior is a function. In the case of operant conditioning, this locus is clearly the controlling environment that provides the reinforcing and punishing stimuli that regulate the rate of performance of a response. The organism is acted upon by these consequential stimuli, and its behavior comes to be controlled by behavioral antecedents, that is, discriminative stimuli that set the occasion for reinforcement or punishment or motivating operations that enhance the relation between a response and a reinforcer. But this attribution of agency to entities other than organisms is perhaps unusual. Okasha (2018, p. 2) says that agential thinking "appeals to the notion of *agents* with *interests, goals, and strategies,*" and distinguishes

Type 1 agency in which the agent is an organism from Type 2 agency in which agents are "genes or groups or mother nature." It is clear from Okasha's mention of agents' having interests, goals, and strategies that agency often involves the ascription of intentionality. Moreover, in connection with the appeal to "mother nature" that derives from Dennett's strategy of predicting an intentional system by ascribing to it the intentionality it "ought" to have given its history and current situation, I would argue that ascribing intentionality might make entities more predictable in a gross and vague way (that is, at the greatest level of generality, not fine-grained predictions that would add to our knowledge of how the entity would act anyway). I am more inclined to ascribe intentionality only to entities that can *demonstrably* make intensional distinctions (whether or not these are veridical).

An agent *acts* (rather than having movement imposed on it). Its doing something is transitive: the moving of gene (what gene does) rather than gene's moving (in the sense of being moved by something external to him). The gerund "moving" is intransitive in the second instance since it refers to his being moved (Dretske, 1988; Hornsby, 1981). The cause of the action is assumed to be the agent's mental states (desires and beliefs), and we can only be certain that the organism has such mental states by virtue of its demonstration of what we might call intensional fluency. Hence, agency involves intensional performance since this is the only means by which we can adduce evidence that the entity in question can be moved by intentionality. Intensional reasoning is necessary though probably not sufficient to allow behavior to be explained intentionally. Indeed, why would we think an entity that was incapable of demonstrating such reasoning would be capable of acting in ways that are caused by its desires and beliefs and other intentionality? This is especially poignant given the evidence that we *can* demonstrate the capacity to possess intentionality in the form of desires and beliefs by means of intensional fluency, even though the propositions it entails may not be veridical (perhaps *because* it *can be* nonveridical). This reasoning carries the import that intentional explanation ought to be confined to verbal humans: that is, to entities that can *employ* Dennett's intentional stance to predict/ understand others rather than simply be rendered predictable or intelligible by its being applied to them; to entities that can demonstrate the capacity to exercise metacognition in the understanding of the intentionality by which it claims to behave. This *intensional criterion*, therefore, facilitates a psychological understanding of agency.

8.5.2 Economic agency

Ross (2012) proposes an *economic* conception of agency, arguing that an agent is present wherever a utility function can be identified. This has the implication that any entity that behaves in such a way as to secure provisions for its wellbeing is an agent. The movements of such an agent could be the result of operant or classical conditioning or fixed action patterns rather than intentionality: at any rate, they are stimulus bound and do not merit the ascription of intentionality. Having a utility function does not sound in any way like agency as Okasha understands it.

There is no reason why the treatment of economic agency as a theoretical abstraction rather than a description of manifest human agents (see Ross, 2005, 2007, 2012) should preclude its alternative treatment in terms of what agents actually do. Ross (2012, p. 692) argues that "Whereas people are pretheoretical entities found in the world, economic agency is a theoretical construction elaborated as part of the development of a family of models" and refers to the direct study of people as "an expression of *normative phenomenalism*." I interpret Ross's views as providing a necessary corrective to criticisms of economics, notably from behavioral economists, that claim that economists should analyze human behavior directly by focusing on what people actually do rather than presenting idealized theoretical constructs of agency (see, e.g., Davis, 2003). I see no reason, however, why economic theory should proceed other than in the manner it does given its intellectual purposes; moreover, the difficulties inherent in ascertaining "directly" what it is that consumers and other economic actors actually do renders a wholly empirical stance problematic in itself. As Ross points out, there is no pressure on physicists and other scientists to adopt normative phenomenalism by asking them to deal directly with tables and chairs rather than to the "unobservable objects of reference" on which theory depends; it seems to be a stricture that critics uniquely seek to impose on economists. However, I do maintain that different intellectual purposes require different conceptual and methodological approaches. In the following, I shall, therefore, first describe Ross's position as a point of reference and then present that which I assume.

Ross (2005, p. 87) assumes Robbins's definition of economics as correct, though he prefers to drop the word "human": "the science which studies human behavior as a relationship between ends and scarce means which have alternative uses" (Robbins, 1935, p. 16). Indeed, Ross argues that because an insect's goals and limited range of behavioral options available to achieve them are hardwired and the insect's behaviors are only minimally influenced by environmental factors, wasps are ideally suited to behavioral prediction by means of neoclassical microeconomics (Ross, 2005, p. 95ff). Now, there is strong evidence that wasps' behavior is almost entirely describable and predictable in environmental terms since it is predominantly operant in nature. But, to return to Ross's argument, the wasp's budget constraint is given by the control mechanisms identified by the entomologist. So is what Ross calls its "condition−action repertoire." From the budget constraint and condition−action constraint, the insect's utility function is calculable. There is thus "a one-to-one mapping between the biological individual insect and a well-behaved economic agent" (Ross, 2005, p. 96). This is where microeconomics works best: not among the humans to whom Robbins wished to confine his analysis. Elsewhere, Ross (2007) argues that the basic models of agency should be simple: insects are prototypically agential because they are simple (not because of an attempt at reductionism). Their behavior is not subject to apparent preference reversals: "an entire biological bug does map relatively neatly onto representation as a single agent" (Ross, 2007, p. 198). In the case of humans, however, the appearance of a novel set of preferences means that we are dealing with a novel agent.

The argument that it is legitimate in the face of Ross's reasoning to conceive of agency in different terms is borne out by the complexities inherent in human economic decision-making that are not reproduced in the experience of most if not all animals, let alone bugs. Ross's analysis ignores the fact that human consumers' utility bundles are more complex than those of insects but are equally calculable given the conceptual development of reinforcement found in Intentional Behaviorism. Humans' utility bundles comprise utilitarian *and* informational reinforcement, whereas those of insects are presumably confined to the former. Informational reinforcement accounts for much of the complexity inherent in human economic behavior. Given that we can measure both utilitarian and informational reinforcement and include them in a utility function to determine the point of consumer equilibrium, consumers turn out to be remarkably well behaved too. If a well-defined utility function is the mark of agency, there is no reason to deny this status to individual consumers. But it needs to be understood in a specific way that reflects its complexities. Moreover, it is possible to characterize consumers' ultimate utility bundles as consisting in the *pleasure, arousal,* and *dominance* that are the final rewards of consumer behavior (for a full discussion, see Foxall, 2017b).

There is no reason, therefore, to think of humans having agency "by extension" from simpler organisms, as Ross puts it. We can identify their utility functions in terms of bundles of utilitarian and informational reinforcement clearly and successfully. Pattern of reinforcement is the key. While consumers may purchase products and services, what they consume is combinations of utilitarian and informational reinforcement, and ultimately combinations of emotional response. The justification for taking a view of agency that embraces consumers' multiplicity of sources of utility is that this alone will allow us to predict consumer behavior accurately and to explain and interpret it successfully in the later stages of the intentional behaviorist strategy.

The conceptual assumptions and tools of analysis forged in this chapter require application to economic behavior in order that the intentional behaviorist research strategy may be evaluated further. This is the theme of Chapter 9, *Ascribing intentionality*.

Chapter 9

Ascribing intentionality

Chapter Outline

9.1 Modeling consumer choice 181
   9.1.1 The extensional model of consumer choice (BPM-E) 181
   9.1.2 The bounds of behaviorism in consumer psychology 185
   9.1.3 The imperatives of intentionality 188
   9.1.4 The intentional model of consumer choice (BPM-I) 189
9.2 Predictability: attitude−intention−behavior 194
   9.2.1 Predictive validity 194
9.2.2 The attitude revolution 197
9.3 Consumer heterophenomenology 209
   9.3.1 The nature of heterophenomenology 209
   9.3.2 Consumer heterophenomenology 213
   9.3.3 Heterophenomenology in the context of Intentional Behaviorism 215
9.4 Endnote 219

This chapter summarizes the extensional model of consumer choice, which provides the theoretically minimal element of the intentional behaviorist research strategy and shows how the bounds of behaviorism identified in Chapters 5−7 apply to it. It goes on to summarize the intentional model and the construction of the intentional consumer situation. These themes, which are the subjects of the first section, have been covered in greater length elsewhere (e.g., Foxall, 2016a, 2016b, 2017a, 2017b). The questions of how far an intentional interpretation can provide testable hypotheses through which its veracity can be ascertained is raised and illustrated by reference to multiattribute attitude—intention—behavior models such as the theory of reasoned action and the theory of planned behavior (Section 9.2). The conclusion is drawn that theoretical minimalism is an inescapable prerequisite of intentional interpretation. Finally, the relationship between first-personal subjective experience (knowledge-by-acquaintance) and third-personal scientific data (knowledge-by-description) is discussed in light of Dennett's heterophenomenological methodology (Section 9.3).

9.1 Modeling consumer choice

9.1.1 The extensional model of consumer choice (BPM-E)

The process of psychological explanation comprises two parts: the formation of an intentional interpretation which is followed by its justification in terms of a cognitive interpretation (Foxall, 2016a, 2016b). This chapter shows how these two stages in the intentional behaviorist research strategy are composed and related to one another. The discussion begins, however, with the role of the theoretically minimalist initial stage, which proceeds in extensional terms. The discussion is primarily conceived within the framework of conceptualization and analysis provided by the Behavioral Perspective Model (BPM) of consumer choice, though there is no inherent reason why the discussion in this chapter would not apply equally well to managerial behavior and the actions of the firm or other organization.

The extensional model of consumer choice (BPM-E) is shown in Fig. 9.1. The essence of the model is found in the idea of the consumer situation, which is conceived as the immediate precursor of consumer behavior. In the extensional model, the consumer situation is composed of the consumer behavior setting in interaction with the consumer's learning history, particularly her consumption history. The consumer behavior setting is in turn composed of the discriminative stimuli and motivating operations of which consumer behavior is a function. These have gained their functional ability to exert stimulus control of behavior through their constituting the setting in which behavior has previously been enacted and reinforced or punished. The reinforcing and punishing consequences generated by consumer behavior are of two fundamental kinds: utilitarian and informational.

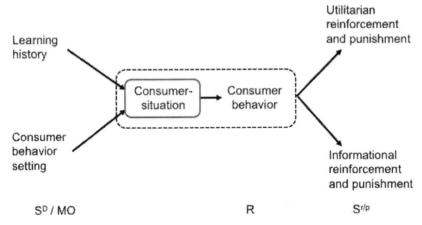

FIGURE 9.1 **The extensional model of consumer choice (BPM-E).** The essence of the model is the consumer situation and consumer behavior. The figure shows also how the consumer situation is determined by the consumer's learning history, particularly her consumption history, and the discriminative stimuli and motivating operations that compose the consumer behavior setting. For completeness' sake, it also shows the outcomes of consumer behavior, namely, utilitarian and informational reinforcement and punishment, though strictly speaking these are understood by the elements of the consumer behavior setting. *BPM*, Behavioral Perspective Model; *MO*, motivating operations; *R*, response; S^D, discriminative stimuli; $S^{r/p}$, reinforcing and punishing stimuli.

Utilitarian reinforcement consists in the functional benefits of owning and consuming products and services, while informational reinforcement consists in the social and symbolic benefits thereof. Each of these sources of reinforcement is equally a source of punishment and consumer behavior entails both sorts of consequence. At the very least consumer behavior meets the aversive consequence of the consumer's having to surrender potential generalized purchasing power in the form of money; and while the consumption of many products and services attracts positive social esteem as others observe it, it may also engender negative consequences in the form of ridicule or jealousy or simple disapproval. Each of the variables that compose the consumer behavior setting is primed by the consumer's history of reinforcement and punishment.

The *scope* of the consumer behavior setting consists in the number of behavior programs that the setting permits. A relatively closed setting allows one or at best a few behaviors to be enacted—retail banks present consumers with settings that are normally confined to members who can enact a limited number of behaviors, typically transactive operations linked to the orderly conduct of the bank's business and the consumer's requirements. Extraneous activity is strongly discouraged, and its persistence punitively dealt with. A social interaction such as a party is, by contrast, a setting in which multiple courses of behavior are available to participants. Most consumer situations fall between these extremes. A variety store, for instance, allows multiple consumption related activities but actively excludes some extraneous behavior. In the extensional model, the consumer situation is defined simply as the scope of the consumer behavior setting, which is a function of the current stimulus field as primed by the consumer's learning history. All of the elements of the extensional model have proven amenable to empirical measurement and analysis, and the magnitude that consumers maximize has been shown to be a bundle of utilitarian and informational reinforcement. In the extensional model, the consumer situation is equivalent to the scope of the consumer behavior setting.

The large volume of empirical research inspired by the extensional model has been reviewed in detail recently (Foxall, 2017a), but it will be instrumental to later discussion to note one aspect of this here, namely, the determination, based on Cobb—Douglas utility function analysis, that what consumers maximize is a bundle of utilitarian and informational reinforcement. Oliveira-Castro and Foxall (2017) used the function,

$$U_{(x_1,x_2)} = x_1^a x_2^b \quad (9.1)$$

where U is the utility, x_1 is the quantity of utilitarian reinforcement, x_2 is the quantity of informational reinforcement, and a and b are empirically obtained parameters, to examine purchases of fast moving food products (see also Oliveira-Castro, Cavalcanti, & Foxall, 2016a, 2016b). More precisely, we can say that on the basis of several investigations, consumers maximize the utility that derives from particular combinations of utilitarian and informational reinforcement subject to the constraint imposed by their budget for the goods in question.

Another important research theme has been concerned with identifying the emotional reactions to the various consumer situations defined by higher or lower utilitarian reinforcement, higher or lower informational reinforcement, and the scope of the consumer behavior setting. Eight such kinds of consumer situation can be defined (Fig. 9.2).

A number of research projects have tested the hypotheses that utilitarian reinforcement will be associated with a higher rather than lower degree of *pleasure* (P); informational reinforcement, with a higher rather than lower degree of *arousal* (A); and the scope of the setting with a higher rather than lower degree of *dominance* (D), which is greater the more open the setting. These hypotheses have been supported by the evidence (Fig. 9.3); the

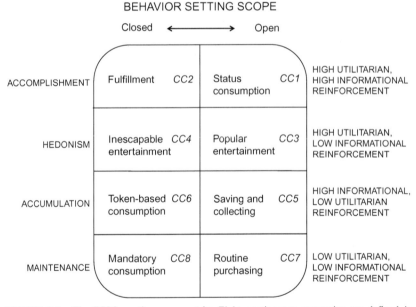

FIGURE 9.2 The BPM contingency matrix. Eight contingency categories are defined in terms of the relative levels of utilitarian and informational reinforcement and the scope of the consumer behavior setting represented. The levels of high/low utilitarian reinforcement and high/low informational reinforcement determine the operant class of consumer behavior: accomplishment, hedonism, accumulation, and maintenance. The nature of the consumer situation involved is determined by the operant class and the scope of the setting (ranging from closed to open). The idealized consumer situations are described arbitrarily but these descriptions have proved remarkably resilient in empirical research (see, e.g., Foxall, 2017a). *BPM*, Behavioral Perspective Model.

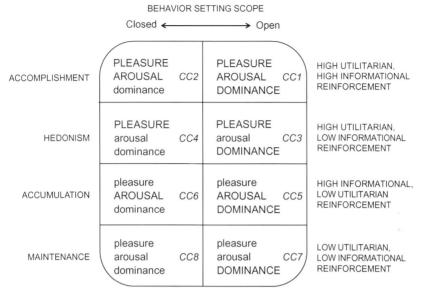

FIGURE 9.3 **The BPM emotional contingency matrix.** Each of the eight contingency categories is associated with a high or low level of pleasure, arousal, and dominance (P^-, A^-, D^-). The uppercase designations of these emotions indicate a higher level of emotional reaction (P^+, A^+, D^+).; lowercase indicates a lower level of emotional reaction (P^-, A^-, D^-). The figure summarizes the hypothesized relationships between the contingencies of reinforcement and punishment represented by each contingency category and the patterns of emotional response. *BPM*, Behavioral Perspective Model.

research and its implications are discussed in detail in Foxall (2011, 2017b) and Foxall, Yani-de-Soriano, Yousafzai, and Javed (2012). In terms of the extensional model, these results indicate only the verbal responses of consumers in response to descriptions of the patterns of contingencies that represent each of the eight contingency categories defined by that model. Nevertheless, the consistency of the results across cultures and languages offer a remarkable pattern of response to the variables defined by the BPM.

9.1.2 The bounds of behaviorism in consumer psychology

9.1.2.1 Behavioral continuity and discontinuity

The extensional BPM is not able to offer an explanation of consumer behavior when no stimulus field is empirically available. The bounds of behaviorism discussed in Chapters 5–7 are operative in this domain as well as in behavioral science generally. For instance, consumer innovativeness exemplifies the inability of radical behaviorism to cope with behavioral continuity and discontinuity in the realm of consumer choice. In order to account for a consumer's trialing a new brand in an established product class, a behavioral interpretation would have to assume stimulus/response generalization or functional equivalence of stimuli. However, these are just descriptions at best and have no causal force. How do they, in any case, come about, how are they efficacious? Not only is behavioral interpretation intellectually dishonest: it is explanatorily inadequate. Advertising might well lay down rules suggesting that the new brand is equivalent to existing brands, but we still need a mechanism to explain how an individual integrates such rules and acts accordingly. In new brand trial, there is no learning history, no stimulus field. There is no mechanism for learning stimulus generalization or equivalence in the absence of a learning history or stimulus field—no discriminative stimuli can have formed. *The learning takes place without these.* It is cognitive. Even a *similar* learning history or consumer behavior setting requires a mechanism: analogizing, for instance. In the case of a new product which inaugurates a new product class, there is not even a similar learning history or consumer behavior setting. Purchasing such an item relies entirely on verbal description, observation: we must invoke symbols and intentionality in order to explain this.

9.1.2.2 The personal level of exposition

There are central consumer phenomena that are inexplicable without resort to a personal level of exposition. An important example is consumer choice itself, the selection between a smaller but sooner-to-appear reinforcer [smaller-sooner reinforcer (SSR)] and a later occurring but larger reinforcer [larger-later reinforcer (LLR)]. At t_1 the consumer contemplates the possibility of these reinforcers (in whatever combination of utilitarian and informational consequences they promise to enrich her life) and the emotional rewards that will be their outcomes. At this time, neither actually exists in her experience (though she may have a learning history or memory in which they appear); yet she is able to imagine them and attach relative valuations to them to reach a determination of which she will select. It is highly likely that she will prefer the LLR at this point since both reinforcers exist in the relatively remote future and the exigencies of waiting what seems just a little longer for the superior benefit do not seem particularly to outweigh those of having to wait for the inferior (Foxall, 2017b, pp. 25–29). Subsequently, however, just before the availability of the SSR (at t_2), it is likely that its value will increase substantially compared with that of the LLR: the former is about to appear and to be consumable while the later seems a long way off. If this is the case, the consumer is said to discount the future hyperbolically (Foxall, 2016a, Chapter 2). That the SSR will be chosen, thereby precluding the attainment of the LLR, is in these circumstances highly probable. But at this point, though it may become easier to imagine the SSR and while it may actually be visible to the would-be consumer, the LLR still exists only in vaguer imagination. Yet the consumer is able to contemplate both the more concrete imminent reinforcer and emotional rewards promised by the SSR and the more abstract LLR, of which she is fully conscious that it will provide a quantitatively larger benefit and reward, to the extent that she can reverse her previous preference. The consumer who does not discount hyperbolically, whose preference remains unchanged, and who, during t_3, patiently awaits the superior benefits of the LLR (which will become available at t_4) is similarly working on reinforcers and values that exist at that point only within her mind. What sustains this consumer, enabling her to withstand the temptation to obtain and consume the SSR at the earliest opportunity, and to exhibit what is often called self-control for a prolonged period is her perception of the situation, her understanding of the benefits of waiting, her memory of the times she has held out for a superior consequence in the past. We cannot explain the behavior of either consumer without employing notions of her desires and beliefs, valuations, memories, and imaginings. A similar mechanism of intrapersonal decision-making is necessary in order to comprehend the process that Ainslie (1992) refers to as "bundling," a theme which Chapter 10, *Grounding intentionality*, will revisit.

Of course, behaviorists may counter that they are interested only in behavior and that at a descriptive level. By ascertaining the learning history of both consumers, it might prove possible to predict their behavior simply in terms of the contingencies of reinforcement and punishment. But it is difficult to credit this methodology when one considers that the contingencies that control present and future behaviors are those that exist not only in the intrasubjectively available world of natural settings but those that are present in the thoughts of the consumer. We saw that similar considerations apply in the case of schedule insensitivity. A broader consideration that arises is the possibility that there is little or no conditioning in human or nonhuman animals in the absence of cognition (Brewer, 1974; Kirsch, Lynn, Vigorito, & Miller, 2004).

9.1.2.3 Delimiting behavioral interpretation

The problem that arises here for the behavioral interpretation of consumer choice may be illustrated by the adoption/diffusion of innovations. The feasibility of a radical behaviorist interpretation of the adoption and diffusion of innovations has been demonstrated in consumer behavior analysis (Foxall, 1994, 2017a). The decision process itself and the elements in terms of which adoption may be understood at various stages of the process of diffusion can be related systematically to the contingencies of reinforcement and punishment. However, the consequences of choosing an innovative good may ramify indefinitely, and the interpreter is under an obligation to show how the consequences that could feasibly have acted as reinforcers and punishers in an individual innovator's experience can be plausibly identified. The relevance and credibility of a behavioral interpretation must be in doubt if this cannot be accomplished. Clearly, our interpretation must be constrained by what the consumer could have known at the time of her selecting the novel item, and this entails an intentional interpretation. Sources of intentional interpretation might include, for instance, knowledge of those elements of an innovation that ensure its more rapid diffusion: relative advantage, compatibility, complexity, conspicuousness, trialability, and comprehensibility (see also Foxall et al., 1998; Rogers, 2004). These are factors that the innovator would be likely to take into consideration in trialing and subsequently adopting a new product or service and are also likely to be emphasized by the supplier of the innovation. Additional elements in terms of which the intentional interpretation might be phrased, if these can be ascertained by the interpreter, might include personality and cognitive style of the innovator (Foxall, 1995). Only if attempts are made to circumscribe the nature and extent of the motivators of the innovative process can the behavioral interpretation be reliably confined to feasible elements of the environment of which innovative behavior might have been a function, while avoiding fanciful speculations about the role of remote consequences on the decision procedure. It is unlikely that behavioral interpretation can stand alone; therefore a credible interpretation relies also on the ascription of intentionality.[1]

9.1.3 The imperatives of intentionality

Each of the three bounds of behaviorism gives rise to an imperative of intentionality, an opportunity to employ intentional idioms in the explanation of action. The problem of being unable to demonstrate the stimulus-defined foundations of continuous or discontinuous behaviors requires a turning to the desires, beliefs, emotions, and perceptions in terms of which the consumer perceives her consumption history and its outcomes, the current behavior setting with its indications of the consequences that are contingent upon the execution of particular consumer behaviors, and the nature of the pattern of utilitarian and informational reinforcement that she expects to be the result of her behavior. These perceptions also generate expectations of the emotional rewards that will ensue. Similarly, the adoption of an intentional personal level of exposition allows the consideration of the mental processing that takes place when the consumer contemplates the situation in which she is about to act, that in which she purchases and consumes economic and social goods, and that in which she evaluates her behaviors and consumption experiences. Decision-making, including the comparative evaluation and determination of desired consumption outcomes, the representation of future events, and the revaluing of current options must all feature in an intentional account of consumer behavior. Finally, the necessity of

---

1. For additional behavioral interpretations of consumer choice which rely for their ultimate credibility on the ascription of intentionality, see Foxall (2017a, Chapter 3).

delimitation of behavioral interpretation begs the question what could the individual have known at the point of behaving? What consequences of her behavior could not possibly have impinged on the performance or frequency of the behavior (i.e., what was not known to her)?

9.1.4 The intentional model of consumer choice (BPM-I)
9.1.4.1 Behavioral Perspective Model-I
The objective of the psychological explanation is to formulate an intentional understanding of behavior for which no stimulus field is empirically available and, as was said in Chapter 8, *The intentional behaviorist research strategy*, to derive therefrom hypotheses that can be tested by the extensional sciences of neurophysiology and consumer behavior analysis. The initial stage of the psychological explanation proposes an intentional interpretation of the behavior in question basing its suggestion of contingency-representations on the general findings of the examination of the behavior through the theoretically minimalist lens of an operant analysis of consumer behavior in general.[2]

The intentional interpretation is tested by reference to its capacity to predict, which as I have said, is likely to be minimal, and its consistency with cognitive psychology. A central concern of this cognitive interpretation is to show how the various levels of exposition that enter the explanation of consumer activity are interrelated. This is an essential component of resolving the illata issue. The relevant economic analysis is then employed to derive testable hypotheses for empirical research: this is in fact a reiteration of the initial stage: the current iteration of the research process is complete.

Cognitive psychology is predicated on the operation of central processes that receive information from the environment which, through its processing, eventuates in behavioral outputs. On a materialist philosophical foundation, the central processes involved are portrayed as either physical or functionally defined operations the realization of which may be physiological (Hamlyn, 1990). In other words, we use intentional language to account for the functions of the brain that we cannot account for in terms of neuroscience or operancy.[3] What we are saying in intentional language must nevertheless be consistent with the *class of behaviors* we are thus interpreting, that is, the class of consumer behavior defined by the pattern of reinforcement and punishment. Neuroscience and operancy constrain our interpretations While the ontological position is entirely materialistic, the methodological standpoint is that both extensional and intentional languages are necessary in order to

---

2. The intentional consumer-situation and the concept of contingency-representation are described at length in Foxall (2017b).
3. I use the term "operancy" to refer to the procedure inherent in the learning process described by the three-term contingency.

provide a fully functional as well as structural account of brain and behavior; hence, we invoke two distinct modes of explanation, which are immiscible and must consequently be kept scrupulously separate in our account of behavior. It is incumbent upon us, however, to attempt to show how they relate (hence, the concept of Janus variables will be introduced in Chapter 10: *Grounding intentionality*), not least insofar as each is used to critically examine and, where necessary, circumscribe the other. This research strategy is consonant with the understanding that biconditionals are, to say the least, unlikely and that the only conceptions we necessarily have to work with belong to distinct levels of exposition. Given that McGinn's search for biconditionals is going to be abortive at least for the conceivable future, the employment of both extensional and intentional language, coupled with the recognition of their immiscibility and their belonging to different levels of exposition, seems a reasonable way forward. This strategy requires two things: a means of connecting the levels of exposition at least logically though not conceptually and a route to the empirical investigation of the claims of the intentional interpretation.

9.1.4.2 Construction of the intentional consumer situation

The intentional consumer situation is not a matter of fantasy just because it is an interpretation and not directly amenable to empirical investigation. People do think about future contingencies they have never encountered in life, plan what they would do in these circumstances, and decide a course of action which they implement. It is false to say that their projective thinking, planning, and deciding are unreal or noncausal. Similarly, we cannot conclude that their perceptions of future consequences of actions yet to be performed cannot be part of their causal texture that leads to one course of action rather than another, that they cannot feel the consequences of imagined behaviors. The intentional consumer situation has been discussed at length elsewhere (Foxall, 2017b) and the present exposition continues that discussion by concentrating on the links between the intentional interpretation and the cognitive interpretation in psychoanalytical terms.

The intentional consumer situation comprises the desires and beliefs that are appropriate to the consumer's learning history and current consumer behavior setting (Fig. 9.4). We may take beliefs to include perceptions, including emotional anticipations of the reinforcing and punishing outcomes of consumer behavior and the beliefs and other propositional attitudes entertained by consumers as guides to action. Such propositional attitudes include beliefs-proper, neurotic beliefs, and fantasies as cognitive and affective foundations of the intentional consumer situation. The reconstruction of these desires and beliefs permits an interpretation of observed consumer choice. It is a matter, first, of proposing the propositional attitudes that are appropriate to the consumer's situation. The general knowledge of the variables of which

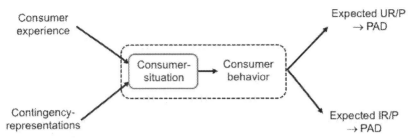

FIGURE 9.4 The intentional model of consumer choice (BPM-I). The variables employed in the extensional model are redefined in intentional terms. Hence, the intentional consumer situation as is derived from contingency-representations of the consumer's history, and of the current consumer behavior setting, namely, desires, beliefs, emotions, and perceptions. The consumer's learning history thereby becomes her experience that may be recalled from memory and have a direct influence on her current behavior or act implicitly on current choice (see, e.g., Bargh, 2007; Gawronski & Payne, 2010). The stimulus field that composes the consumer behavior setting is active now insofar as it is represented by the consumer's contingency-representations, especially with respect to the utilitarian and informational reinforcement that will ensue from particular behaviors. The essence of the model is again the consumer situation→consumer behavior relationship. The expected utilitarian and informational reinforcement and punishment are indicated for completeness. The ultimate outcome of the consumer behavior, which determines its future rate of recurrence, is the emotional reward (pleasure, arousal, and dominance). *A*, Arousal; *D*, dominance; *IR/P*, informational reinforcement or punishment; *P*, pleasure; *UR/P*, utilitarian reinforcement or punishment.

consumer behavior is a function provided by the extensional model is of inestimable value here; it not only suggests the appropriate propositional attitudes that render intelligible the observed behavior of the consumer, for which no obvious stimulus field is apparent, but also identifies the likely intentional objects that will form part of these propositions. The empirical research that has identified the importance of essential value to consumer choice indicates, for instance, the attitude a consumer is likely to have toward changes in the price/quantity relationships that the consumer faces. Similarly, the finding that consumers maximize utilitarian and informational reinforcement bundles is instrumental in suggesting the desires and beliefs of the consumer. But there is more to the reconstruction of the intentional consumer situation, namely, the emotional contingency-representations that can be attributed to the consumer whose behavior is interpreted. The levels of pleasure, arousal, and dominance felt by the consumer in a particular consumer behavior setting that promises particular levels of utilitarian and informational reinforcement contingent upon her purchasing and consumption actions are also of enormous value in suggesting why she acted as she did.

A key question is how to make the transition from the intentional interpretation to the cognitive interpretation so that we may be sure that we are talking about the same manner of cognitive experience and relating like to like. The Freudian conception of primary and secondary mentation from which the categories of belief previously mentioned are taken provides a clear linkage between the intentional interpretation and the cognitive interpretation, especially insofar as the latter is conceived within the ambit of dual- and tri-process modeling of cognitive architectures and events. Consumers' emotional reactions to the contingency categories defined by the variables of the extensional BPM can, in light of the intentional model, be interpreted as indicative of their subjective responses to the contingencies of reinforcement and punishment that are indicated by the current consumer behavior setting in which they have the option to act and, having acted, the emotional rewards that are the outcome of their receipt of utilitarian and informational reinforcement. This consideration will become critical in Chapter 10, *Grounding intentionality*, which considers the means by which Intentional Behaviorism proposes how the separate levels of exposition are interconnected in a comprehensive explanation of consumer action.

This conception embraces not only the components of the intentional consumer situation but also the kinds of cognitive psychology, which can justify the interpretation on which it depends. Theories, such as Bickel's neurobehavioral decision systems model and Stanovich's tri-process model, which provide exemplars of micro-cognitive psychology; Ainslie's picoeconomics that I have referred to as a meso-cognitive psychology; and operant consumer behavioral economics that relies on rates of temporal discounting, are all prefigured by the Freudian distinction. Freud's model is not identical with any of these, all of which are more specific in their predictions and more elaborate in their explanations. What Freud's model does, however, explain very specifically is the kinds of neurotic beliefs and fantasies that people adopt in their verbal behavior and subsequent nonverbal behavior. It is, therefore, essentially compatible with the dual process theories. Although the Freudian distinction has been discussed in the context of the intentional consumer situation at some length (Foxall, 2017b), it bears brief recapitulation in the current discussion. In Brakel's terms, primary processes "lack (rather than violate) the principles of everyday logic, so that opposites are not mutually exclusive, contradictions are tolerated, and neither reality testing nor contextualizing in terms of time is employed" (Brakel, 2018, p. 177). It is primary process mentation that accounts for individuals' inability to differentiate the nature of the propositional attitudes on which they act, mistaking neurotic beliefs for beliefs-proper, for instance, and suppositional thinking for reality-tested logic. By contrast, secondary processes embody "ordinary conscious, wakeful, largely rational operations." The contrast is evidenced in that "primary process is faster, closer to the drives, affect and impulse-linked; whereas secondary process thought can be more independent of emotions and drives, is more deliberate, and entails more mental/psychological work" (Brakel, 2018). Since it is a-rational rather than irrational, primary process can be seen as a "developmentally earlier form of organization" rather than an irrational one. It is not necessarily pathological as witness its instrumentality in achieving creative goals and its promotion of survival strategies involved in evolutionary tasks. The intentional consumer situation is composed of the consumer's beliefs-proper and neurotic beliefs and the role of secondary mentation in promoting the reality testing thereof provides a strong link to the role of executive functions' capacity to correct and overcome the operation of the impulsive system in dual- and tri-process models cognitive functioning.

9.1.4.3 Informational reinforcement

Several of the considerations raised by Bandura's social learning theory, which were discussed in Section 5.1 are closely related to informational reinforcement, for example, the valuation of behaviors, the appraisal of self-performance, the ascription of self-esteem, all involve, ultimately, activities at the personal level of exposition. An operant account of informational reinforcement requires that the antecedent and consequential stimuli involved function simply as (1) discriminative stimuli or motivating operations and (2) secondary reinforcers, respectively, via their physical (e.g., visual and auditory properties). They are stimuli, the effects of which are established in the course of conditioning and they receive their capacity to control behavior simply by being paired with utilitarian reinforcers. This is how they must be understood in the BPM-E account which, true to the requirements of radical behaviorism, is concerned solely with behavior, its prediction and possible control. At this level, rule-governed behavior is simply a matter of additional physical stimulation that controls behavior through associative learning. The verbalizations employed in the expression of a rule do not differ from the nonlinguistic sounds employed by nonhumans. This is consonant with Skinner's (1957) view that the *meaning* of verbal behavior inheres in the functions it performs: in school, being able to say "Pass the bread, please" in French gets you a good mark; in France, it gets you the bread. The analysis is purely extensional in nature: informational reinforcement consists in variables that can be incorporated into laboratory experiments as easily as utilitarian reinforcement. This is the nature of the extensional consumer situation.

In the intentional consumer situation, however, we recognize the intentional nature of the verbalizations, the fact that speech, writing, and thinking are *about* something other than themselves, and that employing them to explain the behavior of others entails a different kind of explanation from that of the extensional radical behaviorist account. Informational reinforcement is now something that the individual accords him/herself, sometimes simply by noting his/her progress toward standards of behavioral performance he/she has set, sometimes because the standards set by others have been achieved, sometimes on the basis of others' behavior that indicates performance feedback.

The intentional model (BPM-I) is concerned to provide an account of behavior by treating the consumer as an idealized system and detailing the intentionality he/she would exhibit given his/her history and current circumstances. As a result the consumer situation has become intentionally specified, in terms of the desires, beliefs, emotions, and perceptions in accordance with which the individual would be acting if she were a utility-maximizer who optimized bundles of utilitarian and informational reinforcement. We would specify not only the utilitarian reinforcement she received but also the informational reinforcement that would explain her behavior in this idealized context. We have the advantage of a well-developed extensional model of choice on which to base this intentional interpretation.

There are two ways in which we can ascertain the empirical validity of intentional interpretations: the prediction of behavior based on intentional constructs such as attitude and intention (the latter in the psychological sense of prebehavioral determination) and the translation of first-personal experience into third-personal scientific data (employing a methodology akin to Dennett's *heterophenomenology*). To these we turn.

9.2 Predictability: attitude–intention–behavior

9.2.1 Predictive validity

The criterion of predictive accuracy has been invoked by Dennett as a means of justifying the IST and it is a possible source of verification for the intentional interpretation of Intentional Behaviorism, but one that has been criticized on the grounds of the necessary generality and vagueness of the projections involved.[4] This section, first, clarifies Dennett's position and, second, draws on social psychological research to examine what can be expected of predictions based on intentional constructs.

Philosophers and psychologists frequently overestimate the extent to which purported measures of beliefs, attitudes, intentions, and other items of intentionality actually predict and explain behavior. Nor do verbal expressions of intentionality, as behaviorists would characterize them, succeed except in the most situationally bound circumstances. It is a continuing enigma of social cognitive psychology that in the absence of measures of these cognitive and behavioral variables that are *situationally* constrained in the severest fashion the simple correlations that simple theories of behavior would anticipate can rarely be demonstrated (Foxall, 1983, 1997a, 2005; Kuhl & Beckman, 1985). The following discussion argues that the improving

---

4. I have presented the argument summarized here in greater detail in the context of consumer psychology: see Foxall (1983, 1997a, 1997b, 2002b). The attitude–intention–behavior models discussed in this chapter are in fact examples of subpersonal cognitive psychology, which transcend the predictive goal of folk psychology by proposing causal structures to account for behavior at the cognitive level. See Dennett (1987a, Chapter 3; cf. Yu & Fuller, 1986).

success of social cognitivists in predicting and explaining behavior may stem from their adoption of something akin to the intentional behaviorist approach advocated here, that is, the addition of a heuristic overlay based on the intentional stance to the findings of researchers implicitly employing the contextual stance.

The intentional strategy requires the attribution to an assumed rational system of the beliefs and desires it *ought* to have and thereby to predict the behavior of the system; if its behavior proves predictable by this method, we are justified in calling it an intentional system. The question that arises is how this abstract formula is to be translated into a practical means of predicting the behavior of intentional systems. Dennett's (1982, 1991b) means of investigating consciousness, heterophenomenology, involves applying the intentional stance to people's verbal behavior, treating it as a text to be interpreted in terms of their beliefs and desires. Much as one examines the text of a character in a novel in terms of what he or she says, what they do and what others say of them, plus background information about the author and his or her other writings, so one can produce an intersubjective account of the text provided by another person. The heterophenomenology of the person consists in an account of *"what it is like to be* that subject — in the subject's own terms, given the best interpretation we can muster" (Dennett, 1991b, p. 98). The resulting account is, like a scientific hypothesis, subject to testing in the face of the evidence, and hence corrigible.

There is, then, little doubt that Dennett intends the heuristic overlay of intentional ascription to be accomplished on the basis of observation of the system's behavior. This is also a conclusion drawn by some of Dennett's critics such as Webb (1994) who have emphasized the philosophical downside of Dennett's failure to show how behavioral evidence is to be used by the intentional stance. According to Webb, any attempt by Dennett to do so will lead him into either "a radical irrealism or logical behaviorism" (p. 457). These possible consequences do not impinge on the quest to find a practical means of predicting intentional systems. Although I outline Webb's argument here, therefore, the solution for present purposes lies beyond his analysis. Yet his analysis is fruitful for what it reveals of the relevance of the contextual stance to the problem of correct intentional attribution. Failure to consider and take proper account of behavioral evidence will lead to inaccurate attributions of intentionality. The desires and beliefs the system ought to have must in part be derived from "important facts the system has been exposed to" (Webb, 1994, p. 459), or as Dennett (1987a, p. 19) himself puts it, "that the system's experience to date has made available." In the terminology of the contextual stance, this means that the system's learning history and behavioral history need to be taken into account. But how?

A clue is that the correct beliefs and desires arise out of consideration of the logical consequences of the beliefs the system has previously held, which introduces issues that the contextual stance would attribute to learning history plus the current behavior setting and the consequences it portrays as contingent on behaving. The big problem is that Dennett does not give a concise and useable answer to the question of just which of the many available potential consequences of behavior are to be taken into consideration in this process. Dennett raises the problem that the logical consequences of behavior are infinite in number. Webb seeks the answer in the witnessed behavior of the system, a thesis he expands by discussing the three sources of attributable desires identified by Dennett (1987a, p. 20) in what he described as his "flagship" exposition of the intentional stance.

First, there are the fundamental desires for basic goods: "survival, the absence of pain, food, comfort, and entertainment." Second are those desires that can be rationally deduced from the system's goals and situation. Finally, Dennett introduces a form of witnessed behavior as a source of intentional ascription, one that is confined to consideration of verbal behavior. This raises problems of its own, however, since "The capacity to express desires in language opens the floodgates of desire attribution" (Dennett, 1987a, p. 20). Dennett says little more about this means of belief attribution other than that these are beliefs the agent could not have had without language. As Webb points out, it would be useful here had Dennett made clear "just how we recognize utterances that call for desire attributions and how we know (based on what we hear) which desires to attribute." (p. 460). He notes however that Dennett's proposed method of intentional attribution: it allows for the attribution of desires on the basis of linguistic behavior. Dennett moreover is silent concerning any other attributions on the basis of witnessed behavior, but without some means of making these delimiting ascriptions of content, any attributions made in order to operationalize the intentional stance are likely to be implausible.

If the intentional stance is to be practically applicable as a means of accurate behavioral prediction, it is necessary that the process of intentional ascription be corrigible in the light of accruing information about the behavior of the system and its environment. There is no means to this end other than the incorporation of witnessed behavior. It is interesting that Webb adopts something closely akin to reasoning that is at the heart of radical behaviorism here. Ideally, he argues, only behavior that has actually been witnessed should be considered but this impracticable. For instance, a person who has never smoked cigarettes before may write on a shopping list "Carton of cigarettes": the attribution of intentionality here cannot depend on whether someone else reads the shopping list. It is thus necessary to consider therefore behavior that is only available in principle (Webb, 1994, p. 463). In radical behaviorist terms, the person making the list is a witness to his/her own behavior; it is immaterial that this opportunity is available only to him/her.

An important boundary condition that Webb introduces is that any behavior the intentional stance considers must be displayed at the surface of the system that is being predicted (Webb, 1994, p. 464). Neuronal activity cannot be brought in to solve problems of the stance: only external behavior is permissible. Using information about brain states would make the intentional stance a subset of the design stance and make impossible its intended capacity to identify a pattern of behavior more abstract that given by the design stance. Only behavior that systems display at their surface is thus admissible. This is witnessed behavior. Webb's initial plan is to "incorporate all behavioral evidence available in principle into the intentional stance. An intentional state is thus defined as whatever intentional state would be attributed on the basis of the intentional system's environment and exhibited behavior, where the 'exhibited behavior' is to include all and only the behavior which (actually) occurred prior to its attribution" (p. 464).

The import of Webb's analysis is that Dennett has shown no means by which the intentional stance can attribute intentionality on the basis of witnessed behavior. Webb suggests that in incorporating some such method, Dennett would reveal himself as a behaviorist, a designation he does not necessarily deny but which he claims to abhor. None of this impinges on the argument being pursued here. My reading of Dennett fully accepts the necessity of attributing intentionality on the basis of witnessed behavior; Webb's analysis is a useful corroboration. Social cognitive psychology has evolved its own method of incorporating both the contextual and intentional stances and provides a means of overcoming the problems Webb raises, at least on a practical level. The import of the remainder of this chapter is twofold: first, the program of social cognitive psychology is incapable of implementation without the prior use of the contextual stance and second, the methods evolved by social cognitivists can be usefully employed to provide one level of conceptual link between the extensional behavioral science and intentional cognitive psychology.

9.2.2 The attitude revolution

When Dennett first published *Content and Consciousness* in 1969, attitude psychology, which lies at the heart of social cognitive explanation, had apparently failed. Its subsequent effectiveness is due to cognitive psychologists' adopting the contextual stance as the means of providing the syntactic structure to which they can ascribe semantic content in order to predict behavior. The verbal measures of beliefs, attitudes, and intentions, which cognitive psychologists had employed and to which they attributed propositional content when using them indexically of mental constructs, simply failed to predict the behaviors to which they referred. Only by introducing elements of the contextual stance into their models have cognitivists been able to predict behavior.

Attitude research is nowadays staunchly cognitive in its theoretical orientation: it is a quest to predict behavior by identifying and understanding the mental structures and processes that allegedly underlie it, giving it shape and direction (Ajzen, 1987, 1988; Eagly & Chaiken, 1993; Fishbein & Ajzen, 1975, 2010). As such, it exhibits the intentional idiom, attributing to individuals the attitudes and other belief-based propositional content necessary to predict their actions. Attitude research presents an opportunity *nonpareil* to observe the intentional stance in operation in psychology. (Throughout this discussion of recent developments in attitude theory and research, it will be necessary to refer extensively to "attitudes" and "intentions," as the social psychologist does, in the sense of underlying mental structures and relationships. Attitudes and intentions in this sense are always intentional in the philosophical sense: they refer to something else, one always has an attitude *about* something else. A psychological attitude is, therefore, an example of a propositional attitude, as are several other belief-based constructs, which will be spoken of in the following account: subjective norms (SNs), intentions, perceived behavioral control (PBC), and so on. When I refer to the propositional attitudes per se I always employ that full term; talk simply of attitudes refers to the particular mental structures I have so designated here).

Careful examination of these developments in attitude research indicates that the ascription to intentional systems of propositional attitudes such as beliefs and intentions requires the antecedent interpretation of the system's behavior in terms of the contextual stance. That is, human behavior must first be conceptualized as due to the interaction of the current behavior setting and the system's learning history.

There has been a revolution in attitude research over the last three decades. Current emphases in attitude theory and research stem from the dire assessments of the evidence for attitude–behavior consistency published in the late 1960s and early 1970s. Wicker (1969) showed that early attitude research (from the 1930s to the 1960s) generally revealed positive but insipid relationships between attitudes and behaviors. The extent to which attitudinal variance accounted for behavioral variance was small indeed. Rather, as Fishbein (1972) noted, the evidence favored the prediction of attitudes from behavior rather than the expected position. In a judgment that was to foreshadow the role of specificity in future research, Fishbein registered that the relationships probed by earlier research were generally between global measures of attitude toward an object and very particular indices of behavior toward the object.

More recent work has generated much higher correlations for two of the attitude–behavior models, which will be described in greater detail later. A metaanalysis of studies using the theory of reasoned action undertaken by Sheppard, Hartwick, and Warshaw (1988) reported an average correlations between the *behavioral intentions* that are determined by these various cognitive variables and the *behaviors* to which they refer of 0.53; a more recent metaanalysis for this theory reported by Van den Putte (1993) found an average correlation of 0.62. In the case of the theory of planned behavior, Ajzen

(1991) reports, for a small selection of studies, an average multiple correlation of 0.71 between the cognitive variables and behavior. (Rather lower correlations have been observed, however, for both theories in a variety of contexts; see for instance Davies et al., 2002.) The amount of variance in behavior accounted for by variance in the prebehavioral variables posited in these models is thus (for the studies analyzed) within the approximate range of 25%−50%, a significant improvement on the typical level of "less than 10%" found by Wicker (1969). (For more recent results and analysis, see Ajzen & Cote, 2008).

The accurate prediction and explanation of behavior require an understanding of why this change has come about. This is not an easy task since, despite the increasing cognitivist rhetoric of those attempting to explain the results of such work, the underlying methodologies are increasingly behavioristic. Those methodologies are of two broad kinds. Some researchers (e.g., Fazio & Zanna, 1978a, 1978b, 1981) have sought a solution to the original problem of understanding the consistency between global attitude toward an object and specific behaviors toward that object. Others (e.g., Ajzen, 1988; Ajzen & Fishbein, 1980; Bagozzi & Warshaw, 1990; Fishbein & Ajzen, 1975) have concentrated on predicting specific behaviors from various combinations of equally specific measures of the reasoning involved in forming attitudes, reacting to social pressure, and assessing one's self-efficacy and one's prior behavior.

Fazio (1990) proposes that these approaches are complementary in that (1) the "global" approach deals with spontaneous attitude elicitation that requires little or no mental processing and that leads directly to action; hence, this approach is known as spontaneous processing theory and (2) the "reasoned" approach draws attention to the deliberation on the consequences of performing a behavior prior to forming an intention to do so; hence, deliberative theory. However, our interest is primarily that research on attitude−intention−behavior relationships conducted in both traditions leads to two conclusions: attitude research has actually pointed up the situational influences on behavior rather than shown that behavior's alleged cognitive precursors are its best predictors and attitude researchers increasingly measure respondents' behavioral histories in order to predict their behavior, though they conceptualize their measures and achievements in cognitive terms.

9.2.2.1 Spontaneous processing theory

Fazio (1986, p. 214) defines an attitude as involving "categorization of an object along an evaluative dimension": specifically, an attitude is an association between a given object and a given evaluation (Fazio, 1989. p. 155). The definition of attitude in terms of evaluation or affect is evidence of the propositional content ascribed to this construct. Spontaneous processing attitude theory (Fazio & Zanna, 1981) highlights how nonattitudinal factors are increasingly taken into consideration in the prediction of behavior from attitudes to objects. The variations in correlations between attitudes and behaviors depend on the variability in nonattitudinal factors from situation to situation, which is considerable. That is, nonattitudinal factors moderate the relationship of attitude toward an object and behavior toward that object (Eagly & Chaiken, 1993). Fazio's (1990) MODE model of the attitude−behavior process thus attempts to answer the question "When is attitude related to behavior?" rather than the more pervasive question "why?". MODE is an acronym for "motivation and opportunity as determinants." The model assumes that social behavior is substantially determined by the way in which the individual perceives the immediate situation in which the attitude object is presented as well as the way the object itself is perceived. Situations are generally ambiguous, and the individual's definition of any particular situation depends on how it is interpreted.

Behavior is guided by perceptions of the attitude object but also by perceptions of the situation in which it occurs: that setting is said to determine the event. For instance, behavior toward a particular person (attitude object) naturally depends on the individual's perception of him or her: but the style of that behavior will differ depending on whether the attitude object is encountered in his or her home, or a store, or at a party, or in church. "It is this definition of the event—perceptions that involve both the attitude object and the situation in which the object is encountered — that the model postulates to act as the primary determinant of an individual's behavior" (Fazio, 1986, p. 208).

"Spontaneous" attitude research draws attention to the conditions under which attitudes have been formed: whether by direct experience with the attitude object, the role of experience in the formation of object-evaluation, and the verbal rehearsal of evaluations prior to behavior. The methodological procedures emanating from the deliberative models are actually measuring learning histories under the guise of addressing cognitive influences. The findings of research conducted within this framework bear this out. Major emphasis is placed on how past behavior is implicated in attitudinal dynamics. The extent to which an attitude guides behavior depends on the manner of its formation. Attitudes formed from direct experience with the attitude object are expected to differ from those stemming from indirect experience (e.g., word of mouth, advertising) in terms of their capacity to predict behavior. Especially when they have to articulate an attitude, for example, to a researcher or to fill out a questionnaire, people draw on past experiences that "are organized and transformed in light of current contingencies" (Rajecki, 1982, p. 78). There is corroborative empirical evidence that the attitudes of people who have had direct experience with an attitude object (target) correlate moderately with subsequent attitude-relevant behaviors; attitudes where such experience is lacking correlate only weakly.

Attitude—behavior consistency is higher when the preceding sequence has been behavior-to-attitude-to-behavior, rather than when it has been simply attitude-to-behavior.

A second emphasis is the effect of experience on the efficacy of verbal behavior. Whether an attitude guides behavior depends also on the accessibility of the attitude from memory. Research indicates that (1) attitudes formed behaviorally lead to a stronger object-evaluation bond than those formed indirectly and are as a result more easily accessed from memory. (2) The difficulty people encounter in assessing their attitudes (their evaluations of an object) is overcome by engaging in behavior with the object or by observing their own behavior with it. (3) Information gained through behavior or behavioral observation is more trustworthy than that presented by another person or medium.

The influence of repeated verbal expression also receives emphasis. An attitude's strength is also increased through its repeated verbal expression, though repeated expression is also related to attitude polarization. Accessible attitudes are, moreover, activated automatically in the presence of the attitude stimulus—without conscious and volitional cognitive processing. Not surprisingly, therefore, the role of prior knowledge is also stressed. Prior knowledge about the attitude object increases attitudinal—behavioral consistency presumably because such knowledge is attained through direct experience. As will be documented, there is empirical evidence that such verbal repetition increases the chance that the evaluative behavior described as an attitude will become a self-instruction that guides further responding.

It is also most relevant that direct experience with the attitude object is accorded central significance. A feasible deduction from Fazio's demonstration of the significance of direct experience with the attitude object is that the consequences of relevant past behavior are responsible wholly or partly for the probability of current responding in the presence of the attitude object. Current behavior could then be explained as having come under the stimulus control of the attitude object, such control having been established through the reinforcement resulting from previous experience with the stimulus. In other words, the entire episode might be depicted as operant conditioning and investigation might be directed toward identifying the consequences of behavior that accounted for its future probability. However, the explanation that has predominated is cognitive: attitudes formed through direct experience are held to be more accessible from memory than those formed indirectly. And accessibility, measured as verbal response latency (that is the speed with which the attitude is activated or recalled in the presence of the attitude object), is hypothesized to be directly proportional to behavior change. The strength of an attitude, its capacity to influence behavior in the presence of the attitude object, increases with such structural attitude qualities as clarity, confidence, stability, and certainty (Albarracin & Johnson, 2018; Petty & Krosnick, 1995).

9.2.2.2 Deliberative theory

We have noted that some researchers have concentrated on predicting specific behaviors from various combinations of equally specific measures of the reasoning involved in forming attitudes, reacting to social pressure, and assessing one's self-efficacy and one's prior behavior. Each of these explanatory variables is assessed through the elicitation of respondents' beliefs, as the following brief account of the principal deliberative models—the theory of reasoned action and the theory of planned behavior—attests. (The most comprehensive account defense of these theories is to be found in Fishbein & Ajzen, 2010.)

In the case of the theory of reasoned action, reasoned behavior that is under the individual's volitional control is assumed to approximate intentions toward its performance (Fishbein & Ajzen, 1975). The theory of reasoned action holds that behavioral intentions are determined by two belief-based cognitions: (1) *attitude toward performing the target behavior*, is measured as the respondent's belief that a particular action will have a given outcome or consequence, weighted by his or her evaluation of that outcome. (2) *SN*, the respondent's perceptions of the evaluations that important social referents (significant others) would hold toward the respondent's performing the target action, weighted by the respondent's motivation to comply with them. SN is an attempt to capture the nonattitudinal influences on intention and, by implication, behavior. By permitting this consideration of perceived social pressure to enter the calculation of behavioral intentions, the theory takes account of some at least of the situational interventions that may reduce the consistency of the attitude—behavior sequence.

Consideration of the ways in which the components of the theory of reasoned action are disaggregated and measured by users of this method confirms both the propositional content of the underlying theory and the ways in which these components refer in practice to elements of behavior setting and learning history. *Attitude toward the act* is operationalized as "The person's beliefs that the behavior leads to certain outcomes and his evaluations of those outcomes. [Hence] [a]ccording to our theory, a person's attitude toward a behavior can be predicted by multiplying her evaluation of each of the behavior's consequences by the strength of her belief that performing the behavior will lead to that consequence and then summing the products for the total set of beliefs" (Ajzen & Fishbein, 1980, p. 8, 67). Sample measurement protocols are suggested in the box. The definitive guide remains (Ajzen & Fishbein, 1980, but see also the Appendix to Fishbein & Ajzen, 2010).

Sample measurement protocols for the theory of reasoned action and the theory of planned behavior

The measurement technique involves respondents' engaging in verbal behavior that rates the attitudinal behavior in question according to a small number of its consequences (those representing *salient* behavioral beliefs that have been ascertained in previous qualitative research). An individual's attitude toward a behavior (A_B) is directly proportional (α) to the sum of her beliefs (b) weighted by her subjective evaluation of the belief's attribute (Ajzen & Cote, 2008, p. 291):

$$A_B \alpha \sum b_i e_i \qquad (9.2)$$

In the case of the behavior: buy*ing organically grown vegetables*, and its context: *at your usual supermarket next time you shop for groceries*, the required behavior might be elicited thus (the example uses only two belief dimensions for ease of exposition—there would normally be three or four—and shows the reversal of the rating dimension). Hence, the statement,

Buying organic vegetables when I shop for groceries is ...

would be rated on semantic differential scales in terms of, say, (1) expensive–inexpensive and (2) environmentally harmful–environment friendly.

In order that the belief statements elicited in this way can be weighted by the individual's strength of expectation that the behavior will actually lead to the stated positive or negative consequence, the respondent will be asked a question such as, *How certain are you that buying organic vegetables will prove environmental friendly?* and will be asked to answer "Not at all certain", "Slightly certain", "Quite certain" or "Extremely certain." Verbal behavior of this kind requires experience in the form of a learning history, and it can be argued that this history is in fact what is being measured by means of this technique.

Similarly, SN is conceptualized and measured as a set of beliefs about what the respondent believes a significant other thinks about the respondent's performing the behavior in question. SN is directly proportional to the individual's normative beliefs (n) weighted by her motivation to comply with them (m) (Ajzen & Cote, 2008, p. 303):

$$SN \alpha \sum n_i m_i \qquad (9.3)$$

For example,

My partner thinks that I should...I should not buy organic vegetables,

the two polar opposites being separated by a semantic differential scale indicating the level of agreement with the statement. This is weighted by the respondent's motivation to comply with the perceived wishes of the significant other, elicited by an answer to a question such as:

In general, how much do you want to do what your partner thinks you should do?

Responses to this might vary from "Not at all" to "strongly."
Intentions are measured in a way that will by now be familiar:

(Continued)

> **(Continued)**
>
> *I will buy organic vegetables on my next shopping trip,*
>
> a statement that is rated on a semantic differential ranging from "Probable" to "Improbable."
>
> The theory of planned behavior incorporates an additional variable, *PBC*, in addition to the cognitive variables that form the theory of reasoned action (Ajzen, 1985; Fishbein & Ajzen, 2010). PBC is directly proportional to control beliefs (*e*) weighted by perceived power (*p*) (Ajzen, 1985; Fishbein & Ajzen, 2010):
>
> $$\text{PBC} \alpha \sum e_i p_i \tag{9.4}$$
>
> PBC is posited—along with attitude toward the act and SN—to determine behavioral intentions. Further, on those occasions when perceived and actual behavioral control coincide or are closely approximate, PBC is expected to exert a direct determinative influence on behavior. The theory thus applies to behaviors over which volitional control is limited. This is in contrast to the theory of reasoned action that is adamantly a theory for volitional behavior. Moreover, the extent to which PBC adds significantly to the prediction of intentions is apparent from Ajzen's (1991) analysis of the results of several studies employing his theory, which was mentioned in the text, which shows that the average multiple correlation was 0.71.
>
> *PBC* might be measured as a response to the question,
>
> *How much control do you have over the kinds of vegetables you buy?*
>
> with semantic differential responses ranging from "Complete control" to "Very little control."
>
> Another example would be
>
> *For me, to buy organic vegetables is*
>
> rated from "Very difficult" to "Very easy."
>
> Or,
>
> *If I wanted to, I could buy organic vegetables every time I shop,*
>
> rated from "Extremely likely" to "Extremely unlikely."

The reasoned approach indicates that in order to obtain high correlational consistency among attitude, intention, and behavior, these variables must be measured at identical levels of situational specificity. The first source of evidence concerns measurement specificity. The systematic processing group of attitude theories revolves around the belief that the degrees of specificity with which attitudinal and behavioral measures are each defined must be identical if high correlations are to be found between them. Generic attitude measures are therefore consistent with multiple-act measures of behavior toward the attitude object. It follows that the prediction of single acts is only likely to result from equally narrow measures of attitude, those that correspond exactly in level of specificity to the act to be predicted; those, moreover, that are framed as measures of the respondent's attitude toward performing that act in closely designated circumstances (Ajzen & Fishbein, 1980; Fishbein & Ajzen, 1975, 2010).

A second source of evidence is the quest for setting correspondence. Ajzen and Fishbein's (1977) analysis of numerous studies of attitudinal—behavioral consistency revealed that high correlations are probable only when the measures of attitude and behavior coincide with reference to the *target* toward which the action is to be directed, the precise *action* to be performed, the *context* in which the action would occur, and its *timing*. (These four provisos are sometimes summarized by the acronym TACT.) Evidence is finally available from the insistence on temporal contiguity. An important recognition was that measures of the cognitive precursors of attitude will be highly predictive only when there is maximal temporal contiguity of the behavioral and antecedent measures (Ajzen & Fishbein, 1980). The greater the temporal gap between attitude or intention and the behavior to which they refer, and hence the extent of situational intervention that potentially separates them, the lower will be their correlative consistency. It is the intention which *immediately* precedes behavior that is predictive.

The implication of the tight situational compatibility requiring measures of target behavior and its antecedent cognitive predictors (Ajzen & Fishbein, 1977) is that situational factors are highly significant for the correlational consistency of attitudes/intentions and behavior. Only when the situational influences governing both the prebehavioral and the behavioral variables are functionally equivalent are high correlations found. That the intertemporal period between prebehavioral and behavioral measures must be minimal if high correlations are to be found corroborates this view by pointing to the undesirability of unexpected situational demands that reduce the predictive value of measured intentions. Context and situation deserve a more central place in the explanation of behavior, and this is denied them by the partiality inherent in the preeminence of the cognitive paradigm among consumer researchers. The explanatory power of past behavior is frequently sufficient to make cognitive variables superfluous; a behavior analytic theory may be capable of explaining or interpreting the evidence on attitudinal—behavioral consistency in full; and in any case the reason for including a behaviorist perspective is to identify the consequences that past behavior has produced to account for the consistency of that prior responding and thus to use those consequences to predict future behavior.

This approach has proved successful in as much as the prediction of behavior, albeit under the specialized circumstances to which the theory applies, has been achieved. Hence, the technological achievement of the theory of reasoned action is that as long as its variables are measured under conditions maximally conducive to high correlations, which, as noted, refer to conditions of close situational correspondence, high correlations are usually obtained. However, the deficiencies of the theory of reasoned action identified by researchers all point up the importance of further incorporating behavior setting influences on an individual's behavior.

First among these is the disregard of behavioral outcomes. The theory of reasoned action predicts behavioral intentions and behaviors rather than the outcomes of behaviors: it would, for example, predict the likelihood of one's studying for a test, not of one's passing it (Sheppard et al., 1988). The amount of studying actually undertaken is under personal volitional control but whether one's hard studying leads to success in the test depends on factors that lie beyond that control: others in the household or library must cooperate, required books must be available at the right time, the necessary time and effort must have been invested in acquiring relevant study skills, to name but three. Even the individual who is strongly motivated and tries hard may find that circumstances may impede performance and achievement. The second deficiency stems from the recognition of uncompeting behaviors. The theory of reasoned action also concentrates on the prediction of single, specified behaviors that are not in competition with other behaviors. It thus avoids situations of choice within the class of intended behaviors or consequences.

The role of nonattitudinal influences in determining the incidence and consistency of behavior is the third source of deficiency. Most significantly, the theory of reasoned action has been criticized for not taking into consideration the full gamut of nonattitudinal personal and situational factors likely to influence the strength of the attitude–behavior relationship or to enhance the prediction of behavior. The authors of the theory of reasoned action are adamant that behavior is determined by behavioral intention and that all contributing influences are subsumed by the two elements that determine it: attitude toward performing the target act and SN with reference to performing that act. Yet this principle of sufficiency has proved inaccurate in empirical work that has incorporated additional factors to increase the predictability of intentions and/or behavior. Factors not comprehended by the theory have been found to improve the predictability of behavior including personal norm; self-identity; self-schemas; size and content of consideration set; availability of relevant skills, resources, and cooperation; action control; past behavior; amount of reasoning during intention formation; perceived control/confidence; and attitude functions.

Finally, deficiencies of the theory of reasoned action become apparent when one considers skills, resources, and cooperation. Behavior that requires one or more of these items in order to be enacted is especially problematical. Much behavior requires all three, yet restricting the theory of reasoned action to behavior that is volitional means it requires only motivation on the part of the individual. Studies that have supported the model have dealt with only simple behaviors that require little if anything by way of resources and skills. Fishbein and Ajzen argue that such considerations have an effect on intention and thus were taken care of in their model (Foxall, 2005).

The theory of reasoned action (Fishbein & Ajzen, 1975) probes respondents' learning histories by asking them to identify and evaluate (1) the utilitarian consequences of behaving in a particular manner and referring to this as an "attitude" and (2) the individual's socially determined rule-governed behavior (SN). The theory of planned behavior (Ajzen, 1985) adds to these a measure of how successful the respondent expects to be; this variable delineates personal rule-formation and -following but is cognitively construed as "PBC." This does not mean, however, that cognitively framed propositions can be simply "translated away" into extensional terminology. Although some antecedents of Fishbein and Ajzen's work can be found in that of the behavioristically inclined Dulany (1968), their theory is unquestionably cognitive. The suggestion has been made by Schnaitter (1999) that a sound starting point for behaviorists' taking intentionality into consideration would be (in my words, not his) to parse intentional statements in the functional terms suggested by Skinner's *Verbal Behavior*. Hence, in the statement, "I believe it is going to rain," an autoclitic modifies the tact that lies at the heart of the sentence: "'I believe' is a response *following from* the tact 'It is going to rain'" (Schnaitter, 1999, p. 243). It need not, therefore, be the case, he argues, that "I believe" is a "response directed *toward* the tact," which would be the intentional interpretation. All of the statements used in the measurement of the variables contained in the theories of reasoned action and planned behavior can be translated in this manner.

Attitudinal beliefs were measured in the example given earlier in terms of responses to the statement, "Buying organic vegetables is expensive/inexpensive." Behavior analysis can provide a nonintentional understanding of what is going on here, which makes clearer the role of the contextual stance in the elicitation and use of these responses. Following Schnaitter's (1999) methodology for providing a behavior analytical interpretation of intentional sentences, the verbal behavior of a respondent to this kind of inquiry is a kind of tacting or naming and the stated rule is a track (Zettle & Hayes, 1982). From this, it is possible to derive an interpretation of the individual's relevant learning history since, according to the logic of radical behaviorism, it would be difficult to understand how a person could be capable of engaging in tacting/naming and tracking of this sort without a behavioral repertoire based on a learning history that is the basis of his or her answers. SN, measured in the example in terms of responses to the statement, "My partner thinks that I should/should not buy organic vegetables," can be similarly expressed in the nonintentional terms of manding and pliance, and these verbal responses can once again be attributed to an appropriate learning history.

A statement used to elicit behavioral intention, such as "I will buy organic vegetables on my next shopping trip," can be construed as eliciting a tact, which is modified by the autoclitic "I intend to" or "I will" (the present tense of "to will" (which is a propositional attitude in the intentional interpretation) rather than the future tense of "to be"). Such a locution expresses an augmental (there is no corresponding functional element in the verbal behavior of a speaker). The augmental is "I *will* buy organic vegetables!". There is nothing intentional about this expression: the response "I will" follows from the tact; it is not directed toward it. Finally, the verbal responses to which social cognitive psychologists attribute the mental process or state they call PBC is explicable in behavior analytical terms without resort to propositional content: as response such as "I believe that I can achieve this" is simply a tact "I can achieve this" modified by the autoclitic "I believe." The motivating force with which this is held and expressed may transform the expression into an augmental.

In itself, this approach is entirely consistent with principles of behaviorist interpretation, especially as they are evinced in Skinner's (1957) *Verbal Behavior*, which concentrates on the verbal behavior of the speaker, and in recent work on the verbal (rule-following) behavior of the listener (e.g., Hayes, 1989). It is valuable in so far as it demonstrates that a consistent interpretation of verbal behavior is feasible that is devoid of propositional content; it demonstrates the capacity of a functional analysis of verbal behavior to cope with this aspect of language on its own level. As such it is on a par with the reasoning that underlies the application of the intentional stance. But it has a drawback due to its provenance: whatever its persuasive impact on intentionalists, it may seem less than plausible to behavior analysts on account of the impossibility of subjecting it to an experimental analysis or other empirical means of generating data consistency with its premises and conclusions. Like much behaviorist interpretation in the mold of *Verbal Behavior*, it is plausible to those who accept the basic principles of behavior analysis. But can behaviorism satisfactorily handle intentionality in this way?

The answer has to be that while Schnaitter's procedure maintains the extensional consistency of a behaviorist account of this aspect of language (or verbal behavior), it does not deal with the entire range of human experience available to psychology. Specifically, it does not handle the personal level of analysis. In this regard, it is similar to the broader approach to explanation of which it is part. Nor does it account for *how* rules delivered verbally at one time influence behavior much later and in different circumstances. Nor yet for how the same rule can produce vastly different responses, different rules the same behavior. Parsing sentences functionally will not do.

9.2.2.3 The indispensability of an extensional model

The tight situational correspondence between measures of intentionality and measures of behavior that is essential for high BI:B correlations in the deliberative models makes an underlying extensional model of consumer choice essential to a proper intentional model. The theories of reasoned action and planned behavior implicitly include the understanding that is inherent in the extensional model of consumer choice. Attitude toward performing the specific consumer behavior in question (A_B) is measured in terms of a verbal assessment of the functional attributes of purchasing and consuming the product, that is, its utilitarian reinforcement as determined by prior consumer behavior. SN is measured by a verbal assessment of the social consequences of consumption, which reflects prior consumer behavior and contemplation of the interpersonal effects of past and future purchasing, that is, its informational reinforcement. PBC is measured by a verbal assessment of the consumer's felt self-efficacy, which again manifests prior consumer behavior and reflection on it. The verbal assessments are all of elements which inhere in the extensional model. Responses to questions eliciting these assessments consist, of course, in verbal *behavior* but that is no barrier to their being interpreted cognitively, as they are in the deliberative models. Figs. 9.5 and 9.6 summarize the argument.

9.3 Consumer heterophenomenology

9.3.1 The nature of heterophenomenology

Heterophenomenology is

> the neutral *path leading from objective physical science and its insistence on the third-person point of view, to a method of phenomenological description that can (in principle) do justice to the most private and ineffable subjective experiences, while never abandoning the methodological principles of science* (Dennett, 1991a, 1991b, p. 72).

This seems uncontroversial as a practical methodology for turning knowledge-by-acquaintance into knowledge-by-description. However, in line with his thinking earlier reviewed, Dennett argues that it is possible to study

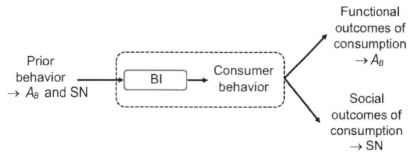

FIGURE 9.5 The theory of reasoned action captures the variables inherent in the extensional model of consumer choice. *AB*, Attitude toward a behavior; *BI*, behavioral intention; *SN*, subjective norm.

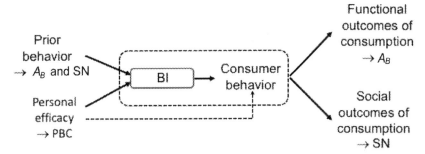

FIGURE 9.6 The theory of planned behavior captures the variables inherent in the extensional model of consumer choice. *AB*, Attitude toward a behavior; *BI*, behavioral intention; *PBC*, perceived behavioral control; *SN*, subjective norm.

all there is to know about first-person consciousness at the level of third-person analysis without leaving a significant residue (Dennett, 2005, pp. 29–30). Dennett's, again uncontroversial, conception of scientific method as third-person analysis based on intersubjective agreement on terminology and observations cannot access directly human conscious experience. Heterophenomenology, then, sets out the steps required to for obtaining such a third-person understanding of the contents of consciousness which are directly apprehended only subjectively, that is, in the first-person terms of the individual who is conscious of them (Dennett, 1982, 1991a, 1991b). The essential character of this experience is its *privacy*. The task, if such experience is to be of scientific worth, is to tap into this experience, given that the individual's account (say, in verbal expression) is not necessarily accurate. Heterophenomenology provides a *bridge* between the subjective experience or consciousness of the individual and the physical sciences (Dennett, 2005). At one end, the bridge must be securely affixed to the objective or third-person perspective pursued by the physical sciences in its conventional spheres of operation. The causation implied or invoked is that of standard conservative physics, or we might say, the extensional mode of explanation that is central to scientific explanation (Dennett, 1969).

The practice of heterophenomenology would begin with "recorded raw data," the transcribed verbal behavior of the subject, that is, her description of her first-person thoughts, expressed in words and then transformed into data for heterophenomenological investigation. This transcription is itself an act of interpretation since it transforms sounds into syntactical sentences. It could also be that the subject responds to the investigator's instructions by means of key-presses (perhaps on a computer keyboard): these are then transformed into speech acts. However they are obtained, these speech acts constitute a *text* for further, third-personal, linguistic analysis, similar in principle to the text of a novel which is subjected to literary critique.

To clarify the nature of the fundamental data of heterophenomenology, we must note Dennett's (2005) response to Levine's (1994) argument that these data ought to consist in actual conscious experiences rather than beliefs, judgments, or other intentional expressions *about* those experiences. Dennett replies by proposing four levels from "raw data" to "heterophenomenological worlds":

1. conscious experiences
2. beliefs about these conscious experiences
3. verbal expressions of these beliefs
4. utterances

Dennett asks which of these represents the "primary data." For the heterophenomenologist, he says, it is the sounds or utterances, (4). But these data can be interpreted via speech acts, (3), to beliefs about experiences, (2). These, he maintains, are the primary *interpreted* data, the QED, "organized into heterophenomenological worlds, for a science of consciousness" (Dennett, 2005, pp. 44–45). It is not possible, however, to go back as far as (1), that is, to locate our primary data in conscious experience itself; for, if (1) exceeds (2), indicating that the subject has conscious experiences she is not aware she has, these experiences are inaccessible to her exactly as they are to anyone else; and if (2) exceeds (1), indicating that she believes she has conscious experiences that she does not in fact have, then the beliefs are what has to be explained rather than the nonexisting experiences. Therefore (2), beliefs about one's subjective conscious experience, emerges as the "maximal set of primary data."

Given that conscious experience (1) is ruled out as data for scientific analysis on the grounds that it is simply not empirically available for third-person analysis, the closest a scientific investigation of consciousness can get to the raw primary data is by reconstructing what the subject believes about her subjective experience (2). This believing, when it is the unreconstructed mentalizing of the individual, is also a first-person occurrence, also not publicly available. But the subject is able to give it verbal expression (3) and, in the course of a heterophenomenological investigation, to make utterances based on it (4). The heterophenomenologist takes (4), the basic recorded data, and employs the intentional stance to interpret them as expressions of beliefs and to infer the subject's beliefs themselves from the expressions. This is the heterophenomenological methodology. The subject describes what *seems* to be going on her consciousness (on which she is the authority), not what is actually going on (on which she is not). She knows as no other what it is like to be herself.

Chapter 2, *A kind of consilience*, pointed out that the intentional stance requires that, in order to account for the behavior of an intentional system, the investigator must ascribe to it the beliefs, desires, and other intentions that enable the behavior to be predicted (Dennett, 1987a, 1987b).

An intentional system is any entity the behavior of which is predictable by the ascriptions of such intentionality. The beliefs and desires that are ascribed for this purpose are those the system "ought" to have, given its history and its current circumstances. In the terms of the BPM, these are its learning history and its current behavior setting. As we have noted several times, all there is to believing is to be predictable by the intentional stance. The point of the interpretive phase of the heterophenomenological enterprise is, therefore, to reconstruct the intentional structure that would be consistent with the utterances made by the subject. Dennett is careful to note that even in the process of transcribing these utterances into sentences (typified by but not limited to the work of an audio-stenographer transcribing a recorded voice) interpretation is taking place: the utterances are being organized into sentences that follow a particular syntactic logic; perhaps at some stage sentence structure is altered to make the utterances more intelligible (to whom?); perhaps the sentences themselves are later reordered to construct or preserve a narrative. But the application of the intentional stance requires another form of interpretation: the assignment of the beliefs and desires necessary to predict the behavior of the intentional system, beliefs and desires that are judged (by whom and by what criteria?) to be those the system "ought to have" (as determined by whom and on what basis?) given its history and circumstances. I propose here that the bases for the ascription of intentionality are twofold: a pattern of molar operant behavior and an underlying neurophysiological foundation. Before I say more about the rationale for this methodology, let me examine the form it would need to take.

Of course, if we were to know the precise operant learning history of a subject, together with her neurophysiology, we would have no difficulty in constructing an intentional framework within which to interpret her behavior. This is an unlikely prospect, however. Rather, we are thrown back on a general understanding of the kinds of behavior and its outcomes that the person is characterized by and its neurophysiological underpinning. In the case of the social and economic behavior of consumers, however, we have an advantage. We are aware of the general factors toward which such behavior is directed and the environmental stimuli that shape and maintain that behavior. They are the very subject of the BPM and the empirical research that it has inspired. We also have an understanding of the neurophysiological bases of these behavior patterns, the role of neuronal firing in the selection of behavior in regard to economic goals and behavioral norms. Knowing the potential and the limits of the methodology, we can now say more of its rationale. The point is not that we can pinpoint the exact causal texture of the consumer behavior the interpretation of which preoccupies us: rather, we can use behavioral science and neuroeconomics to delimit the scope of our intentional interpretations of behavior, which otherwise might grow Topsy-like into the unfalsifiable generalizations of the cognitive.

9.3.2 Consumer heterophenomenology

Dennett argues that the intentional stance is inevitable in transforming heterophenomenological data into interpretations. I would add that the content of such ascribed intentionality (in the context of consumer choice in which we are operating) is provided in the context of consumer choice by the structural variables of the BPM. Moreover, as the model proceeds from a purely extensional portrayal of consumer choice through the intentional and cognitive portrayals, it acquires more intentionally based constructs in terms of which the heterophenomenological interpretation should proceed such as that of the *symbolic consumer situation* and *symbolic reinforcement* (Foxall, 2013). The following account does not present a comprehensive example of consumer heterophenomenology but aims to show how such a study would need to adhere to the requirements of interpretive practice on the basis of consumer behavior analysis.

The distinctive mode of heterophenomenological interpretation may be illustrated by reference to research which sought to test the BPM by investigating the emotional reactions elicited by descriptions of consumer situations based on the structural components of the model described earlier. The research has been briefly described in Section 9.2, and more detailed analyses are available in Foxall (2017b) and Foxall et al. (2012). A comprehensive analysis in terms of heterophenomenology requires a four stages research exercise, each stage of which would complement the others. The necessary analyses are as follows:

1. *A statistical analysis of aggregated results.* This would proceed in terms of a third-person investigation of the ways in which consumer respondents react to written scenarios of consumer situations that reflect the levels of utilitarian and informational reinforcement and the scope of the consumer behavior setting as defined by the BPM. The responses would be cast in terms of answers to psychometric measures of the emotional dimensions appropriate to testing hypotheses about the consumer situations. The results would be interpreted according to the model's expectations of consumer choice in these various situations. Results for a large sample of consumers would be aggregated and subjected to statistical analyses.

    This has been accomplished. The responses to scenarios of consumer situations, which embody sources of high versus low utilitarian reinforcement, high versus low informational reinforcement, and relatively open/closed consumer behavior settings in terms of the emotional reactions of consumer respondents allow the process to be illustrated (Foxall, 1997b). The scenarios depict each of the eight contingency categories shown in Fig. 9.2. The psychometric instruments employed to elicit consumers' reactions are the scales for the assessment of *pleasure, arousal,* and *dominance* devised and tested by Mehrabian and Russell (1974). The working hypothesis of the studies we have conducted in several cultural contexts, two languages and for a wide range of consumer scenarios, was that pleasure would be more strongly reported for situations embodying higher levels of utilitarian reinforcement, arousal for situations embodying higher levels of informational reinforcement and stronger dominance for more open settings. In the eight studies, we have now conducted thus far, these hypotheses have been supported. Fig. 9.3 shows the results.

2. *An individual-level analysis of a single respondent member of this sample.* This would still entail using the psychometric measure of emotional reactions. The verbal responses of this consumer would be interpreted according to the model from which the hypotheses in (1) were derived. Individual-level results could also be interpreted in terms of the results gained from (1).
3. *An individual-level interpretation of the verbal behavior of a single consumer* (i) requested to respond ad lib to each of the scenarios presented in (1) in terms of his/her first-person experience of the situations depicted. This would enable a wider range of verbal responses to be sampled than those made available in the psychometric measures.
4. *An individual-level interpretation of the verbal behavior of a single consumer* (ii) requested to respond ad lib in describing their subjective experience of whatever consumer situations they choose to speak about. This is probably closest to the spirit of heterophenomenology since it imposes the fewest interviewer-defined categories on the respondent.

From the point of view of the heterophenomenological method, the verbal behavior provided by each respondent, when properly transcribed, provides a third-person account of the first-person feelings and experiences that that person felt on reviewing the stimuli presented in each scenario. The results summarized in Fig. 9.3 are aggregated for statistical analysis and ease of presentation but the analyses to which methods (2)–(4) refer could be undertaken for each of the consumer respondents in turn at the individual level. The pattern of responding revealed by the aggregate analysis (1) might provide a means of interpreting the verbal behavior of the individual respondent but the extent to which this is feasible or desirable is as yet an open question. Similarly, the information gained in the more interpretive analyses (2)–(4) might provide important insight into the actual experiences of consumers and allow the scope of the statistical patterns revealed by (1) to be more accurately assessed. The relationship between (1) and (2)–(4) is that of quantitative social science to qualitative.

Now, the advantage of conducting this multistage research is that the quantitative stage (1) allows us to compare the content of the propositional attitudes employed by individual respondents in the later stages with that which a psychometric study imposes by regulating the range of responses the consumer is permitted. This is especially so with respect to the most nebulous stage (4) in which the consumer is seeking to reveal his/her beliefs, desires, emotions, and perceptions in the context of any experience as a consumer he/she chooses to speak about.

Are the categories on which the psychometric measures are based those in terms of which the consumer normally thinks when formalizing his/her prior behavior? Do the settings he/she chooses to speak of resemble those scenarios selected on the basis of the BPM's contingency categories (Fig. 9.2)? Do consumers naturally think in terms of utilitarian and informational reinforcement, the functional and social/symbolic benefits provided, in describing their consumption experiences? Stages (2) and (3) facilitate a closer comparison of heterophenomenologically revealed consumer experience with the results of the psychometric work since they are based on greater situational continuity of the imagined scenarios. There is no ultimate need to confine the experimental stimuli to prewritten consumption scenarios, of course; the possibility arises of obtaining scripts that serve as texts for further analysis actually in the consumption situations populated by consumers.

The literary critique that is the methodology of the analysis of plays or novels or other written works is in my view not sufficient for the heterophenomenological analysis of texts produced by stages (2)–(4). In the case of consumer behavior, we can draw upon a much broader field of knowledge as our interpretive base, a functional model of consumer choice, which can be subjected to empirical test by means of the third-person methodology of science, as well as a third-person description of the first-person experience of consumers that is as close as we are likely to get to the subjective mentality of consumption.

9.3.3 Heterophenomenology in the context of Intentional Behaviorism

The situations of explanation in which the imperatives of intentionality hold—where the continuity/discontinuity of behavior cannot be related appropriately to the discriminative and reinforcing stimuli required to fulfill the requirements of the three-term contingency, where the personal level of interpretation becomes necessary, and where behavioral interpretations must be delimited—are especially relevant to these heterophenomenological considerations. The extensional model of consumer behavior depicted in Fig. 9.1 is insufficient to cope with these requirements and Intentional Behaviorism has been proposed as a methodology that can take them fully into account by responsibly ascribing intentionality. Although it is beyond the scope of this section to provide a complete account of the methodology of Intentional Behaviorism (see, for instance, Foxall, 2007a, 2007b, 2008, 2009), I should like to illustrate the relevance to it of this discussion of heterophenomenology by reference to the derivation of appropriate intentional idioms.

The schedule-insensitive behavior of many human adults on matching tasks can be explained by the concurrent schedules of reinforcement in operation, as was noted in Section 5.2.2. If, in phase 1 of an experiment, pressing key A is reinforced every 10 seconds as long as at least one press has been made and pressing key B once every 20 seconds as long as at least one press has been made, then we can predict according to the matching law that the participant will allocate 66.6% of responses to key A and 33.3% to B. In addition, he/she will obtain similar proportions of reward, respectively, from each key. Similar results are obtained for human and nonhuman animals. But if, in phase 2 of the experiment, the schedules are modified so that different periods must elapse before responding receives reinforcement, nonhumans adapt quickly to the new schedule while human participants tend to retain the former response pattern. We cannot explain humans' insensitivity to the altered schedules by reference to the discriminative and reinforcing stimuli now in operation since their behavior is by definition not influenced by them. The sole explanatory factor within the scope of orthodox radical behaviorism is the private events (thoughts and feelings) that are a central, even defining, element in this philosophy of psychology. The rules that participants devise for themselves to comply with the schedules in force during phase 1 of the experiment and that are enshrined in their thoughts are held to be carried over to the new situation defined by phase 2 and to lead the individual to continue the behavior pattern that was reinforced in phase 1 but not phase 2.

An alternative strategy of explanation might be to maintain that it is the individual's learning history that carries over from phase 1 to phase 2 that he/she is constrained by previous reinforcement patterns to repeat the behavior under the new stimulus conditions.

Neither of these explanations is acceptable within a science of behavior because each deals in unobservables that cannot enter either an experimental or correlational analysis. Any statements about the verbal rule-formulations that entered into the decision-making of an experimental participant are mere fabrications, untestable conjectures, and explanatory fictions. Similarly, any appeal to a learning history that is not empirically available is not an entity that can enter a scientific explanation. They are speculations the purpose of which is to save the theory on which the accompanying explanation of behavior rests. These are precisely the sorts of explanatory fiction that behaviorists such as Skinner sought to eliminate from scientific inquiry. The fact that they proceed in the terminology of behavior analysis may seduce the reader into thinking that they do not "appeal to events taking place somewhere else, at some other level of observation, described in different terms, and measured, if at all, in different dimensions" (Skinner, 1953, p. 193). In fact, they contravene Skinner's strictures on every count. Resort to private verbal behavior or to an unobserved learning history is necessarily an appeal to otherwise-located events, observed by who knows whom, and discriminable only in different dimensions. It would be intellectually dishonest to provide accounts of this kind simply to prop up the radical behaviorist ideology of explanation or to appeal to some form of "action-at-a-distance" to fill in the gaps that scientific observation is unable to fill. The fact of the matter is that the behavior cannot be explained in terms of the extensional language that is the hallmark of behaviorist psychology and perhaps its very raison d'être.

More satisfactory is to acknowledge the explanatory gap that arises when the stimuli responsible for a behavior pattern cannot be identified using intentional language to account for the behavior. But how is such an interpretation to be constructed and justified?

The construction of an interpretation in intentional terms depends on establishing how a pattern of behavior that *is* amenable to explanation in operant terms (because the antecedent and consequent stimuli that control the behavior and their relationships to the behavior can be identified) could be understood in terms of the putative desires, beliefs, emotions, and perceptions that need to be ascribed to account for its emergence and persistence. So, the behavior of an adult human participant in a matching experiment could be interpreted in terms of his desire to achieve successful outcomes, his belief that this could be achieved by pressing keys A and B in a particular sequence, his feelings of pleasure, arousal and dominance on achieving a winning outcome, and his perception of the efficacy of the keys pressed in producing rewards at a particular rate. Yes, these desires, beliefs, emotions, and perceptions amount to explanatory fictions but, faute de mieux, we have no alternative to employing them, given the absence of any means to ascribe the behavior to observable contingencies of reinforcement. To ascribe the schedule-insensitive behavior of the matching participant to the contingencies that were obtained in phase 1 would not square with the influence of the contingencies obtaining in phase 2 to which he/she is currently subject.

This strategy takes a pattern of behavior that is as close as can be achieved to the pattern to be explained and extrapolates an intentional interpretation from the former to the latter. The behavior that is the subject of the extrapolated interpretation must be consistent with selection by consequences at the levels of (1) natural selection and (2) operant conditioning.

1. The first criterion seeks a rationale for the interpreted behavior in the general neurophysiology of the individual. This is not the same as saying that his/her behavior is *caused by* neuronal activity: only that the organism would have evolved in such a way as to acquire a neuronal system that behaves consistently with the behavior pattern being interpreted. I have in mind here the formation and operation of reward prediction errors, the release of dopamine as a preparation for reinforced behaviors,

the further reward of reinforced behaviors through the experience of emotion, and so on. An important demonstration in our work is therefore that the consumer behaviors we are investigating are rewarded by emotional feelings. Rolls's (1999) theory of emotion provides an underlying rationale for the necessary links between emotion and reinforcement. Rolls proposes that any reinforcing stimuli present in the extra-individual environment can act as an eliciting stimulus to generate corresponding emotions (Foxall, 2011).
2. To reach this level of corroboration it is necessary to determine that the behavior in question is amenable to reinforcement; hence, the requirement that selection by consequences be demonstrated by showing that the behavior is subject to operant conditioning. Operant conditioning is determined by applying the correlational law of effect (Baum, 1973) to the molar behavior pattern observed during the period when the contingencies of reinforcement can be ascertained (phase 1 in the matching experiment t). The purpose of determining this is that an intentional interpretation of behavior that is under contingency control can be logically extended to that for which contingency control is not obvious, that is, similar behavior that is interpreted because its explanation is not possible in view of the lack of observable contingencies.

This interpretation is broadly similar to that obtained in the case of consumers' emotional reactions to various consumption environments by means of psychometric analysis. At least it is as close as we can get to understanding the behavior of consumers in extensional terms and constructing an intentional interpretation that fits the "facts" so established. However, useful as this may be when extensional analysis is no longer possible, it is corrigible through the use of heterophenomenological methods (2)–(4). The possibility of reconstructing the consumer's actual experience of decision-making by eliciting his/her desires, beliefs, emotions, and perceptions by heterophenomenology adds immensely to the warrant of assertibility we can assume as interpreters of behavior.

Moreover, this example of a behavioral situation requiring interpretation that goes beyond the explanation of which the three-term contingency alone is capable illustrates the three imperatives of intentionality: the fundamental problem is one of accounting for the continuity of behavior in the absence of supporting stimuli, be they antecedent or subsequent to the behavior; this necessitates a personal-level interpretation based on intentional language; and finally, the range of interpretation invoked is limited by the scrupulous use of intentional language rather than explanatory fictions in the form of invented learning histories, private verbal behavior or rule-governance. Although this example is drawn from experimental analyses of behavior, its invitation to interpret behavior intentionally is also a common feature of consumer choice; for example, when a new brand is incorporated into the consumer's consideration set in the absence of prior experience with it (Foxall, 2007, 2008).

9.4 Endnote

Social cognitive psychology clearly cannot do without the contextual stance any more than it can avoid the intentional. But equally, radical behaviorist interpretation is incomplete on the level of explanation (though not necessarily prediction) by virtue of its attempt to ignore intentionality. Indeed, an extensional operant interpretation of behavior raises three difficulties for a comprehensive psychology of complex human behavior: the accommodation of what Dennett designates the personal level of analysis, providing an account of the factors responsible for behavioral continuity, and dealing with the problem of equifinality and the need to delimit operant accounts of complex human behaviors. The problem that arises in connection with the personal level of analysis is that neither physiological theories (which operate at a subpersonal level) nor environment-behavior theories (which operate at a superpersonal level) capture what the person as a whole knows (what pain is, for instance). In the case of behavioral continuity, the problem is that radical behaviorism lacks a mechanism to account for the continuity of behavior between situations and over time. Continuity is sought in the discriminative and other setting stimuli that are constant from setting to setting. This is problematic in accounting for such phenomena as generalization and discrimination. Finally, the problem stemming from considerations of equifinality and delimitation is that of ambiguity surrounding the behavioral response enacted, the precise discriminative stimuli that should be held responsible for it, and the particular consequences that should be implicated in its shaping and maintenance.

These problems may be examined in relation to three approaches to radical behaviorist interpretation, each of which illustrates a particular difficulty. First, Skinner's solution to the problem of providing an extra-laboratorial account of behavior is to assume that such behavior is determined by the consequences of previous behavior of a similar kind. Skinner seeks to avoid teleology by concentrating on history. Hence, the person gazing at his desk, moving papers to look underneath them, is according to Skinner "looking for his glasses." He can say this only because the last time he behaved in this way he came across them. His knowledge of what he is doing is gained from the same source as our knowledge of what he is doing: external observation. Second, Hayes' solution is to define in greater depth the stimulus basis of the behavior setting by showing how stimuli transfer their functions one to another by participating in relational frames. Third, Rachlin's solution is to claim that the causes of behavior are its final consequences, the effects it has on the environment, and these are nested within each other or to change the metaphor spreading out as do the ripples on a pond when a pebble is thrown into it. Each element of the contextual stance—history, behavior setting, and consequences—is thus explored. In examining them, there is no intention to criticize the approaches to radical behaviorist interpretation, which are used to exemplify each of the problems of interpretation and the solutions offered by an intentional framework. Indeed, the analysis strengthens the position of each as an approach to extensional behavioral science. The aim is only to draw attention to the role of intentionalism in order to enhance their explanatory contribution.

Dennett's IST is subject in his system to critical review through the medium of its predictive validity, the intentional behaviorist research program is based on the belief that such prediction can be at best somewhat nonspecific in its referential purview by which I mean likely to proceed in terms of the testing of hypotheses that are so general as to be difficult to disconfirm. The intentional behaviorist research strategy overcomes this to a degree by insisting on an account of economic behavior based on extensional behavioral science prior to the formulation of an intentional interpretation. This means that the intentional component is guided by an empirically justified knowledge base and also, therefore, constrained by an independently attained body of knowledge. Dennett's scheme also proposes that the ability of the intentional constructs generated through the operations of SPCP will become part of psychological theories and thereby subject to further empirical validation. The major vehicle for the evaluation of the intentional interpretation in Intentional Behaviorism is through an assessment of its consistency with cognitive psychologies, which seek to explain mental structure and functioning. This may lead to empirical investigations, which derive from considerations raised by these psychologies, but the intentional behaviorist research program currently lacks means by which the empirical testing of hypotheses generated directly by the intentional interpretation might occur. While the investigation of economic behavior based on extensional behavioral science continues to refine the theoretically minimalist knowledge base, this process is independent of the intentional interpretation stage of the research program. Although the intentional interpretation may be examined critically in light of the findings of cognitive psychology, it does not eventuate in its own right in the kind of empirical investigation that marks the psychological sciences. Chapter 10, *Grounding intentionality*, proposes a solution to this problem through the possibility that each of the cognitive psychologies on which grounding intentionality rests is related to an economic methodology that can provide a more exacting appraisal. Hence, neuroeconomics, picoeconomics, and operant behavioral economics present themselves as potential links to a program of empirical and interpretive testing.

Chapter 10

Grounding intentionality

Chapter Outline

10.1 Evaluating the intentional interpretation 221
10.2 Janus-variables and valuation 225
10.3 Relating the levels of exposition 229
    10.3.1 Micro-cognitive psychology as a basis for picoeconomic interaction 229
    10.3.2 Picoeconomic analysis: the determination of V_2 236
    10.3.3 Macro-cognitive psychology as a basis for picoeconomic interaction 247

This chapter represents the culmination of the preceding analyses and the findings of the intentional behaviorist research program. It first summarizes the approach taken to the evaluation of the intentional interpretation, going on to introduce the idea of Janus-variables and the candidacy for this status of personal valuation of the corps (Section 10.1). Next, it turns to the question of how levels of exposition can be related one to another. In doing so, it proposes the concept of Janus-variables in relation to processes of valuation at the various levels of exposition (Section 10.2). It develops picoeconomic analysis in the context of the valuation of competing reinforcers at different times and goes on to consider the relevance of micro-cognitive psychology to the strategic interaction of picoeconomic interests within the individual and the influence of the outcome thereof on the rate at which the consumer discounts the future in economic and social decision-making (Section 10.3). Section 10.3 continues by applying insights from consumer behavioral economics (CBE) to the analysis of picoeconomic interests, employing the concept of bilateral contingency, originally developed in the context of corporate relations, to understand the processes of intrapersonal evaluation and decision-making.

10.1 Evaluating the intentional interpretation

Chapter 2, *A kind of consilience*, alluded to the problem that the cognitive psychologies employed in Intentional Behaviorism to evaluate and substantiate the intentional interpretation lack a direct empirical component, that is, one that relates specifically to the verification of an intentional interpretation.

Dennett's three kinds of intentional psychology scheme evaluates the IST level interpretation of the idealized intentional system according to its predictive success. The IST is also, ideally, confronted with empirical rigor in the research program of subpersonal cognitive psychology (SPCP) that seeks the variables of psychological theories in the *illata* that comprise physical entities, such as neurons, that are intentionally characterized. Intentional Behaviorism, however, has hitherto sought to provide its justification of the intentional interpretations it generates in the cognitive theories to which the intentional constructs in which they are couched belong, on the grounds that intentionality-based predictions are likely to be so vague as to be easily supported by observation and, therefore, unlikely to clinch the predictive validity of the intentional interpretation (Foxall, 2016b). Dennett also links the IST and SPCP phases of his research strategy by means of the ready transferability of intentional idioms from the personal to the subpersonal level, a move we have a priori outlawed on the grounds that it invites the mereological fallacy. The possibility of biconditionals was, equally, judged to be an unlikely solution to the need to link the levels of exposition entailed in the explanation of human economic behavior. However, the problem of empirically embedding the intentional interpretation of Intentional Behaviorism persists. This chapter seeks a means of conjoining the concerns of the super-, sub-, and personal levels of exposition which relies neither on flipping between them nor on concepts that attempt to be at once both intentional and extensional. It briefly reviews the nature of the cognitive psychologies before introducing the idea of Janus-variables which are intentional in nature, but which reach backward to the causative components of neuroeconomics, and forward to those of operant behavioral economics.

A predominant strand of cognitive theory explains a spectrum of behaviors from impulsive choice to delayed gratification in terms of the interaction of two types of metacognitive system. Models based on this dichotomy can be found in various forms, but the following characteristics are common. The first kind of system, fast-acting, automatic, associative, effortless, and nonconscious, acts in parallel and without the support of working memory. These metacognitive systems, often designated "S1," are responsible, if unchecked, for impulsive behaviors. The second kind, which is working memory-based, is slower, rule-based, effortful and conscious, and acts serially. These "S2" metacognitive systems may override the actions of S1 systems and promote a more considered pattern of behavior that is careful of the organism's longer term welfare (see, for instance, Kahneman, 2011). Some authors argue that while the cognitive functions proposed by these models share some common properties, the systems and subsystems these models variously propose are fundamentally dissimilar (e.g., Evans, 2010). Proponents of another batch of models that seemingly deal in the same subject matter couch their ideas in terms of mental or cognitive modules and, in some cases, central processing units (e.g., Fodor, 1983). These considerations are germane to each of the three kinds of cognitive model employed in the evaluation of the intentional interpretation.[1]

A brief overview of these cognitive psychologies (which are described in detail in Foxall, 2016a, 2016b) is useful at this point in order to proceed to a discussion of Janus-variables, and then a longer description of the cognitive psychologies in relation to the economic analyses that derive from them and their roles in the determination of value.

> Micro-cognitive psychology *links the personal and sub-personal levels, though it also has implications for the super-personal. It embodies a theory of neuro-cognitive behavior systems (e.g., Bickel's competing neuro-behavioral decision systems (CNDS) model or Stanovich's tripartite theory) which links neurophysiology functioning, decision-making, and behavior/action (see Bickel et al., 2011; Stanovich, 2011). Although the terminology differs from model to model, micro-cognitive psychology proposes two or three of these neuro-cognitive behavior systems; at its simplest, an* impulsive or autonomous system *that is based in the limbic system and an* executive system *based in prefrontal cortex. Either of these may be hypo- or hyper-active and the balance between them is a determinant of the strength of the interaction of picoeconomic interests, which determines the rate at which the consumer discounts future events.*

> Meso-cognitive psychology *is exemplified by picoeconomics (Ainslie, 1992), a psychology of the personal level, which presents us with the strategic interaction of competing interests within the individual. The first is a short-range interest (SRI) that seeks more immediate satisfaction; it eventuates in behavior that discounts the future steeply; and experientially it approximates the primary mentation of which Freud spoke. The other is a long-range interest (LRI) that seeks to defer gratification if this increases the overall wellbeing of the individual; it leads to behavior that discounts the future shallowly; and at the phenomenal level it approximates Freud's secondary mentation.*

> Macro-cognitive psychology *intertwines the personal and super-personal levels, though it also links in the sub-personal. It embodies a theory of collective intentionality such as Searle's (1995, 2010) which establishes the origins of informational reinforcement. Collective intentionality is the creation and enforcement, by human agents, of the contingencies of reinforcement and punishment that will control their behavior/action. This procedure is part of what makes actions actions (Foxall, 2017b). In a nutshell, what makes actions actions is that the contingencies of reinforcement and punishment that govern the relevant activities' recurrence within the individual's repertoire are determined by the social activities of groups as well as by the individual herself.*

---

1. Brakel (2013) attributes dual-process thinking to Freud. Interestingly, Frankish (2015) argues that Dennett's distinction between two kinds of awareness in *Content and Consciousness* (Dennett, 1969) embodies a dual-process model of reasoning.

Action is activity that is governed by collective and/or individual intentionality (Foxall, 2016b). This is the foundation of informational reinforcement and of self-esteem (pride/shame: $P^+A^+D^+ / P^-A^-D^-$) as the ultimate reinforcer (punisher) of human choice (Foxall, 2016a, 2017b).

Freud's dichotomy between primary and secondary processes, to which allusion was made in Chapter 9, *Ascribing intentionality*, not only provides a link between the structure and functions of the intentional consumer situation but may also act as an integrating element in the cognitive interpretation by bringing together the sources of explanation variously contained within the micro-, macro-, and mesophases of cognitive psychology and the economic hypotheses and interpretations to which they may lead. Each of the three cognitive psychologies gives rise to a particular mode of translating Freud's model into a way of testing predictions from the BPM. The rationale for using Freud's model as an integrative device is to overcome the problem that the three cognitive psychologies could be said to be arbitrary or isolated from one another, each with its own rationale but not belonging to an overarching justification for a unified cognitive interpretation. The rationale for this is that this way there is continuity from the expression of the intentional interpretation (in terms of beliefs-proper and neurotic beliefs) and the cognitive psychologies that are used to justify the intentional interpretation and lead on to the economic hypotheses that enable empirical testing. The intended sequence is shown in Fig. 10.1.

This figure suggests how the cognitive psychologies have a common link with the intentional interpretation through Freud's model of primary and

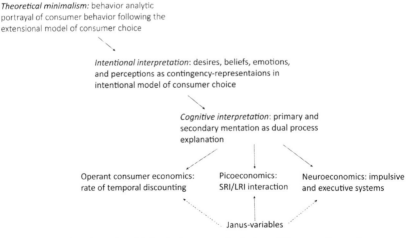

FIGURE 10.1 The intentional behaviorist research strategy. Primary and secondary mentation link the intentional and cognitive interpretations, while Janus-variables serve as an additional integrative device for the cognitive psychologies.

secondary mentation. We now need to progress to an understanding of how these three cognitive psychologies are linked in an empirical program of investigation. This is accomplished by the concept of Janus-variables which are intentional constructs (and, therefore, do not of themselves enter empirical research), which have counterparts in the extensional neuro- and behavioral sciences (which do).

10.2 Janus-variables and valuation

Micro-cognitive psychology, emphasizing the operation of neuro-cognitive behavior systems, is associated with *neuroeconomics*, specifically *neurocellular economics* (NE; Ross, 2012). Ross (2008) defines NE as the application of economic techniques such as constrained maximization and equilibrium analysis to the modeling of neural activities. NE is concerned primarily with what he terms "relatively encapsulated functional parts of brains." Macro-cognitive psychology, emphasizing collective intentionality and the social creation of the contingencies of reinforcement and punishment that will govern action, is closely associated with with CBE (Foxall, 2016d, 2017a). Mesocognitive psychology, emphasizing intrapsychic bargaining, is modeled by *picoeconomics* (Ainslie, 1992). The subtitle of Ainslie's book is *The Strategic Interaction of Successive Motivational States Within the Person*. The relationships between the cognitive psychologies and economic analyses are summarized in Fig. 10.2. The problem that remains is that of relating these sources of cognitive explanation to one another, given that we have rejected Dennett's notion of *illata* as entities that are both physically and intentionally

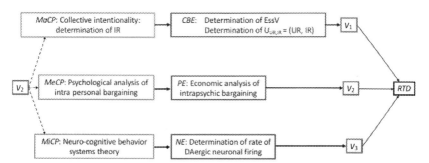

FIGURE 10.2 Value and the determination of RTD. *RTD* is the outcome of the three valuations depicted as V_1, V_2, and V_3. V_2 is determined by reference to psychological intrapersonal bargaining. It is a Janus-variable that links the three notions of valuation through cognitive theories. *CBE*, Consumer behavioral economics; *DA*, dopamine.; *EssV*, essential value; *IR*, informational reinforcement; *MaCP*, macro-cognitive psychology; *MeCP*, mesocognitive psychology; *MeCP* = mesocognitive psychology; *MiCP*, micro-cognitive psychology; *NE*, neurocellular economics; *PE* = picoeconomics; *RTD*, rate of temporal discounting; U, utility; UR, utilitarian reinforcement; V_1, exchange value as expressed in market transactions; V_2, personal understanding of value; V_3, computed valuation as expressed in rate of neuronal firing.

characterizable, as inviting the mereological fallacy. This expedient is denied us by virtue of the assumption that the separation of the levels of exposition and their inherent modes of explanation must be maintained. This stricture limits the nature of the kind of explanation that can be offered. While we are not at liberty to posit the existence of entities that transcend the levels and their explanatory uniquenesses, however, something that would require the biconditionals which McGinn points out we do not possess, we can employ linguistic links that suggest a solution.

Each of the modes of economic analysis contains, for instance, an understanding of *value* that is peculiar to it, but which is conceptually related to the use of this term in the other modes. These economic analyses suggest both novel ways of interpreting further observed consumer action cognitively, and thereby strengthening the cognitive interpretation stage of Intentional Behaviorism, and specific hypotheses that may be employed in testing aspects of the intentional interpretation at an empirical level. Hence, the key to linking variables that exist at multiple levels—such as value at the subpersonal level of neuroscience, the personal level of intentionality, and the superpersonal level of environmental-behavioral relationships—may be to be found in the economic conceptions provided by neuroeconomics and operant behavioral economics which translate into empirically testable extensionally stated hypotheses, and the interpretive contribution of picoeconomics. We can define value, therefore, in the following three ways:

> Value$_1$ (V_1) *is defined at the super-personal level of exposition as an operational, extensional understanding of value which captures the* rate of exchange of work or money (i.e., behavior) for a reinforcer. *This is value located at the super-personal level of exposition: valuation is understood in the objectively specifiable language of extensional behavioral science. The link to consumer behavioral economics is evident here in the relation between informational reinforcement and value, since it is this especially that is determined through collective intentionality by people themselves determining what will act as a reinforcer or punisher for them and how it will operate.*

> Neurocellular economics *is initially concerned with the rate of dopaminergic firing that occurs in anticipation of a reinforcer, but it is also intimately concerned with* V_2. *If informational reinforcement evokes the same neurophysiological operations as utilitarian reinforcement, and it appears it does, then neuroeconomic explanation must also reflect this intentional determination of behavior. When we look to neurophysiology to provide a basis of valuation (V_3) we can, following the definition of V_3, look at the rate of dopaminergic firing. But at a more abstract level we need to be able to relate this to broader neurophysiological functioning that itself relates to cognitive and behavioral events. The competing neuro-behavioral decision systems (CNDS) approach provides a means to conceptualize this since it posits two systems (impulsive system and executive system) that (i) are based in neurophysiological structures*

and functions (the limbic system and prefrontal cortex (PFC), respectively), (ii) relate to behavior (operancy, rate of temporal discounting), and (iii) are cognitively-grounded by virtue of their being decision *systems (Figure 10.c).*

Value$_2$ *(V$_2$) is defined at the personal level of exposition in terms of the subjective representation of worth of an object (reinforcer).* V$_2$ *is what the consumer would be willing to pay rather than walk away from a transaction, one's fallback position. A notional concept, it is what gives rise to consumer surplus. It is what one would be willing to receive for an exchanged item one owns. This is a purely mental operation, a representation. It is necessarily an intentional expression of value: knowable by the individual to whom it belongs, though not necessarily consistently and is ascribable in the course of using folk psychology and formulating explanations of behavior/action. It is the subjective worth the consumer ascribes to an as yet to be obtained reinforce such as an anticipated reinforcer.* V$_2$ *may first be perceptual — knowledge-by-acquaintance — and only then cognitive — knowledge-by-description. Picoeconomics (Ainslie, 1992) is essential here as a means of comprehending how the objective contingencies of reinforcement that determine* V$_1$ *are translated into a personal valuation of reinforcers in view of the amount of work that must be done for them. And vice versa: how the individual's personal valuation of a reinforcer is translated into an action tendency to accept/reject the reinforcer actually offered at a particular price.*

Picoeconomics *proves a meso-cognitive psychology. At the level of psychological analysis, picoeconomics identifies the SRI, LRI, and their interactions. At the level of economic analysis, it expresses these relationships in economic terms, for example modelling the interests as synchronous or diachronic influences on action (Ross, 2012). The interaction of the interests establishes the nature of* V$_2$ *and thereby influences the individual's rate of temporal discounting. This chapter supplies an economic assessment of the interactive behaviors of SRI and LRI in terms of the components of the BPM and the conceptions of value introduced above. It also makes a major contribution to understanding the personal level of experience. And it reaches out to both NE and CBE: we may confidently say that the conception of value at this level of exposition, i.e.,* V$_2$, *can be described as a "Janus-variable" since it looks toward* V$_1$ *and* V$_3$, *toward* V$_1$ *insofar as it takes the work/reinforcer relation as its object, toward* V$_3$ *by investigator-ascription.* V$_1$ *and* V$_3$ *are extensional and do not "look" anywhere! (We shall return to the metaphor of "looking" when we return to the subject of* illata*).*

Value$_3$ *(V$_3$) is defined at the sub-personal level of exposition as the rate of dopaminergic firing in anticipation of receiving a reinforcer. Especially when alternative courses of action are available, it is possible to evaluate each comparatively in objective way. Different rates of firing can be detected for alternative courses of action as they are contemplated. This is a sub-personal* understanding of valuation and it can be expressed in the objectively available language of neuroscience.

Consumer behavioral economics *is that component of operant behavioral economics whose scope is set by consumer behavior analysis (Foxall, 2016c, 2017a)*. CBE is initially concerned with the objective determination of value in terms of the work the individual is prepared to do or the amount of money she is prepared to surrender in order to obtain the reinforcer. Hence, it is specifically tied to V_1, which is determined by the consumer's utility function and the essential value that characterizes her purchase behavior, especially its sensitivity to changes in the price of commodities. Essential value, the inverse of elasticity of demand, is a measure of how far the consumer is willing to defend her level of consumption in the face of price increases. Hursh and Silberberg (2008) conceptualize value as the rate of change of elasticity of demand. Their analysis captures the curvature of the demand curve in a single parameter in order to determine the effect on consumption of price increases from zero. Essential value reveals the extent to which the consumer is willing to defend or maintain the consumption level that exists at (virtually) zero price in the face of the price increase (measured proportionally, in percentage terms). In other words the extent to which the consumer maintains or defends consumption as price deviates upwards from zero is a measure of how much she values the reinforcer, i.e., what they call the "essential value" of the commodity.

But CBE is also intimately concerned with V_2, because what counts as informational reinforcement is determined by collective intentionality; while this is initially a social judgment and, therefore, intersubjective, it is ultimately a matter of personal judgment and the self-esteem that results from successfully conducting purchase and consumption responses and is, therefore, subjective. V_2 in this post-purchase or post-consumption phase is concerned with the personal level of satisfaction (value) that the consumer has obtained from these responses.

These conceptions of value do not suggest an equivalence between the levels of exposition but a *commonality* that enables communication between the levels. And they invite the possibility of an economics-based source of empirical testing. The commonality of concepts such as value is determined not in terms of levels of exposition that can then be conveniently merged and demerged (as Dennett tends to do) but at the level of the disciplines of CBE, picoeconomics (PE), and NE. It is here that we can understand how value, for instance, has a precise meaning in terms of monetary yardsticks that are related also to subjective beliefs (CBE: $V_1 \to PE/V_2$). Similarly, NE provides an objective yardstick for the levels of anticipation that clearly links to subjective valuation (NE: $V_3 \to PE/V_2$).

In summary, in the third phase of the intentional behaviorist research strategy, *cognitive interpretation*, we ground the intentional interpretation that includes V_2 in concepts that can enter into extensional investigations and explanations. This process has two stages: the first is grounding the intentional interpretation in cognitive psychological theories which, like the intentional interpretation, are couched in terms of *abstracta*. The second is establishing the economic implications of the behavior/action involved in the cognitive interpretation so that empirical observations can be made in extensional terms that reflect V_1 and V_3. While the cognitive theories entail *abstracta*, the economic theories use variables that are capable of entering into testable hypotheses. They are not *illata* because they are not physical entities that can be intentionally characterized; they are simply and only empirically available constructs that are capable of being operationalized. This is consistent with the view that it is the extensional sciences of neurophysiology and behavioral economics that provide the testable variables. Establishing the economic implications of behavior/action that is the focus of the cognitive interpretation depends on V_2 being what I have called a Janus-variable, one that looks both ways out from the intentional interpretation and its personal level stance toward, first, the concrete extensional notion of value-in-exchange (V_1) and, second, toward that of value-computation (V_3). Hence, of the three concepts of value we have identified, only V_2 is a Janus-variable.

To have such a notion of value that looks two ways, we need to show that it can be embedded in theories that themselves look both ways. First, *micro-cognitive psychologies* such as tripartite theory/NBDS theory do this, linking cognition with both the superpersonal (behavioral) level and the subpersonal (neuro) level. Second, *macro-cognitive psychology* such as collective intentionality theory does this too, linking personal value to social judgment via informational reinforcement which also has links to neurophysiology.

Rate of temporal discounting (RTD), which is chosen as our dependent variable since it embodies the idea of consumer choice, is the outcome of the three valuations depicted as V_1, V_2, and V_3. But, specifically, it is determined by V_2 with V_1 and V_3 being inputs to *its* determination. In the case of V_2, we have to explain (1) how it is determined by reference to psychological intrapersonal bargaining (MeCP) and (2) its nature as a Janus-variable that links the three notions of valuation through cognitive theories (MaCP and MiCP) that themselves point two ways (indicated by the dotted lines in Fig. 10.2).

10.3 Relating the levels of exposition

10.3.1 Micro-cognitive psychology as a basis for picoeconomic interaction

Neurophysiologically, micro-cognitive psychology reflects subpersonal functioning in which the rate of firing of dopaminergic neurons for competing reinforcers determines their relative values and motivates action to obtain them (V_3). But it is also concerned with cognitive decision-making through the competing intrapersonal interaction of the short- and long-range picoeconomic interests of mesocognitive psychology (V_2), and the actions that result from this conflict which determines which of several competing reinforcers is selected for consumption (V_1). Micro-cognitive psychology also reaches out toward the patterns of reinforcement and punishment that encourage and inhibit behaviors. It, therefore, potentially links the subpersonal, personal, and superpersonal levels of exposition. Examples of micro-cognitive psychologies are the neuro-behavioral decision systems theory of Bickel et al. (2011), the two minds hypothesis described by Evans (2010), and the triprocessual theory of Stanovich (2009, 2011), though there are many more candidates. The general understanding is of a relatively impulsive mental process (one that is rapid, autonomous, based on parallel processing) and a relatively deliberative mental process (which is slower, computationally demanding, and sequential) which compete to control responses to environmental opportunities and threats. The impulsive or implicit system resembles an array of modules responsible for the processing of sensory information and possibly language, along with the basic emotional reactions to environmental events (for discussion of modality in the context of Intentional Behaviorism, see Foxall, 2017b, pp. 43–46). These modular systems may give rise to operant and respondent reactions based respectively on instrumental and classical conditioning. The neurophysiological element of such systems is the limbic and paralimbic system, which is responsible inter alia for the release of dopamine in response to external signals of reinforcement and punishment. The processes or systems implicated in impulsive response are often referred to as Type 1 process or systems. The executive or explicit system is responsible for reasoned action which results from reflection on the consequences of alternative courses of action, deemphasizing the rush to impulsivity that would be the result of unrestricted Type 1 activity, and promoting the generation of actions that avoid the possibly deleterious implications of rapid response in favor of more considered judgment with respect to longer term outcomes. This kind of activity which, neurophysiologically, involves the prefrontal cortex (PFC), is often referred to as a Type 2 process or system (Kahneman, 2011). Dual- and triprocessual theories are concerned with the cognitive structures and functioning responsible for the interaction of these processes or systems. The reason some authors posit a third process or system is that the individual's overarching cognitive style acts independently of the other systems to enable a characteristic set of values and for the judgments made necessary by conflicts between those systems, a forum within which resolution can occur. (For further discussion in the context of Intentional Behaviorism, see Foxall, 2016a, 2016b, 2016d).

10.3.1.1 The impulsive system

The impulsive system incorporates the amygdala and ventral striatum, a midbrain region concerned with the valence of immediate results of action, and is liable to become hyperactive as a result of "exaggerated processing of the incentive value of substance-related cues" (Bechara, 2005, p. 1459). Drug-induced behaviors correlate with enhanced response in this region when the amygdala displays increased sensitization to reward (Bickel & Yi, 2008; London et al., 2000). The receipt of positive reinforcers of all varieties causes the release of dopamine in the nucleus accumbens. This is true of both utilitarian reinforcers such as drugs of abuse, and the receipt of informational reinforcers such as social reward or self-esteem (Foxall, 2011). It is also the case for of the receipt of money which has both utilitarian and informational aspects. In the case of a drug of abuse, such brain reward is acute. The effect of the drug in inculcating long-term potentiation at specific synapses is recorded in the hippocampus as the result of experience (memory).[2] The amygdala is involved in the creation of a learned (conditioned) response to the stimuli that accompany the use of the drug. These accompanying stimuli might take the form of informational (social) reinforcers and discriminative stimuli. (For discussion of these points, see, inter alia, Gruber & McDonald, 2012; McGaugh, 2004; Phelps, 2006). The resulting focus of research has been on the mesolimbic dopaminergic system and other brain regions such as the amygdala and ventral striatum involved in emotional responses. But there is recent evidence that the insula is important because of its relation to conscious craving for drugs (Naqvi, Shiv, & Bechara, 2006). This role has been revealed by correlation-based fMRI studies that show the increased activity of the insula during self-reported urges to ingest drugs. Such activity is related to the emergence of the secondary reinforcers which tie drug use to specific behavioral and contextual factors and to the

---

2. *Long-term potentiation* (LTP) is an increase in the efficiency of synaptic transmission. It requires activity in order to occur and it may underlie learning. It is associated with a preceding period of intense synaptic activity and a subsequent (postsynaptic) depolarization. It is a component of Hebbian learning since only those synapses capable of engendering LTP are known as "Hebbian." It is interesting to note in retrospect that Hebb's original surmise had no basis in the physiological knowledge of the time he published his book on this (Hebb, 1949). However, the discovery of LTP and its neural basis gave Hebbian learning an extensional basis by providing a mechanism for *synaptic plasticity* (see also Foxall, 2016a, Chapter 2: *A kind of consilience*). The picture revealed by recent research is a far more complicated than this, however. LTP is currently understood as no more than a possible molecular mechanism of learning (see, for instance, Migaud et al., 1998; Uetani et al., 2000). The role of LTD, which has been correlated with learning, is of particular importance. Present knowledge on synaptic plasticity and learning performance, incorporating the learning of drugs' capacity to reward, indicates that LTP and LTD tend toward an optimal balance which may influences memory performance. Memory formation may also be subserved by hippocampal network oscillations in the theta, gamma, and high frequency range and the activity of place-, grid-, time-, and reward-related cells in the brain (Eichenbaum, 2014; Moser et al., 2015; Pan et al., 2005; Sanders et al., 2015).

cognitive drivers of drug use. "Over time, as addiction increases, stimuli within the environment that are associated with drug use become powerful incentives, initiating both automatic (i.e., implicit) motivational processes that drive ongoing drug use and relapse in addiction to conscious (i.e., explicit) feelings of urge to take drugs" (Naqvi et al., 2006, p. 61; see also Naqvi et al., 2006). The consumer behavior setting is key to the repetition of drug use even when the consumer has ceased to enjoy its effects, that is, when *wanting* overrides (lack of) *liking*. The ritualistic practices involved in the preparation of drugs, associated with specific places, apparatus, packages, lighters, and so on, thus become sources of the pleasure that reinforces not only those activities but also the consummatory acts of drug ingestion. These processes, which elicit specific memories of encounters with the contexts and the drugs, are also responsible for differences in the subjective experience of urges for various drugs be they cigarettes, cocaine, or gambling. By ensuring that the individual keeps particular goals in mind, the insula is also involved in (thwarting) the executive functions that might overcome drug urges (cf. Tiffany, 1999). The learning process includes the development of neural plasticity through dopaminergic priming with respect to the impending chain of appetitive events; Naqvi et al. (2006) propose that this dopamine-dependency invokes activity in the insula and associated regions such as the ventromedial PFC and amygdala. The plasticity involves the establishment of representations of the interoceptive outcomes of using drugs and thus engender relapse even after long periods of nonuse.

Neuroeconomic analysis of valuation procedures accord a central role to dopamine. The processing of the relative reward values of alternative courses of action in the midbrain and prefrontal areas occurs predominantly through a feed-forward circuit that links the ventral tegmental area via the ventral striatum to the orbitofrontal cortex. Ross (2011) points out that changes in tonic dopamine concentration in the striatum affect general alertness of and receptiveness to chances of consuming rewards. However, phasic changes in the uptake of dopamine in the nucleus accumbens of the ventral striatum integrate several components of reward functions, including *relative valuation, maintenance of attention, and preparation of motor response.* Dopamine relates the contingencies that predict reward with expected values of the rewards Ross (2011, p. 57). It seems safe to identify this as a source of V_3.

10.3.1.2 The executive system

The executive system, which includes the PFC, is normally associated with the executive functions of planning and foresight (Barkley, 1997, 2012) and is hypothesized to become hypoactive in the event of addiction. In the absence of its moderating function, effects of the hyperactive dopaminergic reward pathway are exacerbated, leading to an imbalance which is implicated in the enactment of dysfunctional behavior. It is this level of balance/imbalance that determines the individual's RTD expressed in her behavior (Bickel & Yi, 2008). The behavioral concomitant of these neurophysiological processes is observable in the rate at which individuals discount the value of future reward in favor of more immediately appearing reinforcers (Bickel & Yi, 2008). In the context of addiction, the competing neuro-behavioral decision systems (CNDS) hypothesis posits that drug seeking results from "amplified incentive value bestowed on drugs and drug-related cues (via reward processing by the amygdala) and impaired ability to inhibit behavior (due to frontal cortical dysfunction)" (Bickel & Yi, 2008, p. 2).

Analysis of the neurobiological pathway proposed to account for the acquisition by the PFC of the capacity to control the higher level cognitive functions involved in the regulation of behavior in the face of environmental programming reveals a two-stage process (Miller & Wallis, 2009). The first stage is the impingement of signals generated via reinforcement learning on the PFC circuitry: reinforced operant behavior is accompanied by the production of signals that associates PFC functioning with aspects of the stimulus field (the setting in which the behavior takes place), the nature of the behavioral response enacted, and the reinforcing and punishing consequences that are its outcomes. Repeated responding in these circumstances is capable of generating strong PFC representations of the contingencies of reinforcement that maintain such behavior. The second stage in the argument is to account for these signals and the actions of dopaminergic neurons of the midbrain. In the course of learning through the repeated performance of behavioral responses, reinforcers initially activate the dopaminergic neurons themselves, but subsequently the stimuli that predict the reinforcers, rather than the reinforcers themselves, come to activate the dopaminergic neurons. Should an expected reward not appear, the rate of firing of the dopaminergic neurons is reduced. The discrepancy between the expectation of reinforcement and its nonappearance, coded by the dopaminergic neurons' activity is known as the reward prediction error and is instrumental in the organism's subsequent ability to direct its actions more effectively toward the achievement of reinforcement (Miller & Wallis, 2009, pp. 103–104; see also Foxall, 2014b).

10.3.1.3 Impact on behavior

The operations of these systems combine to generate behavior that reflects the individual's valuation of future events, his/her degree of "temporal discounting." Hyperbolic temporal discounting is the procedure in which the later occurring of two rewards is diminished in an individual's subjective estimation even though it is the larger, with the result that the more immediate reward is selected in preference despite its being by definition the smaller of the two. This "impulsive" behavior is described by the hyperbolic discounting function

$$V_d = A/1 + kD \qquad (10.1)$$

where V_d is the discounted value of a reward of a particular magnitude or amount, A, received after a delay, D (Madden & Bickel, 2010; Mazur, 1987). The k parameter indicates the extent to which the value of the larger later reinforcer (LLR) diminishes compared to that of the smaller sooner reinforcer (SSR) over time (Stein & Madden, 2013). The major behavioral characteristic of choice described hyperbolically is that the individual is likely to reverse preferences as time advances, an observation which is highly relevant to the extreme drug-use and gambling already mentioned, the making of resolutions to change, and the yielding to temptation that may follow. Behavior that discounts the future is of central importance to the CNDS model insofar as temporal discounting is an index of the extent to which behavior is under the control of the tendency toward disinhibited impulsivity (the selection of an SSR rather than an LLR) as opposed to the inhibiting influence of the executive functions that results in the choice of LLR over SSR ("self-controlled" behavior) (Barkley, 2012; Bickel & Marsch, 2000; Bickel & Yi, 2008). It is reasonable to inquire how the valuation an individual attaches to the outcomes of his/her future behavior should be understood. The CNDS model argues that the neurophysiological tendencies of the impulsive and executive systems eventuate in an individual's degree of temporal discounting behavior which is explicable in operant terms that translate readily into economic considerations (Bickel et al., 2007, 2011). Bickel, Jarmolowicz, Mueller, Gatchalian, and McClure (2012) argue that addiction can be conceptualized as an outcome of "reinforcer pathologies" that can be analyzed in terms of behavioral economics, specifically the inelasticity of demand (manifesting in a willingness to pay an extraordinarily high price for a drug reward) and extremely steep discounting of the future (manifesting as overvaluation of an immediately available reward). The relevance of Hursh and Silberberg's (2008) concept of essential value is evident here. These elements that reveal an excessive valuation of one reinforcer in comparison with other available reward and impulsivity, respectively, are consistent with the pattern of behavior found in addicts who may accordingly be defined as "people for whom the transient benefits of the addictive behavior persistently outweigh the significant short- and long-term costs of these choices" (Bickel et al., 2012, pp. 334–335). The portrayal of these benefits in terms of positively and negatively reinforced behaviors is confirmed by the neurophysiological analysis of addiction that depicts addicts' initial drug administration as determined by the pleasures this confers and their later drug use as a means of avoiding or escaping from deleterious consequences such as withdrawal symptoms (Koob, 2013). Some aversive consequences cannot be avoided by further drug administration; however, the social isolation and damage to health that often result from persistent addiction are examples of the punishing outcomes of such behavior (Foxall & Sigurdsson, 2011; Rachlin, 2000).

In summary, we can observe that, while the impulsive system emphasizes such impulsivities as sensation-seeking, reward sensitivity, behavioral disinhibition, attention deficit, reflection deficit, and impulsive choice, the executive system emphasizes attentiveness, behavioral flexibility, planning, and the valuation of future events. These behavioral tendencies result in an important source of individual differences that characterize the impatience that leads to impulsivity and, if unchecked, addiction, as opposed to the self-control that leads to sobriety. Bickel et al. (2011) point out that the underlying factors governing these behaviors may be described as "reinforcer pathologies." Reinforcer pathologies may be captured in terms of the overvaluation of immediacy on the one hand and elasticity of demand on the other. Some individuals are disposed to value a reinforcer so highly that they cannot wait for it; others are able to show restraint. The former group are also likely to be willing to pay a high price in order to gain their objective, while the latter do not show so strong a readiness to part with their money. (Reinforcer pathology is discussed in the context of Intentional Behaviorism in Foxall, 2016a, pp. 142–146). The resulting behavior pattern can be summarized as a tendency to discount the future at a higher or lower rate (Foxall, 2016a, Chapter 2).[3]

The fundamental assumptions that reinforcement is coded by dopaminergic neurons (Robbins & Everitt, 2002; Schultz, 1992) and that RPEs are also reflected in the firing rates of dopaminergic neurons (Schultz et al., 1997) ground the relationship between neoclassical microeconomics and neuroscience on which neuroeconomics rests (Glimcher, 2011). For present purposes, they serve to integrate operant psychology with these disciplines by promoting a causal connection among reinforcement, neuronal activity, and behavior (Schultz, 2010; Schultz & Dickinson, 2000). Clearly, any dual-process theory must also point out that the subpersonal neurobiological operations underlying the executive system (which is usually presented in personal level cognitive terms) must seek to mitigate the effect of this dopaminergic activity. There are, of course, individual differences among consumers that determine the extent to which this is successful in producing a balance between

---

3. There are several reasons for thinking more formally about the place and function of a cognitive dimension within neurophysiologically based models of decision-making. The principal reason in the current context stems from the fact that the "valuation" involved in temporal discounting is a mental construct that requires an explanation in terms of cognitive representation and evaluation. This, in turn, raises the concern that the present dual process structure of the model may be inadequate to the task of accounting for the metacognitive processes involved in the exercise of self-control. I have elsewhere called attention to the need for a triprocessual model such as that of Stanovich to capture to complexities of cognitive structure and processing (see especially Foxall, 2016d).

the impulsive and executive systems. Some half a percent of individuals in those populations in which measurement has occurred have dopaminergic reward systems that respond to frequent gambling by those individuals by increasing tonic dopamine production on an ongoing basis which Ross (2011, pp. 59–60) argues "turns the slot machine or home computer into an easily self-operated phasic dopamine pump" (see also Ross, Sharp, Vuchinich, & Spurrett, 2008). He defines this as gambling addiction, behavior learned via classical conditioning rather than adaptive learning, the content of which learning having "no everyday description in folk psychology" (Ross et al., 2008). Although this description applies to only a small proportion of the population, it suggests that there may be individual differences in susceptibility to the process in which the dopaminergic reward system responds to repeated behaviors that are high in V_1, reflecting differences in the reinforcer pathologies identified by Bickel et al. (2011).

We have arrived at an example of behavior (controlled by contingencies operating at the superpersonal level) influencing the rate of dopaminergic firing at the subpersonal level and of this effecting a permanent increase in tonic dopamine generation that is responsible for incentive salience within behavior settings that leads to an individual's being unable to control the rate at which he gambles. This is the mechanism that converts an open into a closed consumer behavior setting. An individual who essayed gambling responses in a situation that encouraged many alternative behaviors is now operating within what looks ostensibly like the same physical and social setting that makes a single behavior highly probable, precludes alternatives, and whose stimulus field is augmented in its capacity to influence that behavior by changes deep within the individual's nervous system. Dopamine acts as an intrapersonal measure of valuation (Ross calls it an internal currency). Dopamine neurons within the reward system vary their firing rates according to whether the externally presented reward is greater than predicted (indicated by an increase in tonic firing rate), less than predicted (a reduction), or exactly as predicted (no change) (Ross et al., 2008, p. 125).

10.3.2 Picoeconomic analysis: the determination of V_2

As a first stage in relating the levels of exposition it is necessary is to understand better how the extensional sciences of neuroeconomics and operant behavioral economics impinge upon the intentional level of picoeconomicsand constrain interpretation at the personal level, it is useful to develop the nature of picoeconomicsin light of the concept of Janus-variables. The following analysis is intended to show the changes in valuation that accompany preference reversal (where this occurs) and temporal discounting in the classic instance of consumer choice. It illustrates *process* of consumer choice in terms of the changing valuations it involves for impulsive consumers and self-controlled consumers.

10.3.2.1 Dynamic valuation process of the impulsive consumer

Fig. 10.3 illustrates this classic situation of consumer choice as that in which two reinforcers that offer, respectively, an inferior (smaller) and a superior (larger) reward, are valued by the consumer according to the time of their availability. These mutually exclusive outcomes are known—as we have seen—as the "SSR" and the "LLR," respectively. The valuations shown are the personal valuation processes of an impulsive consumer, that is, one who discounts the future hyperbolically.[4]

---

4. Whereas exponential temporal discounting involves the consumer's valuing the LLR at all times more highly than the SSR, the hyperbolic discounter experiences a large jump in the value of the SSR just prior to its becoming accessible (see figures below; for a full exposition, see Foxall, 2016a, Chapter 2: *A kind of consilience*; see also Foxall, 2017b, pp. 21–9).

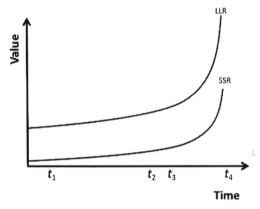

Exponential discounting. The value of the LLR exceeds that of the SSR at all times.

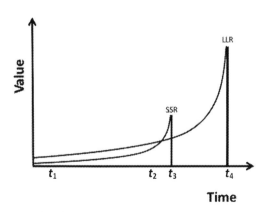

Hyperbolic discounting. The value of the LLR exceeds that of the SSR until shortly before the SSR becomes available, when its value increases dramatically.

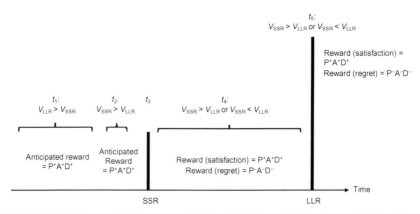

FIGURE 10.3 Temporal influence on valuation: I. *A*, Arousal; *D*, dominance. *IC*, impulsive consumer; *LLR*, later but larger reinforcer; *P*, pleasure; *SSC*, self-controlled consumer; *SSR*, smaller but sooner reinforce; t_1, initial time period; t_2, time immediately prior to availability of SSR; t_3, time of accessibility of SSR; t_4, period subsequent to availability of SSR; t_5, availability of LLR; *V*, present value.

Consumption of the smaller reinforcer will be possible earlier, at the point represented by the shorter vertical line; the larger reinforcer is delayed until the point represented by the longer vertical line. The rewards provided by the ownership and consumption of these reinforcers, as well as by their anticipation, take the form of emotional outcomes in the form of pleasure (P), arousal (A), and dominance (D).[5] The combination of high levels of all three emotional reactions ($P^+A^+D^+$) is summarized as pride or high self-esteem; the reverse ($P^-A^-D^-$), as shame or low self-esteem (see Foxall, 2016a, 2017b). Consumers may prove either impulsive or patient as the availability of the smaller reinforcer approaches. Fig. 10.3 shows the changing valuations of an impulsive consumer, discounting hyperbolically. Comparatively, few consumers start out as "impulsives" at the beginning of this process. There may be some who have failed so often to hold out for the better choice that they have acquired a self-image that leads them to predict even at t_1 that they will select the SSR when it is offered. But most, even if they have a learning history that contains some failures, are likely to commit at this time to selecting the LLR. For this majority, it is as time goes on that the possibility of discounting hyperbolically arises. The values of an exponentially discounting consumer are assumed to remain constant over the

---

5. This typology of emotions is that of Mehrabian and Russell (1974). For explication of its role in the testing of the BPM, see Foxall (1997c), Foxall and Greenley (1998, 1999, 2000), Foxall and Yani-de-Soriano (2005, 2017b). The results of the empirical research program are summarized in Foxall et al. (2012). The most recent comprehensive account of the significance of this work for the intentional behaviorist research program can be found in Foxall (2017b).

entire period; for her, the subjective value of the LLR is always higher than that of the SSR, a pattern that mirrors that of the objective values. The values shown in Fig. 10.3 are V_2s, the personal subjective valuations attached, first, to outcomes that lie in the future and, when opportunities to consume have passed, to those that lie in the past and reflect previous actions. They also presumably reflect V_3s, the changing rates of dopaminergic neuronal firings as reinforcers are first promised, then as they become imminent, then as they are consumed or spurned. They do not, however, reflect any *changes* in V_1s for there are none. The objective nature of the acts of consumption involved and the conditions on which they become available, that is, different lapses of time, do not alter during the process; if there are other conditions involved, such as the surrender of money or payment of some other price, they are unmoving.

At the earliest stage of the process (t_1), these valuations are entirely cognitive projections of the emotions that will be felt either on receipt of the more immediate reinforcer, or during the period of showing patience if this instant gratification is rejected, or on receipt of the more substantial but delayed reinforcer. None of these outcomes exists (i.e., is available) at this stage and so can only be represented intentionally, that is, in the form of desires and beliefs that refer to the expected emotional rewards and sanctions that each situation promises. At this point, the long-range interest (LRI) is in control: it is easy to exercise forbearance when both sources of reward lie in the considerable future. The LLR, therefore, is far more highly valued than the SSR. Both consumers who will prove impulsive and those who will prove patient anticipate the reward of attaining the LLR in terms of positive feelings of pleasure, arousal, and dominance ($P^+A^+D^+$); we refer to this combination of high-level positive emotions for short as *pride*.

The next salient temporal point, t_2, begins just before the SSR becomes available. At this point, there is a tendency for the SSR to be disproportionately highly valued, at least by the consumer who is discounting hyperbolically, so that there is a great temptation to take it, even though this means that the possibility of ever getting the LLR is thereby preempted. The short-range interest (SRI) is asserting itself. The change in subjective valuation is due entirely to the temporal circumstances faced by the individual. There is now only a short delay involved in getting the smaller reward but a considerably longer one in the case of the other. Obtaining the smaller reinforcer leads to the immediate emotional rewards of high levels of PAD, which collectively result in a feeling of pride or high self-esteem, as the individual receives high levels of utilitarian and informational reinforcement and is operating in a relatively open behavior setting that is defined by her personal feelings of uninhibited attainment. It is probable that the impulsive consumer's overall level of utility at t_2 and beyond is nominally as high as that of the patient consumer, both of whom derive $P^+A^+D^+$ from, respectively, opting for immediacy or waiting and exercising self-control. The impulsive consumer receives a lower level of utilitarian reinforcement (UR) in the form of the SSR but also receives immediacy of reward which is a form of informational reinforcement and the self-satisfaction of having acted in her own current interests despite being fully aware of the contingencies. The informational reinforcement that is the outcome of acting in this self-willed manner should not be overlooked: defying the objective logic of a situation, simply because one can, may be a potent source of satisfaction. The impulsive consumer is maximizing her utility just as surely as if she waited for the later reinforcer that provides a higher level of UR. We are making an interpretation of the reinforcement and reward received by each of these categories of consumer and cannot of course say that their rewards, although we denote them as $P^+A^+D^+$ in both cases, are equal in magnitude. Much depends also on the learning history of the consumer in this situation, especially that which pertains to informational reinforcement.

The smaller sooner reinforcer becomes available at t_3.

The period following the availability of the SSR, t_4, might present a very different kind of experience for the person who has taken the SSR from that of her more patient counterpart. The consumer who succumbs to the earlier source of reward experiences euphoria initially: she has received not only the UR inherent in having the commodity but also the IR that stems from being able to behave as one pleases, to exercise self-determination. However, she may become dissatisfied with this state of affairs as the first flush of positive emotion, during the period marked t_4 gives way to regret that the larger source of reward is now blocked. Shame rather than pride is likely to be the outcome (Foxall, 2016a). But there is no knowing this for all impulsive consumers, some of whom will remain entirely satisfied with the choice they have made. The consumer who has deferred gratification, however, may be more likely to begin t_3 with feelings of regret that the short-term reward has been forgone but to experience greater pride as the delay of the more substantial reinforcer diminishes. For her, the LRI remains dominant. Contemplation of the ultimate receipt of the LLR at t_5 is itself, for the self-controlled consumer, accompanied by the pride that results from the receipt of utilitarian and informational reinforcement in an open setting and the emotions that accompany this. There is no point speculating whether this level of pride exceeds that of the impulsive consumer at t_2 since the element of informational reinforcement translates into self-esteem in a very subjective fashion that is individually determined. The temporal point designated for the arrival of the LLR, should this be selected, marks the beginning of t_5. While, as noted, the self-controlled consumer receives the reward of pride, the impulsive one, if she feels anything and is conscious of the arrival of this time period, *may* feel regret but may as easily still be entirely satisfied with her choice (it depends in part on how long she will have to wait for another SSR to become available).

We have not considered thus far the downsides that the choices governed by SRIs and LRIs impose. The interpretation I have given works well for a relatively low-involvement commodity such as a chocolate bar, but if we switch to consider the role of alcohol in the reward mechanism of an addict, the position becomes far more complicated. What is rewarding at one point, say t_2, may have severe deleterious effects thereafter. The consumption of a drug by an addict may not be something that is pleasant even though it is urgently desired. Berridge (2000; see also Berridge & Kringlebach, 2015; Berridge & Robinson, 2012) proposes that the situation in which drug preparation and administration has previously occurred acquires the capacity to increase the saliency of the reinforcer. The key is the release of dopamine, a neurotransmitter associated with arousal. In the case where *wanting* the drug rather than *liking* it is the norm, the role of the drug is to negatively reinforce the approach behavior that it evokes, assuaging the negative emotions and other consequences of prior use rather than bringing positive feelings. This neurophysiological event has the effect of closing the consumer behavior setting and making a specific behavioral response all the more likely.

10.3.2.2 Valuation processes: impulsive and self-controlled consumers

This analysis provides further understanding of what is happening in temporal discounting and preference reversal (Fig. 10.4). At t_1, the consumer, impulsive or self-controlled, has a mental image of the objective or nominal SSR and LLR in the form of V_1s, and their relative valuation in the form of V_2, the subjective valuation that is the immediate precursor of action. V_2 at this stage approximates the objective value of the LLR. At this point, both rewards have objective descriptions, for example, the amounts of a single commodity available at different times or, by projection, at different prices or costs. At t_2 the valuation of the SSR increases dramatically for the

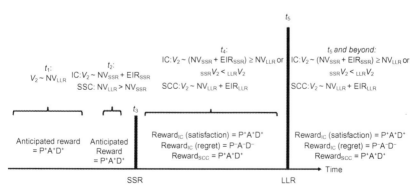

FIGURE 10.4 Temporal influences on valuation: II. EIR_{LLR}, Enhanced IR component of the LLR; EIR_{SSR}, enhanced value of the IR component of the SSR; *IC*, impulsive consumer; NV_{LLR}, nominal value of the LLR (i.e., objective V_1 value of the LLR); NV_{SSR}, nominal value of the SSR (i.e., objective V_1 of the SSR); *SCC*, self-controlled consumer; V_2, personal level valuation.

hyperbolically discounting consumer and may exceed that of the LLR to the point where, despite the fact that $_{LLR}V_1 > {}_{SSR}V_1$ in terms of an objective valuation, the hyperbolically discounting consumer chooses SSR. Clearly, something else is entering into the valuation process. A possible interpretation is that the informational reinforcement of the SSR at t_2 is so high that the overall valuation of the SSR exceeds that of the LLR. At t_1, V_2 approximates the objective value of the LLR, and the objective value of the SSR is seen as greatly inferior. However, at t_2, the valuation of the SSR has been augmented: it comprises the objective value of the SSR plus the subjective valuation of its enhanced informational reinforcement (EIR_{SSR}). This latter subjective evaluation is all that differentiates the impulsive consumer's V_2 from that of the self-controlled consumer, but it is all-important in determining the actions of both. In what does the enhanced informational reinforcement in question inhere? It is presumably a temporal preference for immediacy, and the ability to exercise personal power over circumstances, even in the face of experiencing the loss of the LLR. This may reflect a higher level of reinforcer- and reward-sensitivity. Both lead to enhanced self-esteem at least in the short term. In a situation where a higher pecuniary price is payable for obtaining a reinforcer at t rather than $t+1$, it also reflects that the consumer attaches a lower essential value to the reinforcer, a reduced willingness to defend her level of purchasing in the face of a price increase. This may also reflect the greater level of informational reinforcement the consumer obtains from immediate consumption, a hedonistic style of consumption that is conspicuous to others or simply to the consumer in question. Either way, it is a source of enhanced self-esteem. The impulsive consumer selects the SSR.

For the self-controlled consumer however, the nominal value of the SSR at t_2 remains inferior to that of the LLR, and there is no reason for this consumer to depart from the commitment reached at t_1 to select the LLR. At t_3, both consumers have made their decisions. For the impulsive consumer, at t_4, there is the possibility that she will either be content with the decision she has made, in which case she will remain confident that the nominal (objective) value of the SSR plus the enhancement of informational reinforcement that its choice brings exceeds that of the LLR, in which case her reward will be high self-esteem ($P^+A^+D^+$) or she will feel regret at having passed up the opportunity to acquire the LLR, thereby reaping the aversive emotional outcome of $P^-A^-D^-$. The self-controlled consumer, however, has a subjective evaluation of the situation in which the nominal value of the LLR, enhanced by the informational reinforcement resulting from selecting an option that will deliver the superior reinforcer and reward (EIR_{LLR}), is highly satisfying. Finally, at t_5, the options for the impulsive consumer's valuations remain as at t_4. Though the possibility must be faced that the value of EIR_{SSR} may well be diminishing in all but the most resolute valuer of immediacy. Similarly, for the self-controlled consumer, the option of being highly satisfied with her decisions and ability to see them through is constant, though it is highly likely that the value of EIR_{LLR} will have been enhanced as a result of her fortitude. It is, of course, possible that the emotive language such as "impulsive," "self-controlled," and "fortitude," is misplaced for some consumers; there is bound to be a range of individual differences that make the actions hypothetically recounted above more or less habitual for consumers as a whole.

10.3.2.3 Attempted behavior modification through bundling

Not all consumers with a learning history of choosing the SSR on many or most occasions are destined to retain this behavior pattern. There is always hope for those who wish to change. In this section, we trace the valuation process of an individual who embarks on this path of reform. The sequence is depicted in Fig. 10.5. At t_1, both consumers who will normally prove impulsive and those who will resist temptation begin with a personal subjective value, $V_2 \sim NV_{LLR}$. Let us follow the dynamics of the former's valuation over the course of her waiting for the SSR. Since we surmise that she has a learning history of yielding to the temptation to take the SSR at t_3, we expect that she will discount hyperbolically, experiencing the conflict at t_2 as an overwhelming pull toward the inferior reinforcer. Indeed, if she contemplates each valuation process in the sequence that will constitute her experience with the reinforcer in question, one at a time, she is likely to be overwhelmed every time. At t_2, the subjective value of the SSR will always, for a person who discounts in this way, be far greater than that of the LLR. However, let us make one more assumption about this consumer. Should she have absorbed Ainslie's (1992) *Picoeconomics* in the interval since her last lapse, she may decide to experiment at t_2 with the technique he calls "bundling," bringing together in mind all the SSRs that she will face in the course of her lifetime, at least with this particular reinforcer, as well as the totality of the LLRs that will also be available to her. In this case, bundling the patterns of future reinforcers together, the totality of the LLRs will outweigh that of the SSRs. This may make her present decision easier, and she may forgo the SSR on this occasion and choose to wait for the LLR. This one decision will make it that bit easier on the next choice occasion to select the LLR, just as, if she had given in to temptation on this occasion, it would be just that much easier to succumb next time, and so on.

10.3.2.4 Picoeconomic valuation: synchronicity and diachronicity

If the interests are perceived as acting synchronously, they can be viewed as subagents whose conflict might consist in opposing utility functions or time preferences. The first situation can be modeled economically as a Nash equilibrium game among these agents. The second, invoking the subpersonal

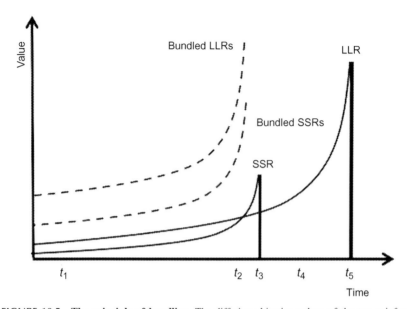

FIGURE 10.5 **The principle of bundling.** The differing objective values of the two reinforcers, observed at t_1, lead the consumer to prefer therefore LLR at this juncture. However, at t_2, while the value of the SSR is augmented by virtue of the addition to its objective worth of the EIR_{SSR} element, reflecting the higher informational reinforcement based on the immediacy of having a sample of the reinforcer, the consumer does not act on impulse as has been her wont. She experiences cognitive dissonance based on her desire for the SSR and her knowledge that selecting it will continue the downward vicious cycle in which she constantly makes a deleterious choice. Perhaps we may also be permitted the assumption that on previous consumption occasions, she has, at t_4, regretted her choice of the SSR and resolved to change her behavior. Aware of the principle of bundling, she now, in imagination, brings together the aggregated SSRs and LLRs that she will encounter. This time, the value of the (aggregated) LLR exceeds that of the (aggregated) SSR, and, from this extended perspective, it is much easier to select the former.

level of neurophysiology, reflects the idea that a hyperbolic time preference emerges from competition between the limbic and paralimbic systems which give rise to steep exponentially discounting and the regions such as PFC which govern the executive functions, giving rise to less steep exponential discounting (Ross, 2012, p. 720). In this case, the bilateral contingency linking the interests involves simultaneous interactions between the subagents, the immediate response to each other's behavior as it acts as a discriminative stimulus or motivating operation for a response. The result of behaving is likely to be seen as emotional reward rather than any obvious reinforcer. This reward, ranging from $P^+A^+D^+$ to $P^-A^-D^-$, is also likely to act as an immediate spur to further behavior. The behavior of the interests consists in the imaginative action of the consumer. Although the consumer remains the agent, the instigator of action, the subagents that exist under her imaginative control may still exert their own pull toward a particular behavior pattern.

If the subagents are seen as acting diachronically, however, each of them is temporarily in control of the consumer's behavior, guarding its unique utility function against the prior encroachment of the opposing interest. But the subagent is at some disadvantage under these arrangements. Ross (2012) points out that, in this situation, each interest not only possesses incomplete knowledge of the other but also finds its utility constrained by the prior investments made by the earlier appearing agent. In this instance, the different consumer situations represented in the bilateral contingency also appear in sequence, though each contains constraining elements generated by the opposing subagent's prior behavior.

The examples that have been given of value analysis in picoeconomics illustrate well the difference between considering SRI and LRI interactions as occurring synchronously or diachronically. The analyses summarized in Figs. 9.3 and 9.4 are concerned with the sequential changes in valuation over the course of a decision process. While the LRI remains in control over the entire sequence for the self-controlled consumer, there is a succession of dominant interests, possibly including some element of synchronicity for a while, in the case of the impulsive. For the latter, the LRI dominates at t_1, while at t_2 the SRI assumes a dominant position. If the impulsive consumer regrets her decision to adopt the SSR then at t_4 she may find that conflict between the aims of the SRI and LRI occurs, introducing an element of synchronicity. If this has remedial effects on the impulsive consumer's thinking it may lead to a determination to select the LLR on the next occasion, maybe as a result of engaging in the mental deliberations required for bundling or some other means of overcoming the onslaught of the SSR's availability at t_3. However, the impulsive consumer may experience none of this regret, remaining content in her having chosen the SSR and reaping the enhanced informational reinforcement (EIR_{SSR}) that comes from both an early opportunity to consume and the fact that her decision to take the earlier reinforcer was self-determined. Similarly, in the period beyond t_5, the impulsive consumer may either regret or accommodate to her decision to consume at t_3, while the self-controlled consumer remains steadfast in her resolve to select only the larger outcome. She is sustained in this view, after t_5 by the enhanced informational reinforcement that accrues to her for her fortitude (EIR_{LLR}).

The procedure that Ainslie (1992) calls bundling involves a near-simultaneous interaction of the interests at t_2, each following the other in rapid succession as the consumer struggles to reach an accommodation of her interests with the contingencies of reinforcement and punishment she is beholding.

Whether the decision process is viewed in terms of the interests occurring synchronously or diachronically, their nature remains the same. In view of the determination in Intentional Behaviorism to maintain the integrity or separation of the levels of exposition, this means that they are facets (rather than aspects) of the entire person who is successively engaging in primary and secondary mentation or whose behavioral tendency is governed by relatively steep or relatively shallow temporal discounting. They are not, therefore, *parts* of the individual, let alone *subpersonal* mental entities (as proposed by Frankish, 2009 and Ross, 2012). They are the whole person acting under differing contingencies of reinforcement and punishment. In synchronicity, as when the consumer engaging in bundling-related deliberation, the conflicting interests may severally exert pressure on the consumer over a very small period of time. The interests may fluctuate in their having control, and their closeness in time may have a joint effect on the emotional reaction of the consumer. But they are discrete in their influence, each taking hold of the entire consumer at one time. In a sense, this rules out synchronicity in an absolute sent of simultaneousness; but it is consistent with a view of synchronicity in which the powers exerted separately by the interests, while temporally discrete, follow hard upon one another. Whatever one makes of this, however, these rapidly alternating forces take hold of the whole person. It would be impossible otherwise to speak of them as desiring and believing, knowing or deciding, without committing the mereological fallacy. The determination of V_2 in these circumstances requires some kind of supra-interest capacity of mind to consider their implications in light of the consumer's overall cognitive style and current desires, beliefs, emotions, and perceptions. This requirement of a forum in which such deliberation can occur is the main reason for favoring a triprocessual micro-cognitive psychology such as Stanovich's (2011) model over a dual process depiction (something I have discussed at length in Foxall, 2016a, 2016b, 2016c). (Fig. 10.6 portrays such a model in terms of picoeconomics). It is legitimate to speak of the person who is dominated by either an SRI or a LRI as an *agent*, however, since she has desires and beliefs and is responsible for a behavioral response. The short-range and long-range dominated agents that the consumer becomes have divergent time preferences which reflect their, at times, hyperbolic

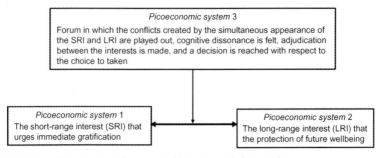

FIGURE 10.6 Triprocessual Construal of Picoeconomic Interaction.

discounting preference is the culmination of "competition between steeply exponentially discounting 'limbic' regions and more patient (less steeply exponentially discounting) 'cognitive' regions" (Ross, 2012, p. 720).

10.3.3 Macro-cognitive psychology as a basis for picoeconomic interaction

10.3.3.1 Macro- and meso-cognitive psychologies

Macro-cognitive psychology is concerned with valuation that is created and maintained through social creation and social judgment. Informational reinforcement enters CBE as a component of the consumer's utility function, the other component being UR. CBE is concerned to determine, first, the essential value the consumer attaches to a particular reinforcer (crucially, the comparative levels of essential value among commodities) and, second, the relative strengths of UR and informational reinforcement in the utility function: $U_{UR,IR} = (UR, IR)$. Essential value and the shape of the utility function influence the RTD in three ways: (1) by motivating the interests that comprise picoeconomics (V_2), (2) by providing the valuation of reinforcers that will have neurophysiological implications for V_3, and (3) by establishing the rate at which the consumer will exchange money/work for reinforcers (V_1).

Mesocognitive psychology as represented by picoeconomics (Ainslie, 1992) identifies, at the level of psychological analysis, the SRI and LRI and their interactions, but it can also express these relationships in economic terms, for example, modeling the interests as synchronous or diachronic influences on action. The interaction of the interests establishes the nature of V_2 and thereby influences RTD. The behaviors of the SRI and LRI have been modeled economically (Ainslie, 1992; Ross, 2012). The present exposition does not seek to rehearse this analysis but, within the confines of Intentional Behaviorism, proposes how they might be represented within an economic-psychological framework (i.e., within the logic of the BPM and associated operant consumer behavior economics) as the interactions of two intrapersonal "consumers" each of whom has a behavior setting that has common elements with the behavior setting of the other. The result is bilateral contingency, which we define as the interaction of behavior settings. Each consumer acts to maximize a bundle of utilitarian and informational reinforcement (and ultimately a bundle of emotionality). The SRI and LRI are treated as parties to a relationship (not a transaction because no literal/objective exchange occurs) that may be of shorter or longer duration depending on its outcomes. (Neurotics may enjoy and therefore prolong the conflict). The relationship takes the form of a bilateral contingency which is a reciprocal interaction of the three-term contingencies that govern the behavior of two parties to a transaction or relationship. The behavior of one party supplies the reinforcing and punishing consequences of the other's behavior;

in addition, the behavior of one party provides discriminative stimuli and motivating operations for the behavior of the other. The meshing of these reciprocal contingencies determines whether the relationship between the parties is of short- or long-term duration; it, therefore, determines whether one or other party will engage in search for alternative arrangements. The concept was first advanced in the context of the exogenous corporate relationships that mark the interactions of the marketing firm with its consumerate (Foxall, 1999; see also Foxall, 2019), but it can also be applied to the intrapersonal picoeconomic interactions of the SRI and LRI. Bilateral contingencies may be symmetrical (lasting, durable, stable) or asymmetrical (leading to one predominant course of action when one party gets the upper hand).

10.3.3.2 Bilateral contingency of the short- and long-range interests

As has been mentioned, modeling these interests economically requires assumptions about their operating synchronously or diachronically (Ross, 2012). We can also see them within the framework that has been advanced here as involving bilateral contingencies that bind the interests to one another. The behavior of each and the consequences thereof act as discriminative stimuli and motivating operations for the behavior of the other (Fig. 10.7).

We model each of the interests as an agent the behavior of which is explicated in terms of a three-term contingency that is intertwined with that of the opposing interest or agent. The term intertwined stresses the *twin* nature of the contingencies that dovetail to form a single unit of analysis. The principal sources of UR in the case of the SRI are the commodity itself: albeit diminished in size, it is high in value. Sources of IR in the case of the SRI include, principally, immediacy. This may itself lead to a sort of self-esteem stemming from the ability to have one's own way. The principal sources of utilitarian punishment in the case of the LRI entail dealing with the delay of the commodity; this is a cost that has to be borne in a number of ways; for example, by diminishing the value of immediacy, by building

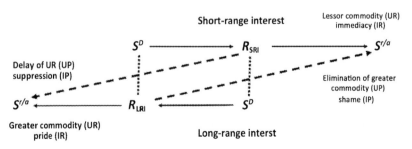

FIGURE 10.7 Intrapersonal bilateral contingency.

up the emotional rewards of patience, in terms of the ultimate pride felt in having waited but also the processual pride that comes from striving to be longsuffering. The sources of informational punishment are, therefore, mixed with coping with waiting for the commodity. The exercise of the LRI leads to UR in the form of a greater amount of the commodity, which has retained its higher value throughout the whole period, which is reflected in the informational reinforcement of enhanced pride and lasting self-esteem.

This view of intrapersonal bilateral contingency is amenable to the understanding of the interests as entities that appear either synchronously or diachronically. The import of synchronicity is evident if we take the case when the addict attempts to overcome dependency on a drug or behavior, for example, through bundling. This is a classic case of the individual attempting to make the interaction of the interests synchronous by bringing the imagined stream of future LRIs into the present so that it can be compared with the corresponding stream of SRIs. It is necessary to bring these streams of SSRs and another of LLRs into a single forum in order to compare them and make a decision as to which is preferable (currently more highly valued) and how to behave on the next available opportunity. In normal course of events the SSR is inevitably more highly valued for the hyperbolic discounter at t_2. In each succeeding instance of t_2, this continues to be the case and the SSR is chosen, the possibility of the LLR foreclosed. However, if the individual can imagine the combined outcome of *all* the SSRs she is going to encounter, on the one hand, and *all* the LLRs she will also potentially be confronted with, the combined value of the former stream will outweigh that of the latter. By "bundling" together, in imagination, these future consequences, the individual may conclude that denial of the SSR on the next occasion is worthwhile and thus enter upon a sequence of choices in which the selection of the LLR over the SSR predicts and encourages future behavior of the same kind. Bundling requires the simultaneous experience of the pulls of the SRI and the LRI. Other forms of self-management also require synchronicity—for example, preparation of emotion (Ainslie, 1992). The simultaneous vying of the SRI and LRI to obtain dominance is a kind of cognitive dissonance which leads to attempts to reduce or eliminate the resulting mental conflict. Bundling and other self-management strategies are methods of dissonance reduction which attempt to eliminate the SRI. This cognitive dissonance is for many the predominant feeling at t_2; the more steeply one discounts hyperbolically, the more intensely is this emotional struggle likely to be borne. Addicts tend to discount more steeply than nonaddicts. At other times, there is likely to be less intensely felt conflict: one or other of the interests is likely to predominate at t_1, t_3, and t_4, though regret and a hankering after an alternative choice, SSR, no longer available may afflict both impulsive and self-controlled consumers during t_3. This is not the same thing as full-on synchronous discord, but it rests on a mental representation of other possibilities, other states which indicate the metacognitive source of the conflict.

V_1 is an intentional object that aids decision-making with respect to the formulation of the V_2 that determines the individual's RTD. At t_1 and t_2, the SSR and LLR only exist for the consumer as intentional objects. At t_2 SSR rockets in value even though it is still just an intentional object, while that of LLR, another intentional object, remains lower than that of the SSR and may indeed diminish. The resulting comparison of $_{SSR}V_1$ and $_{LLR}V_1$ leads to a V_2 that favors the SSR.

10.3.3.3 Bilateral contingency analysis of bundling

Although the concluding chapter will revisit bundling in terms of the manipulation of intentional objects, it is useful to conclude this chapter with a brief exposition of the relevance of bilateral contingency to picoeconomics and bundling. At t_1 where $V_2 \sim NV_{LLR}$, the objective values of both the SSR and the LLR, presented to the consumer in verbal terms, are represented in mind as intentional objects. The *future* SSR and LLR are themselves additional intentional objects since neither exists for the consumer at this point. Their superpersonal level descriptions are, however, extensional objects. At this stage, the LRI is firmly in control. At t_2, in addition to these representations, the consumer holds the aggregated values of future SSRs and future LLRs in mind as intentional objects. The consumer's V_2 which is the immediate precursor of action is based on reasoning with respect to all of these intentional objects and decisions based on them. The consumer is now engaged in a cognitive decision process which is entirely intrapersonal and whose content is a range of propositional attitudes that represent either the SRI or LRI. These interests are engaging with one another as part of this decision process. The outcome of their interaction will determine V_2 and the ensuing action. The mental deliberation that bundling entails at t_2 is extensive and relies on the juxtaposing and comparison of, and judgment among numerous intentional objects. As long as the LRI remains in control of this process, the consumer may opt for, therefore, LLR, but there is always the possibility that the SRI will intervene, proposing the easiest option which is for the consumer to act in accordance with her learning history and select the SSR. Depending on her learning history and susceptibility to steep temporal discounting, the consumer is more or less at the mercy of her neurophysiological functioning. A learning history of extreme consumer choice may mean that even contemplation of the possibility of taking the SSR engenders the kind of dopamine rush that, as we have seen and for a small minority of consumers, Ross (2011) compares to the presence of a "self-activated phasic dopamine pump." Not everyone is at the mercy of such a dramatic intervention by the limbic system but there is, nevertheless, a tendency in most consumers to be susceptible in a degree, depending in part on their consumption histories, to incentive salience.

Part V

Conclusion

Chapter 11

The explanatory significance of Janus-variables

Chapter Outline

11.1 Janus-variables and the intentional consumer-situation 253
    11.1.1 Intentional objects populate the intentional consumer-situation 253
    11.1.2 Decision-making 255
    11.1.3 Bundling revisited 257
11.2 The broader explanatory significance of Janus-variables 260
11.3 Endnote 263

Two overarching questions have guided this inquiry. First, can the antipodal perspectives on the explanation of behavior or action, extensional behaviorism and intentional cognitivism, be brought together into a meaningful and useful framework of conceptualization and analysis while maintaining the integrity of the superpersonal, personal, and subpersonal levels of exposition? Second, can the levels of exposition be shown, nonetheless, to interact meaningfully in the production of that behavior or action? The intentional behaviorist research strategy has been proposed in relation to the former, and the claim has been made that it provides a justifiable integrative perspective. The concept of Janus-variables has been advanced as a means of achieving the latter, eliciting the additional question of the explanatory significance of this conceptual innovation. This is a matter of according a more precise meaning to the metaphor used in Chapter 10, *Grounding intentionality*, to the effect that V_2 "looks toward" V_1 and V_3. This concluding chapter addresses the explanatory role of Janus-variables, first in relation to the construction of the intentional consumer-situation (Section 11.1) and second in terms of how Janus-variables compare with *illata* and the contribution they can make to the interlevel analysis of economic behavior (Section 11.2).

11.1 Janus-variables and the intentional consumer-situation

11.1.1 Intentional objects populate the intentional consumer-situation

The concept of Janus-variables is central to the construction of the intentional consumer-situation; as such, it advances an investigation of the nature of the intentional consumer-situation begun in Foxall (2016b). V_1, the superpersonal determination of value, takes the form of price/quantity relationships (1) of past transactions, forming part of the learning history of the consumer (2) of prospective transactions. These relationships that exist objectively at the superpersonal level become intentional objects at the personal level, evoking pleasure, arousal, and dominance (PAD) reactions where they are part of the subjective experience of the consumer. Equally, price/quantity relationships that exist at the superpersonal level evoke neurophysiological reactions at the subpersonal level that evoke emotions (PAD) at the personal level. The constituents of the intentional consumer-situation are desires, beliefs, emotions, and perceptions, principally *beliefs* about price/quantity relationships and *emotional perceptions*. Hence, occurrences at both the superpersonal and subpersonal levels have an influence on the personal level as V_1 and V_3 are represented in the form of intentional objects at the personal level and, along with other beliefs, influence V_2, and hence the consumer's preferred rate of temporal discounting (RTD) and action. Key beliefs are the essential value that the consumer is willing to evince in her behavior. The desires, beliefs, emotions, and perceptions that comprise the intentional consumer-situation are the determinants of the degree of reinforcer pathology the consumer evinces in her overt behavior.

The procedure of subjectively valuing a prospective reinforcer takes place at the personal level and eventuates in V_2. This procedure, therefore, comprises purely intentional acts, drawing on the contingency-representations that consist in the desires, beliefs, emotions, and perceptions relevant to the decision in question (presumably whether to engage in the proffered transaction). These contingency-representations may include for instance the consumer's desires, what she wants to achieve, and the beliefs she entertains about the nature of the price/quantity relationship implicit in the offer, as well as her judgment about the fairness of this relationship in regard to her budget constraint and her emotional reactions. These contingency-representations are intentional objects, and they include the consumer's understanding of the relationship between the work that must be expended or the money that must be surrendered and the amount of the reinforcer this will yield. The objective counterpart of this is the expression of the proposed deal, its components and its implications, at the superpersonal level, perhaps in a series of verbal statements. These verbal behaviors describe the objective valuation of the deal (V_1). At some point in the decision process, the consumer must translate the parameters of the deal, perhaps as stated by the marketer, into a subjective appreciation thereof. She does this by thinking about, comparing, and evaluating the proposed deal in regard to her desires and her feelings about all of these, the PAD that she experiences in the course of the decision-making procedures she follows. All of these elements, the qualities she subjectively manipulates, are intentional objects, representations of the extensional objects with which she has been presented by the marketer's pitch. This is shown as A in Fig. 11.1. The key relationship is that between the consumer's view of V_1 (something which is inherent in the behavior of the marketer at the superpersonal level of exposition) as a potential valuation of the commodity if the transaction takes place and her personal valuation of the commodity in terms of what it will avail and what it will cost, an intentional element at the personal level that is contributing, via a process of decision-making, to the formulation of V_2. V_1, perhaps as an objective statement of the terms on which a transaction can occur, has become an intentional object of the valuation that takes place at the personal level. V_2, when it is realized, is also in itself an intentional object. It is the mental comparison of these intentional objects that determines whether the consumer participates in the transaction as it is represented by V_1 or continues to negotiate or withdraws from the transaction. Marketer behavior is the objectively available means of conveying an offer to consumers. It can be analyzed via the superpersonal level of exposition in terms of the stimulus field that generates it and the pattern of reinforcement and punishment to which it leads. This marketer behavior provides the V_1 that the consumer internalizes as an intentional object which participates in the process of decision-making. It also evokes neural firing and neurotransmitter transmission at the subpersonal level (B in Fig. 11.1).

11.1.2 Decision-making

Decision-making, which is the central kind of intentional behavior that occurs within the intentional consumer-situation, is essentially the manipulation of intentional objects. Picoeconomic interests each embody a distinct representation of $_{SSR}V_1$ and $_{LLR}V_1$ since each discounts the future at a different rate. Each of the interests also embodies a representation of $_{SSR}V_3$, which is peculiar to it, in the form of emotional reactions. Indeed, these intentional pico-interests can exist and operate only if they hold these varying values as intentional objects. These intentional objects, representations of V_1 and V_3, are the ultimate determinants of V_2, which is responsible for the rate at which the consumer would prefer to discount the future and, therefore, for her actions. In Fig. 11.2 the decision-making unit (mind) contains the desires, beliefs, emotions, and perceptions formed from the consumer's learning history and understanding of the current consumer behavior setting. Among these, it also contains, as intentional objects, what the consumer knows about the smaller−sooner reinforcer (SSR) and larger−later reinforcer (LLR): $_{SSR}V_1$ and $_{LLR}V_1$. From a comparative evaluation of these intentional objects, and in the context of all other relevant desires, beliefs, emotions, and perceptions, the consumer determines V_2 with respect to the two reinforcers: $_{SSR}V_2$ and $_{LLR}V_2$. A final contextualized comparative evaluation of these V_2s leads to the consumer's (mentally) preferred *RTD* (which is itself an intentional object, generated by deliberation, essentially the consumer's final V_2), and this is revealed in action. These mental and overt actions are assumed to be

256 PART | V Conclusion

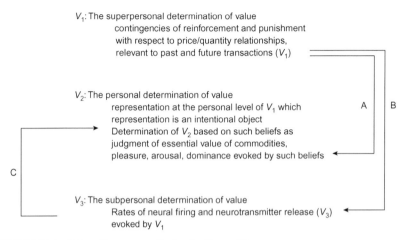

FIGURE 11.1 Interactions among the levels of exposition.
A = Verbal descriptions of the price/quantity relationships promised by a proposed transaction (V_1), acting as CSs or S^Ds, evoke emotional reactions as intentional objects that represent the proposed transaction.
B = Influence of verbal descriptions and behavior at the superpersonal level on neuronal valuation at the subpersonal.
C = Influence of neuronal firing and neurotransmitter release at the subpersonal level on emotional feelings at the personal level.

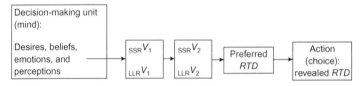

FIGURE 11.2 Intrapersonal valuation: the process of decision-making.

underpinned by appropriate neuronal activity resulting in $_{SSR}V_3$ and $_{LLR}V_3$. This analysis chimes with the description of micro-cognitive psychology activity: $_{SSR}V_1$ and $_{SSR}V_2$ are reached by or at least reflect the activity of the impulsive system, while $_{LLR}V_1$ and $_{LLR}V_2$ are reached by or reflect the activity of the executive system. The comparative evaluations are the fora or mechanisms in which these systems interact and eventuate in a "preferred" *RTD* that manifests in revealed preference. This is an overcognitive view of what happens in the course of decision-making. The behavioral outcomes of the operation of the impulsive system can be automatic and rapid, not allowing for deliberation. It is only if the executive system intervenes that valenced consideration of the alternative courses of action open to the consumer can take place. But when this is the case, the final outcome is the result of reflection, debate, and negotiation. The precise form of this will depend on the consumer's cognitive style and learning history.

The action of decision-making, then, involves the mental comparison of these intentional objects. Let us consider it in the familiar context of consumer choice and the time frames that were proposed in Fig. 10.4. At t_1 the SSR and LLR can for the consumer comprise only mental representations of two V_1s that are slated to appear in the future. The consumer is likely to mentally prefer at this point the mental representation of the LLR as a goal for future action. At t_2 the impatient consumer again represents the SSR and LLR mentally and values the SSR more highly and selects this (displaying a revealed preference for the SSR). The patient consumer at this point still values the LLR more highly and by refusing the SSR reveals a preference for the LLR. At t_3 the impatient consumer may either come to regret her choice of the SSR, repine that she did not wait for the SSR, and incur the punishing emotional outcomes of shame or guilt ($P^-A^-D^-$); or she may look upon her choice of the SSR without regret, reaping the positive rewards of having maximized her utility by selecting an option that has provided a high level of informational reinforcement that leads to her having a sense of self-esteem. The patient consumer at t_3 may remain content with her choice of the LLR, reaping the high levels of informational reinforcement that are consistent with the anticipation of not only gaining a higher level of utilitarian reinforcement when the LLR becomes available but also that of the self-esteem she feels for exercising restraint. Part of the satisfaction she feels during this temporal period is therefore due to the *future* informational reinforcement she will receive on holding out to obtain the LLR. She is reaping a high level of reward even though she has not received any utilitarian reinforcer at this point. Moreover, the reward she experiences ($P^+A^+D^+$) must result solely from informational reinforcement in the form of her expectation of the outcomes of waiting for the LLR. Alternatively, the patient consumer at t_3 may encounter regret that she did not select the SSR, impatience at having to wait so much longer for *any* tangible reinforcer and the rewards contingent upon its delivery to her, and increased longing for the utilitarian reinforcer represented by the LLR. The result is $P^-A^-D^-$, shame, regret. At t_4 the impatient consumer may experience either more of the guilt or shame she encountered at t_3 or the continued high level of PAD due to her exercise of self-control. The patient consumer is likely to enjoy a high degree of $P^+A^+D^+$ on account of the high levels of utilitarian reinforcement embodied in the receipt and consumption of the LLR and informational reinforcement that derive from her enhanced self-esteem that results from her exercise of self-control.

11.1.3 Bundling revisited

The proposed explanation of decision-making is clear in the case of bundling. Indeed, bundling is an operation that relies almost exclusively on the manipulation of intentional objects. In Fig. 10.5, at t_1 the *descriptions* of the contingencies for obtaining SSR and LLR constitute V_1s, though the rewards themselves will only become actual at later times. These descriptions are the rules that exist objectively for the acquisition of a reinforcer. They exist at the superpersonal level. However, they can become intentional objects at the personal level and thereby contribute to the formulation of a V_2 that influences preferred RTD and action. Assume that $_{SSR}V_1$ = the objective value of the SSR and $_{LLR}V_1$ = the objective value of the LLR, both as *described* to the consumer. These V_1s enter the personal level by becoming intentional objects that the consumer manipulates, along with others, in the course of computing V_2. In the absence of bundling, at t_2 the $_{LLR}V_1$ and $_{SSR}V_1$ remain unchanged; what has changed is the imminence of the SSR if chosen. The intentional objects that consist in personal-level portrayals of $_{SSR}V_1$ and $_{LLR}V_1$ may change, however (in the case of the tempted consumer), because her contemplation of the SSR evokes high levels of PAD in anticipation of the early reward. She may either withstand this temptation and wait for the LLR or find that the high level of anticipated reward for the SSR means that it wins out. (The consumer who discounts exponentially simply ignores SSR and is not tempted). Bundling is an attempt to overcome the situation in which $_{SSR}V_1 > {_{LLR}V_1}$ by ignoring the simple dichotomy presented by the SSR versus LLR choice and inculcating longer term reasoning into the definition of the situation. Bringing forward in mind the cumulative outcomes of choosing a stream of LLRs for comparison with the outcomes that will accrue from a stream of associated SSRs may indicate to the consumer that the former is more rewarding and therefore preferable. The amended stream of behavior that results from this reasoning, and the associated emotional reactions, must, however, begin with the present situation, which must eventuate in the selection of the LLR. Each succeeding adherence to the strategy of choosing the LLR strengthens the probability that the consumer will maintain this behavior pattern on succeeding occasions. Any lapse makes further aberration more likely.

Can this reasoning provide a means of bridging the divide between the personal and subpersonal levels? The firing of neurons cannot in itself be represented in mind at the personal level. But the feelings, for example, of pleasure or arousal or dominance, to which such firing gives rise, can be so represented. These feelings—perhaps of pleasure in response to endorphin production, or of arousal as a result of the firing of dopaminergic neurons— can be registered at the personal level and contribute to the formation of a valuation (V_2 again) that determines the consumer's discount rate and hence her economic behavior, or of serotonin which may enhance confidence and, therefore, feelings of dominance. In fact, those feelings *are* the personal-level representations of neurophysiological activity, and they do feed directly into the consumer's decision-making and behavior (C in Fig. 11.1). These feelings are the intentional objects that represent V_3 but at the personal level, just as the consumer's beliefs are personal-level representations of the value (V_1) proposed by a prospective deal. Together these representations determine the values the consumer attaches to particular courses of action—past or future—that is, V_2, and V_2 determines the RTD she is willing to display and her actual consumer behavior. Hence, the experience of valuation that inheres in the formulation V_2 is linked to the rate of neuronal firing that indexes V_3. This latter is not on the surface a matter of holding V_3 as an intentional object since this would not be empirically demonstrable; to present it in such terms would be to engage in unnecessary abstraction. Nevertheless, to speak of the intentional representation of V_3 at V_2 does make sense insofar as emotional responses, inaugurated at the subpersonal level through neural firings and neurotransmitter release, are felt at the personal level. These felt emotions are intentional objects that influence the formulation of V_2 and hence action.[1]

The determination of V_2 at the personal level is the construction and operation of the intentional consumer-situation. We can take a modular approach to all this in which sensory modules (Fodor, 1983), plus emotional modules encompassing PAD (Foxall, 2017b), determine the beliefs the individual forms with respect to the appropriateness of values offered her (V_1s) that, in turn, determine V_2 which then determines the consumer's preferred RTD and then action. Janus-variables, such as personal valuation (V_2), are not *illata*. *Illata* are, according to Dennett, intentionally characterized physical entities. Their aim is to allow the conceptual divide between knowledge-by-acquaintance and knowledge-by-description to be bridged through the assumption that physical entities can be spoken of as though they were intentional. This, as we have seen, commits the mereological fallacy and does not explain scientifically. Janus-variables are intentional idioms, propositional attitudes. They exist at the personal level of exposition and may take related extensional constructs as intentional objects (i.e., behaviors that exist or are projected in mind to exist at the superpersonal level of exposition such exchanging, valuing, a commodity X at $\$Y$. In other words, these objects may be the revealed preference of the consumer or a projected action). But they are not intentionally characterized by physical entities. Insofar as they take other acts of valuation as their intentional objects, they relate different levels of exposition, that is, the personal and superpersonal.[2] Let us look at this from the viewpoint of action at the super-personal level, i.e., the enactment of an economic exchange that reveals preference and therefore value. (Such action occurs at the super-personal level because it is controlled or

---

1. Dennett, as we have repeatedly seen, gets around a broadly similar problem of marrying together the intentional and the extensional—but one that is by no means identical to that raised here—by positing *illata* that involve crossing the level of exposition divide and commits the mereological fallacy. There is no equivalent legerdemain available to my way of thinking.
2. *Super*personal because, as an exchange behavior, it is controlled or explained by its consequences.

explained by its consequences.) If the consumer subsequently thinks about this exchange then she performs a personal level action (i.e., her thinking *of*, or thinking *that*). The exchange, as the consumer experiences it at this personal level of intentionality, has become an intentional object. The actions that make up the exchange which are portrayed in extensional language at the super-personal level, are now being represented at the personal level of intentionality. This still does not make it a physical entity that is intentionally characterized (an *illatum*), but it does transform it into a rather special sort of thing. It is an extensionally definable/specifiable action that is intentionally created but not intentionally characterized in Dennett's sense. That is, it is not something that has (or is considered to have) desires and beliefs in its own right in order that it may be predicted. It is not an intentional system, therefore, in his sense. It is an intentional object. But it is still something that crosses levels of exposition. Moreover, it is something that can *influence* V_2—a consumer's desire/belief about a value exchange that has taken place, will take place, or may take place is an important modifier of the subjective valuation of a future transaction, and the action that will be taken based on it. Occurrences at the subpersonal level of exposition do not, however, fulfill a similar role, since persons do not conceive of their actual rates of neuronal firing as representations of value, though they may do so of neuronal action in general. But that is a very different thing from what has been posited at the superpersonal/personal levels in the case of intentionally conceived exchange actions. Hence, Janus-variables are not *illata*; nor yet are they the biconditionals that McGinn identifies as necessary to resolve the mind–body problem. But, in maintaining the principle of the separation of levels of exposition, while still showing how they are related, they may be the closest we can get to such a resolution.

11.2 The broader explanatory significance of Janus-variables

Are Janus-variables, or at least the intentional objects that are their components, really not intentionally characterized physical entities? We have defined the intentional objects that contribute to the calculation at the personal level of V_2 as extensionally defined items such as objective valuations presented to the consumer in superpersonal terms (V_1). This may seem, superficially, to be comprehensible as a physical (or at least extensional) object that is realized at an intentional level. However, Dennett's idea of "physical entities that are intentionally-characterized" refers to physical objects that are treated as intentional systems by virtue of the ascription to them of desires and beliefs such as to render them predictable. We never leave the realm of the physical here. The intentional characterization of a physical object in Dennett's system is simply a heuristic overlay that is not a part of the physical item, which remains exactly as the physicist would apprehend it. All that is gained by treating it as an *illatum* is that we investigators assume the right to speak of it in the vocabulary of intentionality. The intentional objects that contribute to V_2, however, are subjectively experienced entities that enjoy intensional inexistence as part of the personal experience of the individual who entertains them. This is consistent with the definition of intentionality reached in Section 8.3.

Janus concepts can, therefore, be defined *only* intentionally and are to be located exclusively at the personal level of exposition. Hence, extensionally characterized terms are not Janus-variables. Janus-variables cannot, therefore, overcome the problem raised by McGinn to the effect that we can overcome the mind−body problem only by devising concepts that are *both* applicable to knowledge-by-acquaintance and knowledge-by-description. We are left with conceptual dualism, but we can perhaps see more clearly how the extensional and intentional concepts are related and how they figure in explanation. Dennett's idea of *illata is* a single conception that does not do the job because it invokes the mereological fallacy. *Illata* are physical concepts to which Dennett applies the intentional stance but without logic or justification since the physical stance is clearly the applicable stance here. What of his argument that by using the intentional stance we can better *predict* phenomena? Now that might be true, but it amounts to a folk-psychological truism rather than a scientifically relevant explanation. By instead using the physical stance—albeit at the cost of greater unwieldiness and inconvenience—we can arrive at explanations in ontologically relevant terms. Physical things are caused by physical things.

Janus-variables are not *physical* entities that are intentionally characterized: they are intentional entities that can take extensional behaviors that are under operant control (i.e., controlled by their consequences as revealed in exchange) as their intentional objects. These exchange actions are not intentional entities: they are superpersonal extensional happenings that can be represented at the intentional level of exposition. This is as close as we can come to an intermingling of the levels of exposition, as near as we can currently come to the biconditionals that McGinn identifies as necessary for the solution of the mind−body problem. But each conception (be it objectified exchange at the superpersonal level, intentional valuation at the personal level, or neuronal evaluation at the subpersonal) exists in its own conceptual sphere. There is no attempt to cross over, flip, or encompass. The mystery that is the capacity to represent extensionality as an intentional object remains the essence of the mind−body problem.

Dennett, in my view, goes as far toward solving the mind--body problem (without directly alluding to it as far as I can discern) as anyone. In the absence of genuine biconditionals, his three kinds seems as close an approximation to what is required as we can achieve. But the approach is problematic. It is obvious from the foregoing that the results at which Chapter 10, *Grounding intentionality*, arrived, rely on several basic components of the intentional behaviorist research program that are not found in his scheme.

The first is an insistence on *theoretical minimalism* as the founding stage. The existence of a basis for theoretical minimalism that delineates the point at which intentional explanation becomes necessary and the shape it should assume. The existence of a theoretically minimal model of economic behavior also ensures that intentional interpretation is grounded in the demonstrable bases of the variables of which consumer behavior is a function. Radical behaviorism is doubly qualified: positively, it acts as a methodology for the identification of those behaviors whose rate of recurrence can be assigned to environmental stimuli; negatively, its explanatory potency degrades, revealing the imperatives of intentionality. The extensional model also provides a means of identifying the nature of the intentional objects that enable the consumer to formulate V_2 that determines preferred RTD and subsequent action. The Behavioral Perspective Model research program identifies the emotions that reflect neuronal firing rates (V_3) and the beliefs that derive from judgments of the contingencies available at V_1. The intentional consumer-situation, as I argued it should be constructed in terms of contingency-representations (Foxall, 2017b), provides the basis of the nature and structure of Janus-variables.

The second is an understanding of *intentionality as subjective experience* rather than as that which must be ascribed to an entity in order to predict its behavior. There *is* more to being an intentional system than is implied by being so amenable to prediction. The understanding of intentionality and intensionality on the basis of Searle's and Strawson's analyses renders intentionality a capacity of minds; intensionality, of sentences. Derived intentionality cannot, therefore, be entertained, and according to Dennett, there is no other variety. Moreover, Dennett's case for the ascription of content rests on the understanding that, because some neural events, states, and structures must be interpreted as being about other things in order to make sense of what an animal is doing—that is, inanimate objects are to be taken as intentional—it is possible to ascribe content to them, to apply concepts and variables that we have reasoned apply only at the personal level of exposition to the subpersonal. Now, this might be a useful *façon de parler*, but it is not a scientific argument. It entails the equation of intentionality with aboutness but, as Strawson points out, aboutness is not the index of intentionality: as I quoted him in Chapter 8, *The intentional behaviorist research strategy*, "No states of nonexperiential entities are ever really about anything at all" (Strawson, 2010, p. 330). In short, Dennett's understanding of intentionality is not sufficient because, for him, intentionality is a matter of external ascription rather than something that is subjectively experienced.

The third is the rigorous s*eparation of levels of exposition and their appropriate mode of explanation*. In addition to Dennett's pioneering proposal, Intentional Behaviorism includes the superpersonal level of exposition, without which the concept of Janus-variables could not be. The key factor, however, is that in Intentional Behaviorism, intentionality applies to the person as a whole and cannot cross the expository barrier. Conceptual terms such as *value*, *arousal*, and *attitude* have both intentional and extensional connotations/characterizations. They are words that are employed at all three levels of exposition. It is not the case, however, that the three usages cohere into a single concept or term. Rather, they may correlate positively with one another, as when a high rate of dopaminergic firing coincides with the payment of a high price and self-reported high valuation. Hence, Janus thinking maintains the conceptual separation of extensional and intentional variables while arguing that they are closely bound together in the explanatory process. But rather than switch between levels of exposition for a single concept, as Dennett's system does, it maintains the appropriateness of extensional language to the superpersonal and subpersonal levels and intentional language to the personal level.

Chapter 3, *The basis of the intentional stance*, noted, moreover, Dennett's proposal that intentionality can be applied to neurophysiological events through the provision of a "heuristic overlay" that answers such question as how the organism "knows" what response to select from its repertoire as an appropriate resolution of the problem brought about by the detection of a particular stimulus. I have argued that this move is unacceptable because it breaches the principle of separation of levels of exposition and rests on the mereological fallacy. Neurophysiology belongs to the extensional subpersonal level, and the question of how the animal "knows" what to do is as readily accommodated by reference to its learning history as by this kind of intentional heuristic intervention. Heuristic overlaying is simply a device for transferring explanatory variables from the personal level of exposition where they belong to the subpersonal level.

Intentional Behaviorism proposes something rather different that permits a bringing together of the personal and superpersonal levels of exposition. The variables that exist at the superpersonal level, such as objective behaviors that mark particular exchange values, can be represented at the personal level. Objective valuations that have been revealed at the superpersonal level (e.g., the price the consumer paid for a given quantity of a commodity) can be represented in thought (e.g., as a contribution to the belief that she paid too much). Or the amount that she is offered for the surrender of a particular further payment, which takes the form of a track or a ply, can be represented at the personal level as a valuation that is too high or enticingly low and can enter into the formulation of the valuation (V_2) that determines the extent to which the consumer is prepared to discount the future by making or forgoing a transaction.

11.3 Endnote

The levels of exposition are conjoined through the ability of the personal level to incorporate as intentional objects the elements of the superpersonal and subpersonal levels that exist objectively as extensional objects. This does not, of course, remove the mind−body problem, but it offers a tentative solution to the problem of how far we can go to resolve it within a framework defined by the assumption of inevitable conceptual duality. Janus-variables differ from *illata* in this crucial regard. *Illata* are physical items that can be intentionally characterized by means of a heuristic overlay that attributes intentionality to them in a third personal manner. What this means is that there need be no actual subjective experience of desires and beliefs on the part of the physical entity; there need only be an external ascription to it of desires and beliefs in order to make it predictable. This reflects Dennett's view of intentionality as something ascribed by an external agent rather than something experienced by a person, as well as his other conclusions that were reviewed in Chapter 3, *The basis of the intentional stance*. However, the definitions of intentionality and extensionality adopted in this study (Section 8.3) entail that the former is a subjective experience of a sentient being; moreover, the intensional criterion (Section 8.4.1) requires that intentional explanation be confined to verbal humans. This rules out the ascription of intentionality to animals and inanimate entities, except as a *façon de parler* that aids understanding without constituting part of a scientific explanation. The question how we ascribe intentionality to persons remains. We cannot know their personal experience (knowledge-by-acquaintance); nor can it enter directly into a scientific inquiry, which we understand to rely on third personal knowledge. We can gauge it only via something such as heterophenomenology (Dennett, 1981, 2005). The only evidence of first personal experience comes in this derived fashion. But that does not mean that first personal experience does not exist. On the contrary: it plays a vital part in the explanation of action in intentional terms.

Bibliography

Adger, D. (2019). *Language unlimited*. Oxford: Oxford University Press.
Ainslie, G. (1986). Beyond microeconomics: Conflict among interests in a multiple self as a determinant of value. In J. Elster (Ed.), *The multiple self* (pp. 133–175). Cambridge: Cambridge University Press.
Ainslie, G. (1989). Freud and picoeconomics. *Behaviorism, 17*, 11–19.
Ainslie, G. (1992). *Picoeconomics: The strategic interaction of successive motivational states within the person*. Cambridge: Cambridge University Press.
Ainslie, G. (2001). *Breakdown of will*. Cambridge: Cambridge University Press.
Ainslie, G. (2007). Emotion: The gaping hole in economic theory. In B. Montero, & M. D. White (Eds.), *Economics and the mind* (pp. 11–28). London and New York: Routledge.
Ainslie, G. (2010). Procrastination: The basic impulsive. In C. Andreou, & M. D. White (Eds.), *The thief of time* (pp. 11–27). Oxford University Press.
Ainslie, G. (2011). Free will as recursive self-prediction: Does a deterministic mechanism reduce responsibility? In J. Poland, & G. Graham (Eds.), *Addiction and responsibility* (pp. 55–87). Cambridge, MA: MIT Press.
Ainslie, G. (2013). Money as MacGuffin: A factor in gambling and other process addictions. In N. Levy (Ed.), *Addiction and self-control: Perspectives from philosophy, psychology, and neuroscience* (pp. 16–37). Oxford: Oxford University Press.
Ainslie, G. (2016). The cardinal anomalies that led to behavioral economics: Cognitive or motivational? *Managerial and Decision Economics, 37*, 261–273.
Ainslie, G., & Monterosso, J. (2003). Hyperbolic discounting as a factor in addiction: A critical analysis. In R. E. Vuchinich, & N. Heather (Eds.), *Choice, behavioural economics and addiction* (pp. 35–70). Oxford: Pergamon.
Ajzen, I. (1985). From intentions to actions: A theory of planned behavior. In J. Kuhl, & J. Beckman (Eds.), *Action control: From cognition to behavior* (pp. 11–39). Berlin: Springer-Verlag.
Ajzen, I. (1987). Attitudes, traits, and actions: Dispositional prediction of behavior in personality and social psychology. In L. Berkovitz (Ed.), *Advances in experimental social psychology* (20, pp. 1–63). San Diego, CA: Academic Press.
Ajzen, I. (1988). *Attitudes, personality and behavior*. Milton Keynes: Open University Press.
Ajzen, I. (1991). The theory of planned behavior. *Organizational Behavior and Human Decision Processes, 50*, 179–211.
Ajzen, I., & Cote, N. G. (2008). Attitude and the prediction of behavior. In W. D. Crano, & R. Prislin (Eds.), *Attitude and attitude change* (pp. 289–311). London and New York: Psychology Press.
Ajzen, I., & Fishbein, M. (1977). Attitude-behavior relations: A theoretical analysis and review of empirical research. *Psychological Bulletin, 84*, 888–918.
Ajzen, I., & Fishbein, M. (1980). *Understanding attitudes and predicting social behavior*. Englewood Cliffs, NJ: Prentice-Hall.

Albarracin, D., & Johnson, B. T. (Eds.), (2018). *The handbook of attitudes. Volume 1: Basic principles* (2nd ed.). London and New York: Routledge.

Alcaro, A., Huber, R., & Panksepp, J. (2007). Behavioral functions of the mesolimbic dopaminergic system: An affective neuroethological perspective. *Brain Research Review, 56*, 283–321.

Alhadeff, D. A. (1982). *Microeconomics and human behavior*. Los Angeles, CA: University of California Press.

Allen, C., & Bekoff, M. (1997). *Species of mind: The philosophy and biology of cognitive ethology*. Cambridge, MA: MIT Press.

Amsel, A. (1989). *Behaviorism, neobehaviorism, and cognition in learning theory: Historical and contemporary perspectives*. Hillsdale, NJ: Erlbaum.

Amsel, A., & Rashotte, M. E. (Eds.), (1984). *Mechanisms of adaptive behavior: Clark L. Hull's theoretical papers, with commentary*. New York: Columbia University Press.

Angulo, M. C., Staiger, J. F., Rossier, J., & Audinat, E. (1999). Developmental synaptic changes increase the range of integrative capabilities of an identified neocortical connection. *Journal of Neuroscience, 19*, 1566–1576.

Anninou, J., & Foxall, G. R. (2019). The reinforcing and aversive consequences of customer experience: The role of consumer confusion. *Journal of Retailing and Customer Service, 51*, 139–151.

Anninou, J., Foxall, G. R., & Pallister, J. G. (2016). Consumer confusion: A BPM perspective. In G. R. Foxall (Ed.), *The Routledge companion to consumer behavior analysis* (pp. 400–416). London and New York: Routledge.

Anon. (1970). Status of the mental. *Times Literary Supplement, 3546*, 152, 12 February.

Anscombe, G. E. M. (1957). *Intention*. Oxford: Blackwell.

Arntzen, E. (2012). Training and testing parameters in formation of stimulus equivalence: Methodological issues. *European Journal of Behavior Analysis, 13*, 123–135.

Arntzen, E., & Nartey, R. K. (2018). Equivalence class formation as a function of preliminary training with pictorial stimuli. *Journal of the Experimental Analysis of Behavior, 110*(2), 275–291.

Audi, R. (1972). Review of Dennett: Content and consciousness, *Philosophy Forum* (12, pp. 206–208).

Baars, B. J. (2003). The double life of B. F. Skinner. *Journal of Consciousness Studies, 10*, 5–25.

Bach, K. (1978). A representational theory of action. *Philosophical Studies, 34*, 361–379.

Bagozzi, R. P., & Warshaw, P. R. (1990). Trying to consume. *Journal of Consumer Research, 17*, 127–140.

Baker, L. R. (1991). Dretske on the explanatory role of belief. *Philosophical Studies, 63*, 99–111.

Baker, L. R. (1995). *Explaining attitudes: A practical approach to the mind*. Cambridge: Cambridge University Press.

Bandura, A. (1977). *Social learning theory*. Englewood Cliffs, NJ: Prentice Hall.

Bandura, A. (1978). The self system in reciprocal determinism. *American Psychologist, 33*(4), 344–358.

Bandura, A. (1986). *Social foundations of thought and action: A social cognitive theory*. Englewood Cliffs, NJ: Prentice-Hall.

Bandura, A. (1997). *Self-efficacy: The exercise of control*. New York: W. H. Freeman and Company.

Banich, M. T. (2009). Executive function: The search for an integrated account. *Current Directions in Psychological Science, 10*, 89–94.

Bargh, J. A. (Ed.), (2007). *Social psychology and the unconscious: The automaticity of higher mental processes.* London and New York: Psychology Press.

Barkley, R. A. (1997a). Behavioral inhibition, sustained attention, and executive functions: Constructing a unified theory of ADHD. *Psychological Bulletin, 121,* 65–94.

Barkley, R. A. (1997b). *ADHD and the nature of self-control.* New York: Guilford Press.

Barkley, R. A. (2001). The executive functions and self-regulation: An evolutionary neuropsychological perspective. *Neuropsychology Review, 11,* 1–29.

Barkley, R. A. (2012). *Executive functions: What they are, how they work, and why they evolved.* New York: Guilford Press.

Barkley, R. A. (2013). Attention-deficit/hyperactivity disorder, self-regulation, and executive functioning. In K. D. Vohs, & R. F. Baumeister (Eds.), *Handbook of self-regulation: Research, theory, and applications* (2nd ed., pp. 551–563). New York: Guilford Press.

Baum, W. (1973). The correlation based law of effect. *Journal of the Experimental Analysis of Behavior, 20,* 137–153.

Baum, W. (1994). *Understanding behaviorism: Science, behavior, and culture.* New York: HarperCollins.

Baum, W. (2000). Alive and kicking: A review of handbook of behaviorism. *Journal of the Experimental Analysis of Behavior, 33,* 263–270.

Baum, W. M. (2017). *Understanding behaviorism: Behavior, culture, and evolution* (3rd ed.). Chichester: Wiley-Blackwell.

Bechara, A. (2005). Decision-making, impulse control and loss of willpower to resist drugs: A neurocognitive perspective. *Nature Neuroscience, 8,* 1458–1463.

Bechara, A. (2011). Human emotions in decision making: Are they useful or disruptive? In O. Vartanian, & D. R. Mandel (Eds.), *Neuroscience of decision making* (pp. 73–95). Hove and New York: Psychology Press.

Bechara, A., & Damasio, D. R. (2005). The somatic marker hypothesis: A neural theory of economic decision. *Games and Economic Behavior, 52,* 336–372.

Bechara, A., Damasio, H., & Damasio, A. R. (2000). Emotion, decision making and the orbitofrontal cortex. *Cerebral Cortex, 10,* 295–307.

Bechtel, W. (1978). Indeterminacy and intentionality: Quine's purported elimination of propositions. *Journal of Philosophy, 75,* 649–662.

Bechtel, W. (1988). *Philosophy of mind: An overview for cognitive science.* Hillsdale, NJ: Lawrence Erlbaum Associates.

Bechtel, W. (2008). *Mental mechanisms: Philosophical perspectives on cognitive neuroscience.* London and New York: Psychology Press.

Bem, D. (1972). Self-perception theory. In L. Berkovitz (Ed.), *Advances in experimental social psychology* (6, pp. 1–61). San Diego, CA: Academic Press.

Bennett, M. R. (2007). Neuroscience and philosophy. In M. Bennett, D. Dennett, P. Hacker, & J. Searle (Eds.), *Neuroscience and philosophy: Brain, mind, and language* (pp. 49–69). New York: Columbia University Press.

Bennett, M. R., & Hacker, P. M. S. (2003). *Philosophical foundations of neuroscience.* Oxford: Blackwell.

Bennett, M. R., & Hacker, P. M. S. (2007). The conceptual presuppositions of cognitive neuroscience: A reply to critics. In M. Bennett, D. Dennett, P. Hacker, & J. Searle (Eds.), *Neuroscience and philosophy: Brain, mind, and language* (pp. 127–170). New York: Columbia University Press.

Bermúdez, J. L. (2000). Personal and sub-personal: A difference without a distinction. *Philosophical Explorations, III,* 63–82.

Bermúdez, J. L. (2003). *Thinking without words.* Oxford: Oxford University Press.

Bermúdez, J. L. (2005). *Philosophy of psychology*. New York and London: Routledge.
Berridge, K. C. (2000). Reward learning: Reinforcement, incentives, and expectations. In D. L. Medin (Ed.), *The psychology of learning and motivation* (49, pp. 223–278). San Diego, CA: Academic Press.
Berridge, K. C., & Kringelbach, M. L. (2015). Pleasure systems in the brain. *Neuron, 86,* 646–664.
Berridge, K. C., & Robinson, T. E. (2012). Drug addiction as incentive sensitization. In J. Poland, & G. Graham (Eds.), *Addiction and responsibility* (pp. 21–53). Cambridge, MA: MIT Press.
Berwick, R. C., & Chomsky, N. (2016). *Why only us? Language and evolution*. Cambridge, MA: MIT Press.
Bickel, W. K., Jarmolowicz, D. P., Mueller, E. T., & Gatchalian, K. M. (2011). The behavioural economics and neuroeconomics of reinforcer pathologies: Implications for etiology and treatment of addiction. *Current Psychiatry Reports, 13,* 406–415.
Bickel, W. K., Jarmolowicz, D. P., Mueller, E. T., Gatchalian, K. M., & McClure, S. M. (2012). Are executive function and impulsivity antipodes? A conceptual reconstruction with special reference to addiction. *Psychopharmacology, 221,* 361–387.
Bickel, W. K., Kowal, B. P., & Gatchalian, K. M. (2006). Understanding addiction as a pathology of temporal horizon. *Behavior Analyst Today, 7,* 32–47.
Bickel, W. K., & Marsch, L. A. (2000). The tyranny of small decisions: origins, outcomes, and proposed solutions. In W. R. Bickel, & R. E. Vuchinich (Eds.), *Reframing health behavioral change with behavioral economics* (pp. 341–391). Mahwah, NJ: Erlbaum.
Bickel, W. R., & Yi, R. (2008). Temporal discounting as a measure of executive function: Insights from the competing neuro-behavioral decision system hypothesis of addiction. *Advances in Health Economics and Health Services Research, 20,* 289–309.
Biglan, A. (1995). *Changing cultural practices: A contextualist framework for intervention research*. Reno, NV: Context Press.
Bindra, D. (1978). How adaptive behavior is produced: A perceptual–motivation alternative to response reinforcement. *Psychological Review, 81,* 199–213.
Blake, A. G. E. (1969). Review of content and consciousness by D. C. Dennett. *Systematics, 7,* 261–263.
Bohner, G., & Wänke, M. (2002). *Attitudes and attitude change*. London and New York: Psychology Press.
Bolles, R. C. (1972). Reinforcement, expectancy, and learning, *Psychological Review* (79, pp. 394–409).
Bolles, R. C. (1979). *Learning theory* (2nd ed.). New York: Holt, Rinehart and Winston.
Bouton, M. E., & Franselow, M. S. (Eds.), (1997). *Learning, motivation, and cognition: The functional behaviorism of Robert C. Bolles*. Washington, DC: American Psychological Association.
Brakel, L. A. W. (2001). Phantasies, neurotic beliefs, and beliefs-proper. *American Journal of Psychoanalysis, 61,* 363–389.
Brakel, L. A. W. (2002). Phantasy and wish: A proper function account of a-rational primary process mediated mentation. *Australasian Journal of Philosophy, 80,* 1–16.
Brakel, L. A. W. (2009). *Philosophy, psychoanalysis, and the a-rational mind*. Oxford: Oxford University Press.
Brakel, L. A. W. (2010). *Unconscious knowing and other essays in psycho-philosophical analysis*. Oxford: Oxford University Press.
Brakel, L. A. W. (2013). *The ontology of psychology: Questioning foundations in the philosophy of mind*. New York and London: Routledge.

Brakel, L. A. W. (2015a). Two fundamental problems for philosophical psychoanalysis. In S. Boag, L. A. W. Brakel, & V. Talvitie (Eds.), *Philosophy, science, and psychoanalysis: A critical meeting* (pp. 119–143). London: Karnac.

Brakel, L. A. W. (2015b). Unconscious knowing: Psychoanalytic evidence in support of a radical epistemic view. In S. Boag, L. A. W. Brakel, & V. Talvitie (Eds.), *Psychoanalysis and philosophy of mind: Unconscious mentality in the twenty-first century* (pp. 193–237). London: Karnac.

Brakel, L. A. W. (2016). Animals are agents. *Animal Sentience, 103*, 1–3.

Brakel, L. A. W. (2018). The primary process: Bridges to interdisciplinary studies of mind. *Psychoanalytical Inquiry, 38*, 177–185.

Brakel, L. A., & Shevrin, H. (2003). Freud's dual process theory and the place of the a-rational. *Behavioral and Brain Sciences, 26*, 527–528.

Bratman, M. E. (1994). Intention. In S. Guttenplan (Ed.), *A companion to the philosophy of mind* (pp. 375–379). Oxford: Blackwell.

Brentano, F. (1995). *Psychology from an empirical standpoint*. London and New York: Routledge. (First published, Leipzig, 1874).

Brewer, W. F. (1974). There is no convincing evidence for operant or classical conditioning in adult humans. In W. B. Weimer, & D. S. Palermo (Eds.), *Cognition and the symbolic processes* (pp. 1–42). Hillsdale, NJ: Erlbaum.

Broadbent, D. E. (1961/1978). *Behavior*. London: Methuen. (Reprinted in 1986 by Greenwood Press, Westport, CT).

Brook, A., & Ross, D. (Eds.), (2002). *Daniel Dennett*. Cambridge: Cambridge University Press.

Brown, J. R. (2001). *Who rules in science? An opinionated guide to the wars*. Cambridge, MA: Harvard University Press.

Bry, A. (1975). *A primer of behavioral psychology*. New York: NEL.

Burgos, J. E., & Donahoe, J. W. (2000). Structure and function in selectionism: Implications for complex behavior. In J. C. Leslie, & D. Blackman (Eds.), *Experimental and applied analysis of human behavior* (pp. 39–57). Reno, NV: Context Press.

Catania, A. C. (1992). *Learning* (3rd ed.). Englewood Cliffs, NJ: Prentice-Hall.

Catania, A. C. (1998). *Learning* (4th ed.). Upper Saddle River, NJ: Prentice-Hall.

Catania, A. C., & Harnad, S. (Eds.), (1988). *The selection of behavior. The operant behaviorism of B. F. Skinner: Comments and consequences*. New York: Cambridge University Press.

Catania, A. C., Matthews, B. A., & Shimoff, E. (1982). Instructed versus shaped human verbal behavior: Interactions with nonverbal responding. *Journal of the Experimental Analysis of Behavior, 38*, 233–248.

Chance, M. R. A. (1960). Köhler's chimpanzees—How did they perform? *Man, 60*, 130–135.

Chance, P. (1999). Where does behavior come from? A review of Epstein's cognition, creativity, and behavior. *The Behavior Analyst, 22*, 161–163.

Cherniak, C. (1981). Minimal rationality. *Mind, 90*, 161–183.

Chisholm, R. (1957). *Perceiving: A philosophical study*. Ithaca, NY: Cornell University Press.

Chisholm, R. (1960). *Realism and the background of phenomenology*. Glencoe: The Free Press.

Chomsky, N. (1959). Review of Skinner's verbal behavior. *Language, 35*, 26–52.

Chomsky, N. (1969). *Aspects of the theory of syntax*. Cambridge, MA: MIT Press.

Chomsky, N. (2006). *Language and mind* (3rd ed.). Cambridge: Cambridge University Press.

Churchland, P. M. (1981). Eliminative materialism and the propositional attitudes. *Journal of Philosophy, 78*, 67–90.

Churchland, P. S. (1986). *Neurophilosophy: Toward a unified science of the mind/brain*. Cambridge, MA: MIT Press.

Crane, T. (1998). Intentionality as the mark of the mental. *Royal Institute of Philosophy Supplement, 43*, 229–251.

Crane, T. (2001). Intentional objects. *Ratio, 14*, 336–349.
Crane, T. (2009). Intentionalism. In B. P. McLaughlin, A. Beckerman, & S. Walter (Eds.), *The Oxford Handbook of philosophy of mind* (pp. 474–493). Oxford: Oxford University Press.
Crane, T. (2016). *The mechanical mind* (3rd ed.). London and New York: Routledge.
Dahlbom, B. (1993a). *Dennett and his critics: Demystifying mind*. Oxford and Cambridge, MA: Blackwell.
Dahlbom, B. (1993b). Mind is artificial. In B. Dahlbom (Ed.), *Dennett and his critics* (pp. 161–183). Oxford: Blackwell.
Dahler-Larsen, P. (2018). Theory-based evaluation meets ambiguity: The role of Janus variables. *American Journal of Evaluation, 39*, 6–21.
Dancy, J. (2000). *Practical reality*. Oxford: Oxford University Press.
Davey, G. C. L., & Cullen, C. (Eds.), (1988). *Human operant conditioning and behavior modification*. Chichester: Wiley.
Davidson, D. (2001). How is weakness of will possible? In D. Davidson (Ed.), *Essays on action and events* (pp. 21–42). Oxford: Oxford University Press.
Davies, J., Foxall, G. R., & Pallister, J. G. (2002). Beyond the intention—behaviour mythology: an integrated model of recycling. *Marketing Theory, 2*, 29–113.
Davis, J. B. (2003). *The theory of the individual in economics: Identity and value*. London and New York: Routledge.
De Brigard, F. (2015). What was I thinking? Dennett's content and consciousness and the reality of propositional attitudes. In C. Muñoz-Suárez, & F. De Brigard (Eds.), *Content and consciousness revisited* (pp. 49–71). Berlin: Springer.
Delgado, M. R., & Tricomi, E. (2011). Reward processing and decision making in the human striatum. In O. Vartanian, & D. R. Mandel (Eds.), *Neuroscience of decision making* (pp. 145–172). New York and Hove: Psychology Press.
Delprato, D. J., & Midgley, B. D. (1992). Some fundamentals of B. F. Skinner's behaviorism. *American Psychologist, 47*, 1507–1520.
Dennett, D. C. (1969). *Content and consciousness*. London: Routledge.
Dennett, D. C. (1978). *Brainstorms*. Montgomery, VT: Bradford.
Dennett, D. C. (1981). Three kinds of intentional psychology. In R. Healy (Ed.), *Reduction, time and reality*. Cambridge: Cambridge University Press. (Reproduced in Dennett, 1987a).
Dennett, D. C. (1982). How to study human consciousness empirically, or nothing comes to mind. *Synthese, 59*, 159–180.
Dennett, D. C. (1983). Intentional systems in cognitive ethology: The "Panglossian paradigm" defended. *The Behavioral and Brain Sciences, 6*, 343–390.
Dennett, D. C. (1987a). *The intentional stance*. Cambridge, MA: MIT Press.
Dennett, D. C. (1987b). Reflections: Interpreting monkeys, theorists, and genes. In D. C. Dennett (Ed.), *The intentional stance* (pp. 269–286). Cambridge, MA: MIT Press.
Dennett, D. C. (1988). Out of the armchair and into the field, *Poetics Today* (9, pp. 205–221). (Reprinted in Dennett, D. C. (1998). *Brainchildren: Essays on designing minds*. Cambridge, MA: MIT Press).
Dennett, D. C. (1991a). Real patterns. *Journal of Psychology, 88*, 27–51. (Reproduced in Dennett, 1998).
Dennett, D. C. (1991b). *Consciousness explained*. New York: Little, Brown and Co.
Dennett, D. C. (1994). Dennett, Daniel C. In S. Guttenplan (Ed.), *A companion to the philosophy of mind* (pp. 236–244). Oxford: Blackwell.
Dennett, D. C. (1995). *Darwin's dangerous idea: Evolution and the meanings of life*. New York: Simon and Shuster.

Dennett, D. C. (1996). *Kinds of minds: Toward an understanding of consciousness*. London: Weidenfeld and Nicolson.
Dennett, D. C. (1998). *Brainchildren: Essays on designing minds*. Cambridge, MA: MIT Press.
Dennett, D. C. (2003). *Freedom evolves*. London: Allen Lane.
Dennett, D. C. (2005). *Sweet dreams: Philosophical obstacles to a science of consciousness*. Cambridge, MA: MIT Press.
Dennett, D. C. (2013). *Intuition pumps and other tools for thinking*. London: Allen Lane.
Dennett, D. C., & Haugeland, J. C. (1987). Intentionality. In R. L. Gregory (Ed.), *The Oxford companion to the mind* (pp. 383–386). Oxford: Oxford University Press.
Dent, N. J. H. (1970). Review of Dennett: Content and consciousness. *Philosophical Quarterly*, *20*, 403–404.
Deutsch, D. (1997). *The fabric of reality*. Harmondsworth: Penguin.
Deutsch, J. A. (1960). *The structural basis of behavior*. Chicago, IL: Chicago University Press.
Dickinson, A. (1980). *Contemporary learning theory*. Cambridge: Cambridge University Press.
Dinsmoor, J. A. (1985). The role of observing and attention in establishing stimulus control. *Journal of the Experimental Analysis of Behavior*, *43*, 365–381.
Donahoe, J. W., & Palmer, D. C. (1994). *Learning and complex behavior*. Boston, MA: Allyn and Bacon.
Donahoe, J. W., Palmer, D. C., & Burgos, J. E. (1997). The S-R issue: Its status in behavior analysis and in Donahoe and Palmer's learning and complex behavior. *Journal of the Experimental Analysis of Behavior*, *67*, 193–211.
Dretske, F. (1981). *Knowledge and the flow of information*. Cambridge, MA: MIT Press.
Dretske, F. (1988). *Explaining behavior: Reasons in a world of causes*. Cambridge, MA: MIT Press.
Dretske, F. (1991). How beliefs explain: Reply to Baker. *Philosophical Studies*, *63*, 113–117.
Dretske, F. (1995). *Naturalizing the mind*. Cambridge, MA: MIT Press.
Dretske, F. (2001). Where is the mind? In A. Meijers (Ed.), *Explaining beliefs: Lynne Rudder Baker and her critics* (pp. 39–49). Stanford, CA: Center for the Study of Language and Information.
Dub, R. (2015). The rationality assumption. In C. Muñoz-Suárez, & F. De Brigard (Eds.), *Content and consciousness revisited* (pp. 93–110). Berlin: Springer.
Dulany, D. E. (1968). Awareness, rules, and propositional control: A confrontation with S-R behavior theory. In D. Hornton, & T. Dixon (Eds.), *Verbal behavior and S-R behavior theory* (pp. 340–387). Englewood Cliffs, NJ: Prentice-Hall.
Eagly, A. H., & Chaiken, S. (1993). *The psychology of attitudes*. Fort Worth, TX: Harcourt Brace Jovanovich.
Eichenbaum, H. (2014). Time cells in the hippocampus: a new dimension for mapping memories. *Nature Reviews Neuroscience*, *11*, 732–744. Available from https://doi.org/10.1038/nrn3827.
Elton, M. (2000). Consciousness: Only at the personal level. *Philosophical Explorations*, *III*, 25–41.
Epstein, R., Kirshnit, C., Lanza, R., & Rubin, L. (1984). Insight in the pigeon: Antecedents and determinants of an intelligent performance. *Nature*, *308*, 61–62.
Evans, J. S. B. T. (2010). *Thinking twice: Two minds in one brain*. Oxford: Oxford University Press.
Fagerstrøm, A., Foxall, G. R., & Arntzen, E. (2010). Implications of motivating operations for the functional analysis of consumer choice. *Journal of Organizational Behavior Management*, *30*(2), 110–126.

Fagerstrøm, A., & Ghinea, G. (2011). On the motivating impact of price and online recommendations at the point of online purchase. *International Journal of Information Management, 31*(2), 103−110.

Fagerstrøm, A., Stratton, J. P., & Foxall, G. R. (2015). The impact of corporate social responsibility activities on the consumer purchasing situation. *Journal of Organizational Behavior Management, 35*(3−4), 184−205.

Fazio, R. H. (1986). How do attitudes guide behavior? In R. M. Sorrentino, & E. T. Higgins (Eds.), *Handbook of motivation and cognition: Foundations of social behavior* (pp. 204−243). Chichester: Wiley.

Fazio, R. H. (1989). On the power and functionality of attitudes: The role of attitude accessibility. In A. R. Pratkanis, A. J. Breckler, & A. G. Greenwald (Eds.), *Attitude structure and function* (pp. 153−180). Hillsdale, NJ: Erlbaum.

Fazio, R. H. (1990). Multiple processes by which attitudes guide behavior: The MODE model as an integrative framework. In M. P. Zanna (Ed.), *Advances in experimental social psychology* (23, pp. 75−109). San Diego, CA: Academic Press.

Fazio, R. H., & Zanna, M. P. (1978a). Attitudinal qualities relating to the strength of the attitude-behavior relationship. *Journal of Experimental Social Psychology, 14*, 398−408.

Fazio, R. H., & Zanna, M. P. (1978b). On the predictive validity of attitudes: The roles of direct experience and confidence. *Journal of Personality, 46*, 228−243.

Fazio, R. H., & Zanna, M. P. (1981). Direct experience and attitude-behavior consistency. *Advances in Experimental Social Psychology, 14*, 161−202.

Feyerabend, P. (1962). Explanation, reduction, and empiricism. In H. Feigl, & G. Maxwell (Eds.), *Minnesota studies in the philosophy of science*. Minneapolis, MN: University of Minnesota Press.

Feyerabend, P. (1970). Consolations for the specialist. In I. Lakatos, & A. Musgrave (Eds.), *Criticism and the growth of knowledge* (pp. 197−230). Cambridge: Cambridge University Press.

Feyerabend, P. (1975). *Against method*. London: NLB.

Fishbein, M. (1972). The search for attitudinal-behavioral consistency. In J. S. Cohen (Ed.), *Behavioral science foundations of consumer behavior*. New York: Free Press.

Fishbein, M., & Ajzen, I. (1975). *Belief, attitude, intention and behavior*. Reading, MA: Addison-Wesley.

Fishbein, M., & Ajzen, I. (2010). *Predicting and changing behavior: The reasoned action approach*. London and New York: Psychology Press.

Flanagan, O. (1991). *The science of the mind*. Cambridge, MA: MIT Press.

Fodor, J. A. (1983). *The modularity of mind*. Cambridge, MA: MIT Press.

Fodor, J. A. (2000). *The mind doesn't work that way: The scope and limits of computational psychology*. Cambridge, MA: MIT Press.

Fodor, J. A., & Piattelli-Palmarini, M. (2011). *What Darwin got wrong*. London: Profile Books.

Foxall, G. R., & Sigurdsson, V. (2011). Drug use as consumer behavior. *Behavioral and Brain Science, 34*, 313−314. Available from https://doi.org/10.1017/S0140525X11000707.

Foxall, G. R. (1983). *Consumer choice*. London: Macmillan; New York: St. Martin's Press.

Foxall, G. R. (1990/2004). *Consumer psychology in behavioral perspective*. London and New York: Routledge, Reprinted 2004 Beard Books, Frederick, MD.

Foxall, G. R. (1994). Behavior analysis and consumer psychology. *Journal of Economic Psychology, 15*, 5−91.

Foxall, G. R. (1995). Science and interpretation in consumer research: A radical behaviourist perspective. *European Journal of Marketing, 29*(9), 3−99.

Foxall, G. R. (1996/2015). *Consumers in context: The BPM research program*. London and New York: Routledge.

Foxall, G. R. (1997a). Explaining consumer behaviour: From social cognition to environmental control. In C. L. Cooper, & I. T. Robertson (Eds.), *International review of industrial and organizational psychology* (12, pp. 229–287). Chichester: Wiley.

Foxall, G. R. (1997b). *Marketing psychology: The paradigm in the wings.* London: Macmillan.

Foxall, G. R. (1997c). Affective responses to consumer situations. *International Review of Retail, Distribution and Consumer Research, 7,* 191–225.

Foxall, G. R. (1998). Radical behaviorist interpretation: Generating and evaluating an account of consumer behavior. *The Behavior Analyst, 21,* 321–354.

Foxall, G. R. (1999). The contextual stance. *Philosophical Psychology, 12,* 25–46.

Foxall, G. R. (2002a). *Consumer behavior analysis: Critical perspectives.* London and New York: Routledge.

Foxall, G. R. (2002b). Marketing's attitude problem – And how to solve it. *Journal of Customer Behaviour, 1,* 19–48.

Foxall, G. R. (2004). *Context and cognition: Interpreting complex behavior.* Reno, NV: Context Press.

Foxall, G. R. (2005). *Understanding consumer choice.* London and New York: Palgrave Macmillan.

Foxall, G. R. (2007). Explaining consumer choice: Coming to terms with intentionality. *Behavioural Processes, 75,* 129–145.

Foxall, G. R. (2007). Intentional behaviorism. *Behavior and Philosophy, 35,* 1–56.

Foxall, G. R. (2008). Intentional behaviorism revisited. *Behavior and Philosophy, 37,* 113–156.

Foxall, G. R. (2009). Ascribing intentionality. *Behavior and Philosophy, 37,* 217–222.

Foxall, G. R. (2010a). Invitation to consumer behavior analysis. *Journal of Organizational Behavior Management, 30,* 92–109.

Foxall, G. R. (2010b). *Interpreting consumer choice: The behavioral perspective model.* New York and London: Routledge.

Foxall, G. R. (2011). Brain, emotion, and contingency in the explanation of consumer behaviour. *International Review of Industrial and Organizational Psychology, 26,* 26–52.

Foxall, G. R. (2013). Intentionality, symbol, and situation in the interpretation of consumer choice. *Marketing Theory, 13,* 105–127.

Foxall, G. R. (2014a). The marketing firm and consumer choice: implications of bilateral contingency for levels of analysis in organizational neuroscience. *Frontiers in Human Neuroscience, 8*(Article 472), 1–14. Available from https://doi.org/10.3389/fnhum.2014.00472.

Foxall, G. R. (2014b). Cognitive requirements of competing neuro-behavioral decision systems: some implications of temporal horizon for managerial behavior in organizations. *Frontiers in Human Neuroscience, 8*(Article 184), 1–17. Available from https://doi.org/10.3389/fnhum.2014.00184.

Foxall, G. R. (2016a). *Addiction as consumer choice: Exploring the cognitive dimension.* London and New York: Routledge.

Foxall, G. R. (2016b). *Perspectives on consumer choice: From behavior to action, from action to agency.* London and New York: Palgrave Macmillan.

Foxall, G. R. (Ed.), (2016c). *The Routledge companion to consumer behavior analysis.* London and New York: Routledge.

Foxall, G. R. (2016d). Operant behavioral economics. *Managerial and decision economics, 37,* 215–223.

Foxall, G. R. (2016e). Metacognitive control of categorial neurobehavioral decision systems. *Frontiers in Psychology, 7*(170), 1–18. Available from https://doi.org/10.3389/fpsyg.2016.00170.

Foxall, G. R. (2016f). Consumer heterophenomenology. In G. R. Foxall (Ed.), *The Routledge companion to consumer behavior analysis* (pp. 417–430). London and New York: Routledge.

Foxall, G. R. (2017a). *Advanced introduction to consumer behavior analysis.* Cheltenham and Northampton, MA: Edward Elgar.

Foxall, G. R. (2017b). *Context and cognition in consumer psychology: How perception and emotion guide action.* London and New York: Routledge.

Foxall, G. R. (2017c). Behavioral economics of consumer behavior analysis. *The Behavior Analyst, 42,* 309–314.

Foxall, G. R. (2020). The theory of the marketing firm. *Managerial and Decision Economics, 41,* 164–184.

Foxall, G. R., & Greenley, G. E. (1998). The affective structure of consumer situations. *Environment and Behavior, 30,* 781–798.

Foxall, G. R., & Greenley, G. E. (1999). Consumers' emotional responses to service environments. *Journal of Business Research, 46,* 149–158.

Foxall, G. R., & Greenley, G. E. (2000). Predicting and explaining responses to consumer environments: An empirical test and theoretical extension of the behavioural perspective model. *The Service Industries Journal, 20,* 39–63.

Foxall, G. R., & James, V. K. (2002). Behavior analysis of consumer brand choice: A preliminary analysis. *European Journal of Behavior Analysis, 2,* 209–220.

Foxall, G. R., & James, V. K. (2003). The behavioral ecology of brand choice: How and what do consumers maximize? *Psychology and Marketing, 20,* 811–836.

Foxall, G. R., & Oliveira-Castro, J. M. (2009). Intentional consequences of self-instruction. *Behavior and Philosophy, 37,* 87–104.

Foxall, G. R., Oliveira-Castro, J. M., & Schrezenmaier, T. C. (2004). The behavioral economics of consumer brand choice: Patterns of reinforcement and utility maximization. *Behavioural Processes, 65,* 235–260.

Foxall, G. R., & Schrezenmaier, T. C. (2003). The behavioral economics of consumer brand choice: Establishing a methodology. *Journal of Economic Psychology, 24,* 675–695.

Foxall, G. R., & Yani-de-Soriano, M. M. (2005). Situational influences on consumers' attitudes and behaviour. *Journal of Business Research, 58,* 518–525.

Foxall, G. R., Goldsmith, R. E., & Brown, S. (1998). *Consumer psychology for marketing* (2nd ed.). London and New York: International Thompson Business Press.

Foxall, G. R., Yani-de-Soriano, M., Yousafzai, S., & Javed, U. (2012). The role of neurophysiology, emotion and contingency in the explanation of consumer choice. In V. K. Wells, & G. R. Foxall (Eds.), *Handbook of developments in consumer behaviour* (pp. 461–522). Cheltenham, Glos. and Northampton, MA: Edward Elgar.

Frankish, K. (2009). Systems and levels: Dual-system theories and the personal—Sub-personal distinction. In J. S. B. T. Evans, & K. Frankish (Eds.), *In two minds: Dual processes and beyond* (pp. 89–107). Oxford: Oxford University Press.

Frankish, K. (2015). Dennett's dual-process theory of reasoning. In C. Muñoz-Suárez, & F. De Brigard (Eds.), *Content and consciousness revisited* (pp. 73–92). Berlin: Springer.

Frankish, K., & Evans, J. S. B. T. (2009). The duality of mind: An historical perspective. In J. S. B. T. Evans, & K. Frankish (Eds.), *In two minds: Dual processes and beyond* (pp. 1–29). Oxford: Oxford University Press.

Franklin, R. L. (1970). Review of content and consciousness by D. C. Dennett. *Australasian Journal of Philosophy, 48,* 264–273.

Freud, A. (1937). *The ego and the mechanisms of defence* (C. Baines, Trans.). London: Hogarth. (Originally published, Vienna 1936).

Freud, S. ([1895]1964). Project for a scientific psychology. In *The standard edition of the complete psychological works of Sigmund Freud* (J. Strachey, Trans., Vol. 1). London: Hogarth Press.
Freud, S. ([1900]1953). The interpretation of dreams. In *The standard edition of the complete psychological works of Sigmund Freud* (J. Strachey, Trans., Vols. 4–5). London: Hogarth Press.
Freud, S. ([1911]1958). Formulations on the two principles of mental functioning. In J. Strachey, & A. Freud (Eds.), *The standard edition of the complete works of Sigmund Freud* (Vol. 12, pp. 218–226). London: Hogarth Press.
Fryling, M. J., Johnston, C., & Hayes, L. J. (2011). Understanding observational learning: An inter-behavioral approach. *Analysis of Verbal Behavior*, 27, 191–203.
Gardner, S. (2000). Psychoanalysis and the personal/sub-personal distinction. *Philosophical Explorations*, III, 96–119.
Garrett, R. (1996). Skinner's case for radical behaviorism. In W. O'Donohue, & R. F. Kitchener (Eds.), *The philosophy of psychology* (pp. 141–148). London: Sage.
Gawronski, B., & Payne, B. K. (Eds.), (2010). *Handbook of implicit social cognition: Measurement, theory, and applications*. New York and London: Guilford Press.
Gazzaniga, M. S., Ivry, R. B., & Mangun, G. R. (1998). *Cognitive neuroscience: The biology of the mind*. New York: W. W. Norton.
Glimcher, P. W. (2003). *Decisions, uncertainty, and the brain: The science of neuroeconomics*. Cambridge, MA: MIT Press.
Glimcher, P. W. (2011). *Foundations of neuroeconomic analysis*. Oxford: Oxford University Press.
Griffin, D. R. (1976). *The question of animal awareness*. New York: Rockefeller University Press.
Gruber, A. J., & McDonald, R. J. (2012). Context, emotion, and the strategic pursuit of goals: Interactions among multiple brain systems controlling motivated behavior. *Frontiers in Behavioral Neuroscience*, 6(50). Available from https://doi.org/10.3389/fnbeh.2012.00050.
Gunderson, K. (1972). Content and consciousness and the mind-body problem. *Journal of Philosophy*, 69, 591–604.
Guttenplan, S. (1994). Intensional. In S. Guttenplan (Ed.), *A companion to the philosophy of mind* (pp. 374–375). Oxford: Blackwell.
Hacker, P. M. S. (2007). *Human nature: The categorial framework*. Chichester: Wiley-Blackwell.
Hacker, P. M. S. (2013). *The intellectual powers: A study of human nature*. Chichester: Wiley-Blackwell.
Hacker, P. M. S. (2018). *The passions: A study of human nature*. Chichester: Wiley-Blackwell.
Hackett, P. M. W., & Foxall, G. R. (2017). Why consumer psychology needs neurophilosophy. In L. Moutinho, & M. Sokele (Eds.), *The Palgrave handbook of innovative research methods in management* (pp. 28–42). London and New York: Palgrave Macmillan.
Hamlyn, D. W. (1970a). Conditioning and behaviour. In R. Borger, & F. Cioffi (Eds.), *Explanation in the Behavioural Sciences* (pp. 139–152). Cambridge: Cambridge University Press.
Hamlyn, D. W. (1970b). Reply. In R. Borger, & F. Cioffi (Eds.), *Explanation in the Behavioural Sciences* (pp. 162–166). Cambridge: Cambridge University Press.
Hamlyn, D. W. (1990). *In and out of the Black Box: On the philosophy of cognition*. Oxford: Blackwell.
Hansen, S., & Arntzen, E. (2018). Eye-movements during conditional discrimination training and equivalence class formation. *European Journal of Behavior Analysis*, 19, 1–18.

Harman, G. (1998). Intentionality. In W. Bechtel, & G. Graham (Eds.), *A companion to cognitive science* (pp. 602–610). Oxford: Blackwell.

Harzem, P. (2000). Toward a new behaviorism. *European Journal of Behavior Analysis, 1,* 51–60.

Hayes, L. J., & Ghezzi, P. M. (Eds.), (1997). *Investigations in behavioral epistemology.* Reno, NV: Context Press.

Hayes, S. C. (1986). The case of the silent dog—Verbal reports and the analysis of rules: A review of Ericsson and Simon's protocol analysis: Verbal reports as data. *Journal of the Experimental Analysis of Behavior, 45,* 351–363.

Hayes, S. C. (Ed.), (1989). *Rule-governed behavior: Cognition, contingencies, and instructional control.* New York: Plenum.

Hayes, S. C. (1992). Verbal relations, time, and suicide. In S. C. Hayes, & L. J. Hayes (Eds.), *Understanding verbal relations* (pp. 109–118). Reno, NV: Context Press.

Hayes, S. C. (1994). Relational frame theory: A functional approach to verbal events. In S. C. Hayes, & L. J. Hayes (Eds.), *Behavior analysis of language and cognition* (pp. 9–29). Reno, NV: Context Press.

Hayes, S. C. (1997). Behavioral epistemology includes nonverbal knowing. In L. J. Hayes, & P. M. Ghezzi (Eds.), *Investigations in behavioral epistemology* (pp. 35–43). Reno, NV: Context Press.

Hayes, S. C., Barnes-Holmes, D., & Roche, B. (Eds.), (2001). *Relational frame theory: A post-Skinnerian account of human language and cognition.* New York: Kluwer Academic/Plenum.

Hayes, S. C., & Brownstein, A. J. (1986). Mentalism, behavior-behavior relationships and the purpose of science. *The Behavior Analyst, 7,* 135–190.

Hayes, S. C., Brownstein, A. J., Haas, J. R., & Greenway, D. E. (1986). Instructions, multiple schedules, and extinction: Distinguishing rule-governed from schedule controlled behavior. *Journal of the Experimental Analysis of Behavior, 46,* 137–147.

Hayes, S. C., & Hayes, L. J. (1989). The verbal action of the listener as a basic for rule-governance. In S. C. Hayes (Ed.), *Rule-governed behavior: Cognition, contingencies, and instructional control* (pp. 153–190). New York: Plenum.

Hayes, S. C., Hayes, L. J., Reese, H. W., & Sarbin, T. R. (Eds.), (1993). *Varieties of scientific contextualism.* Reno, NV: Context Press.

Hayes, S. C., Strosahl, K. D., & Wilson, K. G. (1999). *Acceptance and commitment therapy: An experiential approach to behavior change.* New York: The Guilford Press.

Hayes, S. C., Wilson, K. G., & Gifford, E. V. (1999). Consciousness and private events. In B. A. Thyer (Ed.), *The philosophical legacy of behaviorism* (pp. 153–197). Dordrecht: Kluwer.

Hayes, S. C., Zettle, R. D., & Rosenfarb, I. (1989). Rule-following. In S. C. Hayes (Ed.), *Rule-governed behavior: Cognition, contingencies, and instructional control* (pp. 191–220). New York: Plenum.

Hebb, D. O. (1949). *The organization of behavior: A neuropsychological theory.* New York: Wiley.

Hefferline, R. F. (1962). Learning theory and clinical psychology: An eventual symbiosis? In A. J. Bachrach (Ed.), *Experimental foundations of clinical psychology* (pp. 97–138). New York: Basic Books.

Heil, J. (1998). *Philosophy of mind.* London and New York: Routledge.

Heil, J. (2013). Mental causation according to Davidson. In G. D'Oro, & C. Sandis (Eds.), *Reasons and causes: Causalism and anti-causalism in the philosophy of action* (pp. 75–96). Basingstoke: Palgrave Macmillan.

Herrnstein, R. J. (1997). In H. Rachlin, & D. I. Laibson (Eds.), *The matching law: Papers in psychology and economics*. New York: Russell Sage Foundation; Cambridge, MA: Harvard University Press.

Heyes, C. (2008). Beast machines: Questions of animal consciousness. In L. Weiskrantz, & M. Davies (Eds.), *Frontiers of consciousness* (pp. 259–274). Oxford: Oxford University Press.

Heyes, C. (2018). *Cognitive gadgets: The cultural evolution of thinking*. Cambridge, MA: Harvard.

Hofmeyr, A., Ainslie, G., Charlton, R., & Ross, D. (2010). The relationship between addiction and reward bundling: An experiment comparing smokers and non-smokers. *Addiction, 106*, 402–409, add_3166 402.409.

Horne, P. J., & Lowe, F. C. (1993). Determinants of human performance on concurrent schedules. *Journal of the Experimental Analysis of Behavior, 59*, 29–60.

Horne, P. J., & Lowe, F. C. (1996). On the origins of naming and other symbolic behavior. *Journal of the Experimental Analysis of Behavior, 65*, 185–241.

Horne, P. J., & Lowe, C. F. (1997). Toward a theory of verbal behavior. *Journal of the Experimental Analysis of Behavior, 68*, 271–296.

Hornsby, J. (1981). *Actions*. London: Routledge and Kegan Paul.

Hornsby, J. (2000). Personal and sub-personal: A defence of Dennett's early distinction. *Philosophical Explorations, III*, 6–24.

Hull, C. L. (1952). *A behavior system*. New Haven, CT: Yale University Press.

Hursh, S. R. (1980). Economic concepts for the analysis of behavior. *Journal of the Experimental Analysis of Behavior, 34*, 219–238.

Hursh, S. R. (1984). Behavioral economics. *Journal of the Experimental Analysis of Behavior, 42*, 435–452.

Hursh, S. R., & Roma, P. G. (2016). Behavioral economics and the analysis of consumption and choice. *Managerial and Decision Economics, 37*, 224–238.

Hursh, S. R., & Silberberg, A. (2008). Economic demand and essential value. *Psychological Review, 115*, 186–198.

Jarmolowicz, D. P., Reed, D. D., DiGennaro Reed, F. D., & Bickel, W. K. (2016). The behavioral and neuroeconomics of reinforcer pathologies: Implications for managerial and health decision making. *Managerial and Decision Economics, 37*, 274–293.

Kacelnik, A. (1993). Leaf-cutting ants tease optimal foraging theorists. *Trends in Ecology and Evolution, 8*, 346–348.

Kagan, J. (2006). *An argument for mind*. New Haven, CT and London: Yale University Press.

Kahneman, D. (2011). *Thinking fast and slow*. London: Allen Lane.

Kandel, E. R. (2001). The molecular biology of memory storage: A dialogue between genes and synapses. *Science, 294*, 1030–1038.

Kane, R. H. (1970). Review of Dennett: Content and consciousness. *Review of Metaphysics, 23*, 740–741.

Keller, F. S. (1958). The phantom plateau. *Journal of the Experimental Analysis of Behavior, 1*, 1–13.

Kelley, J. S. (1990). Review of content and consciousness (2nd edition). *Idealistic Studies, 20*, 83–84.

Kincaid, H., & Ross, D. (Eds.), (2009). *The Oxford Handbook of Philosophy of Economics*. Oxford: Oxford University Press.

Kirsch, I., Lynn, S. J., Vigorito, M., & Miller, R. R. (2004). The role of cognition in classical and operant conditioning. *Journal of Clinical Psychology, 60*, 369–392.

Kitchener, R. F. (1977). Behavior and behaviorism. *Behaviorism, 5*, 11–71.

Kitchener, R. F. (1979). Radical naturalism and radical behaviorism. *Scienta*, *114*, 107−116.
Kitchener, R. F. (1996). Skinner's theory of theories. In W. O'Donohue, & R. F. Kitchener (Eds.), *The philosophy of psychology* (pp. 108−125). London: Sage Publications.
Köhler, W. (1925). *The mentality of apes*. London: Routledge and Kegan Paul.
Koob, G. E. F. (2013). Neuroscience of addiction. In B. S. McCrady, & E. E. Epstein (Eds.), *Addictions: A comprehensive guidebook* (2nd edn, pp. 17−35). New York: Oxford University Press.
Kuhl, J., & Beckman, J. (Eds.), (1985). *Action control: From cognition to behavior*. Berlin: Springer-Verlag.
Kuhn, T. S. (1970). *The structure of scientific revolutions* (2nd ed.). Chicago, IL: Chicago University Press.
Lacey, H. M. (1995/1996). Behaviorisms: Theoretical and teleological: A review of John Staddon's behaviorism: Mind, mechanism and society, and Rachlin's behavior and mind: The roots of modern psychology. *Behavior and Philosophy*, *23*, 61−78.
Lacey, H. M., & Schwartz, B. (1987). The explanatory power of radical behaviorism. In S. Modgil, & C. Modgil (Eds.), *B. F. Skinner: Consensus and controversy* (pp. 165−176). New York: Falmer.
Lakatos, I. (1978). In J. Worrall, & G. Currie (Eds.), The methodology of scientific research programmes. Philosophical papers (Volume I). Cambridge: Cambridge University Press.
Laparojkit, S., & Foxall, G. R. (2016). Collective intentionality and symbolic reinforcement: The case of Thai car-consumer clubs. In G. R. Foxall (Ed.), *The Routledge companion to consumer behavior analysis* (pp. 379−399). London and New York: Routledge.
Leahey, T. H. (1987). *A history of psychology: Main currents in psychological thought*. Englewood Cliffs, NJ: Prentice-Hall.
Lee, V. L. (1988). *Beyond behaviorism*. London: Erlbaum.
Levine, J. (1994). Out of the closet: A qualophile confronts qualophobia. *Philosophical Topics*, *22*, 107−126.
Lewin, K. (1936). *Principles of topological psychology*. New York: McGraw-Hill.
London, E. D., Ernst, M., Grant, S., Bonson, K., & Weinstein, A. (2000). Orbitofrontal cortex and human drug abuse: Functional imaging. *Cerebral Cortex*, *10*, 334−342. Available from https://doi.org/10.1093/cercor/10.3.334.
Lowe, C. F. (1983). Radical behaviorism and human psychology. In G. C. L. Davey (Ed.), *Animal models of human behavior* (pp. 71−93). Chichester: Wiley.
Lyons, W. (1995). *Approaches to intentionality*. Oxford: Clarendon Press.
MacCorquodale, K., & Meehl, P. R. (1954). Edward C. Tolman. In W. K. Estes, S. Koch, K. MacCorquodale, P. E. Meehl, C. G. Mueller, W. N. Schoenfield, et al. (Eds.), *Modern learning theory* (pp. 177−266). New York: Appleton-Century-Crofts.
MacKay, D. M. (1956). Toward an information flow model of human behavior. *British Journal of Psychology*, *XLVII*, 30−43.
Mackenzie, B. (1988). The challenge to Skinner's theory of behavior. In A. C. Catania, & S. Harnad (Eds.), *The selection of behavior. The operant behaviorism of B. F. Skinner: Comments and consequences* (pp. 111−113). New York: Cambridge University Press.
Mackenzie, B. D. (1977). *Behaviorism and the limits of scientific method*. Atlantic Highlands, NJ: Humanities Press.
Madden, G. J., & Bickel, W. K. (Eds.), (2010). *Impulsivity: The behavioral and neurological science of discounting*. Washington, DC: American Psychological Association.
Mäki, U. (2012). *Philosophy of economics (Handbook of the philosophy of science, volume 13)*. Amsterdam: Elsevier.

Malcolm, N. (1977a). *Thought and knowledge*. Ithaca, NY: Cornell University Press.
Malcolm, N. (1977b). Behaviorism as a philosophy of psychology. In N. Malcolm (Ed.), *Thought and knowledge* (pp. 85–103). Ithaca, NY: Cornell University Press. First published in Wann, T. W. (Ed.) (1964). *Behaviorism and phenomenology: Contrasting bases for modern psychology* (pp. 141–162). Chicago, IL: University of Chicago Press.
Malott, R. W. (1986). Self-management, rule-governed behavior, and everyday life. In H. W. Reese, & L. J. Parrott (Eds.), *Behavior science: Philosophical, methodological and empirical advances* (pp. 207–228). Hillsdale, NJ: Lawrence Erlbaum.
Malott, R. W. (1989). The achievement of evasive goals: Control by rules describing contingencies that are not direct acting. In S. C. Hayes (Ed.), *Rule-governed behavior: Cognition, contingencies, and instructional control* (pp. 269–324). New York: Plenum.
Malott, R. W., & Malott, M. E. (1992). Private events and rule-governed behavior. In L. J. Hayes, & P. N. Chase (Eds.), *Dialogues on verbal behavior* (pp. 237–254). Reno, NV: Context Press.
Mazur, J. (1987). An adjusting procedure for studying delayed reinforcement. In M. Commons. In J. Mazur, J. Nevin, & H. Rachlin (Eds.), *Quantitative analysis of behavior: The effect of delay and of intervening events on reinforcement value* (vol. 5, pp. 55–73). Hillsdale, IL: Erlbaum.
McClure, S. M., Laibson, D. L., Loewenstein, G., & Cohen, J. D. (2004). Separate neural systems value immediate and delayed monetary rewards. *Science, 306*(5695), 503–507.
McFarland, D. (2016). *The biological bases of economic behaviour*. London and New York: Palgrave Macmillan.
McFarland, D., & Bösser, T. (1993). *Intelligent behavior in animals and robots*. Cambridge, MA: MIT Press.
McGaugh, J. L. (2004). The amygdala modulates the consolidation of memories of emotionally arousing experiences. *Annual Review of Neuroscience, 27*, 1–28. Available from https://doi.org/10.1146/annurev.neuro.27.070203.144157.
McGinn, C. (2004). *Consciousness and its objects*. Oxford: Oxford University Press.
McKim, V. R. (1970). Review of content and consciousness by D. C. Dennett. *New Scholasticism, 44*, 272.
Mehrabian, A., & Russell, J. A. (1974). *An approach to environmental psychology*. Cambridge, MA: MIT Press.
Michael, J. (1982). Distinguishing between discriminative and motivational functions of stimuli. *Journal of the Experimental Analysis of Behavior, 37*, 149–155.
Michael, J. (1993). Establishing operations. *The Behavior Analyst, 16*, 191–206.
Midgley, B. D., & Morris, E. K. (1998). Nature-nurture in Skinner's behaviorism. *Mexican Journal of Behavior Analysis, 24*, 111–126.
Migaud, M., Charlesworth, P., Dempster, M., Webster, L. C., Watabe, A. M., Makhinson, M., et al. (1998). Enhanced long-term potentiation and impaired learning in mice with mutant postsynaptic density-95 protein. *Nature, 396*, 433–439. Available from https://doi.org/10.1038/24790.
Mill, J. S. (1859). On liberty. In J. S. Mill (Ed.), *Utilitarianism, liberty and representative government*. London: Dent.
Miller, E. K., & Wallis, J. D. (2009). Executive function and higher-order cognition: Definition and neural substrates. In L. R. Squire (Ed.), *Encyclopedia of neuroscience* (vol. 4, pp. 99–104). Oxford: Academic Press.
Moore, J. (1998). On behaviorism, theories, and hypothetical constructs. *The Journal of Mind and Behavior, 19*, 2115–2142.

Moore, J. (1999). The basic principles of behaviorism. In B. Thyler (Ed.), *The philosophical legacy of behaviorism* (pp. 41−68). Dordrecht: Kluwer Academic Publishers.

Moro, A. (2015). *The boundaries of Babel: The brain and the enigma of impossible languages.* Cambridge, MA: MIT Press.

Moser, M.-B., Rowland, D. C., & Moser, E. I. (2015). Place cells, grid cells, and memory. *Cold Spring Harbor Perspectives in Biology, 7*, a021808. Available from https://doi.org/10.1101/cshperspect.a021808.

Muñoz-Suárez, C. (2015). Introduction: Bringing together mind, behavior, and evolution. In C. Muñoz-Suárez, & F. De Brigard (Eds.), *Content and consciousness revisited* (pp. 1−27). Berlin: Springer.

Munñoz-Suárez, C., & De Brigard, F. (2015). *Content and consciousness revisited.* London and New York: Springer.

Nagel, T. (1995). Dennett: Content and consciousness. In T. Nagel (Ed.), *Other minds: Critical essays 1969−1994* (pp. 82−85). New York: Oxford University Press, First published in *The Journal of Philosophy, 69*, 1972, 220−224.

Naqvi, N., Shiv, B., & Bechara, A. (2006). The role of emotion in decision making. *Current Directions in Psychological Science, 15*, 260−264.

Okasha, S. (2018). *Agents and goals in evolution.* Oxford: Oxford University Press.

Oliveira-Castro, J. M., Cavalcanti, P., & Foxall, G. R. (2016a). What consumers maximize: Brand choice as a function of utilitarian and informational reinforcement. *Managerial and Decision Economics, 37*, 360−371.

Oliveira-Castro, J. M., Cavalcanti, P., & Foxall, G. R. (2016b). What do consumers maximize? The analysis of utility functions in light of the behavioral perspective model. In G. R. Foxall (Ed.), *The Routledge companion to consumer behavior analysis* (pp. 202−212). London and New York: Routledge.

Oliveira-Castro, J. M., & Foxall, G. R. (2017). Consumer maximization of utilitarian and informational reinforcement: Comparing two utility measures with reference to social class. *The Behavior Analyst, 42*, 457−476.

Ostrom, T. (1994). Foreword. *Handbook of social cognition. Vol. I: Basic processes* (pp. vii−xii). Hillsdale, NJ and Hove: Lawrence Erlbaum Associates.

Over, D. E. (2003). *Evolution and the psychology of thinking: The debate.* Hove and New York: Psychology Press.

Overskeid, G. (1995). Cognitive or behaviourist − Who can tell the difference? *British Journal of Psychology, 86*, 517−522.

Pan, W. X., Schmidt, R., Wickens, J. R., & Hyland, B. I. (2005). Dopamine cells respond to predicted events during classical conditioning: evidence for eligibility traces in the reward-learning network. *Journal of Neuroscience, 25*, 6235−6242. Available from https://doi.org/10.1523/JNEUROSCI.1478-05.2005.

Parrott, L. J. (1986). The role of postulation in the analysis of inapparent events. In H. W. Reese, & L. J. Parrott (Eds.), *Behavior science: Philosophical, methodological, and empirical advances* (pp. 35−60). Hillsdale, NJ: Erlbaum.

Pepper, S. C. (1942). *World hypotheses: A study in evidence.* Berkeley: University of California Press.

Perry, J. (1994). Intentionality (2). In S. Guttenplan (Ed.), *A companion to the philosophy of mind* (pp. 386−395). Oxford: Blackwell.

Petty, R. E., & Cacioppo, J. T. (1986). *Communication and persuasion.* Berlin: Springer.

Petty, R. E., & Krosnick, J. A. (Eds.), (1995). *Attitude strength: Antecedents and consequences.* Mahwah, NJ: Erlbaum.

Phelps, E. A. (2006). Emotion and cognition: insights from studies of the human amygdala. *Annual Review of Psychology, 57*, 27−53. Available from https://doi.org/10.1146/annurev.psych.56.091103.070234.

Phillips, D. C. (1987). *Philosophy, science, and social inquiry: Contemporary methodological controversies in social science and related applied fields of research.* Oxford: Pergamon.

Phillips, D. C., & Orton, R. (1983). The new causal principle of cognitive learning theory: Perspectives on Bandura's "reciprocal determinism. *Psychological Review, 90*(2), 158–165.

Philosophical Topics. (1994). The philosophy of Daniel Dennett. *Philosophical Topics, 22*(1&2), 1–568.

Pinker, S. (1997). *How the mind works.* London: Allen Lane.

Plotkin, H. (1997). *Evolution in mind.* London: Allen Lane.

Politser, P. (2008). *Neuroeconomics: A guide to the new science of making choices.* New York: Oxford University Press.

Posner, R. A. (1990). *The problems of jurisprudence.* Cambridge, MA: Harvard University Press.

Posner, R. A. (1995). *Overcoming law.* Cambridge, MA: Harvard University Press.

Prelec, D., & Herrnstein, R. J. (1991). Preferences or principles: Alternative guidelines for choice. In R. J. Zeckhausser (Ed.), *Strategy and choice.* Cambridge, MA: MIT Press.

Quine, W. V. O. (1960). *Word and object.* Cambridge, MA: MIT Press.

Quine, W. V. O. (1969). *Ontological relativity and other essays.* New York: Columbia University Press.

Rachlin, H. (1974). Self-control. *Behaviorism, 2,* 94–107.

Rachlin, H. (1989). *Judgment, decision, and choice: A cognitive/behavioral synthesis.* San Francisco, CA: Freeman.

Rachlin, H. (1994). *Behavior and mind: The roots of modern psychology.* New York: Oxford University Press.

Rachlin, H. (2000). Teleological behaviorism. In W. O'Donohue, & R. Kitchener (Eds.), *Handbook of behaviorism* (pp. 195–215). San Diego, CA: Academic Press.

Rachlin, H., Battalio, R., Kagel, J., & Green, L. (1981). Maximization theory in behavioral psychology. *The Behavioral and Brain Sciences, 4,* 371–417.

Radoilska, L. (2013). *Addiction and weakness of will.* Oxford: Oxford University Press.

Rajecki, D. W. (1982). *Attitudes: Themes and advances.* Sunderland, MA: Sinauer Associates.

Reese, H. W. (1986). On the theory and practice of behavior analysis. In H. W. Reese, & L. J. Parrott (Eds.), *Behavior science: Philosophical, methodological, and empirical advances* (pp. 1–34). Hillsdale, NJ: Lawrence Erlbaum Associates.

Reuter, M., & Montag, C. (Eds.), (2016). *Neuroeconomics.* Berlin: Springer.

Rice, Z. C. (1971). Review of Dennett: Content and consciousness. *Modern Schoolman, 48,* 177–178.

Ringen, J. (1976). Explanation, teleology, and operant behaviorism: A study of the experimental analysis of purposive behavior. *Philosophy of Science, 43,* 223–253.

Ringen, J. (1999). Radical behaviorism: B. F. Skinner's philosophy of science. In W. O'Donohue, & R. Kitchener (Eds.), *Handbook of behaviorism* (pp. 159–178). San Diego, CA: Academic Press.

Robbins, L. (1935). *An essay on the nature and significance of economic science.* (2nd ed.). London: Macmillan.

Robbins, T. W., & Everitt, B. J. (2002). Dopamine: Its role in behavior and cognition in experimental animals and humans. In G. Di Chiara (Ed.), *Dopamine in the CNS II* (pp. 173–211). Berlin: Springer.

Rogers, E. M. (2004). *Diffusion of innovation* (4th ed.). New York: Free Press.

Rolls, E. T. (1999). *The Brain and Emotion.* Oxford: Oxford University Press.

Rolls, E. T. (2009). From reward value to decision-making: Neuronal and computational principles. In J.-C. Dreher, & L. Tremblay (Eds.), *Handbook of reward and decision making* (pp. 97–133). Amsterdam: Academic Press.

Rolls, E. T. (2012). *Neuroculture: On the implications of brain science.* Oxford: Oxford University Press.
Rolls, E. T. (2014). *Emotion and decision-making explained.* Oxford: Oxford University Press.
Rosenberg, A. (1992). *Economics—mathematical politics or science of diminishing returns?* Chicago, IL: Chicago University Press.
Rosenberg, A. (2016). *Philosophy of social science* (5th ed.). Boulder, CO: Westview.
Ross, D. (2007). The economic and evolutionary basis of selves. In D. Ross, D. Spurrett, H. Kincaid, & G. L. Stephens (Eds.), *Distributed cognition and the will: individual volition and social context* (pp. 197−226). Cambridge, MA: MIT Press.
Ross, D. (2008). Two styles of neuroeconomics. *Economics and Philosophy, 24*, 473−483.
Ross, D. (2011). Hayek's speculative psychology, the neuroscience of value estimation, and the basis of normative individualism. In L. Marsh (Ed.), *Hayek in mind: Hayek's philosophical psychology. Advances in Austrian economics* (Vol. 15, pp. 51−72). Bingley: Emerald Group Publishing.
Ross, D. (2012). The economic agent: Not human, but important. In U. Mäki (Ed.), *Philosophy of economics* (pp. 691−736). Amsterdam: Elsevier.
Ross, D. (2014). *Philosophy of economics.* London and New York: Palgrave Macmillan.
Ross, D. (2015). A most rare achievement: Dennett's scientific discovery in content and consciousness. In C. Muñoz-Suárez, & F. De Brigard (Eds.), *Content and consciousness revisited* (pp. 29−48). Berlin: Springer.
Ross, D., Brook, A., & Thompson, D. (Eds.), (2000). *Dennett's philosophy: A comprehensive assessment.* Cambridge, MA: MIT Press.
Ross, D., Sharp, C., Vuchinich, R. E., & Spurrett, D. (2008). *Midbrain mutiny: The picoeconomics and neuroeconomics of disordered gambling.* Cambridge, MA: MIT Press.
Ross, D. R. (2005). *Economic theory and cognitive science: Microexplanation.* Cambridge, MA: MIT Press.
Rossiter, J. R., & Foxall, G. R. (2008). Hull-Spence behavior theory as a paradigm for consumer behavior. *Marketing Theory, 8*, 123−141.
Roth, M. (2015). I am large, I contain multitudes: The personal, sub-personal, and thee extended. In C. Muñoz-Suárez, & F. De Brigard (Eds.), *Content and consciousness revisited* (pp. 128−142). Berlin: Springer.
Rumbaugh, D. M. (1995). Emergence of relations and the essence of learning: A review of Sidman's equivalence relations and behavior: A research story. *The Behavior Analyst, 18*, 365−375.
Rumbaugh, D. M. (1997). The psychology of H. F. Harlow: A bridge from radical to rational behaviorism. *Philosophical Psychology, 10*, 197−210.
Russell, B. (1912). *The problems of philosophy.* London: Home University Library of Modern Knowledge.
Russell, B. (1940). *An inquiry into meaning and truth.* London: George Allen and Unwin.
Ryle, G. (1949). *The concept of mind.* London: Hutchinson.
Sanders, H., Rennó-Costa, C., Idiart, M., & Lisman, J. (2015). Grid cells and place cells: an integrated view of their navigational and memory function. *Trends in Neuroscience, 38*, 763−775. Available from https://doi.org/10.1016/j.tins.2015.10.004.
Sandis, C. (Ed.), (2009). *New essays on the explanation of action.* London and New York: Palgrave Macmillan.
Sandis, C. (2012). *The things we do and why we do them.* London and New York: Palgrave Macmillan.

Scheerer, E. (1996). Radical behaviorism: Excerpts from a textbook treatment. In L. D. Smith, & W. R. Woodward (Eds.), *B. F. Skinner and behaviorism in American culture* (pp. 151–175). Bethlehem: Lehigh University Press, London: Associated University Presses.

Schnaitter, R. (1988). "Behaviorism at fifty" at twenty. In A. C. Catania, & S. Harnad (Eds.), *The selection of behavior. The operant behaviorism of B. F. Skinner: Comments and consequences* (pp. 353–354). New York: Cambridge University Press.

Schnaitter, R. (1999). Some criticisms of behaviorism. In B. A. Thyer (Ed.), *The philosophical legacy of behaviorism* (pp. 209–249). Dordrecht: Kluwer.

Schoenfield, W. N., & Cumming, W. W. (1963). Behavior and perception. In S. Koch (Ed.), *Psychology: The study of a science: Vol. 5. The process areas, the person, and some fields: Their place in psychology and in science* (pp. 213–245). New York: McGraw-Hill.

Schultz, W., & Dickinson, A. (2000). Neuronal coding of prediction errors. *Annual Review of Neuroscience*, 23, 473–500. Available from https://doi.org/10.1146/annurev.neuro.23.1.473.

Schultz, W. (1992). Activity of dopamine neurons in the behaving primate. *Seminars in Neuroscience*, 4, 129–138. Available from https://doi.org/10.1016/1044-5765(92)90011-P.

Schultz, W. (2010). Dopamine signals for reward value and risk: Basic and recent data. *Behavioral and Brain Function*, 6, 24. Available from https://doi.org/10.1186/1744-9081-6-24.

Schultz, W., Dayan, P., & Montague, P. R. (1997). A neural substrate of prediction and reward. *Science*, 275, 1593–1599. Available from https://doi.org/10.1126/science.275.5306.1593.

Schwartz, B., & Lacey, H. (1982). *Behaviorism, science, and human nature*. New York: Norton.

Schwartz, B., & Lacey, H. (1988). What applied studies of human operant conditioning tell us about humans and about operant conditioning. In G. Davey, & C. Cullen (Eds.), *Human operant conditioning and behavior modification* (pp. 27–42). Chichester: Wiley.

Scruton, R. (2012). *The face of god: The Gifford Lectures 2010*. London and New York: Continuum.

Searle, J. (1981). Intentionality and method. *Journal of Philosophy*, 78, 720–733.

Searle, J. (1994). Intentionality (1). In S. Guttenplan (Ed.), *A companion to the philosophy of mind* (pp. 379–386). Oxford: Blackwell.

Searle, J. (1999). *Mind, language and society: Philosophy in the real world*. London: Weidenfeld and Nicolson.

Searle, J. R. (1980). Minds, brains, and programs. *Behavioral and Brain Sciences*, 3, 417–458.

Searle, J. R. (1983). *Intentionality: An essay in the philosophy of mind*. Cambridge: Cambridge University Press.

Searle, J. R. (1995). *The construction of social reality*. New York: Free Press.

Searle, J. R. (2000). Consciousness. *Annual Review of Neuroscience*, 23, 557–578.

Searle, J. R. (2001). *Rationality in action*. Cambridge, MA: MIT Press.

Searle, J. R. (2004). *Mind: A brief introduction*. Oxford: Oxford University Press.

Searle, J. R. (2010). *Making the social world: The structure of human civilization*. Oxford: Oxford University Press.

Searle, J. R. (2015). *Seeing things as they are: A theory of perception*. Oxford: Oxford University Press.

Seyfarth, R. M., & Cheney, D. L. (2002). Dennett's contribution to research on the animal mind. In A. Brook, & D. Ross (Eds.), *Daniel Dennett* (pp. 117–139). Cambridge: Cambridge University Press.

Sheppard, B. H., Hartwick, J., & Warshaw, P. R. (1988). The theory of reasoned action: A meta-analysis of past research with recommendations for modifications and future research. *Journal of Consumer Research*, 15, 325–343.

Shettleworth, S. J. (1998). *Cognition, evolution, and behavior*. Oxford: Oxford University Press.

Shettleworth, S. J. (2010). *Cognition, evolution, and behavior* (2nd ed.). Oxford: Oxford University Press.

Shull, R. L. (1995). Interpreting cognitive phenomena: Review of Donahoe and Palmer's learning and complex behavior. *Journal of the Experimental Analysis of Behavior, 63*, 347–358.

Sidman, M. (1989). *Coercion and its fallout*. Cambridge, MA: Authors Cooperative.

Sidman, M. (1994). *Equivalence relations and behavior: A research story*. Boston, MA: Authors Cooperative.

Skinner, B. F. (1945). The operational analysis of psychological terms. *Psychological Review, 52*, 270–277.

Skinner, B. F. (1948). *Walden two*. New York: Macmillan.

Skinner, B. F. (1950). Are theories of learning necessary? *Psychological Review, 57*, 193–216.

Skinner, B. F. (1953). *Science and human behavior*. New York: Macmillan.

Skinner, B. F. (1956). A case history in scientific method. *American Psychologist, 32*, 221–233.

Skinner, B. F. (1957). *Verbal behavior*. New York: Appleton-Century-Crofts.

Skinner, B. F. (1963). Behaviorism at fifty. *Science, 140*, 951–958.

Skinner, B. F. (1969a). *Contingencies of reinforcement*. New York: Appleton-Century-Crofts.

Skinner, B. F. (1969b). An operant analysis of problem solving. In B. F. Skinner (Ed.), *Contingencies of reinforcement*. New York: Appleton-Century-Crofts.

Skinner, B. F. (1971). *Beyond freedom and dignity*. New York: Knopf.

Skinner, B. F. (1973). Answers for my critics. In H. Wheeler (Ed.), *Beyond the punitive society* (pp. 256–266). San Francisco, CA: Freeman.

Skinner, B. F. (1974). *About behaviorism*. New York: Knopf.

Skinner, B. F. (1977). Why I am not a cognitive psychologist. *Behaviorism, 5*, 1–10.

Skinner, B. F. (1981). Selection by consequences. *Science, 213*, 501–504.

Skinner, B. F. (1988a). Reply to Schnaitter. In A. C. Catania, & S. Harnad (Eds.), *The selection of behavior. The operant behaviorism of B. F. Skinner: Comments and consequences* (p. 354). New York: Cambridge University Press.

Skinner, B. F. (1988b). Reply to Mackenzie. In A. C. Catania, & S. Harnad (Eds.), *The selection of behavior. The operant behaviorism of B. F. Skinner: Comments and consequences* (pp. 113–114). New York: Cambridge University Press.

Skinner, B. F. (1988c). Reply to Stalker and Ziff. In A. C. Catania, & S. Harnad (Eds.), *The selection of behavior. The operant behaviorism of B. F. Skinner: Comments and consequences* (pp. 207–208). New York: Cambridge University Press.

Skinner, B. F. (1988d). Reply to Zuriff. In A. C. Catania, & S. Harnad (Eds.), *The selection of behavior. The operant behaviorism of B. F. Skinner: Comments and consequences* (p. 217). New York: Cambridge University Press.

Skinner, B. F. (1988e). Reply to Stich. In A. C. Catania, & S. Harnad (Eds.), *The selection of behavior. The operant behaviorism of B. F. Skinner: Comments and consequences* (pp. 364–365). New York: Cambridge University Press.

Skinner, B. F. (1989). The origins of cognitive thought. *American Psychologist, 44*, 13–18.

Smart, J. C. (1970). Critical notice: Content and consciousness. *Mind, 79*, 616–623.

Smith, L. D. (1986). *Behaviorism and logical positivism: A reassessment of the alliance*. Stanford, CA: Stanford University Press.

Smith, L. D., & Woodward, W. R. (Eds.), (1996). *B. F. Skinner and behaviorism in American culture*. Bethlehem: Lehigh University Press, London: Associated University Presses.

Smith, T. L. (1994). *Behavior and its causes: Philosophical foundations of operant psychology*. Dordrecht: Kluwer.

Soriano, M. Y., & Foxall, G. R. (2002). Emotional responses to consumers' environments: An empirical examination of the behavioural perspective model in a Latin American context. *Journal of Consumer Behaviour, 2*, 138–154.

Staats, A. W. (1996). *Behavior and personality: Psychological behaviorism*. New York: Springer.
Staddon, J. (2014). *The new behaviorism*. London and New York: Psychology Press.
Staddon, J. E. R. (2001a). *Adaptive dynamics: The theoretical analysis of behavior*. Cambridge, MA: MIT Press.
Staddon, J. E. R. (2001b). *The new behaviorism*. Philadelphia, PA: Psychology Press.
Staddon, J. E. R., & Cerutti, D. T. (2003). Operant conditioning. *Annual Review of Psychology*, *54*, 115–144.
Stalker, D., & Ziff, P. (1988). Skinner's theorizing. In A. C. Catania, & S. Harnad (Eds.), *The selection of behavior. The operant behaviorism of B. F. Skinner: Comments and consequences* (pp. 206–207). New York: Cambridge University Press.
Stanovich, K. E. (2009a). Distinguishing the reflective, algorithmic, and autonomous minds: Is it time for a tri-process theory? In J. S. B. T. Evans, & K. Frankish (Eds.), *In two minds: Dual processes and beyond* (pp. 55–88). Oxford: Oxford University Press.
Stanovich, K. E. (2009b). *What intelligence tests miss: The psychology of rational thought*. New Haven, CT and London: Yale University Press.
Stanovich, K. E. (2011). *Rationality and the reflective mind*. Oxford: Oxford University Press.
Stanovich, K. E., & West, R. F. (2000). Individual differences in reasoning: Implications for the rationality debate? *Brain and Behavioral Sciences*, *23*, 645–726.
Stanovich, K. E., & West, R. F. (2003a). The rationality debate as a progressive research program. *Behavioral and Brain Sciences*, *26*, 531–533.
Stanovich, K. E., & West, R. F. (2003b). Evolutionary versus instrumental goals: How evolutionary psychology misconceives human rationality. In D. E. Over (Ed.), *Evolution and the psychology of thinking: The debate*. Hove and New York: Psychology Press.
Stanovich, K. E., & West, R. F. (2011a). A taxonomy of rational thinking problems. In R. E. Stanovich (Ed.), *Rationality and the reflective mind* (pp. 95–119). Oxford: Oxford University Press.
Stanovich, K. E., & West, R. F. (2011b). Intelligence as a predictor of performance on heuristics and biases tasks. In R. E. Stanovich (Ed.), *Rationality and the reflective mind* (pp. 121–154). Oxford: Oxford University Press.
Stanovich, K. E., West, R. F., & Toplak, M. E. (2012). Intelligence and rationality. In R. Sternberg, & S. B. Kaufman (Eds.), *Cambridge handbook of intelligence* (pp. 784–826). Cambridge: Cambridge University Press.
Stein, J. S., & Madden, G. J. (2013). Delay discounting and drug abuse: Empirical, conceptual, and methodological considerations. In J. MacKillop, & H. de Wit (Eds.), *The Wiley-Blackwell handbook of addiction psychopharmacology* (pp. 165–208). Chichester: Wiley.
Sterelny, K. (2003). *Thought in a hostile world: The evolution of human cognition*. Oxford: Blackwell.
Stevens, J. R. (Ed.), (2017). *Impulsivity: How time and risk influence decision making*. Berlin: Springer.
Steward, H. (2012). *A metaphysics for freedom*. Oxford: Oxford University Press.
Stich, S. P. (1981). Dennett on intentional systems. *Philosophical Topics*, *12*, 39–62.
Stich, S. P. (1983). *From folk psychology to cognitive science*. Cambridge, MA: MIT Press.
Stout, R. (1996). *Things that happen because they should: A teleological approach to action*. Oxford: Clarendon Press.
Strawson, G. (2010). *Mental reality* (2nd ed.). Cambridge, MA: MIT Press.
Strawson, G. (2019). A hundred years of consciousness: "a long training in absurdity". *Estudios de Filosofía*, *59*, 9–43.
Symons, J. (2002). *On Dennett*. Belmont, CA: Wadsworth/Thomson Learning.
Terrace, H. S., Petitto, L. A., Sanders, R. J., & Bever, T. G. (1979). Can an ape create a sentence? *Science*, *206*(4421), 891–902.

Thyer, B. (Ed.), (1999). *The philosophical legacy of behaviorism*. Dordrecht: Kluwer Academic Publishers.
Tiffany, S. T. (1999). Cognitive concepts of craving. *Alcohol Research and Health, 23*, 215–224.
Toates, F. (1986). *Motivational systems*. Cambridge: Cambridge University Press.
Todes, D. P. (2014). *Ivan Pavlov: A Russian life in science*. Oxford: Oxford University Press.
Tolman, C. (1932). *Purposive behavior in animals and men*. New York: Appleton-Century-Crofts.
Tolman, E. C. (1948). Cognitive maps in rats and men. *Psychological Review, 55*, 189–208.
Tomasello, M. (2014). *A natural history of human thinking*. Cambridge, MA: Harvard.
Tomasello, M. (2016). *A natural history of human morality*. Cambridge, MA: Harvard.
Tomasello, M. (2019). *Becoming human: A theory of ontology*. Cambridge, MA: Harvard.
Tomasello, M., & Rakoczy, H. (2003). What makes human cognition unique? From individual to shared to collective intentionality. *Mind and Language, 18*, 121–147.
Uetani, N., Kato, K., Ogura, H., Mizuno, K., Kawano, K., Mikoshiba, K., et al. (2000). Impaired learning with enhanced hippocampal long-term potentiation in PTPδ-deficient mice. *EMBO Journal, 19*, 2775–2785. Available from https://doi.org/10.1093/emboj/19.12.2775.
Valentine, E. R. (1992). *Conceptual issues in psychology*. London and New York: Routledge.
Van den Putte, B. (1993). *On the theory of reasoned action* (Unpublished doctoral dissertation). University of Amsterdam.
Vaughan, M. (1989). Rule-governed behavior in behavior analysis: A theoretical and experimental history. In S. C. Hayes (Ed.), *Rule-governed behavior: Cognition, contingencies, and instructional control* (pp. 97–118). New York: Plenum Press.
Viger, C. (2000). Where do Dennett's stances stand? Explaining our kind of mind. In D. Ross, A. Brook, & D. Thompson (Eds.), *Dennett's philosophy: A comprehensive assessment* (pp. 131–145). Cambridge, MA and London: MIT Press.
Vuchinich, R. E., & Heather, N. (Eds.), (2003). *Choice, behavioral economics and addiction*. Amsterdam: Pergamon.
Watson, A. J. (1970). Comment. In R. Borger, & F. Cioffi (Eds.), *Explanation in the Behavioural Sciences* (pp. 153–161). Cambridge: Cambridge University Press.
Watson, J. B. (1913). Psychology as the behaviorist views it. *Psychological Review, 20*, 158–177.
Webb, S. (1994). Witnessed behavior and Dennett's intentional stance. *Philosophical Topics, 22*, 457–470.
Wicker, A. W. (1969). Attitudes versus actions: The relationship of verbal and overt behavioral responses to attitude objects. *Social Issues, 25*, 41–78.
Wilhelms, E. A., & Reyna, V. F. (2015). *Neuroeconomics, judgment, and decision making*. London and New York: Psychology Press.
Wilkinson, S. (2015). Dennett's personal/subpersonal distinction in the light of cognitive neuropsychiatry. In C. Muñoz-Suárez, & F. De Brigard (Eds.), *Content and consciousness revisited* (pp. 111–127). Berlin: Springer.
Yu, P., & Fuller, G. (1986). A critique of Dennett. *Synthese, 66*, 453–476.
Zettle, R. D., & Hayes, S. C. (1982). Rule-governed behavior: A potential framework for cognitive-behavioral therapy. In P. C. Kendall (Ed.), *Advances in cognitive-behavioral research and therapy* (pp. 73–117). New York: Academic Press.
Zuriff, G. R. (1979). Ten inner causes. *Behaviorism, 7*, 1–8.
Zuriff, G. R. (1985). *Behaviorism: A conceptual reconstruction*. New York: Columbia University Press.

Index

Note: Page numbers followed by "*f*" refer to figures.

A

Abstracta, 160, 172, 228–229
Accessible attitudes, 201
Analysis of behavior, 22–23
Antiadaptionism, 57
Antiperspirant market, 70
Applied behavior analysis, 22–23
Arousal, 179, 184–185, 213–214
Ascribing intentionality
  attitude revolution, 197–209
    deliberative theory, 202–208
    extensional model, indispensability, 208–209
    spontaneous processing theory, 199–202
  heterophenomenology, 209–219
    consumer heterophenomenology, 213–215
    Intentional Behaviorism, 215–219
    nature, 209–212
  modeling consumer choice, 181–194
    behaviorism in consumer psychology, 185–188
    extensional model of consumer choice, 181–185, 182*f*
    intentionality, imperatives of, 188–189
    intentional model of consumer choice, 189–194
  predictive validity, 194–197
Ascription
  of content, 52–55
  extensional science and intentional, 51–52
  of intentionality, 63–64
  intentional stance, 55
  prelude to, 55–57
Attention deficit, 235
Attitude – behavior consistency, 200–201
Attitude – behavior relations, 116
Attitude – intention – behavior model, 181
Attitude psychology, 197
Attitudes, 20–21, 42, 80–81, 123–124, 140–141, 165, 197–198, 200–204
  polarization, 201

revolution, 197–209
  deliberative theory, 202–208
  extensional model, indispensability of, 208–209
  spontaneous processing theory, 199–202
theory and research, 123–124
Attitudinal – behavioral consistency, 205
Attitudinal beliefs, 207
Automatic reinforcement, 83–84, 101
Aversive stimulus, 54

B

Bandura's social learning theory, 193
Behavior, 200
  contextual stance, 75
  environmental determination, 106
  experimental analysis of, 131
  intermittent schedules, 96
  principles, 131–132
Behavioral contingency, 22–23
Behavioral continuity, 89, 94–95, 98, 104, 106
Behavioral continuity and discontinuity, 175–176, 185–186
  appeal to physiology, 103–106
  appeal to private events, 106–109
  appeal to rules, 109
  appeal to verbal analysis, 109–110
  beyond the stimulus field, 93–99
  symbolic behavior, 99–103
    schedule insensitivity, 102–103
    stimulus equivalence revisited, 99–102
Behavioral disinhibition, 235
Behavioral economics, 157–158
Behavioral flexibility, 235
Behavioral interpretation, delimiting, 127–130. *See also* Delimiting behavioral interpretation
Behavioral interpreter, 136–137
Behavioral Perspective Model-E, 181–185
Behavioral Perspective Model-I, 189–190
Behavioral science, 77–82, 112–113

287

Behavioral – scientific methodology, 156
Behavioral shaping, 21–22
Behavioral variation and selection, 104–105
Behavior analysis, 18–21, 65
Behavior analysts, 41–42, 119–120, 127–128
  interpretations, 83–84
Behavior analytic interpretation, 128–129
Behavior and Mind, 141–142
Behaviorism, 19, 22–23, 25, 32, 34–35, 46–47, 85, 152–153
  cognitivism, 152–153
  in consumer psychology, 185–188
    behavioral continuity and discontinuity, 185–186
    delimiting behavioral interpretation, 187–188
    personal level of exposition, 186–187
Behaviorist psychology, 216–217
Behaviorists, 19–22, 29–30
Behavior modification, 95–96
Behavior(s)
  class of, 189–190
  setting and learning history, 75
  of systems, 20–21
  theory, 82–85
Behaviour (1961/78), 94–95
Belief-based cognitions, 202
Beliefs, 20–21, 42–43, 50, 56, 153–156, 161–162, 165, 172–173
Believing, 118–119
Bickel's neurobehavioral decision systems model, 192–193
Bilateral contingencies, 247–248
  short- and long-range interests, 248–250
Brainstorms (1978), 57–58
Bundling, 186–187, 257–260
  attempted behavior modification through, 243
  bilateral contingency analysis of, 250
  principle, 244f
  self-management strategies and, 249

C

CBE. *See* Consumer behavioral economics (CBE)
Central route to persuasion, 73
Cobb – Douglas utility function analysis, 183–184
Cognition, 86
Cognitive content, 19–20

Cognitive explanation, 25–26, 41–43
Cognitive interpretation, 152, 174–176, 228–229
Cognitive ontology, 27
Cognitive phenomena, 87–89
Cognitive psychologies, 19–21, 23–25, 42, 44, 75, 113–114, 134–135, 162–163, 189–190, 223–224
Cognitive representation and processing, 97–98
Cognitive revolution, 133
Cognitive science, 32–33
Cognitive uniqueness, 174–176
  intentional behaviorist research strategy, 174–176
Cognitivism, 22–23, 27–28, 35, 85, 104–105, 133–134, 157
  in psychology, 17–18
Cognitivists, 19, 22, 29–30, 34–35
Collective intentionality theory, 222–223, 229
Combinatorial entailment, 71–72
Competing neuro-behavioral decision systems (CNDS) model, 222–223, 226–228
Comprehensive explanatory system, 74
Conditioned stimulus (CS), 87–89
Consciousness, 115
Consilience
  insight into insight, 21–25
  intentional behavior, 17–21
  radical behaviorism and intentionality, 25–29
  rationale, 32–37
Consumer behavioral economics (CBE), 192–193, 221, 226–228, 247–248
Consumer's
  behavior, 4, 183
  choice, 4
  emotional reactions, 191–192, 218
  heterophenomenology, 213–215
  innovativeness, 185–186
  learning history, 182–183
  psychology, behaviorism in, 185–188
Consumer-situation, 190–193, 213, 253–260.
  See also Intentional consumer situation
  bundling revisited, 257–260
  decision-making, 255–257
  intentional objects populate, 253–255
  and learning history, 136
Content, 58
Content and Consciousness (1969), 43–44, 57–59, 197
Contextualism, 75

Contextual stance, 7–10, 20, 32–33, 69, 75, 133–134, 172
  behavior theory, 82–85
  comparison, 75–77
  contextual strategy, 72–74
  contingencies, 69–72
  extensional behavioral science, 77–82
  radical behaviorism, nature, 63–69
  radical behaviorism's claim to uniqueness, 85–89
Contextual strategy, 72–74, 134
Contingencies, 74
  of reinforcement, 115
Contingency-shaped behavior, 59–60, 72–73, 79
Continuity/discontinuity of behavior, 63–64
Continuity of behavior, 26–27, 94–95
Conventional behaviorist, 53–54
Counter-inductivism, 31–32
Covert behavior, 19
Cultural learning, 174

D

Decision-making, 20–21, 73, 132–133, 188–189, 254–257
  action, 257
  and behavior, 258–259
  intrapersonal, 186–187
  intrapersonal valuation, 256f
Deliberative processing, 73
Deliberative theory, 202–208
Delimiting behavioral interpretation, 187–188
  analogic guesses, 136–140
  behavioral interpretation, 127–130
  interpretive stances, 133–136
  radical behaviorist interpretation, 141–145
  teleological behaviorism, 140–141
Delineating radical behaviorism, 32
Dennett, Daniel, 28
Derived intentionality, 167–171
  intentional behaviorist research strategy, 167–169
Descriptivism, 129–130
Design stance, 42
Desires, 50, 56–57, 153–156, 161–162, 165
Diachronicity, 243–247
Discrimination of emergent relationships, 100
Discriminative stimulus, 65, 83–84
Discriminatory behavior, 51–52
Dominance, 179, 184–185, 213–214
Dysfunctional behavior, 232–233

E

Economic activity, 3–5
Economic behavior, 253, 258–259, 261–262
Economic-psychological framework, 3–5, 18, 247–248
Emergent relationships, 100
Emitted behavior, 46–47
Emotional contingency-representations, 190–191
Emotional perceptions, 253–254
Emotive language, 242–243
Enhanced informational reinforcement (EIR$_{LLR}$), 245
Enhanced informational reinforcement (EIR$_{SSR}$), 241–242, 245
Environmental-behavioral relationships, 226–228
Environmental contingencies, 115–116
Environmental stimuli, Intentional Behaviorism, 152–153
Environment – behavior linkages, 157
Environment-behavior sphere, 112
"Epistemological anarchy", 31–32
Equifinality, 89
Essential value, 226–228
Establishing operation (EO), 70
Executive system emphasizes attentiveness, 235
Existential inference, 166
Expectancy, 86
Experimental investigation, 18–19
Explanation levels, 52–53
Explanatory stance, 32–33
Exponentially discounting consumer, 238–239
Extensional behavioral, 77–82
  science, 156
Extensional investigations and explanations, 228–229
Extensionality, 163, 165–166
Extensional language psychology, 66
Extensional object, 166–167
Extensional operant analysis, 58
Extensional science
  and intentional ascription, 51–52
  and interpretation, 100–101

F

First-order intention, 56–57
First-person accounts, 114–122
First-person psychological sentences, 119–120

First-person/third-person perspectives, 122–126
Folk psychology, 44, 160
Four-term contingency, 64–65
Freudian distinction, 192–193
Freud's dichotomy, 224
Functional language, 56
Function-altering stimulus, 70

G

Generic attitude, 204–205
Grounding intentionality
  intentional interpretation, 221–225
  Janus-variables and valuation, 225–229
  macro-cognitive psychology, 247–250
    bilateral contingency analysis of bundling, 250
    bilateral contingency of short- and long-range interests, 248–250
    macro- and meso-cognitive psychologies, 247–248
  micro-cognitive psychology, 229–236
    executive system, 232–233
    impact on behavior, 233–236
    impulsive system, 231–232
  picoeconomic analysis, 236–247
    attempted behavior modification through bundling, 243
    impulsive and self-controlled consumers, 241–243
    impulsive consumer, dynamic valuation process, 237–241
    synchronicity and diachronicity, 243–247

H

Hebbian learning, 231–232
Heterophenomenology, 115, 123, 195, 209–219
  consumer heterophenomenology, 213–215
  Intentional Behaviorism, 215–219
  nature, 209–212
  practice, 210
  raw data to, 211
  research exercise, 213–214
  theory of planned behavior, 210f
Human cognitive capacity, 174
Human economic behavior, 19, 221–222
Hyperbolic discounting consumer, 238–239
Hyperbolic temporal discounting, 233–235

I

Identity theory, 55–56
Illata, 8–9, 13, 160–161, 170, 221–222, 225–229, 253, 259–261, 263–264
Imperatives of intensionality, 171–172
Impulsive and self-controlled consumers, 241–243
Impulsive choice, 235
Impulsive consumers, 236–243
Impulsive – executive interactions, 162–163
Impulsivities, 235
Individual innovator's experience, 187–188
Individual's volitional control, 202
Inductive behavior science, 131
Informational reinforcement, 162–163, 179, 182–183, 191–194, 247, 257
Informational reinforcers, 231–232
Information-processing theories, 48
Insensitivity, 102–103
  of human participants' behavior, 102–103
Intellectual civilization, 125
Intellectual diversity, 35–36
Intellectual engagement, 36
Intellectual progress, 17–18
Intelligent decision-making, 54
Intelligent information storage, 51
Intelligent storage, 51
Intending, 118–119
Intensional behavioral science, 59
Intensional criterion, 170–174
  intentional behaviorist research strategy, 170–174
Intensional explanation, 161–162
Intensionality, 161–163, 170, 172–173
  and extensionality, 165
Intensional sentences, 168–169
Intentional ascription, 51–52
  extensional descriptions, 54
Intentional behavior, 17–21, 25–26, 51
Intentional Behaviorism, 5–7, 9, 11, 112–113, 152
  cognitive interpretation, 152
  heterophenomenology, 215–219
  incommensurability, 18
  intentional interpretation, 152
  mutual indispensability, 18
  radical behaviorism, 22–23
  research strategy, 64–65, 152, 224f
  theoretical minimalism, 152
Intentional behaviorist paradigm, 5–6
Intentional behaviorist research strategy, 189
  cognitive uniqueness, 174–176

derived intentionality, 167–169
economic agency, 177–179
extensionality, criteria of, 165–166
intensional criterion, 170–174
intensionality and extensionality, 165
Intentional Behaviorism, 152
intentionality, 163–165
intentional objects, nature of, 166–167
intentional states and intensional statements, 167
objections, 169–170
psychological agency, 176–177
psychological explanation, 158–163
stages, 153, 153f
theoretical minimalism, 153–158
Intentional consumer situation, 253–260
bundling revisited, 257–260
construction, 190–193
decision-making, 255–257
desires and beliefs, 190–191
emotional contingency-representations, 190–191
intentional objects populate, 253–255
propositional attitudes, 190–191
Intentional content, 26–27
Intentional explanation, 43–50
Intentional − extensional distinction, 46–47
Intentional idioms, 165
Intentional inexistence, 166–167
Intentional interpretation, 5, 8–9, 11–13, 152–156, 162–163, 221–225
Intentionalism, 32, 34–35, 47
Intentionality, 19–20, 32–33, 44–45, 163–165, 167–170
Intentionality-based predictions, 221–222
Intentional language, 161, 170
Intentional model of consumer choice, 189–194
Behavioral Perspective Model-I, 189–190
informational reinforcement, 193–194
intentional consumer situation, construction, 190–193
Intentional object, 166–167
Intentional phenomena, 47
Intentional psychology scheme, 49–50, 59, 161–162, 221–222
Intentional stance, 7–8, 19–21, 43–44, 75–77, 83–84, 135, 172
awareness, 59–61
cognitive explanation, 41–43
intentional explanation, 43–50
behaviorism, 48–49

irreducibility, 47–48
psychology, 49–50
prelude to ascription, 55–57
realism, 50–55
ascription of content, 52–55
extensional science and intentional ascription, 51–52
The Intentional Stance (1987), 43–44, 57–58
Intentional states and intensional statements, 167
Intentional strategy, 134
Intentional systems theory (IST), 8–9, 19–20, 44, 160, 170–171, 221–222
Intentional theory, 53
Intentions, 20–21, 42, 140–141, 197–198
Interpretation, 111–113
Interpretive stances, 133–136
assertion, 133–134
philosophical position, 133–134
preempirical, 133–134
universal of application, 133–134
Intrapersonal bilateral contingency, 248, 248f
Intrapersonal decision-making, 186–187
Intrapersonal interpretation, 162–163
Intrinsic intentionality, 168–169
Introspectionism, 116–117
Irreducibility, 47–48
hypothesis, 49–50

J

Janus-variables, 228–229
Behavioral Perspective Model research program, 261–262
concept, 253–254
explanatory significance of, 260–263
intentional consumer-situation, 253–260
bundling revisited, 257–260
contingency-representations, 254–255
decision-making, 255–257
intentional objects populate, 253–255
intentional entities, 261
intentionality as subjective experience, 262
levels of exposition and appropriate mode of explanation, 262–263
objective valuations, 263
radical behaviorism, 261–262
theoretical minimalism, 261–262
and valuation, 225–229

K

Knowledge
compartmentalization, 17–18

Knowledge (*Continued*)
  sources, 112–113
Knowledge-by-acquaintance, 159–160, 259–261
Knowledge-by-description, 159, 181, 209–210, 259–261

L

Language, 20–21
  and behavior, 103
  of science, 45–46
Larger – later reinforcer (LLR), 186–187, 233–235, 255–257
Learning
  definition, 87–89
  history, 73–74, 79, 103, 113
    and consumer-situations, 136
    explanatory significance, 94–95
    verbal behavior, 119–120
Levels of exposition, 5–7, 256*f*
Linguistic entities, 56
LLR. *See* Larger – later reinforcer (LLR)
Logical behaviorism, 195
Logical positivism, 107–108
Long-range interest (LRI), 222–223, 239
Long-term potentiation (LTP), 231–232

M

Macro-cognitive psychology, 162–163, 225–226, 229, 247–250
  analysis of bundling, bilateral contingency, 250
  bilateral contingency of short- and long-range interests, 248–250
  macro- and meso-cognitive psychologies, 247–248
Managerial behavior, 4
Managerial choice, 4
Mand, 80
Marketer behavior, 254–255
Matching, 95–96, 102–103
Mental capacity, 170–171
Mental entities, 52
Mentalistic constructs, 56–57
Mentalistic terms, 115
Mental language, 100
Mental phenomena, 118–119, 140–141
  of pain, 52–53
Mental sentences, 164–165
Mental simulation, 73–74
Mereological fallacy, 8–9, 61, 161–162, 170–174, 221–222, 225–226, 245–247, 259–261, 263
"Merge", 176
Meso-cognitive psychology, 162–163, 192–193, 222–223, 225–226, 247–248
Methodological behaviorism, 127–128, 130–131, 140–141
Methodological explorations, 4–5
Micro-cognitive psychology, 162–163, 222–223, 225–226, 229–236, 255–256
  executive system, 232–233
  impact on behavior, 233–236
  impulsive system, 231–232
  neuro-behavioral decision systems theory, 229–230
  reinforcement and punishment, 229–230
Mind – body problem, 259–262
Misrepresentation, 175–176
Modeling consumer choice, 181–194
  behaviorism in consumer psychology, 185–188
  extensional model of consumer choice, 181–185, 182*f*
  intentionality, imperatives of, 188–189
  intentional model of consumer choice, 189–194
Modern behavior analysis, 20–21
Molar environmental – behavioral sequences, 63–64
Motivating operations (MOs), 64–65
Motivation, extraenvironmental source, 123
Mutual entailment, 71–72

N

Natural selection, 53
  evolution, 63–64
Neo-behaviorisms, 25–28, 135–136
Neo-behaviorist psychology, 85
Neoclassical microeconomics, 235–236
Neurobehavioral decision systems, 162–163
Neurocellular economics (NE), 225–228
Neuro-cognitive behavior systems, 222–223, 225–226
Neuroeconomics, 225–226
Neurophysiological – behavioral patterns, 63–64
Neurophysiology and action, 162
Noncognitive learning and environmental history, 19

Non-intentional characterizations, 46
Nonlaboratory behavior patterns, 131–132

O

Observational learning, 96
Operant behavior, 23, 71, 79–80, 152–153, 157, 211–212, 233
Operant behavioral economics, 3–4, 152–153, 161–163, 220–222, 226–228, 236
Operant conditioning, 22–23
Operant psychology, 3–4, 22–23
Operationism, 129–130
Organizational behavior management, 95–96
Orientation
  economic behavior, 3–5
  exposition level, 5–7
Orthodox behavior analysis, 42

P

Pain, 140–141
  personal-level phenomenon, 100
Painfulness, 52–53
Pattern of reinforcement, 179
Patterns of environmental contingencies, 5–6
PBC. *See* Perceived behavioral control (PBC)
Perceived behavioral control (PBC), 197–198, 204, 208–209
Personal level
  acknowledging personhood, 111–113
  of exposition, 186–187
  first- and third-personal perspectives, 122–126
  more on first-person accounts, 114–122
  Skinner's third-person account, 113–114
Personal rule formation and following, 73–74
Personal valuation, 259–260
Phenomena of pain, 52
Philosophical anthropology, 6
Philosophy of psychology, 6
Physical entities, 260–261
Physicalism, 116–117
Physical stance, 43, 161, 172
Physiological activity, 103–104
Physiological psychology, 27, 59, 111–112
Physiology, 100–101
Picoeconomic analysis, 226–228, 236–247
  attempted behavior modification through bundling, 243
  impulsive and self-controlled consumers, 241–243

impulsive consumer, dynamic valuation process, 237–241
  synchronicity and diachronicity, 243–247
  triprocessual construal of, 246*f*
Planning, 235
Plausible interpretation, 128–129
Plausible operant account, 134
Pleasure, 179, 184–185, 213–214
Pleasure, arousal, and dominance (PAD) reactions, 253–254
Pliance, 80–81
Pluralistic methodology, 31–32
Positivism, 129–130
Poverty of the stimulus, 71
Pragmatism, 129–130
Prebehavioral beliefs, 56–57
Prebehavioral variables, 198–199
Predictive validity, 194–197
Premature physiology, 53–54
Principle of pluralism, 31–32
Principle of proliferation, 31–32
Principles of behavior, 112–113
Private events, 120–121, 127–128
  behavioral continuity and discontinuity, 106–109
Private verbal behavior, 103
Problem-solving activity, 82–83, 113–114
Propositional attitudes, 43–44, 75–76, 135, 164–165
Psychological agency, 176–177
Psychological attitude, 197–198
Psychological explanation, 158–163
  assumption of materialism, 158–159
  consciousness, 159–160
  idealized intentional system, 158
  intentional interpretation, 158
  intentional psychology, 160
  knowledge-by-acquaintance, 159–160
  knowledge by description, 159
  medium of description, 159
  mind – body problem, 158–159
  physical entities, 161
  theoretical minimalism, 153–156
Psychological language, 118–119
Psychological paradigm, Intentional Behaviorism, 157
Psychological rationality, 171–172
Psychological science, 32
Psychological theory, 18–19
Psychology, 34
  intentionalistic, 49–50
  radical behaviorism, 157–158

Psychology (*Continued*)
  social-cognitive school of, 135–136
Public behaviors, 19
Punishers, 65

Q

The Question of Animal Awareness (1976), 50

R

Radical behaviorism, 5, 9, 19–20, 22–25, 32–35, 42, 46–47, 66, 75, 79
  behavioral complexity, 69
  capacity, 25–26
  character, 63
  claim to uniqueness, 85–89
  contingency, 64–65
  criticism, 136–137
  definition, 129–130
  delimiting behavioral interpretation, 127–128
  environmental and behavioral events, 68–69
  expositions, 64–65
  inability, 99–100, 102–103
  and intentionality, 25–29
  intentional stance masking, 133–134
  nature, 63–69
  physiological change, 103–106
  private events, 106–109
  reliance, 10
  third-personal accounts of behavior, 111
Radical behaviorists, 23–25, 27–28, 42, 98, 128–129
  interpretation, 19, 24–25, 63–64, 73, 94–95, 111–113, 128–129, 141–145
  delimiting behavioral interpretation, 141–145
  principle, 129
Rate of temporal discounting (RTD), 229, 253–254
Rational choice theory (RCT), 153–156
Realism, 50–55
  ascription of content, 52–55
  extensional science and intentional ascription, 51–52
Referential opacity, 169–170
Referential transparency, 169–170
Reflection deficit, 235
Reinforcements, 97, 102–103, 112
  and punishment, 113, 153–156, 162
Reinforcers, 3–4, 65
  informational, 231–232

  pathologies, 233–235
Relational Frame Theory, 34–35, 71, 99–100, 124
Relational framing, 100–102
Repeated verbal expression, 201
Reward prediction error, 233
Reward sensitivity, 235
Root metaphor, 75
Rule-governance, 100–101
Rule-governed behavior, 109, 118
Rules, behavioral continuity and discontinuity, 109
Rules of correspondence, 131–132

S

Schedule-insensitive behavior, 216
Schedule insensitivity, 102–103
Second-order intentional system, 56–57
Self-awareness, 82–83
Self-control, 82–83
Self-controlled consumers, 236, 241–243
Self-esteem, 193, 231–232, 240
Self-management strategies and bundling, 249
Self-performance, 193
Self-regulated reinforcement, 97
Self-reward, 97
  control, 97
Sensation-seeking, 235
Shared intentionality, 174
Short-range interest (SRI), 222–223, 239–240
"Silent Dog technique", 124
Skinner box, 65
Skinnerian psychology, 22–23
Skinnerism, 34–35
Skinner – Zuriff approach, 68
Smaller – sooner reinforcer (SSR), 186–187, 233–235, 255–257
Social behavioral science, 27
Social cognition models, 135
Social cognitive explanation, 197
Social cognitive psychology, 20, 26–27, 128–129, 135–136, 197
Social cognitivists, 30, 118–120, 197
Social complexity psychology, 25
Social learning approach, 97
Social psychology, 3
Social reward, 231–232
Social scientific disciplines, 17–18
Solipsism, 116
SPCP. *See* Subpersonal cognitive psychology (SPCP)

Spontaneous processing attitude theory, 199–202
SSR. Smaller sooner reinforcer (SSR);. *See* Smaller – sooner reinforcer (SSR)
Stanovich's tripartite theory, 222–223
Stanovich's tri-process model, 192–193
Stimulus equivalence, 70–71, 99–102
Stimulus field, 64–65, 93–99
Subjective mental awareness, 60–61
Subjective norms (SNs), 197–198
Subpersonal cognitive psychology (SPCP), 8–9, 125–126, 160, 221–222
Subpersonal level of analysis, 5–6, 111–112
Substantiable learning history, 107
Substitution criterion, 165–166
Superpersonal level, 5–6, 111–112
Symbolic behavior, 99–103
  schedule insensitivity, 102–103
  stimulus equivalence, 99–102
Symbolic consumer situation, 213
Symbolic reinforcement, 213
Synaptic plasticity, 231–232
Synchronicity, 243–247
Systematic processing, 73

T

Teleological behaviorism, 116–117, 140–142
Temporal discounting, 233–235
Tempted consumer, 257–258
Theoretical minimalism, 152–158, 162–163
  intentional behaviorist research strategy, 153–158
Theory of mind, 174
Theory of reflexes, 41–42

Thinking, 20–21
Third-person account, 113–114
Three-term contingencies, 10, 65–66, 96, 113, 128–129, 131–132, 138, 218–219
Token functionalism, 56
Tracking, 80–81
Transfer of function, 100–101
Trial-and-error learning, 21–22

U

Utilitarian reinforcement (UR), 182–184, 213–214, 239–240
  informational reinforcement and, 179

V

Vague analogic guesses, 132–133
Value, definition, 226–228
Verbal analysis, behavioral continuity and discontinuity, 109–110
Verbal behavior, 67, 70, 82–83, 100–101, 103, 121, 201
  human interaction, 133
  learning history, 119–120
Verbal Behavior, 132–133
Verbal behaviors, 254–255
Verbalizations, 52–53
Verbal response latency, 201–202

W

Wanting, 118–119
Warrant of assertibility, 128–129
Working approximation, 32–33

Printed in the United States
By Bookmasters